Analyzing DECnet/OSI Phase V

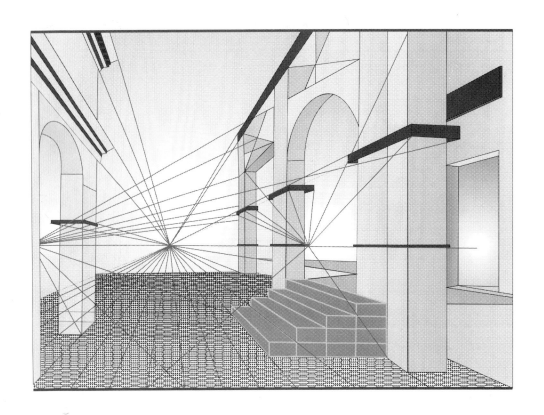

Analyzing DECnet/OSI Phase V

Carl Malamud

VNR VAN NOSTRAND REINHOLD
New York

Library of Congress Catalog Card Number 90-22230
ISBN 0-442-00375-7

Printed in the United States of America

Van Nostrand Reinhold
115 Fifth Avenue
New York, New York 10003

Chapman and Hall
2-6 Boundary Row
London, SE1 8HN, England

Thomas Nelson Australia
102 Dodds Street
South Melbourne 3205
Victoria, Australia

Nelson Canada
1120 Birchmount Road
Scarborough, Ontario MIK 5G4, Canada

16 15 14 13 12 11 10 9 8 7 6 5 4 3 2 1

Cover based on an original perspective drawing by Jan Vredeman de Vries (1527–
1604), reprinted in *Perspective*, Dover Pictorial Archive Series (Dover Publications,
1968). Color was added without the participation of the original artist.

Library of Congress Cataloging-in-Publication Data

Malamud, Carl, 1959—
    Analyzing DECnet/OSI Phase V / Carl Malamud.
        p. cm.
    Includes index.
    ISBN 0-442-00375-7
    1. Local area networks (Computer networks) 2. DECnet 3. Computer network archi-
tectures. 4. OSI (International standards) I. Title.
TK5105.7.M35 1990
621.39'81—dc20   90-22230
                                                                  CIP

Contents

Preface

Analyzing DECnet/OSI Phase V is the second in a three volume series analyzing networks. Whereas the first book, *Analyzing Novell Networks*, looked at the simplistic architecture of Novell's NetWare, this one examines the opposite extreme—DEC's Digital Network Architecture (DNA). The third volume, *Analyzing Sun Networks*, examines TCP/IP, NFS, and other protocols used in the Internet and in many distributed networks.

Phase V of DNA is, without a doubt, one of the more complex network architectures ever invented. Incredible flexibility in network configuration and applications functionality have led to a degree of complexity surpassing even IBM's System Network Architecture. This book takes the major pieces of that architecture (and several related architectures) and puts them into perspective, allowing the reader to see how an individual protocol fits into the larger picture.

DECnet/OSI Phase V is really three different networks: a subset of OSI, a set of services backwardly compatible with DECnet Phase IV, and a new set of modern, proprietary services from Digital. We will see how these three parallel universes coexist in DECnet/OSI Phase V. We will also look at related architectures, such as LAT, EMA, and MOP which fill in holes left by DECnet. A fourth architecture, TCP/IP, also plays a part in a heterogeneous DECnet environment. The reader is directed to *Analyzing Sun Networks* for more information on TCP/IP, NFS, SNMP, and related protocols.

As we go to press, DECnet/OSI Phase V has resurfaced under a new name, Advantage-Networks. The name may be new, but the architecture is the same as described in this book. Why change a name if the underlying technology stays the same? This mystery can only be answered by the legion of Digital marketing executives.

Carl Malamud
Carl@Malamud.Com

Trademarks

PostScript is a trademark of Adobe Systems.

Apple, AppleShare, AppleTalk, Finder, ImageWriter, LaserWriter, Local-Talk, Macintosh, and Quickdraw are trademarks of Apple Computer.

AT&T Mail, STREAMS, Transport Level Interface, Unix, and Unix System V Release 4 are trademarks of AT&T.

ARCNET and DATAPOINT are registered trademarks of DATAPOINT Corporation.

All-IN-1, DEC, DECconnect, DECmcc, DECnet, DECnet-DOS, DECnet/OSI, DECnet-VAX, DECnet Router, DECnet Router/X.25 Gateway, DECserver, DECUS, DELNI, DELUA, DEMPR, DEREN, DEREP, DESTA, DFS, DNA, DNS, EDE, EMA, Internet, LAN Bridge, MAILbus, Message Router, MicroVAX, Terminal Server, ThinWire, Ultrix, Unibus, VAX, VAXBI, VAX Cluster, VMS, and VT are trademarks of Digital Equipment Corporation.

Ingres is a trademark of ASK, Incorporated.

AS/400, DISOSS, IBM, IBM PC LAN, PC/AT, PC/XT, PROFS, SNA, SNADS, System/370, System/38, and 3270 Display Station are trademarks of International Business Machines, Inc.

MS-DOS and Microsoft are trademarks of Microsoft.

Network General and Sniffer Analyzer are trademarks of Network General Corporation.

Retix is a trademark of Retix.

MAILbridge Server/MHS and Softswitch are trademarks of Softswitch.

Network File System, Open Network Computing, SPARC, Sun, SunOS, and TOPS are trademarks of Sun Microsystems, Inc.

TransLAN and Vitalink are trademarks of Vitalink.

Xerox is a trademark of Xerox.

Carl Malamud is a trademark of Carl Malamud.

CHAPTER 1

Introduction

Introduction

This is a book about a hybrid network architecture, Digital's DECnet/OSI Phase V. DECnet is an implementation of Digital's own proprietary network architecture, the Digital Network Architecture (DNA). DNA has gone through four "Phases" with Phase IV being the most recent. In Phase V, Digital took the Phase IV base and added a variety of OSI protocols, new proprietary protocols, and a few de facto standards. This mix of open and proprietary protocols is bundled together under the umbrella of Phase V.

Open protocols means the specifications are published in sufficient detail to allow other vendors to provide their own implementations. Many open protocols that Digital is using come from the Open Systems Interconnection (OSI) protocol suite. Examples of protocols used in DECnet/OSI Phase V are the network layer packet format (ISO 8473) and the File Access, Transfer, and Management (FTAM) standards for data access.

OSI is one of those truth and beauty concepts: nobody does all of OSI; instead, pieces are selected, as in the case of a Government OSI Profile (GOSIP), a subset of OSI used by governments to establish procurement requirements. By using GOSIP as a guide to procurement, the government is able to ensure that components from different vendors will work together.

Supporting GOSIP does not mean that all systems are the same. Rather, OSI is broad enough, and GOSIP is loose enough, to allow considerable variance. In particular, GOSIP only says that an environment must present a certain service (such as FTAM file access protocols) to the outside world. GOSIP requires that a collection of equipment must have a single access point that provides the specified OSI services, providing a link to other GOSIP networks. Inside a particular collection of equipment, any protocols can be used. Instead of FTAM, for example, the network might use some internal protocol better suited to the needs of this particular collection of equipment, such as a distributed file system. FTAM and the internal protocol coexist; FTAM is used to talk to the outside world and the internal protocol is used for local communication.

This is exactly what DECnet/OSI Phase V does. DECnet/OSI Phase V is a collection of many services: Phase IV compatible services, new proprietary Phase V services, a few TCP/IP services, and the OSI basics. In some cases, the services can work together. For file access, for example, a network could easily have five different protocols: FTAM from the OSI world; the Data Access Protocol (DAP) from Digital; the Network File System (NFS) from Sun; the File Transfer Protocol from TCP/IP; and the Distributed File System from Digital.

Some of these protocols have gateways. DAP and FTP can be joined using a gateway on Ultrix (Digital's version of Unix), allowing a DAP user to access resources in the FTP world. DAP and FTAM can also be connected together, using the DAP-FTAM Gateway from Digital.

The relationship of these different protocols is the subject of this book. This is an architecture book: it explains the design of the protocols and their place in the overall architecture. It discusses which protocols provide service to others and which ones provide complementary services. It discusses how the pieces all fit together to provide a collection of services to the user.

Just as OSI is too broad to be fully implemented, so is DECnet/OSI Phase V. Phase V is a philosophy, in great detail, of how a network is put together. Specific products may implement one or more of those pieces.

This book presents a framework from which to examine products. When a vendor, Digital or otherwise, says it supports some specific service, say FTAM, the reader will be able to put that information into perspective. The reader will understand how the FTAM service relates to other file access mechanisms, how it uses the services of the underlying session layer, and what the protocol itself does.

This book also includes topics that are not, by a strict definition, part of Phase V. The Local Area Transport (LAT) is a protocol that is used for terminal servers to communicate with hosts (among other things). Because LAT is a key service provider in a Digital network, one cannot really understand Phase V without understanding what this complementary architecture does. It also discusses network management, the Maintenance Operations Protocol (MOP), and the Naming Service. These topics are pieces that help provide perspective on how a Digital DECnet/OSI Phase V network operates.

There are even a few topics that are not covered at all in this book. The X Windows System, MOTIF, and other aspects of the Graphical User Interface are not covered because it was felt that they deserved their own book. Network-based graphics uses the underlying services of the network, so this book starts where those services end.

Overview of This Book

Chapter 2 begins with the bottom of the protocol stack—the data link and physical layers. The book then climbs up the protocol stack, looking at services that build on each of the lower layers. Before we begin the climb, however, we will provide a quick overview of DECnet/OSI. After all, a climb is much easier if we know what awaits us along the way.

We begin with a caveat. DECnet/OSI, Phase V of DECnet, is a new offering. This means many of its pieces are just becoming clear. Most important, there are pieces, as with any architecture, that have not been defined or that have been defined and will not be used. We therefore discuss DECnet as the Digital architects have envisioned it, not as the engineers have implemented it.

Digital has gone through five stages of the Digital Network Architecture (DNA is the architecture, DECnet is the implementation of that architecture). Phase I was two PDPs with a wire strung between them—not exactly a network by current standards!

Phase IV

Phase IV of DNA is a network centered on Ethernet work groups, strung together with either wide-area bridges or routers. The wide-area systems use Digital's DDCMP data link protocols. Built on top of the data link are proprietary network, transport, and session layers.

Built on top of the Digital session layer is a wide variety of applications. The two most often used applications are the Data Access Protocol (DAP) and the Command Terminal (CTERM) protocols. DAP is a service for access to remote data and provides a variety of record level operations such as searches by index keys. CTERM is used for remote interactive access. CTERM, also known as the "SET HOST" command, allows a remote terminal to appear as a local one to the host system, much as Telnet does in the TCP/IP world.

Over the years, DAP and CTERM were supplemented by a wide variety of other services. Messaging, for example, was first done using the mail-11 message-handling protocols, and lately Digital's proprietary MAILbus. Videotex, remote consoles for network management, booting diskless nodes, distributed bulletin boards, and a host of other services are available for DECnet nodes.

Phase V

To see what DECnet Phase V encompasses, we start at the bottom of the protocol stack. The subnetworks (layers 1, 2, and some of the network layer) in Phase IV included Ethernet, the IEEE 802.3 version of Ethernet, and DDCMP for wide-area communications. In addition, Phase IV supports X.25 networks, but only with permanent virtual circuits. Finally, the IEEE token-passing bus is also supported for MAP/TOP networks.

Phase V has dramatically increased the support for subnetwork technologies. In addition to DDCMP, Digital has added the HDLC protocols. In addition to IEEE 802.3, it has added the FDDI services for faster LANs. More important, Digital has added two proprietary services that allow public data networks to be incorporated into a Digital environment. First, the Modem Control protocol, a physical layer service, allows a modem service such as V.25 or the Hayes AT command set to be dynamically established by a higher layer. The higher layer, in this case the network layer, has a Dynamically Established Datalink (DED) component. The DED service will set up a modem call, an X.25 switched circuit or any other dynamic link, on demand. It will then keep that circuit up for a period of time, determined by management, in case more traffic comes through. After a period of inactivity, it brings the circuit down.

Thus, for data links, Digital supports HDLC, including dynamic X.25 or V.25 circuits. For LANs, Digital supports the IEEE Logical Link Control (LLC). LLC, in turn, makes it possible for DECnet to easily incorporate Ethernet, FDDI, and maybe Token-Ring.

Network Layer

At the network layer, there are two issues that need to be addressed. First is whether any two nodes will be able to read each other's packets. ISO 8473 defines a standard format for data and error packets that DECnet/OSI uses.

The second issue is how nodes find out about each other. Networks are composed of end systems and intermediate systems. If two end nodes on the same network want to communicate, the question of finding each other is not too difficult. The difficult issue is when an intermediate system needs to be used to route packets between different subnetworks (or within a single very large subnetwork). The question of routing information is addressed at two levels.

First, ISO defines an End System to Intermediate System (ES-IS) routing exchange protocol that allows end systems and intermediate systems sharing a common subnetwork to find each other. This is accomplished through End System (ES) and Intermediate System (IS) hello packets which are multicast on an ISO-defined address. DECnet/OSI uses this protocol, defined in ISO 9542.

The more difficult question for routing information is dynamic exchange of routing information between different IS systems. ISO 9542 defines how an ES tells an IS about its existence. Currently, there is no ISO protocol for IS systems to tell other IS systems about the end systems they can service.

The Digital protocol for this information exchange is the link state packet IS-IS protocol, which forms the basis for the current ISO draft. Digital's IS-IS enables two routers to exchange routing information dynamically. It does this through the exchange of link state packets. A link state packet, which contains information on all a node's neighbors, is issued by each intermediate system and sent to every other intermediate system on the network. After the packets are flooded through the network, the collection of ISs have a common view of the state of the network—the link state database.

In addition to the link state database, every IS also keeps two other kinds of information. First, it has static routing information entered by network management. Second, there is a database of adjacencies, compiled from the ISO 9542 hello packets that have come in. Given these three sources of information, the routing decision process is able to decide which of the adjacent neighbors would be able to move a packet for a given destination one hop closer to its destination.

To simplify the routing decision, Digital segments networks into areas. Within an area, the routing decision is made on the individual node address and is known as level 1 routing. Outside an area, the routing decision is made solely on the area address, and is known as level 2 routing.

If a packet is forwarded via level 2 routing, eventually it will reach the destination area. There, it is handed off to a level 1 router for delivery to the actual node. Segmentation of routing into a hierarchy permits large networks to be built. Level 1 routers exchange link state packets that give the location of all nodes within an area. Level 2 routers exchange link state packets that show the location of all areas.

Area-based routing is one way that Digital networks can coexist with other OSI-compliant networks. The Digital view of the world is a series of networks, connected together by public networks. Within a network, dynamic routing information is exchanged. Across network boundaries, routing information is manual.

Interoperability at the network layer is thus achieved in two ways. If a vendor has an ISO 8473 compliant end system, the node can easily become part of a DECnet area. If the node also meets the ISO 9542 ES-IS protocols, the system will automatically configure itself (using an IS hello message). An alternative to making another vendor's equipment part of the DECnet routing domain is to keep the networks segmented and connect the intermediate systems together using a common subnetwork (i.e., X.25) and static routing information.

At the transport layer, Digital has traditionally used the Network Services Protocol (NSP), a reliable transport mechanism similar to TCP or the ISO

TP4 protocols. In Phase V, Digital supports three of the TP classes: 0, 2, and 4. TP4 is the primary transport protocol for Digital applications; TP0 and TP2 are there simply for interconnection to primitive non-Digital systems.

Upper Layers

At this point, the DECnet is a pretty faithful OSI network, with a few additional features for backward compatibility such as DDCMP, and a few supplemental features such as the Dynamically Established Datalink and Modem Control services.

At the Session Layer, Digital supports two different session layers. The OSI Session Layer service is supported for OSI application services. Digital application services use another session layer service, the Digital Session Control protocol. We actually have here three kinds of networks: pure OSI, DECnet Phase V, and DECnet Phase IV. The pure OSI network (i.e., FTAM between two hosts) would use OSI Session, TP4, and the relevant lower layer protocols. Communication between Phase IV and Phase V would use the NSP transport and two interconnected routing domains. The Phase V network would use the Digital Session Control, TP4, and the Digital Phase V routing protocols.

The number of possible combinations of protocol stacks in such an environment is potentially quite large. To keep track of the path available to a given application, Digital uses a concept of towers. A tower is a series of addresses from the network layer on up. One tower might be Digital routing, TP4, Digital Session Control, and DAP. Another tower might be the same, but with the NSP protocols substituted for TP4. Each node keeps a set of towers, showing the possible combinations of protocols to be used for communication.

To communicate between two nodes and/or applications, the Digital session layer compares the tower sets and comes up with a common subset that can be used. If there is more than one possible set of towers in common, it is up to the initiating node to decide which one is best.

The use of towers is thus one aspect of the Digital Session Control service that is different from the generic OSI service. Another aspect is the integration with the DNA Naming Service (DNS). DNS is a distributed, replicated naming service used by the Session Control layer to keep node names and application names and their corresponding tower sets (addresses).

The integration of DNS allows the user and application to communicate across the network using a logical name. The Session Control layer will translate the name into a tower set, which will then be handed down to the appropriate transport layer for initiation of a virtual circuit.

The name server is used in more than just the Session Control layer. It is also an integral part of the Distributed File Service, and will presumably form the foundation for any Digital X.500 offerings.

Towers and DNS are strictly for use within the DECnet Phase V domain. For interconnection to the outside world, Digital uses the OSI Session layer. Built on top of that, Digital has two major services: FTAM and X.400.

Digital's FTAM implementation is fairly robust. It supports the first three document types (unstructured text, sequential string, and unstructured binary). Digital has implemented the recovery functional unit. In addition, it has an FTAM/DAP gateway, which allows DECnet nodes to access non-DECnet FTAM systems.

Digital implements X.400 as a gateway into its own proprietary message-handling system, MAILbus. Within a DECnet environment, the Message Router is the Message Transfer Agent of MAILbus. It moves messages between user interfaces such as ALL-IN-1 and gateways. Digital has implemented gateways for Telex, IBM's SNADS and PROFS, TCP/IP SMTP, and X.400.

The gateway takes an incoming MAILbus message and, using Digital's Distributed Directory product, translates the address. It also does any translation of the message body (i.e., ASCII to EBCDIC for the IBM world). The message is then sent into the next message handling system. Digital does not really do X.400; it gateways into that environment, which is equivalent as far as the user is concerned (and is fully compliant with X.400 and GOSIP standards).

True OSI?

Is DECnet/OSI OSI? At the lower layers, Digital is using OSI internally. The data link, network layer, and transport layer protocols are compliant with OSI, and Phase V applications will use those protocols. Other protocols, such as NSP, are provided for backwards compatibility, but the OSI services are the primary Phase V infrastructure. At the session layer, Digital diverges into two coexistent networks. Pure OSI is used for interconnection to the outside world; Digital protocols are used internally.

The issue is one of philosophy. Is this a true OSI network if most of the application effort seems to be focused in a Digital proprietary stack? The Digital marketing position is that they are adding value and that as the OSI standards stabilize and mature, we can expect to see things shift over to the OSI side of the stack.

As an example, consider name servers. Integration of logical naming into the network has an important implication for a wide variety of different services. Digital uses the name server in the Distributed File System, for example, as a way of providing transparent mounting of remote file systems.

Another area where Digital supplements OSI is network management. Both Digital and pure OSI network management are based on the CMIP protocols. Digital has supplemented these in two ways. First, Digital has architected the agents and event loggers on an individual node. Different network modules are able to give events to an event logger, which then uses the CMIP Management Event Notification subset to send the events to a variety of event sinks on the network. Likewise, Digital architected the management agent on a node, so incoming management directives are dispatched to the appropriate network modules. These supplemental architectures mean that each module is not forced to implement its own CMIP initiators and responders.

The second area Digital has architected for network management is the management director. It has done this at two levels. First, there is a network command language (NCL) which specifies how a user can input a CMIP directive and how it is parsed into CMIP. NCL also specifies the way in which results are displayed back on the user's terminal or console.

NCL is a fairly primitive, command-line based management director. A more ambitious effort is Digital's Enterprise Management Architecture (EMA) and the associated Management Control Center (DECmcc) product. EMA splits the function of the director up into three pieces:

- access modules
- function modules
- presentation modules

The access module is responsible for communicating with manageable entities. A CMIP access module would be used for communicating with a DECnet Phase V entity, whereas a bridge management access module would use a different protocol for managing bridges. In addition to bridges and CMIP, Digital will be supporting T1 multiplexors and the LAT (used for terminal servers).

Presentation modules are responsible for communicating with user devices. Digital presentation modules include DECwindows and traditional line-oriented interpreters. Finally, there are function modules. The point of this architecture is that a function (such as initializing an entity) can be applied over a variety of different network protocols at the same time. It is the responsibility of each of the access modules to communicate with its entities.

Subnetworks

CHAPTER 2

Subnetworks

In the tradition of networking books, this chapter begins with a discussion of physical wiring, synchronous protocols, and other issues in the domain of providing bandwidth: lots of bits available to higher-level network services. It will, however, quickly leave these issues behind and concentrate on the data link part of the network.

The purpose of a data link is to move a packet of data between two nodes. Since a data link may have many nodes on it, we refer to this service as a subnetwork. A variety of subnetworks exists, each suited to a different kind of environment. Chapter 3 will discuss how the network layer brings all these subnetworks together to form an integrated, cohesive internetwork. This chapter, however, concerns itself with the details of the different subnetworks used in a Phase V network.

The basic service of all these technologies is to move a packet of data between any two nodes connected to the subnetwork. Although the data link and physical layers may be quite complex—as in the case of FDDI, for example—the service is delivery of a datagram between any two nodes. In this sense, we can view all subnetwork technologies as a cloud (see Fig. 2-1).

Throughout this book, you will see a variety of users of the data link service. The major user in a DECnet is the Digital Network Architecture network layer. In addition to the network layer, however, we will see that the Local Area Transport (LAT) is a direct user for terminal server to host transfer and the Maintenance Operations Protocol (MOP) uses the data link directly for downline loading operating systems from a remote host. Support protocols, such as the naming service, the time protocol, and remote procedure calls, are also direct users of the service. In addition, other network architectures, such as TCP/IP, may be simultaneously sharing a data link with all these other protocols.

Networks used to consist solely of point-to-point data links meant to tie pairs of individual computers together. These point-to-point protocols were

2-1

Basic Function of the
Subnetwork

often meant to operate in a wide-area environment—this was in the days when computers were expensive and each site had one computer.

An example of these point-to-point protocols is IBM's bisync. In the Digital environment, early PDP and VAX systems used the Digital Data Communications Message Protocol (DDCMP). DDCMP is still used to connect nodes in a wide-area environment.

DDCMP was quickly supplanted in a local environment by the Ethernet protocols. Digital networks have become Ethernet centric: Most Digital computers come with built-in Ethernet adapters, and special-purpose systems such as terminal servers and print servers are all designed to fit on the Ethernet.

The picture of DDCMP for wide-area network (WAN) connections and Ethernet for LANs has been supplemented in Phase V with several other subnetworking protocols. FDDI has been added as a high-speed LAN backbone. X.25, used for years in DEC networks, has been integrated more tightly and is used to establish dynamic wide-area links and for using public data communications networks as a path in the middle of a Digital network. Finally, the HDLC protocols are increasingly being used as a supplement to DDCMP for point-to-point wide-area environments.

As we shall see, the use of HDLC as a native protocol for DECnet/OSI Phase V is an important transition for Digital. The HDLC protocols form the basis for the protocols used in some important wide-area architectures such as the Integrated Services Digital Network (ISDN). By ensuring HDLC compatibility, Digital makes it easier to move to technologies such as ISDN as they mature. It should be noted that Digital controllers have long supported HDLC protocols in packages such as the X.25 Packet Switch Interface (PSI) software. The difference between Phase IV and Phase V is that HDLC plays a more important role in Phase V.

This chapter will look at one additional protocol, Digital's modem connect module. This module resides at the physical layer and allows the network layer to activate a modem-based connection dynamically when it needs a link to a particular destination.

Dynamic data link capability becomes increasingly important as diverse networks interconnect. Interconnected networks are often needed only periodically, and dedicated lines between them would be prohibitively expensive. The modem control protocol at the physical layer, along with the dynamic data link modules in the network layer, allow bandwidth to be allocated as needed.

Although this chapter focuses on the data link layer, it occasionally refers to the physical layer of the network, particularly in the case of the two LAN technologies—Ethernet and FDDI. We will see that because the subnetwork and network protocols are merging somewhat, there is a need to discuss the use of data link-level interconnections (bridges) versus physical layer (repeaters) and network layer (router) strategies.

Ethernets

Ethernet was originally developed at Xerox's Palo Alto Research Center and was subsequently standardized by the IEEE as the 802.3 LAN protocols. This book uses Ethernet to refer to both the original Ethernet and the subsequent 802.3 standards. When it is necessary to distinguish between the two, the term 802.3 refers to the IEEE standard and Ethernet Version 2 refers to the latest version of the original DEC/Xerox/Intel specification.

The basic configuration of any Ethernet is a shared bus. At its simplest, the Ethernet is a single wire with many nodes attached to it. Any one node can send a packet to any other node. As we shall see, the logical picture of a single bus or wire is an oversimplification of most actual physical configurations. Devices called repeaters are used to connect many different segments into a multisegment Ethernet. These multisegment Ethernets can in turn be connected by bridges into an extended Ethernet. The whole tangle of wire looks to the user like a logical bus whereby any node can send a packet to any other node. We will see that this is not quite true: The devices connecting the pieces of the extended Ethernet together, the bridges, can filter out traffic.

CSMA/CD Protocols

The basic operation of the Ethernet uses a protocol that goes under the catchy name of CSMA/CD: Carrier Sense–Multiple Access/Collision Detect. Carrier Sense means all nodes sharing the logical bus can sense whether another node is transmitting. If another node is transmitting, the well-behaved Ethernet node waits. Multiple Access means if the medium is not in use, any node can send without waiting for special permission.

Since any two nodes can send, it is possible that two nodes listen, sense the medium is free, and simultaneously start sending the data. The result is a collision on the network: equivalent to people talking at once. Whereas two people may ignore the resulting collision, in an Ethernet both nodes detect the collision and stop sending.

Both nodes then wait for a random period of time (different for each node), then again listen to the medium. If the medium is free, they can start sending. Although it is theoretically possible for nodes to keep colliding and nothing be sent, in reality this method of sharing a bus works quite well. A typical Ethernet has an average use of around 10–15 percent, which is sufficient for all nodes to send when they want to with very few collisions.

Studies show that when the average use of the Ethernet starts to approach 30–50 percent, the number of collisions begins to increase exponentially. If all of a network's nodes are on a single Ethernet, high growth of network use can indeed saturate the subnetwork.

Realistically, however, most networks use multiple Ethernets. Nodes that frequently communicate with other are put onto a single Ethernet. Then either a bridge or a router is used to connect the multiple work groups into a single, integrated, extended LAN. The backbone of this LAN can be another Ethernet or an FDDI subnetwork.

Ethernet Packet Formats

Figure 2-2 shows the basic format of an Ethernet version 2 packet. Both the source and destination addresses have a 48-bit unique ID. IDs are universally administered and delegated to the manufacturers of Ethernet controller cards. Note that a 46-bit unique ID (after you take into account the flags) is equivalent to 70,254,592,000,000 unique addresses.

The first 2 bits of the ID are used as flags, and are thus not used as part of the individual address. The first bit indicates whether the address is an individual or a group address. A group address is used to refer to many stations (i.e., all DNA Phase V routers). An address of all 1s is a broadcast, which is received by every node on an Ethernet. The use of broadcasts is being strongly discouraged by most network architects, the rationale being that not all nodes on the network need to work just because some subset of

Preamble		
Destination Address		48 bits
Source Address		
Protocol Type		Number not a valid length
Data		Data + Pad ≥ 46
Pad		
Frame Check Sequence		

2-2
Ethernet
Version 2 Format

nodes needs to communicate. Instead, multicast addresses—a group address of more limited scope—are encouraged.

The second bit of the ID indicates whether the address is locally or universally administered. Universal addresses are guaranteed to be unique. It is possible, although not necessarily wise, to administer the address space locally by having the network manager assign addresses. The reason this approach is not considered optimal is that it easily leads to duplicate addresses when previously disjoint address spaces are joined together.

Following the source and destination addresses is the protocol type indicator. This indicator shows for which user of the Ethernet service this particular packet is meant. The protocol type indicator is how, for example, DECnet and TCP/IP can both share the services of a single Ethernet. The Ethernet module will deliver each packet to the appropriate user based on the protocol type field. Note the comment in Figure 2-2, which says the protocol type cannot be a valid length—we shall shortly see that the 802.3 format of Ethernet has a length indicator instead of a type field and this restriction allows us to distinguish the two variations of the packet format.

The length indicator is an optional field that is not part of the Ethernet specification but is sometimes provided so upper-level protocols can determine if padding has been added. If included, it is the third field in the Ethernet packet. The data field in an Ethernet packet must be between 46 and 1500 bytes long. The minimum length requirement for an Ethernet packet ensures that it will remain on the medium long enough for nodes to detect a collision if one occurs. Short packets mean short collisions and thus are hard to discover.

The data part of the packet is transparent to the Ethernet module of the network. It could contain any data. Typically, it contains data for a user, such as the network layer. Thos data, in turn, will consist of a header for the network layer followed by some data, which will be a header for the transport layer and some data, and so on.

Preamble		
Destination Address	▓▓▓▓▓▓	48 bits
Source Address		
Length		
Destination SAP	▓▓▓▓▓▓	802.1 SNAP or "real" SAP
Source SAP		
PDU Type	▓▓▓▓▓▓	XID
Protocol ID	▓▓▓▓▓▓	Only if DSAP = SNAP
Data		
Pad		
Frame Check Sequence		

2-3
IEEE 802.3
Frame Format

The pad is used to increase the data field so it reaches the minimum length requirement for the Ethernet. Following the pad is the frame check sequence (FCS). The frame check sequence is calculated based on the data being transmitted and appended to the end of the packet. The destination node will recalculate the FCS and then compare it to the one received. Ethernet is typically an error-free medium (error rates are in the range of 10^{-9}), so the FCS does not fail often.

IEEE LANs

Some aspects of the Ethernet frame format are protocol dependent; the pad field is not needed in a token ring, for example. When the IEEE began standardizing LAN technology, it broke Ethernet up into two sublayers:

- Logical Link Control (LLC)
- Medium Access Control (MAC)

The LLC is medium independent and applies to all standardized LAN technologies, including the token ring, token bus, CSMA/CD, and FDDI. Underneath the LLC sublayer and on top of the physical layer is the MAC sublayer. Each LAN technology has its own MAC format. Figure 2-3 shows the packet format for an IEEE 802.3 LAN packet. Notice that the preamble, destination, and source addresses are the same as the Ethernet version 2. This is the MAC portion of the field.

After the address fields is a length field. Because the protocol type field in Ethernet was required to be a number that is not a valid length, a node receiving a packet is able to determine which type of Ethernet packet it is and can thus interpret the fields that follow. Ethernet protocol types are greater than the maximum packet length.

Following the length field is a destination service access point (SAP) indicator. The destination SAP is the beginning of the LLC portion of the packet and would be the same for all MAC technologies. This field is somewhat like the protocol type field in Ethernet version 2.

There is a special SAP known as the subnetwork access point (SNAP). The SNAP is a placeholder that indicates that the real address of the user is in the first byte of the data field. If the SAP contains a real address, the first byte of the data contains user data. The source service access point is the address of the program on the sending node that submitted the frame.

Finally, the LLC part of the header contains a protocol data unit (PDU) type field. There are two versions of the logical link control. In LLC Class I, the type used by Digital and most other vendors, the operation is connectionless—each packet is a stand-alone unit of information.

In LLC Class II, which is connection oriented, it is up to the data link layer to ensure that all packets in a stream of data are delivered to the destination SAP in the order they are sent. LLC Class II thus performs error detection and recovery.

LLC Class I is a best-effort delivery service. The packets are delivered, but there is no guarantee a particular packet will make it or that two packets will be delivered in the order they are sent.

Within the LLC Class I operation, there are three types of packets:

- Unnumbered Information
- Exchange ID
- Test

Frames sent by upper-layer service users are almost always Unnumbered Information (UI). The exchange ID (XID) and test frames are used for initialization and maintenance operations.

Figures 2-4 and 2-5 show some typical Ethernet traffic as recorded on Network General's Sniffer Analyzer. The Sniffer decodes each of the frames to show the headers of the different layers of a packet. In Figure 2-4 we see that the data link layer of the packet is Ethernet version 2. There is a destination address, which is a multicast address to all Digital routers. There is an individual source for the frame, followed by the protocol ID, which is the general DECnet identifier.

Following the data link portion of the packet is the data field. The data field is transparent to the Ethernet layer but does have some meaning for the routing layer. This particular packet is an Ethernet Router Hello Message. As far as the data link layer is concerned, however, the data field is transparent.

```
DETAIL
 DLC:
 DLC:
 DLC:  Frame 56 arrived at  17:01:34.5700 ; frame size is 60 (003C hex) bytes
 DLC:  Destination: Multicast AB0000030000, DEC Routers
 DLC:  Source     : Station DECnet002D1C
 DLC:  Ethertype = 6003 (DECNET)
 DLC:
 DRP:  ----- DECNET Routing Protocol -----
 DRP:
 DRP:  Data length = 41
 DRP:  Control Packet Format = 0B
 DRP:               0... .... = no padding
 DRP:               .000 .... = reserved
 DRP:               .... 101. = Ethernet Router Hello Message
 DRP:               .... ...1 = Control Packet Format
 DRP:  Control Packet Type = 05
 DRP:  Version Number  = 02
 DRP:  ECO Number      = 00
 DRP:  User ECO Number = 00
 DRP:  ID of Transmitting Node = 7.45
 DRP:      Information = 01
                          Frame 56 of 153
                         Use TAB to select windows
 1       2 Set            4 Zoom  5          6Disply 7 Prev  8 Next         10 New
  Help    mark             out     Menus      options  frame   frame         capture
```

2-4 An Ethernet Frame

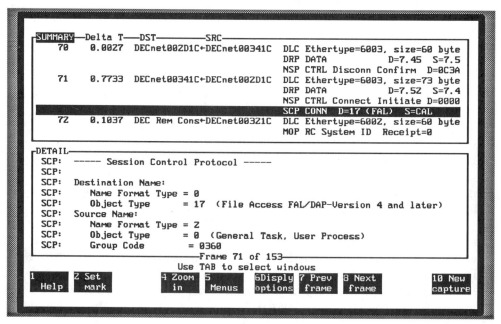

```
SUMMARY  Delta T   DST          SRC
   70    0.0027  DECnet002D1C←DECnet00341C   DLC Ethertype=6003, size=60 byte
                                             DRP DATA        D=7.45  S=7.5
                                             NSP CTRL Disconn Confirm  D=0C3A
   71    0.7733  DECnet00341C←DECnet002D1C   DLC Ethertype=6003, size=73 byte
                                             DRP DATA        D=7.52  S=7.4
                                             NSP CTRL Connect Initiate D=0000
                                             SCP CONN  D=17 (FAL)  S=CAL
   72    0.1037  DEC Rem Cons←DECnet003Z1C   DLC Ethertype=6002, size=60 byte
                                             MOP RC System ID   Receipt=0
DETAIL
 SCP:  ----- Session Control Protocol -----
 SCP:
 SCP:  Destination Name:
 SCP:     Name Format Type = 0
 SCP:     Object Type      = 17  (File Access FAL/DAP-Version 4 and later)
 SCP:  Source Name:
 SCP:     Name Format Type = Z
 SCP:     Object Type      = 0  (General Task, User Process)
 SCP:     Group Code       = 0360
                          Frame 71 of 153
                         Use TAB to select windows
 1       2 Set            4 Zoom  5          6Disply 7 Prev  8 Next         10 New
  Help    mark             in      Menus      options  frame   frame         capture
```

2-5 Typical Ethernet-Based Traffic

Figure 2-5 shows both detailed and summary views of traffic on the Ethernet. Again, we see that the packets are Ethernet version 2 (the indication of an Ethertype means that it is not an 802.3 packet). The first two packets bear the general DECnet protocol ID. The third packet is a specialized protocol, the Maintenance Operation Protocol.

In the first two packets, the concept of an envelope in an envelope is illustrated. The data link layer has a data field, which is actually a routing layer header plus data. Those data, in turn, are the Network Services Protocol (NSP) or transport layer. Finally, the last envelope contains a session control protocol header plus data. In this case, the session layer packet is requesting that a connection be initiated, to exchange data using the application-layer Data Access Protocol.

Again, at this point, we do not really care what is inside these packets. The function of the data link layer is simply to deliver a packet of information from one node to another. How that information is interpreted is the subject of the rest of the book.

Figure 2-6 shows different addresses used in Digital networks. The first section of the figure shows a variety of LAN multicast addresses used in both types of Ethernets. The 48 bits of the address field is split into 12 fields of 4 bits each. Each of the 4 bits is then given a number using the hexadecimal numbering system. All Fs, for example, are equivalent to all 1s in the address field. The last three parts of the figure show protocol types for Ethernet version 2, and the SAP and Protocol ID codes for use in the 802.3 variant of Ethernet.

Basic Ethernet Configuration

Figure 2-7 shows the basic Ethernet configuration. Originally, this consisted of a piece of coaxial cable, also known as ThickWire or Baseband. Since then, a variety of physical media has been approved by the IEEE. These include:

- 10BASE5 (ThickWire), standard coaxial cable. A single segment can be up to 500 meters long with 100 nodes.
- 10BASE2 (ThinWire), a thinner coaxial cable with a smaller maximum length, but less expensive and easier to handle.
- 10BASET which uses unshielded twisted pair.
- Fiber used for security applications.

Fiber is coming into broader and broader use. As an Ethernet segment, fiber is often selected because it is hard to tap unobtrusively. Fiber is also used for connecting repeaters and bridges, and as the basis for the high-speed FDDI LANs.

The details of configuring the specific media are beyond the scope of this book. The typical configuration, however, consists of several components:

LAN Addresses	
09-00-2B-00-00-04	ISO 9542 End System Hello
09-00-2B-00-00-05	ISO 9542 IS Hello
CF-00-00-00-00-00	Loopback Assistance
FF-FF-FF-FF-FF-FF	Broadcast
AB-00-00-01-00-00	MOP Dump/Load Assistance
AB-00-00-02-00-00	MOP Remote Console
AB-00-00-03-00-00	DNA Level 1 Routers
AB-00-00-04-00-00	DNA End Nodes
AB-00-04-01-xx-xx	System Communication Architecture
09-00-2B-00-00-02	VAXeln
09-00-2B-00-00-03	LAN Traffic Monitor
09-00-2B-00-00-07	NetBIOS Emulator (PCSA)
09-00-2B-00-00-0F	Local Area Transport
09-00-2B-01-00-00	All Bridges
09-00-2B-01-00-01	All Local Bridges
09-00-2B-02-00-00	DNA Level 2 Routers
09-00-2B-02-01-00	DNA Naming Service Advertisement
09-00-2B-02-01-01	DNA Naming Service Solicitation
Protocol Type Assignments	
90-00	Ethernet Loopback Protocol
60-01	MOP Dump/Load
60-02	MOP Remote Console
60-03	DNA Routing
60-04	Local Area Transport
60-05	Diagnostics
60-07	System Communication Architecture
80-38	Bridge
80-3B	VAXeln
80-3C	DNA Naming Service
80-3E	DNA Time Service
80-3F	LAN Traffic Monitor
80-40	NetBIOS Emulator
IEEE SAP Assignments	
03	LLC Sublayer Management Function Group SAP
FF	Broadcast SAP
00	Null SAP
02	LLC Sublayer Management Function Individual SAP
AA	SNAP SAP
FE	ISO Network Layer Entity

2-6
Selected
LAN Addresses

IEE Protocol ID Codes for IEEE	
08-00-2B-60-01	MOP Dump/Load
08-00-2B-60-02	MOP Remote Console
08-00-2B-60-03	DNA Routing
08-00-2B-60-04	Local Area Transport
08-00-2B-60-05	Diagnostics
08-00-2B-60-07	System Communication Architecture
08-00-2B-80-38	Bridge
08-00-2B-80-3B	VAXeln
08-00-2B-80-3C	DNA Naming Service
08-00-2B-80-3E	DNA Time Service
08-00-2B-80-3F	LAN Traffic Monitor
08-00-2B-80-40	NetBIOS Emulator
08-00-2B-90-00	MOP LAN Loopback Protocol

2-6 *(Cont.)*
Selected Addresses

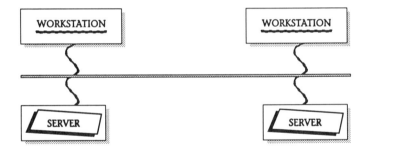

2-7
A Bus Topology

- the medium
- a controller in the workstation, server, or any other device on the network
- a transceiver used to attach to the medium
- a transceiver cable used to connect the transceiver to the controller

In many implementations, a multiport transceiver is used to connect several computers to the medium at one point of attachment. The multiport transceiver can be thought of as a concentrator. The Digital version of this device is known as a DELNI.

Device Class	Device	Notes
Terminal Server	DECserver 200	Up to eight devices
	DECserver 250	Two parallel devices and four asynchronous serial devices
	DECserver 300	Up to 16 asynchronous devices
	DECserver 550	From 8 to 128 asynchronous devices or 4 to 64 IBM 3270 terminals
Remote Terminal Server	MUXserver 100	Links up to DECmux II Remote Terminal Servers for a total of 16 devices
	Muxserver 300/310	Links up to the DECmux 300 Remote Terminal Server to support up to 48 remote devices
Print Server	LPS40	PostScript printer
Routers	DECrouter 100	Supports up to 16 19.2-kbps synchronous links
	DECrouter 200	Up to eight 19.2-kbps asynchronous DDCMP lines
	DECrouter 2000	Two 256-kbps or four 64-kbps synchronous DDCMP lines
Portals	Internet Portal	Allows TCP/IP traffic over a DNA backbone.
	DECnet/Internet Router 2000	Routes both TCP/IP and DECnet traffic
	X25portal 2000	Two 256-kbps links to allow X.25 traffic to use a DECnet backbone
	X25router 2000	Two 256-kbps or four 64-kbps links to allow DECnet users access to X.25 facilities
Gateways	DECnet/SNA Gateway for Synchronous Transport	256-kbps bandwidth link to SNA environment
	DECnet/SNA Gateway for Channel Transport	Channel speed link (1.2 Mbps) to S/370 mainframe
Server	PCLAN/Server 3100	Server for up to 32 PCs
Security	DESNC	Secure Ethernet Controller (works with the VAX Key Distribution Center (KDC) software

2-8 Digital Communications Servers

The controller in the workstation varies according to the type of peripheral bus (and hence type of computer), as well as sustained throughput rate. Controllers also vary based on the type of physical wiring they support. Most controllers that support ThinWire also support unshielded twisted pair (UTP) through the use of a device called a balun (balanced/unbalanced), which couples the ThinWire to the twisted pair.

In addition to standard computers, there is a wide variety of specialized devices that act as servers on the Ethernet. Figure 2-8 lists a variety of these devices from DEC—an up-to-date list can be found in Digital's current *Telecommunications and Networks Buyers Guide*. As with Ethernet controllers and media devices, servers are available from a wide variety of vendors in addition to Digital

Print servers and terminal servers are two of the basic specialized servers that reside on the Ethernet. The terminal server is an inexpensive way of putting many terminals in contact with different hosts on the network. In addition to terminals, the terminal server can connect modems and printers. The terminal server is covered in more detail in Chapter 7 on Local Area Transport protocols.

Routers, covered in Chapter 3, are an alternative to MAC-layer bridges as a way of connecting several Ethernets together. The routers vary based on the number of connections they can support and the amount of throughput they have. As with other devices, routers are available from a wide variety of vendors.

Multisegment Ethernets

A single segment of Ethernet is typically limited to 30–100 nodes: the limits are based on the type of physical wiring used as well as the error rates and availability desired. The Ethernet architecture supports up to 1024 nodes on a single subnetwork. The way this is done is by connecting multiple segments using repeaters.

Figure 2-9 shows a multisegment Ethernet connected together using repeaters. The function of the repeater is to take all signals on one side of the repeater and retime, reamplify, and retransmit them on the other segment. The repeater thus logically extends the wire at the physical layer of the network.

The basic rule of configuration for Digital Ethernets is that there can be at most two repeaters in the path between any two nodes on the network. This means a typical multisegment Ethernet consists of a backbone, with segments running off of it. Nodes on two different segments would go through two repeaters when sending packets of data to each other.

The two-repeater rule is a means of ensuring that a collision will be detected within the architecturally defined parameters of the Ethernet protocol. Every device, including transceivers, repeaters, and the medium itself, introduces delay into the network.

In general, such rules are ways of making sure there is no excessive delay and that the Ethernet will work properly. Many different rules are used, depending on the type of medium and the vendor promulgating the rule. In the case of DEC, the methodology for wiring the Ethernet has been codified in DECconnect, which includes the two-repeater rule. It is important to

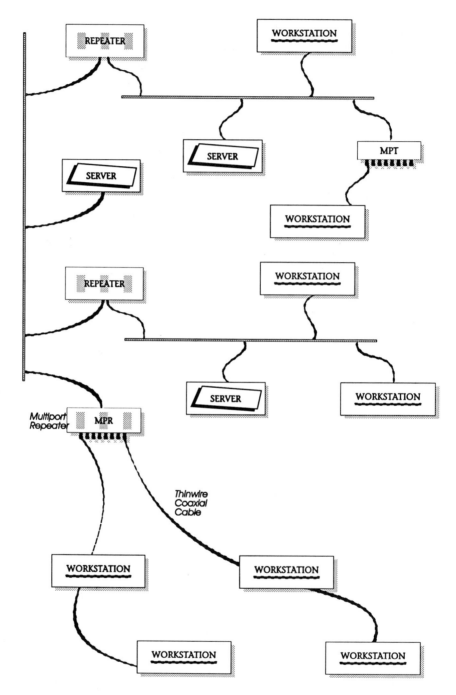

2-9 Repeater Configuration

note that this is just one of many available methodologies, all trying to do the same thing—provide a workable wiring for the Ethernet protocols.

Several different repeaters are available. The typical repeater connects two ThickWire connections together using two transceiver cables. Other repeaters, such as the Digital multiport repeater, connect one piece of Thick-Wire (the backbone) to up to eight segments of ThinWire or unshielded twisted pair. A third type of repeater is the fiber repeater, which enables the segments being connected together to be up to 1000 meters apart. The fiber repeater is actually two half-repeaters, each connected to one of the segments. The fiber is then connected to each of the half-repeaters.

Bridging Ethernets

The bridge is a device that transparently connects multiple subnetworks into an extended subnetwork. Typically, this means connecting two separate Ethernets into an extended Ethernet. The user of the subnetwork still sees the basic property of being able to send a packet of data transparently to any node on the subnetwork.

The difference between a bridge and a repeater is that the bridge only forwards those packets that need to be forwarded, whereas the repeater, operating at the physical level, retransmits every modulation of the signal.

The bridge is thus a filter, selectively sending packets of data based on the source and destination addresses. To do the forwarding, the bridge must learn which nodes are on which side (see Fig. 2-10). When a bridge initializes, it starts listening to each port, noting which source addresses it sees on each side. Based on this information, the bridge knows the location of some nodes. The bridge will not know about every node, however, because not all nodes will transmit information during the initialization period.

When the bridge sees a packet that has both destination and source addresses on the same side, it has no need to forward the packet and ignores it. If the bridge notices that a destination address is located on the other side of the bridge from the source address, the bridge forwards the packet. When a bridge sees an unknown destination address, however, it always "floods" the packet; that is, it sends the packet out of every port it has (this model assumes the bridge has multiple ports, although the typical Ethernet bridge only has two ports).

After a while, the destination of the flooded packet will send a response. The original destination node becomes the source address on the response packet. This information allows the bridge to update its forwarding tables to contain the location of the target node.

Examination of the source portion of the Ethernet packet lets the bridge learn the location of nodes. The model assumes that a node is always on

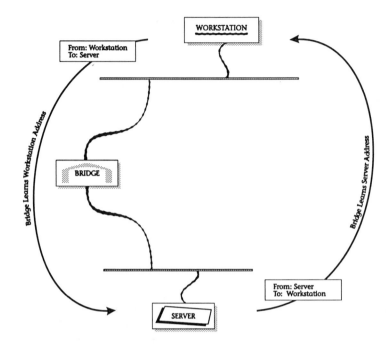

2-10 Bridge Learning Algorithm

one side or the other of a bridge. If there are loops in the bridge topology, however, then this model fails.

To ensure there are no loops, bridges use a spanning tree algorithm which prevents the topology formed by the bridges from containing any routes that form a loop. If two bridges would form a loop, one of the bridges is disabled. Some bridges, such as the ones from DEC, can put themselves in a "hot" backup state, thereby taking over if the active bridge fails. A few vendors still sell bridges that do not use the spanning tree algorithm; these bridges must thus be manually configured to avoid loops.

It is possible for several bridges to be in the path between two nodes (see Fig. 2-11). It is possible, in fact, to have the entire internetwork constructed using bridges. As long as there are no loops, the bridges will continue to forward packets and the entire extended Ethernet will look like one large subnetwork to the user. The problem with this approach is the rather simplistic routing method used by the bridge. We will see that the network layer uses a more sophisticated method to keep track of multiple paths between different nodes, adjusting packet routes based on the relative performance of different paths.

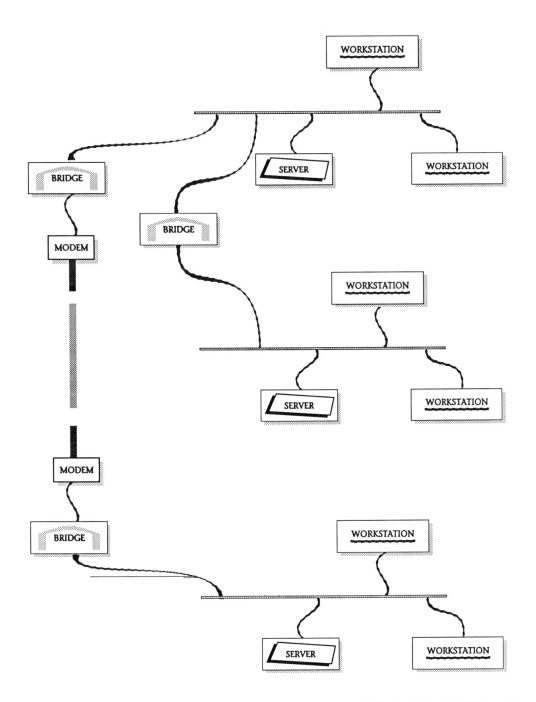

2-11 An Extended Ethernet

Ports	
TransLAN III	1, 4, or 8 ports
TransLAN IV	1 port
TransLAN 350	1 or 8 ports
Serial Line Interfaces	
V.35	1, 4, or 8
RS449/422, 4 or 8	
DS1	1 or 2
Line Speed Support	48 kbps to 2.048 Mbps
Maximum Filtering Rate	14,,880 frames per second
Maximum Forwarding Rate	
TransLAN III	2000 frames per second
TransLAN IV	3000
TransLAN 350	5000
Source: *Telecommunications and Networks Buyers Guide*, p. 2-93	

2-12 TransLAN Wide-Area Bridges

One type of bridge shown in Figure 2-11 is the wide-area bridge. Digital remarkets the Vitalink TransLAN wide-area bridge as a way of connecting Ethernets together. Figure 2-12 shows the characteristics of a few wide-area bridges made by Vitalink. Notice that the TransLAN III and the TransLAN 350 support up to eight wide-area connections to a single Ethernet. The bandwidth is up to 2.048 Mbps. This is one-fifth of the 10 Mbps speed on a single Ethernet. Typically, this will be more than enough bandwidth because only a small fraction of the packets on one Ethernet will need to be forwarded to another Ethernet. If there is enough bandwidth, then the limiting factor for time-sensitive protocols (e.g., LAT) is the latency over the wide-area link.

Many bridges include a filtering capability that allows only certain types of frames to be forwarded. DEC, in its internal network, uses wide-area bridges strictly for forwarding LAT traffic. Other traffic (such as DECnet) is filtered out. If a DECnet node wishes to communicate in a wide-area environment, that traffic is forwarded using a network-layer router.

In addition to filtering by protocol type, many environments will choose to filter out broadcasts by setting the filter function on a MAC-layer bridge. Broadcasts may require an answer from every node. In a multisegment Ethernet, this might involve a few hundred nodes. In an extended Ethernet, this might involve several thousand nodes. If the broadcast results in all nodes broadcasting their answers, a storm of data can quickly incapacitate the network.

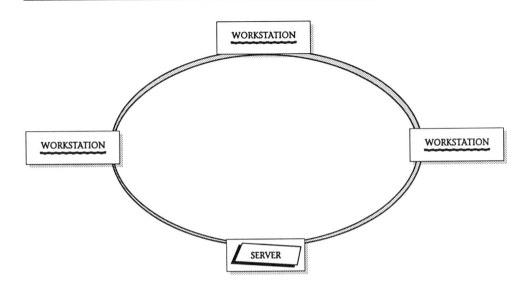

2-13 A Simple Ring

FDDI and Token Ring

Although the Ethernet operates at 10 Mbps, after the overhead of the data link layer and the collision avoidance mechanism, it is rare to see sustained throughput rates of more than 4–5 Mbps per second. Note that often this throughput is sufficient. A typical Ethernet will have 10–15 percent use and can easily support a network of 50–100 nodes doing diskless NFS and other fairly intensive protocols.

There are times, especially with heavy use graphics or in an organizational backbone, when the Ethernet is not enough. A faster network is the Fiber Distributed Data Interface (FDDI) which operates at a gross rate of 100 Mbps; theoretically it can achieve throughput rates of 80 Mbps, and some studies have claimed throughput as high as 90 Mbps.

The basic FDDI configuration is a ring (see Fig. 2-13). Each station on the ring copies incoming data to the next station. In addition to copying the data to the next node on the ring, a node may also make a copy of the data for its own buffers.

FDDI controllers typically also include a bypass function, used when the station is not active (see Fig. 2-14). The bypass function allows the ring to keep operating despite the missing link. When a signal is bypassed at a node, it is not regenerated, and the signal attenuates. If too many consecutive stations are bypassing the signal instead of regenerating it, the signal will become too weak.

The basic FDDI operation is similar to the IEEE 802.5 token ring, which operates at 4 or 16 Mbps. A difference is that FDDI usually consists of two

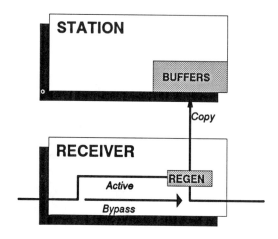

2-14
FDDI Copy Operation

rings. The primary ring is used during normal operation. If there is a break in the primary ring, the optional secondary ring is used to route data back the other way, providing a degree of fault tolerance.

An FDDI configuration can have up to 1000 physical links on a total fiber path of 200 km. If dual rings are being used, this is equivalent to 500 nodes on a 100-km (dual) ring. There is a maximum inter-station distance of 2 km.

The FDDI ring circumference limit is based on a single architectural parameter, the maximum ring latency, which is set at 1.617 ms. The maximum ring latency is the time it takes for a starting delimiter to circulate the ring. From this parameter, the total number of nodes, the maximum distance, and a variety of other ring parameters can be derived.

As an example, assume we have a total path length of 200 km. At the speed of 5085 ns/km, 200 km of fiber introduces a latency of 1.017 ms. If there are 1000 physical connections, with a latency of 600 ns, this introduces a further latency of 0.6 ms. Thus, the total latency of a 200-km, 1000 connection ring is 1.617 ms, equal to the maximum ring latency parameter. Changing the maximum ring latency parameter would change limits on the total number of nodes, the amount of fiber, or even the speed at which the network operates.

Although it is possible to put nodes directly on an FDDI ring, many vendors use a multistation access unit (MAU) as a concentrator. The MAU is a station on the dual ring, connecting to both pieces of fiber. Coming out of the MAU are (typically) 8 or 16 ports. If a station is inoperative, there is no problem with the signal attenuating since the bypass function is provided at the MAU.

One big advantage of the concentrator is that it is less expensive to provide single-ring controllers for workstations and servers than it is to provide a dual-ring attachment. Figure 2-15 shows a possible configuration for a

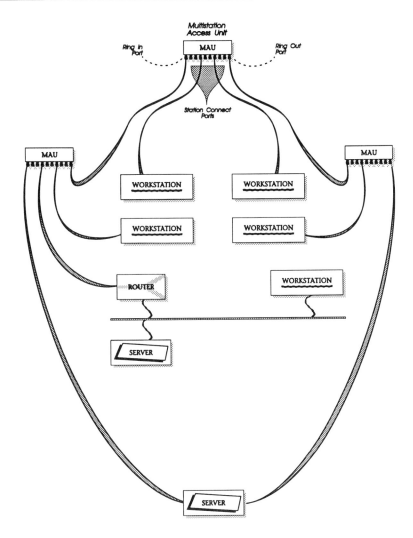

2-15 FDDI Concentrators

concentrator-based ring. Notice that a few stations are directly attached to the main ring. Most stations, however, are attached to the multistation access unit.

The difference between directly attaching a station to the ring and using an MAU is one of philosophy. Digital has come down squarely on the side of using an MAU as an intermediate device, but other companies advocate direct attachment to the ring by a workstation.

If FDDI is used as a backbone, then most stations are even further removed from the ring, being attached to an Ethernet. The Ethernet is con-

Preamble		16 or More Idle Symbols
Starting Delimiter		
Frame Control		Restricted Token?
Ending Delimiter		

2-16
FDDI Token Format

nected to the MAU using a bridge or a router. In the case of the Digital bridge, the device strips off the Ethernet header from the packet, puts on an FDDI header, and retransmits it. The bridge on the other side of the FDDI ring will perform the reverse operation, stripping the FDDI header and putting it back into Ethernet format.

This translating bridge is in contrast to the encapsulating bridge, which merely adds an FDDI header on top of the Ethernet header. The encapsulating bridge only works if the data are destined for an Ethernet, whereas the translating bridge will work on a variety of MAC technologies. Since translating bridges are performing a sort of routing function, it might be simpler to dispense with the bridges altogether and use routers instead.

FDDI Operation

In an Ethernet, any node can transmit if the medium is free. In a token ring such as FDDI, a node can only transmit when it receives a special packet, called the token (see Fig. 2-16). The token is passed from node to node on the ring.

If a node has nothing to transmit, it just copies the token through. If it does have something to transmit, it captures the token. The capture process consists of failing to copy and retransmit the token and, instead, substituting idle symbols where the token would have been. The node then has a set amount of time, governed by the token holding timer (THT), before it must replace the token on the ring. During that time, the node is free to send one or more data frames. A restricted token allows two (or more) nodes to engage in a dialogue by passing the token back and forth to each other without having to worry about other nodes cutting in.

Once a data frame is sent, it will circulate through the ring. Presumably, at some point a node will see its address and copy the data into its buffers in addition to copying the data through to the next station. When the frame goes back to the sending node, it will strip the frame from the ring by replacing the data with idle symbols.

Figure 2-17 shows the format of the data frame. At the end of the frame is the frame status field, which is used to see if a destination node recognized its address. If it did, it flipped the address recognized bit. If it also had enough room in its buffers to copy the frame, it flips the frame copied bit. The error detected bit is used if a frame check sequence fails.

Preamble		16 or More Idle Symbols
Starting Delimiter		
Frame Control		Class Bit: Synch/Asynch
		Address Length Bit
		Frame Type
		00 - MAC/SMT
		01 - LLC
		10 - Implementor
		11 - Future Use
		Priority Bits (LLC Frame)
Destination Address		
Source Address		
Data		
Frame Check Sequence		
Ending Delimiter		
Frame Status Field		Address Recognized?
		Error Detected?
		Frame Copied?

2-17
FDDI Frame Format

The data field is theoretically limited to roughly 8000 bytes, although most users of the FDDI will have much smaller packet sizes. Inside this data field would be the LLC header, followed by the headers for upper layers.

The frame control field is used to govern the basic operation of the ring. The address length bit, for example, selects a 2-byte or the standard 6-byte address. The frame type indicates if this is an internal MAC-management frame, one used for the FDDI station management (SMT) function, or an LLC data frame. More information on the frame type, priority bits, and class bit is presented in the following sections.

Modes of Operation

An FDDI ring operates in two modes:

- Synchronous mode guarantees a certain amount of bandwidth and response time to nodes.
- Asynchronous mode provides dynamic bandwidth sharing.

Asynchronous mode is instantaneously allocated via the token, whereas synchronous bandwidth is allocated ahead of time using SMT protocols. Note that initial FDDI implementations (including Digital's) do not make use of synchronous mode.

Synchronous bandwidth is allocated as a percentage of the target token rotation time (TTRT), which is another way of representing the total bandwidth on the network. The sum of the synchronous allocations should be less than or equal to 100 percent.

Each node with a nonzero bandwidth is allowed to transmit data frames for a period of time, without having to worry about starting the token rotation timer. If, after all nodes complete their synchronous transmissions there is still some bandwidth available, nodes can do asynchronous transmission up to the limit of the token holding timer.

Asynchronous transmission is a two-tier allocation of the bandwidth:

- Nonrestricted mode provides time slicing among all nodes that wish to send data.
- Restricted mode is dedicated to a single extended dialogue.

The normal operation is nonrestricted mode. In this mode, allocation of the token is based on a priority scheme. The priority scheme is based on the amount of time it takes for the token to circulate the ring. Each priority level has a threshold token rotation time.

As the token rotation time (TRT) gets longer and longer, the lower priority levels are cut off. Nodes can then only send data of higher priorities. As the token goes around the ring with a high priority, eventually all nodes will have sent their high priority data. This means the token will go around the ring more quickly, allowing lower priority data frames to be transmitted.

The target token rotation timer is the total bandwidth available on the ring. After the synchronous transmission is finished, there may still be a certain amount of remaining bandwidth, symbolized by the token rotation timer. The difference between the current TRT and the target TRT is thus the available asynchronous bandwidth—the minimum value of the TRT is equivalent to nobody sending synchronous traffic.

When a nonrestricted token is received, restricted mode is entered by two nodes. The first node sends an initial batch of data, then issues a restricted token. The receiving node sends its data, then sends the restricted token back out.

Restricted mode prevents all unrestricted asynchronous traffic (including basic station management tasks such as exchanging neighbor IDs). The decision to enter, terminate, or continue a restricted dialogue is up to the higher layers using FDDI. Since synchronous transmission is unaffected by the token, it is unaffected by the restricted mode.

One of the functions of the station management is to negotiate a maximum restricted mode time. Note that in restricted mode, there is really no need to obey the token holding timer—by its very nature restricted mode has already preempted fairness with other nodes.

Restricted and synchronous modes are optional features in FDDI. Restricted mode would presumably be used by critical functions such as system management. Synchronous mode would be used by time-critical applications such as voice.

Ring Initialization and Recovery

Any station that detects a need to initialize the ring issues a claim token frame. Multiple stations bid for the right to lead the initialization of the ring by continuously transmitting claim frames. Each station engaged in the bidding looks at an incoming claim frame to detect whether the frame is the one it originally sent or is another station's bid. Each frame contains a bid value, and the highest bid wins. A node that lost the bid would start copying frames through. At some point, one node's claim frame will circulate all the way around the ring and arrive back at the sending node, signifying a successful bid.

In the case of conflicting highest bids, arbitration is based on target token rotation time (TTRT), which is used to indicate how long a token should take to circulate the ring continuously. The lowest TTRT wins the bidding process. If there are multiple low TTRT values, then the highest station address wins.

As soon as a station wins the claim token process, it begins the ring initialization process. First, it sets the target token rotation timer to the value in the successful claim frame. It then resets the token rotation timer (used to detect a token that has gone awry) and issues a nonrestricted token.

This token will go through the ring three times before normal data traffic is possible. On the first round, each station sets the TRT value, then sets an internal flag to indicate that the ring is operational again. On the second round, synchronous traffic is issued. On the third round, asynchronous traffic can begin.

The claim token process is timed by each station. If the timer expires and the bidding is still unresolved, a station whose timer expires will begin transmitting a beacon. Note that only stations that are still in the bidding process can send a beacon. If a station is out of bidding and its timer expires, it reenters the bidding process.

The purpose of the beacon frame is to pinpoint where in the ring a problem is occurring. The beacon indicates that a significant logical break in the ring has occurred, either because a station is inoperative or because the medium has a break.

DNA Routing Layer	Maintenance Operations Protocol	User Program
DDCMP		
Satellite	Leased Line	Switched Line

2-18
Multiple
DDCMP Clients

Each ring transmitting beacons will transmit them continuously. As in the case of the claim token, any incoming beacons are examined. If the station address on the incoming beacon is different, it means a station upstream is also sending the beacon and downstream nodes will yield by ceasing to transmit their own beacons.

As each node yields, the source of the beacon gets closer and closer to the break in the ring. At some point, when the ring is fixed, a node will see its own station address in a beacon. This means the ring is operational again, and the claim token process is entered.

DDCMP

The Digital Data Communications Message Protocol (DDCMP) is one of the earlier Digital protocols, initially used for communication between PDP computers. DDCMP is a data link protocol that supports a wide variety of physical media (see Fig. 2-18) as well as a variety of users. The typical user is the DNA routing layer, but it is also used by MOP modules for remote booting. There is also a variety of (typically old) user programs that make direct use of DDCMP for wide-area point-to-point communications.

DDCMP is flexible, operating over a variety of lines including asynchronous and synchronous lines. DDCMP also supports serial, parallel, and multipoint lines. The type of physical connection supported is a function of which communication controller is being used, not the protocol. Figure 2-19 shows some typical communications controllers used on Digital computers. Note that dedicated devices, such as routers, also have DDCMP-based connectors. Also note that the DDCMP controllers vary based on the number of lines and the total bandwidth.

Direct Memory Access (DMA) means the controller can deposit incoming data in memory instead of having to generate a CPU interrupt so the CPU

Controller	Type	Lines	DMA	Maximum Speed	Modem Control
BI Bus					
DMB32	Asynchronous	8	Yes	38.4 kbps	Yes
	Synchronous	1	Yes	64 kbps (HDLC, SDLC),, 19.2 kbps (DDCMP)	Yes
DHB32	Asynchronous	16	Yes	19.2 kbps on two channels	Yes
DSB32	Synchronous	2	Yes	64 kbps (DDCMP),, 19.2 kbps (SDLC/HDLC)	Yes
Q Bus					
CXA16	Asynchronous	16	Yes	38.4 kbps	No
CXY08	Asynchronous	8	Yes	38.4 kbps	Yes
DHF11	Asynchronous	16/32	Yes	38.4 kbps	No
DHQ11	Asynchronous	8	Yes	38.4 kbps	Yes
DLVJ11	Asynchronous	4	No	38.4 kbps	Limited
DPV11	Synchronous	1	No	56 kbps	Yes
DSV11	Synchronous	2	Yes	256 kbps	Yes
DZQ11	Asynchronous	4	No	9.6 kbps	No
MicroVAX 2000					
DHT32	Asynchronous	8	No	38.4 kbps	No
DST32	Synchronous	1	No	19.2 kbps	Yes
DSH32	Asynchronous	8	No	38.4 kbps	No
DSH32	Synchronous	1	No	19.2 kbps	No

2-19 WAN Communications Controllers

can perform the task. Non-DMA access is quite CPU intensive. For example, the DPV11 controller, with no DMA access and a bandwidth of 56 kbps, could easily swamp the resources of a MicroVAX.

Modem control means the controller is able to detect changes in modem signals and transmit that information up to higher-level users. This is important when the line is going to be used by incoming terminal sessions (i.e., a DMB32 in asynchronous mode).

As an example, suppose a user dials in and establishes a session. Then, for some reason the connection is broken. When a second user dials into that same port, he or she is automatically connected to the previous user's session. Modem control ensures that the higher-level user (the VMS operating system) detects the break and terminates the session.

DDCMP Operation

The operation of DDCMP can be broken down into three functional components:

- framing
- link management
- message exchange

Framing is provided by DDCMP at three levels. The lowest level, bit synchronization, is actually done by the physical hardware, such as a modem. Byte synchronization is also part of the physical interface (except for asynchronous or parallel links, where the process is inherent). The highest level of synchronization is at the message level: finding the first and last bytes of the message. This is where the major work for DDCMP is accomplished.

Link management is the process of switching between transmit and receive modes. Message exchange is based on positive acknowledgment and timers.

Several error detection and performance enhancement mechanisms are used in DDCMP. When a user sends data, a timer is set to ensure the data does not go into a black hole. It is the responsibility of the recipient to acknowledge the data.

If an ACK is not received when the timer expires, a special Reply to Message Number (REP) message forces an ACK or NAK from a node.

Positive acknowledgment of messages can be inefficient in an environment with a long transmission delay (such as a satellite link). If a second packet cannot be sent until the first packet is acknowledged, the long delay will reduce throughput to a small fraction of the total bandwidth. DDCMP uses a mechanism called pipelining, which allows several messages to be outstanding. An ACK message acknowledges the receipt of all messages up to the one being specifically ACKed. The combination of pipelining and piggybacked ACKs means DDCMP is efficient for most realistic (i.e., noninterplanetary) situations.

Note that many DDCMP functions can be implemented in hardware. Framing, CRC calculation, and interpretation of some message fields are all likely candidates for hardware implementations.

DDCMP can operate on both asynchronous and synchronous links. For an asynchronous link, it is possible to lose the start of the byte. If so, the module sends a byte of all 1s, followed by an idle for at least 10 bit times. This lets the other end resynchronize itself.

On a synchronous link, byte framing is established by looking for at least two consecutive sync bytes. When a module is sending a start of frame

Message Type		Message Type = 129
Count		Length of Data Field
Flags		Quick Sync (No message following, resynchronize now)
		Select (Reverse transmission on multipoint and half-duplex)
Response Number		
Transmit Number		
Station Address		For Multipoint Links
Header CRC		
Data		
Data CRC		

2-20

DDCMP Data Message

sequence, it sends a total of six sync bytes; after the first two are detected, the remote node will look for another four consecutive synchronization bytes.

Synchronization is not necessary between each frame. It is possible to send several messages abutting each other. If there is space, however, the link needs to be resynchronized.

The remote node will typically buffer all incoming data under the assumption that consecutive frames will be transmitted. This means that a lot of useless data can be buffered before the remote node realizes there is no frame, just line noise. The quick sync flag in a frame tells the remote node that no frames will follow this one and that it should await a start of frame sequence. Once synchronization is achieved on the line, the message framing is accomplished by looking for the 3-byte beginning of message sequence.

Before a line is properly initialized, DDCMP is running in off-line (maintenance) mode. A start message, followed by a start acknowledgment, shifts the line to on-line (operational) mode. The start message is used to resync message numbers.

The reply timer tells a module how long to wait for an acknowledgment before taking error recovery action. On a full-duplex line a typical value would be 3 seconds for a telephone-type, low-bandwidth channel. On a half-duplex line a selection interval indicates the amount of time the other node has to respond.

DDCMP Messages

Figure 2-20 shows the basic DDCMP data message. Notice that the message includes a response number allowing acknowledgment of data to be piggy-backed on the outgoing data message. The transmit number indicates the number of this message, which should be positively acknowledged by the recipient.

The station address is used in a multipoint link environment. In a multipoint link several nodes share a single line. One of the nodes is the master. Communication is between the master and one of the slaves; slave-to-slave communication is not possible. Multipoint DDCMP operation is not supported in DECnet Phase V.

The quick sync flag is used to indicate that the recipient node should resynchronize the line immediately following the message instead of trying to buffer the reverse data. The select flag is an artifact of multipoint operation and indicates which node is allowed to transmit.

The other two message types are the maintenance and control messages (see Figs. 2-21 and 2-22). The maintenance message is used when the link is not initialized for normal operation. A typical user of the maintenance message would be MOP.

The control message is used if a node is forced to NAK a message or send an ACK, but has no normal data message on which to piggyback. The start and start acknowledgment (stack) messages are also subsets of the control message.

Figure 2-23 shows a variety of management parameters kept by the DD-CMP module. All DNA modules keep management information. Some parameters are control parameters, used to set the operation of the module. Other parameters are status parameters, which keep the current status (i.e., number of framing errors detected).

The information in these figures gives you an idea of the scope of the information kept in all DNA modules. Since listing all the information kept by all the DNA modules would easily fill up pages of this book, a sample is shown for a single module.

HDLC

Whereas DDCMP is a Digital proprietary protocol, the High-Level Data Link Control (HDLC) is an international standard. There is therefore a wider variety of implementations available for HDLC-based products than for DD-CMP-based products. Digital is moving away from DDCMP toward HDLC as the method of providing point-to-point, synchronous wide-area communications. DDCMP is still being used for low-cost asynchronous circuits.

The basic HDLC goal is reliable, sequenced, transparent, error-free data delivery over communication links that have significant induced error

Message Type		Message Type = 5
Control Message Type		ACK (Receiver Field has ACK No.)
		NAK (Subtype Field has Reason No.)
		Reply to Message (Asks Slave to ACK or NAK)
		Start (For link initialization)
		Start Acknowledge
Subtype/Modifier		NAK Reasons
		Header CRC Error
		Data CRC Error
		REP Response
		Buffer Unavailable
		Receiver Overrun
		Message Too Long
		Header Format Error
Link Flags		Quick Sync and Select
Message Receiver Field		
Message Sender Field		
Station Address		For multipoint links.
Header CRC		

2-21
DDCMP
Control Message

Message Type		Message Type = 144
Count of Data Field		
Link Flags		Quick Sync and Select
Empty		
Empty		
Station Address		For Multipoint Links
Header CRC		
Data		
Data CRC		

2-22
DDCMP
Maintenance Message

Attribute	Description
DDCMP Module	Child of Node Entity
DNA Version	Current DDCMP Version (5)
Port Entity	Child of DDCMP Module
Name	Simple Name of Port
Client Name	
Link Name	
Station Name	Used for multiport links
Link Entity	Child of DDCMP Module
Protocol	Point-to-Point or Multipoint
Service Module Class	Physical Layer Client (Modem Control
Receive Buffers	Number reserved for link
Dead Timer	Delay between polls of dead tributaries; default is 10,000 ms; used only for the control station of a multipoint link
Delay Timer	Minimum delay between polls for control stations
Retransmit Timer	Maximum time to wait before taking error recovery action; default value is 3000 ms
Scheduling Timer	Time for recalculation of tributary polling priorities (200 ms)
Stream Timer	Time that a half-duplex or tributary station can hold the line (6000 ms)
Service Port Name	Name of the associated physical module
NAKS Received with Receive Overruns	
Message Header Format Errors	
Station Entity	Child of DDCMP Link Entity
Address	Data link address of remote station
Active Base	Base priority for active tributary (default is 255)
Inactive Base	Base priority for inactive tributary (default is 0)
Dying Base	Base priority for dying tributary (default is 0)
Active Increment	Increment to add to active tributary priority (default is 0) when scheduling timer expires
Inactive Increment	Default is 64
Dying Increment	Default is 16
Babble Timer	Time a tributary or remote half-duplex station can transmit (default is 6000 ms)

2-23 Management Information Kept by DDCMP

Attribute	Description
Dead Threshold	Number of times to poll tributary before declaring dead (default is 8)
Dying threshold	Number of times to poll before declaring a tributary dying (default is 2)
Inactive Threshold	Number of times to poll active station before declaring it inactive (default 8)
Transmit Timer	Delay between data messages
Holdback Timer	Delay of acknowledgment; should be 10–20% of Retransmit Timer used by remote station
Transmit Window	Number of outstanding data messages

2-23 *(Cont.)* DDCMP Information

rates. HDLC provides both half- and full-duplex operation. It allows resynchronization of a line in case of temporary failures.

HDLC uses the concept of bit stuffing to locate the beginning and end of messages on a physical link. Within HDLC there are flags, consisting of six consecutive 1s. If the data contained this combination, a message would be prematurely terminated. Whenever there are five consecutive 1s in the data, HDLC adds a 0.

Normally, the gap between two HDLC frames is a sequence of 8 bits: a 0, a flag (six 1s), and a 0. When a second frame follows directly after the first, the line may lose the second frame: It may still be processing the CRC, doing the DMA posting, or checking the address and be unable to copy the incoming data to a buffer. For nodes with limited processing power, it is therefore possible to negotiate a minimum acceptable interframe gap consisting of additional flag sequences.

HDLC is a general-purpose protocol. As such it is too general for general-purpose automatic configuration. When Digital supports HDLC, they are therefore supporting a limited subset of HDLC devices. Digital's support of HDLC does not include support for multidrop (which is basically limited to SDLC-based secondary stations) or asynchronous operation.

Within the general HDLC framework, there is a variety of important subsets, including

- the synchronous data link control (SDLC) used as the basic data link mechanism in IBM SNA networks
- the link access protocol B (LAPB) used in X.25
- the link access protocol D (LAPD) used in ISDN

Digital supports the two basic modes: normal (half-duplex) and balanced (full-duplex). LAPB is a particular variant of balanced mode. LAPX and

LAPD, as well as the now obsolete asynchronous mode are not supported in the current specification.

A variant on normal and balanced mode is extended format. Extended format allows 7-bit sequence numbers instead of 3 bits, thereby allowing more frames to be outstanding. Extended format is needed for efficient operation over long-delay links such as satellite-based transmission.

HDLC, like DDMCP and most other synchronous protocols, is based on pipelining. Each message gets a sequence number. When an acknowledgment is received, it implies receipt of all previous messages (in other words, the acknowledgment sequence number is the next frame expected).

HDLC Frame Structure

Figure 2-24 shows the basic format for the HDLC frame header, known as the control fields. The first 2 bytes of the frame (3 in extended) define the frame type. There are three types used in HDLC:

- The information (I) frame is for user information. It is subject to error recovery and sequence control.
- The supervisory (S) frame is for control information such as acknowledgments, retransmission request, and temporary busy indications. It is used to ensure the correct transfer of I frames.
- The unnumbered (U) frames provide link control functions such as initialization and termination, as well as unacknowledged user data.

Each of these frames can be a command or a response. In a half-duplex mode, one node is the master, the other the secondary. Only the master sends commands; the secondary only sends responses. In balanced mode, either can send commands or responses. To determine which type of frame it is, we look at the station address field. If the sender's address is in the field, it is a command. If the receiver's address is in the field, it is a response.

Each frame has a poll/final bit. In commands, the bit is a poll bit. In responses, it is a final bit. In normal mode (half-duplex) the poll bit set indicates that the slave can send data; this is the beginning of a transmit opportunity. The slave then sends data until it is done, at which point it sets the final bit. The poll/final bit is thus a way of synchronizing two stations.

Error detection is done using either a 16- or 32-bit CRC. Digital always begins the initialization procedure using the 16-bit CRC but switches to the 32 bit in data transfer phase if it is negotiated.

HDLC Control Field Format					
0					Numbered Information
Send Sequence Number					
Poll/Final Bit					P or F
Receive Sequence Number					
1					Supervisory Format
0					
S-Format Flags					00 - Receive Ready (RR)
					01 - Reject (REJ)
					10 - Receive Not Ready (RNR)
Poll/Final Bit					
Receive Sequence Number					
1					Unnumbered Information Format
1					
UI-Format Flags					
Poll/Final Bit					
UI-Format Flags					

Flags					
1	1	P	1	0	0	Set Asynchronous Balanced Mode (SABM)
0	0	P	0	1	0	Disconnect (DISC)
0	0	P	0	0	0	Unnumbered Information Poll (UI)
1	1	P	1	0	1	Exchange ID (XID)
0	0	F	1	1	0	Unnumbered Acknowledgment (UA)
1	0	F	0	0	1	Frame Reject Response (FRMR)
0	0	F	0	0	0	Unnumbered Information Response
1	1	F	1	0	1	Exchange ID Response (XID)

2-24
HDLC Header Format
(Control Fields)

Error Recovery

The basic method for error recovery is checkpointing. When an acknowledgment is received with the final bit sent, it indicates a checkpoint. The checkpoint means that all lower-numbered frames have been received but no higher-numbered frames have been received. In other words, the other node should resend any outstanding higher-numbered frames.

The checkpoint procedure is usually started after the acknowledgment timer expires. By setting the final bit on the acknowledgment, we are indicating to the remote node that we have not received any higher-numbered frames.

Other ways to recover from an error occurs when the node receives an out of sequence frame. Sending a reject forces retransmission. On long-delay links (satellites) there is a refinement to HDLC called selective rejection; this is not specified in the Digital HDLC document.

Link Initialization

Link initialization goes through three phases. First, there is attempt to exchange XID frames. If there is response before a timer expires, we assume the remote node does not support the XID. Next, a disconnect indication is sent to force a disconnected frame. Then, the link is established in normal, balanced, or extended mode.

Flow control is done through the use of the Receive Not Ready (RNR) frame instead of a receive ready. The other station will then test periodically to see if the condition still exists.

HDLC normally assumes two direct users of the line. There is no inherent provision for multiplexing multiple users over a single link. Digital provides this service, but only with the use of unnumbered information frames, by putting a protocol ID as the first piece of the data field. To suppress the use of protocol IDs in UI frames when communicating to non-Digital nodes, Digital allows a link to be started in exclusive mode.

For sequenced information, there can be only one user. Note that this is not the end user—a single user might be the Digital routing protocol.

X.25

At the data link layer, the X.25 protocols are a subset of HDLC. In addition, X.25 defines functions at the physical and the network layer (see Figs. 2-25 and 2-26). The network layer function of X.25 is used to set up a virtual connection between two nodes in the X.25 subnetwork. Then the LAPB protocols define how a user of X.25 interfaces to the network. X.25 is actually used in a wide variety of different portions of the Digital network.

	Routing Module	
Dynamically Established Data Links		*Network Layer*
X.25 Packet Layer		
	LAPB	*Data Link Layer*
	Physical Module	*Physical Layer*

2-25
X.25 Layers

Selected Attribute	Value
Ack Timer	3000 ms default
Extended Mode	Mandatory
Holdback Timer	0 (Time to wait before sending ACK)
Max Data Size	1500
Min Data Size	576
Retry Max	10 (before declaring fatal error)
UID	UID of Link
Maintenance Mode	False
Max Frame Size	Negotiated
Window Size	Negotiated

2-26
The LAPB Subset
of HDLC

X.25 is connection oriented. The user at the network layer sets up a virtual circuit to a remote destination. The virtual circuit can stay permanently in place or can be set up dynamically (a switched virtual circuit).

Figure 2-27 shows a typical X.25 configuration. Notice that X.25 only specifies the interface to the network; the inner workings are implementation dependent and are thus represented as a cloud.

X.25 can be used for a wide variety of purposes. For host-to-host communication, a higher-level program is resident on both computers. Thus, the

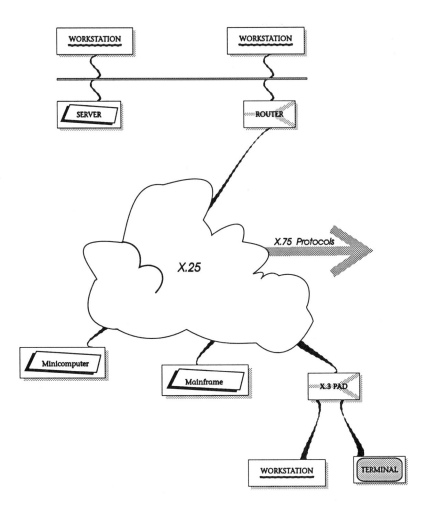

2-27 An X.25 Configuration

router on the Ethernet might set up a virtual circuit to a minicomputer or mainframe or even to another router. In Chapter 3, we will see that X.25 can be used as a means of connecting multiple LANs together.

X.25 is also a means for a terminal to communicate with a host. The X.25 protocols define synchronous data transmission, but terminals are usually asynchronous. A device known as a packet assembler/disassembler (PAD) is used to interface the asynchronous device to the synchronous X.25 network. The operation of the PAD is defined in the X.3 CCITT standard.

Two additional protocols are used to define how the terminal (or the workstation emulating a terminal) and the host communicate with each other. The X.28 protocols define how the terminal interfaces to the PAD. X.28 defines eveents such as when the PAD should take data received and bundle it up in an X.25 packet. The X.29 protocols define how the host can communicate with the PAD and thus control the terminal.

In a Digital environment, it is possible to make a VAX computer emulate an X.3 PAD using Digital's Packet Switch Interface (PSI) software. By emulating a PAD, the PSI software lets users initiate outgoing sessions to hosts. In addition, PSI is able to accept incoming sessions. PSI does not require DECnet for local users, although DECnet allows users to access the services of a remote X.25 gateway.

PSI allows direct use of the X.25 network by users or user programs. A special instance of a user is the Phase V network layer. When X.25 is a service provider for the network layer of a Phase V environment, an X.25 router—a dedicated piece of equipment that interfaces to the Ethernet and to the X.25 network—is used. The X.25 router is the same basic hardware used in DDCMP-based routers with point-to-point connections.

Another variant of X.25 in a Digital environment is the X.25 portal. The X.25 portal allows a DECnet to be used as a backbone for foreign traffic. The X.25 portal accepts incoming messages and encapsulates them inside a DECnet packet. The packet is then sent to a portal on the other side of the network, where the DECnet header is stripped and the data packet is sent back on its way.

X.25 is particularly important in Phase V because the intent of the architecture is to interconnect to other networks easily. Since OSI defines a unified address space, it is technically possible for a network to establish an X.25 call dynamically to a remote network for the purpose of, say, exchanging mail messages.

Most sites would typically pick one X.25 vendor. In the United States this would be Tymnet, Telenet, or one of the other public service providers. In many other countries, the X.25 service provider would be the local PTT.

Once connected to one X.25 network, it is still possible to reach a destination target on another X.25 network. The X.75 protocols define how one X.25 network interconnects to another. A switched virtual circuit could thus be established across national boundaries.

Modem Connect Module

Before leaving the data link layer and subnetworks, we will look at one more module, the modem connect module. This module is part of the physical layer of the network and allows the control of modems. Figure 2-28 shows an HDLC module that connects to a wide-area link via a modem. DDCMP can also use the services of this module.

Once the operation is set up, the HDLC module uses the normal data transmission facility of the physical layer. To set up a call, however, requires capabilities not present in the HDLC protocols. This is where the modem connect module comes in.

Figure 2-29 shows a more detailed view of the modem connect module. The dynamically established data link component of the DNA routing layer is responsible for interfacing to the call control service interface. This interface, in turn, is able to work with a variety of different modem control protocols to establish a connection to a remote location.

Once the connection is established, the network layer (or other user of the data link layer) sends its request for transmission to the data link layer module, which then interfaces to the physical layer of the network. The call control service interface is thus a mechanism used before the link is up and running and is thus not really a network protocol.

Summary

In this chapter, we looked at a variety of different protocols for setting up a subnetwork: a means of connecting multiple nodes together so any two nodes can exchange a packet of data. In the next chapter, we will see how the network layer joins these various subnetworks together into an integrated network.

For the local area network, the Ethernet CSMA/CD protocols are key for Digital. Most servers, such as computers, terminal servers, and print servers, come with built-in Ethernet interfaces. The Digital view of the world is a series of work groups, connected together with Ethernet.

In addition to Ethernet, Digital supports the FDDI local area network, primarily as a means of providing a high-speed corporate backbone. Bridges or routers then connect the FDDI to the Ethernet-based work group.

For wide-area connections, Digital originally supported the DDCMP protocols. DDCMP will be used in Phase V for asynchronous connections, as well as for synchronous connections to provide backward compatibility.

In the wide-area environment, Digital is moving toward HDLC-based connections. HDLC is used for point-to-point connections, and is also the basis for interconnection to X.25 and ISDN.

X.25 (and later ISDN) plays a key role as the interface to the public data communications environment. X.25 allows a switched virtual circuit to be dynamically established, allowing short-term connections to be easily established to a wide variety of different targets.

The last thing we looked at was the modem connect module which, with X.25, presents a choice of ways to provide dynamic wide-area links. X.25 uses the public data network, whereas the modem connect module allows point-to-point links to be established over the public voice network.

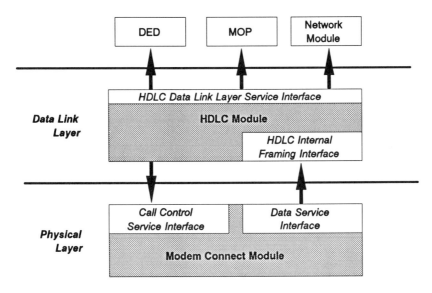

2-28 Modem Connect and HDLC

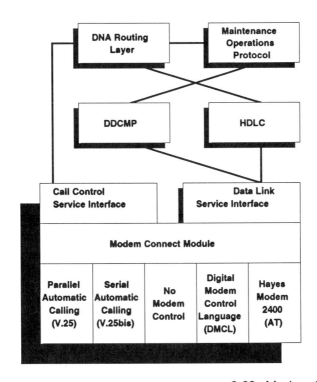

2-29 Modem Control Protocol

Network Layer

CHAPTER 3

Network Layer

The data link layer provides a basic service—transmission of a packet of data between any two nodes on the subnetwork. The DNA architecture allows a variety of different data link technologies, and a node may actually be connected to several different subnetworks.

The function of the network layer is to tie the different subnetworks together (see Fig. 3-1). In this sample configuration, several kinds of subnetworks are being used, each suited to the particular task at hand. FDDI acts as a high-speed backbone, Ethernet is used for work group computing, and HDLC, DDCMP, and X.25 are used for wide-area links. This is just one kind of possible configuration. FDDI, for example, might also be used for work group computing, as in the case of visualization workstations connected to supercomputers.

The basic role of the network layer is to deliver a packet of data from any one node in the network to any other node. The network layer uses the services of the data link to move the packet across a subnetwork, then chooses another subnetwork to move the packet one step closer to its destination.

The problem is knowing which subnetwork to use to move the packet one step forward. With all the nodes on one subnetwork, it is simply a matter of submitting the packet to the data link layer. In a multisubnetwork environment, just knowing which nodes exist is a challenge. A further wrinkle is introduced by multiple paths between any two nodes. Keeping abreast of which nodes exist and the best way to get there is the function of the network layer.

The network layer is a user of the different data link services (see Fig. 3-2). In DECnet, the network layer provides a best-effort delivery service: It tries to move a packet across the network.

The user of the network service will be the transport layers of the network. The transport layer, examined in Chapter 4, makes sure that all packets submitted by a given user are received at the destination node in the

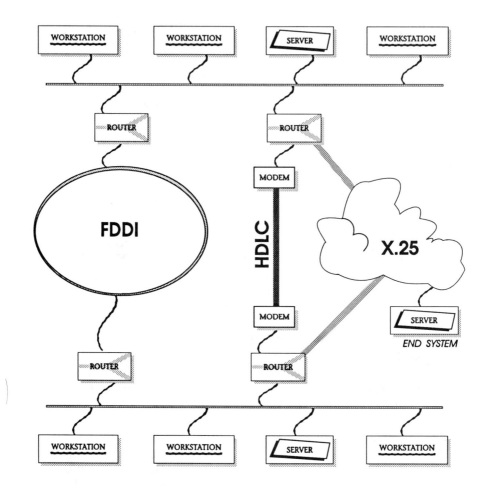

3-1 Multiple Subnetworks

ISO TP 0		ISO TP 2		ISO TP 4	DEC NSP	
DNA Routing Layer						
HDLC		IEEE 802.2			Ethernet	DDCMP
LAPB	LAPD	802.3	802.4	FDDI		

3-2 DNA Routing Layer

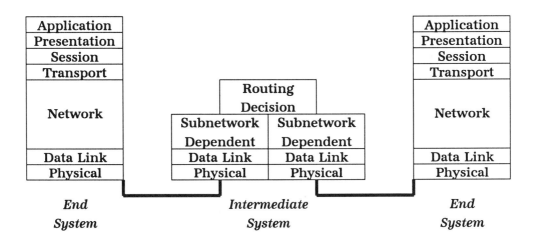

3-3 End Systems and Intermediate Systems

order sent. Using the network layer, the transport layer can be unaware of the topology of the network—the combination of data links that provides a path between two nodes at a given point in time.

We can divide the universe of all nodes that have some form of connection (or potential connection) into three categories:

- Phase V nodes
- Phase IV nodes
- non-DNA nodes

Based on their function we can further divide each of these types of nodes into end systems and intermediate systems (see Fig. 3-3). The corresponding terms for Phase IV networks were end nodes and routing nodes. An end system is able to send and receive traffic on the network but does not route traffic through on behalf of other nodes. A typical end system is a multipurpose server or workstation, but specialized end systems could be terminal servers, print servers, or any other device implementing the network layer functions.

An intermediate system performs a forwarding function on behalf of other nodes. An intermediate system can also be an end system, originating traffic on behalf of itself. It does not have to be a traditional host, such as a VAX. Often, intermediate systems are dedicated hardware and software packaged as a router. In fact, as routing functions become more complex it becomes increasingly important to off-load these functions from general-purpose hosts onto specialized routers.

In most networks, there may be several paths to the destination, each path represented by a different neighboring intermediate system. Which intermediate system to use to move a particular packet of data closer to its destination is the crucial decision in the network layer. A given node may be connected to several different subnetworks. Each subnetwork may have several different intermediate systems connected to it, which in turn are connected to other subnetworks. The number of possible paths to a given destination can thus be very large.

We can examine the network layer from three increasing layers of complexity. At the lowest level of complexity, we assume a simple network topography (or at least a node that has very little knowledge of the topography). Our only concern at this point is to standardize the format of the data packet. This is addressed by the basic ISO standard for the network layer. At this level, we assume that an intermediate system already knows, through some out-of-band mechanism, how to find a destination end system.

The next level of complexity is the mechanism by which a node finds its neighbors: determining the presence of neighboring intermediate systems and end systems. This is the function of the ISO ES-IS Routing Exchange Protocol. By sending out "hello" messages, all nodes on a subnetwork inform their neighbors of their presence.

Finally, at its most complex, we have the IS-IS protocol, which is intended to allow an intermediate system to determine the best path to any node in the network, whether it be a neighbor or not. Digital pioneered this particular protocol, known as the link state protocol or the IS-IS protocol which is on the ISO standards track.

This chapter first considers the problem of assigning unique addresses for a network that could potentially span all computers in the world. Then, it looks at the basic data and error packets. Next, it looks in detail at the DNA Routing Module, the implementation of the network layer on an intermediate system. The routing module consists of two sublayers: the subnetwork dependent and independent sublayers. This chapter looks at the different components of each of these sublayers and how they carry out the functions of the ES-IS and IS-IS services.

Addresses, Areas, and Domains

To provide compatibility with existing systems, ISO has defined a variety of different authorities who can allocate addresses. This hierarchical address allocation scheme allows allocating authorities to handle the specifics within their environments, yet keeps a standard address format for the interchange of data packets. This system is much like the international telephone network, where a U.S. user (with a seven digit number plus a three-digit area code) is able to call other countries that have different length phone numbers and different ways of allocating the digits within the numbers.

The first part of a network address is an Authority and Format Identifier (AFI). It identifies the authority, as well as the encoding method used for the address that follows. The allocating formats that have been defined for network addresses are as follows:

- X.121—a CCITT numbering plan for public data networks.
- Data Country Code (DCC)—an ISO-administered unique ID based on geographical location.
- International Code Designator (ICD)—an ISO-administered unique ID based on organizations.
- F.69—CCITT standard for telex addresses.
- E.163—CCITT numbering scheme for public switched telephone networks.
- E.164—CCITT standard for numbering in an ISDN environment.
- Locally administered address.

Locally administered address formats, while legal, make it much more difficult for a remote intermediate system to decide how to reach the locally administered domain. It would be the equivalent of making up state names (and leaving off country names) in an international postal system.

After the AFI, the address has an Initial Domain Identifier (IDI). The IDI is given to different organizations by whichever authority is specified in the AFI. Together, the AFI and the IDI are known as the Initial Domain Part (IDP). In the United States, the American National Standards Institute (ANSI) is the registration authority for many IDPs.

Following the initial domain part of the address is a Domain Specific Part (DSP). An organization would apply to an authority for an allocation of an IDI. Within the IDI, the organization would be responsible for allocating a unique domain specific part of the address.

An organization would presumably obtain a single IDI allocation for all its different computers, DECnet or non-DECnet. DECnet nodes then have a specific format for the domain specific part (or at least the last 9 bytes of the DSP). It is possible that the organization would use other information in the leading portion of the DSP that would divide nodes up by geographical or administrative areas or by network type. In Figure 3-4, we see how the different portions of the OSI address are formatted for use in a Phase V DECnet. The last 9 bytes have the three portions shown: the local area indicator, the node ID, and the selector. We will look at each of these pieces of the DECnet version of the OSI address in more detail in later sections.

Figure 3-5 shows how different format addresses get encoded. Notice that all addresses are less than or equal to 20 bytes. The network layer is

3-4
ISO Address Format

IDI Format	AFI Value		IDP Length		Maximum DSP Length (Octets)
	Pad IDI with 0	Pad IDI with 1	Decimal	Octets	
Binary DSP Encoding					
X.121	37	53	16	8	9
ISO DCC	39	—	5	3	14
F.69	41	55	10	5	12
E.163	43	57	14	7	10
E.164	45	59	17	9	9
ISO ICD	47	—	6	3	13
Local	49	—	2	1	15
Decimal DSP Encoding			Max IDP Length (Decimal)	Max DSP Length (Decimal)	Max NSAP Length (Octets)
X.121	36	52	16	24	20
ISO DCC	38	—	5	35	20
F.69	40	54	10	30	20
E.163	42	56	14	26	20
E.164	44	58	17	23	20
ISO ICD	46	—	6	34	20
Local	48	—	2	38	20

3-5 ISO Address Encoding

responsible for taking an incoming packet in any of these formats and reading it so that it can then decide how to forward the packet.

An address can be represented as a string of decimal digits or binary octets. In binary encoding, a semioctet (4 bits) is used for each of the digits of the AFI. A digit of 8, for example, would encode as 0100.

After the AFI is encoded, it is necessary to pad the initial domain indicator (since the IDI can be of variable length). A different AFI is allocated for padding with 0s or 1s, allowing the network layer to determine which kind of pad is used. The pad takes a variable length IDP and appends either 0s or 1s to make it the maximum possible length (thus allowing the DSP to be easily identified).

This somewhat complicated procedure allows a variety of different addressing schemes to be used, each of them guaranteeing that each node in the world wide internetwork has a unique address. In a DECnet, the binary encoding is used, with a pad of 1. DNA nodes, however, are fully capable of processing and generating the other address formats when communicating from non-DECnet nodes.

Networks and Areas

Before we continue with the question of addressing and the corollary question of finding a particular address, we will look at a conceptual model of how a network is structured. The basic goal of this structure is to be able to find any node on the network and to get a packet of data to that node.

We start by dividing the networks of the world into public and private networks (see Fig. 3-6). The public network is simply a publicly administered subnetwork, such as a national X.25 network. The private network is the collection of subnetworks under the control of some organization. Although it is an oversimplification, one can think of the public network as the means used to connect different organizations together. In this book, we concentrate on how an organization builds up its private network.

A public network is one that offers dynamic data links. Dynamic data links offer full connectivity between any two private networks. In this sense, subject to security and access control, the world is one big network.

We assume all networks, no matter how administered, share a unique address space as defined by the OSI-compatible network address. A given computer might be on both a public and a private network. Such a computer is the gateway to the outside world.

The real difference between the public and the private networks is how much information is transferred within the network layer about the different paths between different nodes. The public network offers full connectivity, but it is not quite so dynamic in the exchange of routing control information.

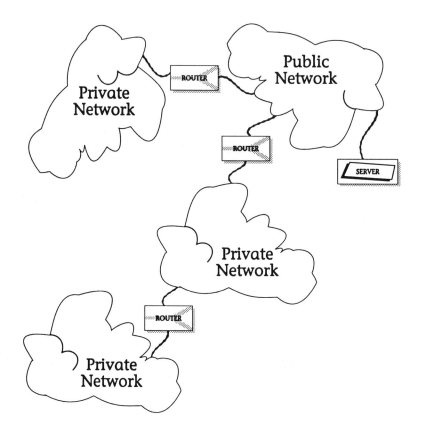

3-6 Private and Public Networks

Inside Private Networks

Inside a private network, there may be a variety of different paths between nodes (see Fig. 3-7). Although the choice of different paths is transparent to the end system, it is important information to the intermediate systems or routers. The intermediate system must respond to topology changes when a line goes up or down. When there are multiple working paths, the intermediate system must choose the best one. One way of making the choice easier is to split the private network up into routing areas (see Fig. 3-8). Remember that one portion of the DSP of a DECnet address is the local area indicator.

Because of areas, routers are able to specialize. A level 1 router knows how to get to every node within its own area. A level 2 router knows how to get to other areas, but not how to get to the individual nodes in those

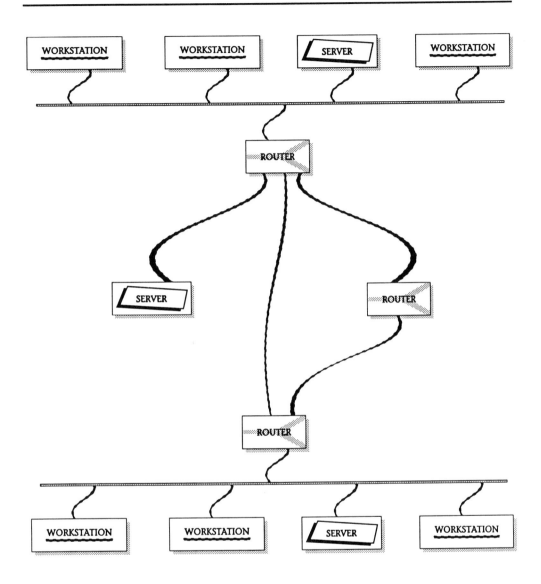

3-7 A DECnet Area

remote areas (although many level 2 routers do double duty as a level 1 router).

This hierarchical routing scheme makes it easier to route information. An end system will send a packet of data over the Ethernet to its nearest level 1 router (known as the designated router). The level 1 router will examine the IDP and the local area indicator of the address.

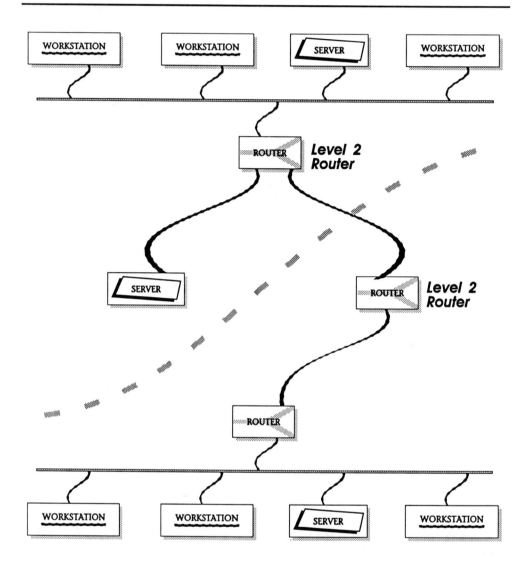

3-8 Multiple DECnet Areas

If both the IDP and the area match the address of the router, then the destination node is in the same area as the sender. The intermediate system will examine its routing tables and choose the appropriate subnetwork to use to send the data. If the IDP or the area indicator are different, however, the level 1 router will forward the packet to a level 2 router. The level 2 router will examine its routing tables and decide the best path to use to get it to the destination area. The destination area might be part of this private network, or may have to cross several public networks to reach a different routing domain.

Eventually, the packet will be forwarded to the destination area using level 2 routing. There, the packet will be handed off to a level 1 router that will get the packet to its eventual destination. Note that an area can be quite simple, as in the case of a single node or a single Ethernet. The area can also be complex with hundreds of nodes and a variety of subnetwork technologies.

The concept of a routing domain, or private network, can also be simple, as in the case of a single end system attached to a public network. It can also be complex, reaching the limit of the 2-byte area space. Several private networks can be administered by the same group, leading to a potential network size that is virtually unlimited.

The total number of possible areas in Phase V of DECnet represents a distinct difference from Phase IV. In Phase IV, there was a maximum of 1023 nodes per area and 63 areas in a DECnet. Phase V has a virtually unlimited address space (the Phase V limit is 280 quadrillion nodes).

This Phase IV limit of 64,449 nodes may not sound like a problem, but the limits were quickly surpassed in two instances. First, extremely large corporate networks, such as Digital's internal EasyNet quickly outgrew the 63 area limit. Second, the limit was achieved in scientific and research communities when several different organizations tried to combine their networks into a common research environment. For example, the High-Energy Physics Network (HEPnet) combines physics groups all over the world into a common DECnet. Although an individual research facility is of moderate size having hundreds or a few thousand systems, the aggregate number of systems used by the high-energy physics community can easily overrun the address space.

DECnet and NonDECnet Nodes

The concept of public and private networks allows other vendor's networks to be reachable from a DECnet private network, as long as they comply with the OSI address scheme. The public network forms the bridge. It is also possible for other vendors equipment to be part of a DECnet area, typically as an end system. In order for the node to be a part of the DECnet area, it must follow several addressing rules.

First, the address, minus the last byte, must be unique. The last byte, called the selector field, is used by DECnet nodes to decide which user of the network service should get the data. In a strict OSI environment, the user is always the OSI transport service. In a Phase V network, there is another transport service, called the Network Services Protocol. Thus, the selector field is an address for the next layer user. The implication of this is that end systems from other vendors cannot use the last byte of the address as a way of making nodes unique. The concept of a selector field was not present in original OSI network layer specifications, but was added into drafts on IS-IS routing.

A second limitation is that the DSP of the address must be at least 9 bytes and that the area portion of the address must match that of a neighboring router. A DECnet area can be known by up to three different area addresses, allowing some flexibility in incorporating non-Digital end nodes.

If the area address does not match, the end system can still participate in a Digital private network, but it must do so as a separate area. In other words, routing to it will not be quite as efficient, although connectivity is still preserved as it would be to any other private network via level 2 routing.

Basic Data Delivery Function

Let us assume for the time being that, using a series of subnetworks, a given router knows how to deliver a packet to a destination node. The first compatibility question is whether the packet can be read by the destination node. The format of a data packet is specified in the ISO standard 8473 (see Fig. 3-9). If two nodes share ISO 8473 compatibility, we know that at the network layer of the network they can exchange data. They must also have some upper layer service protocol in common, such as FTAM, if they are to do useful work.

The OSI-compatible address assures us that we can find the node. The compatibility with ISO 8473 assures us that the destination node can read the packet. In Figure 3-9 we see that both data and error packets share a common format. A lifetime indicator indicates how long the packet should be considered valid. Each intermediate system that receives the packet will decrement this number by at least 1. If a router brings this number down to 0, the packet can be considered worthless and is discarded. Note that a router will always decrement the lifetime indicator by at least 1. If the packet is held for more than a half second, the indicator is decremented by 2 or more units.

Following the lifetime indicator are the control flags. The flags indicate whether, after determining that a particular subnetwork needed to forward the packet has a small packet size limitation, an intermediate system can segment the packet. The flags also indicate there are more segments to this packet (i.e., if it was segmented by a prior router). Reassembly of packets is not done until the packet reaches its ultimate destination.

The error report requested flag indicates if an intermediate system should attempt to send an error report if it has to drop the packet. It might drop the packet if the destination is unreachable, if there is an error in the

Protocol ID		129
Header Length		
Version		1
Lifetime		In 1/2 seconds
Flags		Segmentation Permitted
		More Segments Flag
		Error Report Requested
		Packet Type (Data or Error)
Segment Length		Length of this segment
Checksum		0 for DNA Nodes
DA Length		
Destination Address		
SA Length		
Source Address		
Data Unit Identifier		
Segment Offset		Offset within message.
Total Length		Before fragmentation.
Option Code		204 - Padding
		197 - Security
		200 - Source Routing
		203 - Route Recording
		195 - Quality of Service
		205 - Priority
		193 - Reason for Discard
Option Length		
Option Value		
Data		

3-9

Basic ISO 8473
Packet Format

header format, if the lifetime indicator expires, or for a variety of other reasons.

Note that both the error report and the data packet are a best-effort delivery service. There is no guarantee that the data packet will be delivered. Network layer modules attempt to forward packets, but if buffer overflow or a line goes down, the network layer makes no attempt to recover that particular packet. Because an error report is a packet, there is no guarantee that an error report will be sent if the original packet was discarded. If the error report is sent, there is no guarantee that it will reach the original sender of the data packet.

Following the flags is the segment length—the total length of this segment. The segment offset, given later in the header, indicates where this particular segment fits into the original data packet.

There are three other relevant pieces of information in the header (aside from the data). The header checksum is used to check the integrity of the header and is set to 0 in a DECnet network. If a checksum is received from a non-DNA node, it is checked. The data unit identifier is provided in the case of segmentation and operates as an identifier for the packet. This way, if two different packets are segmented, the destination node can keep track of which segment belongs with which packet. The DECnet routing layer keeps track of which data unit identifiers (DUIs) were last used for nodes that it is communicating with. Each node has a DUI counter, and the counter is incremented every time a packet is sent.

A separate DUI is used for each node instead of keeping a single DUI counter and using it for all nodes. If there are high-bandwidth links and low-bandwidth links, it is possible that a single DUI counter could wrap around (because of the high-bandwidth link) and thus generate a duplicate DUI for the low-bandwidth destination.

If a node is communicating with a very large number of destinations, it may not be possible to keep a separate counter for each destination. In this case, there is a "leftover" counter used for all nodes that would have exceeded the size of the DUI counter cache.

The last part of the packet header is the options section. The OSI standards define a wide variety of different options, each encoded using a code, a length, and a value. As a general rule, DECnet nodes ignore most of the options available. For example, instead of the option-specified quality of service, DECnet nodes use the routing decision process to decide which route a particular packet should take. The priority indicator option is also ignored.

Figure 3-10 shows an example of an ISO 8473-compatible data packet. Notice that the packet has a remaining lifetime of 20 seconds, measured as 40 half-second increments. In other words, this particular packet could go through another 40 intermediate systems before expiring.

The packet is a data packet and has segmentation permitted. Notice that the packet has not been segmented, since the segment length is equal to the total length of 121. Notice also that the data portion of this packet is ISO transport layer.

3-10 ISO 8473 Data Packet

Hello Packets

We now move on to the question of how to find a particular node on the network. The easiest case is when the node is on the same subnetwork. If we know that a desired end system is on the same subnetwork, we can send data directly to it and alleviate the need for using an intermediate system. In fact, in this case, we could have a network with no intermediate systems.

Identifying neighbors is also necessary to find intermediate systems. An end system needs to know of at least one intermediate system to which it can hand off packets with unknown destinations. Neighbor identification lets the end system find this default intermediate system.

Neighbor identification is done via hello messages, a PDU defined as part of the ISO ES-IS routing exchange protocol. The ES hello is used to inform intermediate systems of the presence of an end system. The IS hello tells the end system about the presence of the router. In addition, Digital has defined a private IS-IS hello to inform routers about each other.

Figure 3-11 shows the format of the ES hello message. The packet format includes a holding time, which indicates for how long the presence of this node is valid. The packet also includes one or more source addresses for this node, containing the network addresses. The data link header will contain the data link address. In this way a node can build a cache that con-

Protocol ID	130
Header Length	
Version	1
Type	2
Holding Time	In seconds
Checksum	0 for DNA nodes
Number of SAs	
Source Address Length	2 or 6 octets
Subnet Address	
Source Address Length	
Source Address	
Options	Options are ignored

3-11

ISO 9542 ES Hello

Protocol ID	130
Header Length	
Version	1
Type	4
Holding Time	In seconds
Checksum	0 for DNA nodes
Number of SAs	
Source Address Length	2 or 6 octets
Subnet Address	
Source Address Length	
Source Address	

3-12

IS 9542 IS Hello

tains the network address of the destination as well as the corresponding data link address to use to get to that network address.

The IS hello message is shown in Figure 3-12. In addition to the other fields, this packet contains an ES configuration timer. This option tells an end system how often it should send an ES hello. In a stable topology, the ES hello just adds overhead and we want the timer set as high as possible. In an unstable topology, however, the ES hello is crucial to inform the routers about the end node's presence.

Because network layer packets are not guaranteed for delivery and because destination nodes may be temporarily out of resources, there is the possibility that any given hello message might be lost. One of the assumptions of the architecture is that a message will not be lost several times in a row, that maximum number of lost times being called the holding multiplier.

When an IS decides there might be a network partition or merge, hence a need to find out about the current configuration quickly, it broadcasts a new IS hello with a (lower) ES configuration timer. It sends out that message holding multiplier times ensuring that all nodes receive it. When an ES receives this message, it adjusts its ES timer downward. It then sends out holding multiplier ES hellos, ensuring that the IS knows about its presence. If during that time it receives a new, even lower, suggested timer, it immediately adjusts its own timer. If it receives a higher value, however, it keeps the present lower value to ensure that no IS loses information.

The low value of the ES timer is only kept for a period of time. With the IS hello message, there is an expiration timer for the new value of the configuration timer. Once the expiration timer expires, the ES reverts back to the default value in its configuration.

An option on hello messages for point-to-point links is verification. It is possible that a link will come in dynamically over X.25. Each node has a management parameter indicating whether verification is required. If so, the hello message must contain the verification option with the correct value. The value, a password, is compared against the stored value before a link will finish initializing.

Figure 3-13 shows an end system hello message. Notice that this packet uses the IEEE 802.3 format at the data link control layer. The logical link control include an addresses of FE, which corresponds to the OSI network layer (as opposed to IP for TCP/IP or the Phase IV DNA Routing Layer).

The packet has a holding time of 125 seconds. Presumably, before the 125 seconds have expired, this node will have sent another hello message. The packet contains a single network-layer address, represented here in hexadecimal format.

End Systems and Caches

It is possible for an end node to have more than one active data link. Since the end node does not have a decision process, it does not have a forwarding database. Instead, it uses two types of information to decide on which link to send a packet:

- manual information
- reverse path caching

For a given packet, manually entered information always takes precedence over the dynamic information. The end node looks for any manual adjacencies to use for a given destination, performing load splitting if possible. If there is no manual information, the node uses the end node cache

Courtesy of Network General

```
┌DETAIL┐
│ DLC:    Destination: Multicast 09002B000005, ISO End Stns
│ DLC:    Source      : Station Bridge00FA00
│ DLC:    802.2 LLC length = 33
│ DLC:
│ LLC:    ----- LLC Header -----
│ LLC:
│ LLC:    DSAP = FE, SSAP = FE, Command, Unnumbered frame: UI
│ LLC:
│ ISO_IP: ----- ISO IP Network Layer -----
│ ISO_IP:
│ ISO_IP: Protocol ID = 82 (Routing Exchange Protocol)
│ ISO_IP: Header length = 26
│ ISO_IP: Version / Protocol ID extension = 01
│ ISO_IP: PDU type: End System Hello (ESH)
│ ISO_IP: Holding time is 125 seconds
│ ISO_IP: Checksum = 0000
│ ISO_IP: Number of Source addresses = 1
│ ISO_IP: Source address: 840F454E45000000040003000901
│ ISO_IP:
│ DLC:    Frame padding: 13 bytes
        ─────Frame 255 of 260─────
              Use TAB to select windows
┌─────┐┌─────┐    ┌─────┐┌─────┐┌─────┐┌─────┐┌─────┐       ┌─────┐
│1    ││2 Set│    │4 Zoom││5    ││6Displ││7 Prev││8 Next│      │10 New│
│o Help││ mark│    │ out ││ Menus││options││ frame││ frame│      │capture│
└─────┘└─────┘    └─────┘└─────┘└─────┘└─────┘└─────┘       └─────┘
```

3-13 ES Hello Message

(see Fig. 3-14), whose construction is based on the receipt of IS and ES hellos, as well as redirect messages on broadcast links.

The redirect packet is an instruction from an intermediate system that another IS should be used for a particular destination. If an intermediate system receives a packet and sends it back out the same subnetwork, it should not have received the packet in the first place. Rather than continue to perform this superfluous service, it sends the packet, but also sends a redirect packet which contains a suggestion that for a given destination another router should be used (see Fig. 3-15). The end node (or intermediate system) will use this information to update routing tables. The end node cache assures that the end system can avoid making that same mistake of sending a packet to the wrong router.

In addition, the end node will probe all other circuits to see if they are a potential path to a destination. Every few packets, the end node will send an extra copy of a data packet down these other circuits. The receipt of a redirect message, hello, or data packet will confirm whether or not this circuit is a possible path to the destination.

If the destination node is not directly attached to the end node, but there are multiple paths in the cache, load splitting is performed on all applicable circuits. Load splitting means that if there are multiple paths (up to four total) with the same cost, packets alternate on all the equal, best-cost paths.

DA Length		
Destination Address		
Remaining Time		Time before entry expires
Number of Splits		Number of circuits
Circuit ID		
Data Link Addresses		Max 1 for Phase IV Type
Address Type		Phase IV or Phase V
Directly Connected?		True if directly reachable
Circuit ID		
Data Link Addresses		
Address Type		
Directly Connected?		

3-14
End Node Cache

Protocol ID		130
Header Length		
Version		1
Type		6
Holding Time		In seconds
Checksum		0 for DNA nodes
DA Length		2 or 6 octets
Destination Address		
Subnet Address Length		
Subnet Address		Data link address for destination address
Router Address Length		
Router Address		Suggested router
Option Code		197 - Security
		195 - Quality of Service
		205 - Priority
Length		
Value		

3-15
ISO 9542
Redirect Packet

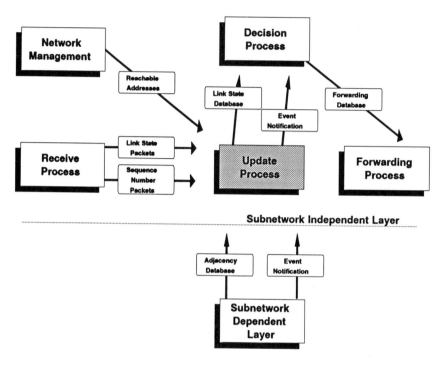

3-16 Update Process

If the destination node is not in the cache, a copy of the packet is sent down every circuit. Presumably, a hello, redirect, or data packet will result, updating the cache for the next time a packet is to be sent.

The transport layer has the option of setting a "try hard" flag on a packet. This flag directs the end node to invalidate all cache entries for that destination. The packet will therefore be sent down all possible circuits until the cache is reconstructed.

Subnetwork Independent Sublayer

Figure 3-16 shows the basic components of the DNA routing layer. The routing layer is broken up into two sublayers. The subnetwork independent sublayer operates at a high layer of abstraction, knowing only about the presence of broadcast and nonbroadcast links. The subnetwork dependent sublayer is responsible for managing functions that differ depending on the type of data link in use. For example, initializing an HDLC circuit is quite different from initializing a CSMA/CD LAN.

We start first with the subnetwork independent sublayer, in which there are four major processes in operation:

- receive
- update
- decision
- forwarding

The receive process takes incoming packets and allocates them to one of the other processes. If the packet has reached its final destination, it is given to the appropriate transport layer module. If the packet is destined for another node, it goes to the forwarding process.

Control packets are either handed back to the subnetwork dependent layer or to the update process. Link state and sequence number packets are part of the IS-IS routing exchange protocol and are given to the update process. Other control packets, such as Exchange ID (used for password exchange among other things) and hello packets are handed back to the subnetwork dependent sublayer. That sublayer maintains a database of adjacencies, which is used by the update process.

The update process is responsible for maintaining a list of all links and nodes in an area, as well as all paths to other areas if it is a level 2 router. The Link State Packet is the primary method used to do this. Sequence Number Packets are used to ensure that all routers have all Link State Packets. The Sequence Number Packet is thus a form of acknowledgment.

The decision process takes the link state database from the update process and the adjacency database from the subnetwork dependent sublayer and decides the best path to any given node. This forwarding database is then used by the forwarding process to decide which adjacency to use to forward a packet to a particular destination.

Update Process

The update process is one of the most complex in the network layer. Its function is to ensure that, within a DNA routing domain (or area), every router knows about every other router and every end node.

To begin, all routers exchange IS-IS hello packets (see Fig. 3-17). The packets allow two neighbors to identify each other as routers and identify which types of routers they are. The packet includes version numbers and minor version numbers (known as Engineering Change Orders or ECOs). In addition, the packet contains identifiers indicating which type of router is sending the information. The node can be a Phase IV or Phase V router and, for each of these, a level 1 or level 2 router. It is possible to be both a level 1 and a level 2 router.

The packet also contains a bid for the designated router. The designated router is the router on an Ethernet that receives, by default, traffic from

Protocol ID		DNA Private Protocol ID
Header Length		
Version		1
Type		15
Version		3
ECO		0
User ECO		1
Circuit Type		Level 1 or 2, Phase IV or V
Source ID		Six-octet node ID
Holding Timer		
Segment Length		Total length of PDU
Priority		Bid for designated router
LAN ID		Designated router ID
Code		1 - Area Addresses
		4 - Phase IV Area Address
		8 - Routing Neighbors
		8 - Padding
Length		
Value		

3-17

DNA IS-IS Hello

end nodes. The packet also contains all valid area addresses, any routing neighbors, and an indication if the node is a designated router.

Link State Packets

Each router on the network constructs a Link State Packet (LSP) which contains information on all neighbors of the router and the cost of reaching those neighbors (see Fig. 3-18). By exchanging LSPs, every router knows the current status of every other router and of that router's neighbors. This information is then used by the decision process to calculate the shortest path(s) between any two nodes.

As seen in Figure 3-18, the LSP includes a sequence number. It is possible that a given node will not be able to fit all the information into a single LSP. The sequence number allows the recipient to distinguish the different parts of the sender's link state database.

Protocol ID		DNA Private Protocol ID
Header Length		
Version		1
Type		20
Version		3
ECO		0
User ECO		1
Segment Length		
Remaining Lifetime		Validity of this LSP
Source ID		
Seguence Number		LSP Sequence Number
Checksum		
Flags		Router Level (I or II)
		Should this LSP be used for cost calculation?
Option Code		1 - Area Addresses
		2 - Router Neighbors
		3 - End Node Neighbors

3-18
DNA Link State Packet

The packet also includes an indicator showing whether the packet is operating at level 1 or level 2. The level 1 packet includes a list of all router neighbors and end node neighbors. The level 2 packet includes a list of all area neighbors. Remember, the level 1 and level 2 decision processes operate separately.

To ensure that LSPs are propagated throughout the network, DNA uses an explicit acknowledgment scheme based on the concept of a Sequence Numbers Packet (SNP). Two different kinds are used. The complete SNP (see Fig. 3-19) is used on broadcast links by the designated router and on nonbroadcast circuits whenever the circuit initializes or reinitializes.

The complete SNP covers a range of LSPs received. For each of these LSPs, the node includes an eight-octet node ID (consisting of the local area and node ID within the network portion of the address) and the LSP sequence number that identifies which of the packets is being acknowledged. The checksum of the LSP is also included as an integrity check.

The beginning LSP ID and ending LSP ID indicate the range of packets included in this acknowledgment. If a particular node falls within this range and there is an LSP, it will be included in the SNP. Using this

Protocol ID		DNA Private Protocol ID
Header Length		33
Version		1
Type		24
Version		3
ECO		0
User ECO		1
Segment Length		
Source ID		Seven-octet node ID
Start LSP ID		First LSP covered
End LSP ID		Last LSP covered
Remaining Lifetime		
Eight Octet LSP ID		
LSP Sequence Number		
Checksum of LSP		
Eight Octet LSP ID		
LSP Sequence Number		
Checksum of LSP		
Remaining Lifetime		
Eight Octet LSP ID		
LSP Sequence Number		
Checksum of LSP		

3-19
Complete Sequence
Numbers Packet

method, a node can see whether it is missing an LSP, or has a packet that the sending node is missing.

The partial SNP is used on nonbroadcast circuits as an explicit acknowledgment of a particular LSP (see Fig. 3-20). Instead of a range of LSPs, this partial sequence number message has a specific list.

Other Inputs

The update process is responsible for keeping the link state database up to date. The basic input to the update process is the LSPs and sequence number packets, delivered by the receive process. There are two types of links

Protocol ID		DNA Private Protocol ID
Header Length		17
Version		1
Type		26
Version		3
ECO		0
User ECO		1
Segment Length		
Source ID		
Seven octet node ID.		
Remaining Lifetime		
Eight Octet LSP ID		
LSP Sequence Number		
Checksum of LSP		
Eight Octet LSP ID		
LSP Sequence Number		
Checksum of LSP		
Remaining Lifetime		
Eight Octet LSP ID		
LSP Sequence Number		
Checksum of LSP		

3-20
Partial Sequence
Numbers Packet

that do not have LSPs: dynamic data links and circuits that have no DNA nodes on them.

For links that do not have LSPs, the subnetwork dependent layer furnishes an adjacency database and notifies the update process of any changes to adjacencies (see Fig. 3-21). The adjacency database is derived from hello messages. It includes an indicator of how long the adjacency information can be considered reliable and whether the information was manually configured or dynamically received from a hello message.

In addition to the adjacency database, one more piece of information is used: a set of manually configured reachable addresses furnished by network management. If a destination area or node lies on the other side of a public network, a network manager can always enter forwarding informa-

ID		ID for End Node
		NET for Router
Remaining Time		1 to 65535 Seconds
Type		Manual or Autconfigure
State		Initializing, Up, Up but Dormant, Failed
LAN Address		
DTE Address		For X.25
Adjacency Type		Unknown, non-DNA IS, DNA IS (L1, L2), DNA ES, Phase IV (End Node, L1, or L2)
LAN Priority		For becoming designated router on the LAN
Area Addresses		For L2 Routers
One entry is kept for each: Point-to-Point (HDLC/DDCMP) Circuit Broadcast Router Adjacency Broadcast Endnode Adjacency (Routers Only) Potential SVC on a DED Circuit		

3-21
Adjacency Database

Address		7 Byte Pseudo ID
Type		Level 1 Router
		Attached Level 2
		Unattached Level 2
LSP Sequence Number		
LSP Age		Remaining Lifetime
Last Sent Timestamp		LSP Sent (Any Circuit)
SRM Flags		Circuits to Send LSP

3-22
The Link State Database

tion manually. By indicating the destination address and which neighbor router to use, we can ensure that any node is reachable.

The output from the update process consists of the link state database, which will be used by the decision process (see Fig. 3-22). The link state database is accessed whenever the decision process is periodically run. In addition, the decision process is triggered by the signal of an event, such as the receipt of a new LSP with different information or the purging of an LSP because its remaining lifetime has expired.

Along with the link state database, the routing layer keeps a circuit database (see Fig. 3-23). This includes information about available circuits and is especially useful in dynamic data links. Notice that the database includes information that indicates how long to wait before reattempting a call, the maximum number of call attempts, and how long to wait before clearing a call when there is no traffic.

Decision Process

The decision process uses the link state database and network management-furnished information to find the shortest path or paths to a given node. The algorithm used is known variously as Djikstra's Algorithm (after the originator), shortest path first, or link state algorithm.

Given a series of nodes and links between them, the basic problem is to find the best path between any two nodes. To decide which path is "best," the network manager defines a cost for each link. Costs have a default by link type or are manually entered by network management presumably reflecting the bandwidth and utilization expected on the link. The best path is represented as the lowest total cost path—the sum of the costs of the individual links.

In the early phases of DECnet (based on a different approach, known as distance-vector routing), the network layer came up with a single best path between any two nodes. In DNA Phase IV, this was modified to allow load splitting. When multiple, equal-cost paths are available, alternate packets are sent down the different possible paths. Note that the load splitting is either a strict round-robin or random basis and does not reflect the actual load on the individual links. This is load splitting, not load balancing.

The result of the decision process is a forwarding database. For each destination within an area, the level 1 forwarding database contains the adjacencies that can be used to move the packet one hop closer to its final destination. The level 2 forwarding database contains a list of address prefixes, and the adjacency to use for each of those prefixes.

Internal Databases

The decision process uses two internal databases as holding areas for the algorithm. The paths database contains the results of the decision process: the shortest path to a given node (see Fig. 3-24). It consists of a series of tuples (records) in the following format:

Name		
Type		802.3, DDCMP, HDLC
Template Name		
Data Link Entity Name		
Hello Timer		Seconds between IS Hellos (default = 10)
ISIS Hello Timer		Default = 3 Seconds
Complete SNP Interval		SNP Packets (10 seconds for designated routers, 300 on nonbroadcast links)
Level 1 Cost		Cost for this level of
Level 2 Cost		traffic (default = 20)
Originating Queue Limit		Number packets, this node
Enable PhaseIV Address?		
L1 Router Priority		To be designated router
L2 Router Priority		(default = 64, max = 127)
Datalink Blocksize		Default = 1492
DNA Neighbor Expected?		
Transmit Verifier		For verifying neighbor.
Explicit Verification?		
Receive Verifier		
Neighbor DTE Address		
Recall Timer		Default = 60 seconds
Max Call Attempts		Retries on failure (default = 10)
Idle Timer		Wait before clearing (30)
Initial Minimum Timer		Initial wait before clearing (55)
Reserve Timer		Reserve SVC for DTE (600)
Max SVC Adjacencies		Max simultaneous calls
Reserve Adjacency?		Reserve 1 SVC for router?
Only L2 Traffic?		
Manual Router Address		IDs of routers (can be empty)
Circuit UID		

N, d(N), { adj (N) }

3-23
Circuit Database

Address		Destination Node for Level 1, Destination Area for Level 2
Cost		Cost of Best Path
Parent ID		Parent in Graph
Adjacency Pointer		Adjacency for Forwarding
Parent ID		Up to MaxPathSplits Entries
Adjacency Pointer		

3-24
DNA Paths Database

For every node N, the paths database contains the shortest distance to N and which adjacencies (routers) to use for that shortest path. When an entry is entered into the paths database, that entry is guaranteed to be the shortest distance to that node N.

The second database is called TENT, for tentative placement. Each record in TENT is being held pending a decision on whether or not it is the shortest path to a given node N. A record in TENT also includes an indication of whether or not the node in question is an end node or a router.

Basic Algorithm

The basic process is as follows. First, the node running the process puts itself into the paths database. Since the distance to this node has a cost of zero and is therefore the shortest possible. Next, the adjacency database is used to preload the TENT database.

The way the algorithm works is to look for all nodes in TENT at a given distance or cost. The first sweep will look for all nodes that have a distance of 1 from the node. The second sweep will look for all nodes that have a distance of 2.

When we find a triplet, we continue to scan TENT and combine any other triplets for that same node with the same distance; that is, any other routes that would fit the load splitting definition of equal-cost paths. While going through the TENT database, if we see a path to the node N with a longer distance, it is removed from the database. In this way, we are discarding paths that are not applicable.

We now add our node to the paths database. If the node was an end node, we go back to TENT and look for additional elements with a distance of 1. If the node was a router, we go to the link state database and take that node's LSPs and add them to TENT. In this way, we are adding not only the route to a node but all other nodes to which it is in turn connected. To convert an LSP to triplets in the TENT database, we must take the shortest cost to our router plus the cost to the neighbors of that router to form a total cost to the neighbor.

For each of the nodes in the LSP, we scan the TENT database. If there is already a shorter route to that node, the record in the LSP is ignored. If the route in the LSP is shorter than the route already in the TENT database, the TENT triplet is discarded and the new one added. If the two are equal cost, they are combined.

In this way, we have added more records to TENT. We now go back to scanning TENT, looking for nodes with a distance of 1. If we find one, we repeat the procedure. If it is an end node, add it to the paths database. If it is a router, add it to the paths database and get the LSP and add it to TENT.

When all records with a distance of 1 have been examined, we look for records with a distance of 2, and so on. If there are no more records in TENT, the process is completed.

The level 2 process is identical with level 1, but instead of looking for a node we look for an area prefix. Anything added to the paths database now consists of area prefixes and the associated adjacency to use. Since the forwarding database is derived from the paths database, it too consists of area prefixes for level 2 routing.

There are two possible complications. One is the unattached router. There are level 2 routers that are not connected to any other areas, and are sometimes known as stub routers. For these routers, the LSP contains the infinite hippity cost bit. If the decision process sees that, it only processes end nodes in the LSP.

The second possible complication is the limitation on the number of possible equal-cost paths to a given node. If the number of adjacencies in TENT is larger than the total number of allowable path splits, one or more of the possible paths must be arbitrarily discarded (arbitrarily since they are of equal cost).

Pruning the paths is based on the ID of nodes, circuits, and LAN adapters. First, we attempt to throw out adjacencies with the highest node ID. If a node has multiple circuits to it, and has the highest node ID, we throw out the highest circuit. It is possible to have multiple LAN adapters on a single circuit—we throw out the adjacency with the highest LAN address.

Once TENT is empty, and therefore the paths database complete, we construct the actual forwarding database (see Fig. 3-25). The forwarding database is a subset of the paths database: the node in question (or area prefix) and which adjacencies to use. The forwarding database also needs one more piece of information if it is a level 1 node—the nearest level 2 router.

Address		Destination Node for Level 1, Destination Area for Level 2
Number of Splits		Number of Paths Available
Next Hop Pointer		Adjacency for Forwarding
Next Hop Pointer		

3-25
Forwarding Database

We look for the nearest level 2 router that advertises itself as attached to another area.

Forwarding Process

The forwarding process takes packets from the transport layer and the update and receive processes and sends them down to the data link layer for forwarding. The transport layer sends down originating packets; the update process sends link state and sequence number packets; and, the receive process passes along packets destined for other nodes.

The forwarding decision is based on a portion of the address. The forwarding process will look at the address and see if the packet area address matches any of the area addresses of the router. If so, the packet stays in this area via level 1 routing. Otherwise, it is forwarded using level 2 routing.

For any given node (or area prefix for level 2 routing), the forwarding database returns one or more adjacencies. One of these adjacencies is picked for forwarding this particular packet, either on a round-robin or random basis.

If there is no entry for the particular destination address and this is a route-through packet, it is dropped. If the error report requested flag is included, an error report is generated. If the packet is a local packet, however, it is handed off to a random adjacent router.

The forwarding process is responsible for maintaining the data unit identifiers used to identify a packet uniquely in case of fragmentation. The sequence numbers are kept in a cache (see Fig. 3-26). Note that the cache has a limited size—a single DUI is used for all nodes that do not fit into the cache.

Address		20 Byte Node ID
Data Unit ID		Last ID Used (16 Bit)
Timestamp		Last PDU Sent
Address		
Data Unit ID		Up to Cachesize Entries
Timestamp		
Address		
Other Data Unit ID		For All Remaining Destinations

3-26
Data Unit
Identifier Cache

Redirection

One of the jobs of the forwarding process is to notice when a packet is being forwarded back out the same circuit on which it was received. If this is the case the router should never have gotten the packet in the first place. The data or error packet is sent back out the circuit, and an additional redirect packet is also sent out, informing the sending node of a better possible route to the destination.

The redirect packet includes not only the addresses to use but the length of time for which the redirection is valid. The holding time is extracted from the LSP holding time. Thus, a node may have used a manually entered adjacency for forwarding a packet. When that manually entered router gets the packet, it may inform the node that there is a better path, at least for a while.

Partial Source Routing

A special option in OSI is known as partial source routing whereby the originating node includes specific routing directions with the packet. This is useful when a packet must cross several different routing domains that are not sharing a common routing exchange protocol. Partial source routing is parameter 200 at the end of a data or error packet. The parameter consists of an offset to use for the next network, followed by a list of network addresses.

When the forwarding process sees a packet that uses partial source routing, it looks at the offset number, then uses that offset to find the next applicable network. It then forwards the packet based on that address, updating the offset number to point to the one after that. If the offset points beyond the last network, the partial source routing list has been exhausted. At this point, the node goes back to the destination address in the header of the packet and attempts to send it directly to the destination NSAP.

Congestion Control

One of the jobs of the forwarding process is to perform congestion control. This function is actually performed by four subprocesses:

- the flusher
- the originating packet limiter
- the square root limiter
- the congestion experienced indicator

The flusher is responsible for flushing all packets on a queue for a circuit or adjacency that is down. By flushing unneeded traffic, bandwidth and processing on the network are preserved.

The originating packet limiter ensures that a portion of the resources on a router is available for route-through traffic. This prevents a local user from using all resources, leading to buffers filling up and route-through packets being dropped. The theory is, we have an investment in the route-through packets and it thus makes sense to keep them flowing.

The packet limiter works on a per-queue basis. For each queue, it only allows a certain number of originating data packets to be on the queue at any one time, as determined by network management. Note that in many cases there will be no originating data packets if the router is a dedicated router and all users are on end systems.

The square root limiter prevents any one circuit from taking up all buffer space on the router. A threshold limit is determined for each queue. If a packet is added that would exceed the threshold, the packet is dropped (and an error message is sent if possible and requested).

The square root limiter is based on the total number of routing layer buffers and the total number of active circuits. The formula is:

$$threshold = \left| \frac{TotalRoutingLayerBuffers}{\sqrt{NumberActiveCircuits}} \right|$$

As an example, consider 4 circuits and 4 buffers. The rule ensures that any one circuit does not take more than 2 buffers or 50 percent of the total resources. On the other hand, if there are 16 buffers for 16 circuits, any individual circuit can have only 4 buffers.

The last mechanism is the congestion experienced bit. Whenever the routing layer sees that a packet sits in a queue with the average queue length greater than an architectural constant (usually 1), then the congestion experienced bit is set in that packet. The congestion experienced bit is then used by the transport layer to adjust the window size and thus reduce congestion on the network.

Receive Process

The receive process is fairly simple: it forwards packets up the protocol stack to the appropriate user. By the time a packet gets there, it has reached its ultimate destination.

In addition to sending the packet up to the transport layer, the receive process is also responsible for checking the packet to see that it is in valid format and for reassembling any fragments into a complete packet. If a packet is invalid, an error message is formulated and given to the forwarding process.

In addition to transport layer users, a packet may be received for internal routing layer modules. An LSP, for example, is given to the update process. A Phase IV update message is given to the Phase IV update process. Hello, XID, and redirect messages are given back down to the subnetwork dependent sublayer.

Subnetwork Dependent Sublayer

The subnetwork independent sublayer only saw two generic kinds of links: broadcast and nonbroadcast. Network layer functions that differ depending on the type of data link are handled by the subnetwork dependent sublayer. These functions include the following:

- Call setup on dynamically established data links, either based on operator demand for static links or on traffic receipt for dynamically assigned DEDs.
- Data link initialization, including specification of user parameters such as maximum block size.
- Determination of adjacency identification, including the NSAP and Network Entity Title, as well as the type of node: end or intermediate system; Phase IV or Phase V.
- Autoconfiguration of the end node portion of the area address.
- Identification verification of adjacent nodes.
- Detection of neighbor failures through polling via hello message exchange.
- Moving messages between the independent sublayer and the data link layer by putting in data link specific information (i.e., protocol ID, IEEE SNAP, or DDCMP multipoint address).
- Clearing dynamic data links either through operator intervention or because of timer expiration.
- Specification of static routing information on dynamically allocated DEDs that do not exchange LSPs.

Identification verification is done using an XID packet, which is a simple way of verifying that two nodes are meant to communicate (see Fig. 3-27).

Protocol ID		DNA Private Protocol ID
Header Length		12
Version		1
Type		23
Version		3
ECO		0
User ECO		1
DNA Routing Protocol ID		
Data Link Block Size		
Option Code		7 - Verification Data
Length		
Value		

3-27
DNA XID Packet

A simple verification code (equivalent to a password) is stored locally in the circuit database. When an XID packet is received, the verification value is compared to the stored value.

Static Routing

LSPs are used in a DNA network to exchange routing information. Non-DNA nodes, however, are not able to issue an LSP (unless they implement the same IS-IS protocols). This means that the routing database needs to be manually updated to include information about these nodes. In addition, dynamically assigned DEDs do not have LSPs, and it is necessary to add information about these circuits manually.

On a dynamically assigned DED, there is a management entity called a reachable address. The reachable address consists of a series of reachable address prefixes (i.e., an area address) that is associated with this particular dynamic data link. Associated with each reachable address prefix is a data link address, such as an X.25 address. This is the address of the "router" that will forward packets for that particular address. A cost indicator is also associated with each of these addresses, just as an LSP would include cost information for adjacencies.

When a dynamic circuit is initialized, the subnetwork dependent layer will issue an adjacency cost change event for each of the address prefixes, which will be transmitted to the update process. The update process will then issue a new LSP to inform other nodes on the network about the availability and cost of a particular area.

A second form of manual information is the manual adjacency, used for broadcast circuits. Most ISO-compliant end nodes (and all DNA end nodes)

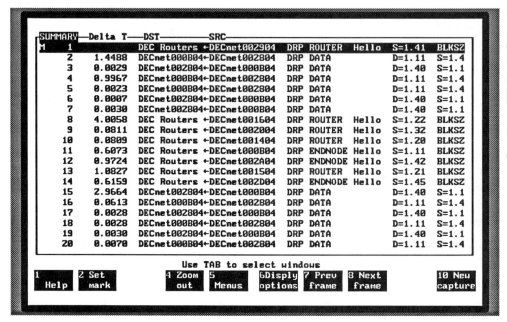

3-28 Phase IV Routing Traffic

will use the ISO ES-IS hello message to inform routers about their presence. It is possible that some end systems do not use the ES-IS protocol but do conform to the ISO 8473 format for data packets. By entering a manual adjacency into the router's database, we tell the router about these nodes.

The last form of manual routing information is for nonDNA routers. An end system can be informed about the presence of these nodes, allowing the DNA end system to work with nonDNA routers on a LAN. Again, manual adjacency information is only necessary on a LAN since a nonbroadcast link has only a fixed, known number of adjacencies.

Autoconfiguration

In a Phase IV environment, it was necessary to enter all the addressing information for each node manually. In Phase V, it is possible for end nodes to configure themselves automatically.

An end node has a unique 48-bit ID for the LAN adapter. This 48-bit ID matches the size of the 6-byte network-layer node ID. All that needs to be added is the local area and the initial domain part. This information can easily be found from an IS hello message.

Autoconfiguration works for all end nodes that can read hello messages; in other words, nodes compatible with ISO 9542. If a node is compatible with the data format (ISO 8473) but not with ISO 9542, it can participate in

```
┌DETAIL──────────────────────────────────────────────────┐
│DRP: ----- DECNET Routing Protocol -----                 │
│DRP:                                                      │
│DRP: Data Length = 38,  Optional Padding Length = 1       │
│DRP: Data Packet Format = 26                              │
│DRP:        0... .... = no padding                        │
│DRP:        .0.. .... = version                           │
│DRP:        ..1. .... = Intra-Ethernet packet             │
│DRP:        ...0 .... = not return packet                 │
│DRP:        .... 0... = do not return to sender           │
│DRP:        .... .110 = Long Data Packet Format           │
│DRP: Data Packet Type = 6                                 │
│DRP: Destination Area     = 00                            │
│DRP: Destination Subarea  = 00                            │
│DRP: Destination ID       = 1.11                          │
│DRP: Source Area          = 00                            │
│DRP: Source Subarea       = 00                            │
│DRP: Source ID            = 1.40                          │
│DRP: Next Level 2 Router  = 00                            │
│DRP: Visit Count          = 0                             │
│DRP: Service Class        = 00                            │
│DRP: Protocol Type        = 00                            │
│DRP:                                                      │
│NSP: ----- Network Services Protocol -----                │
│NSP:                                                      │
│NSP: Message Identifier = 60                              │
│NSP:        0... .... = Non-extensible field              │
│NSP:        .110 .... = Begin-End Data Message            │
│NSP:        .... 00.. = Data Message                      │
│NSP:        .... ..00 = always zero                       │
│NSP: Type     = 0  (Data Message)                         │
│NSP: Sub-type = 6  (Begin-End Data Message)               │
│NSP: Logical Link Destination = 0491                      │
│NSP: Logical Link Source      = C039                      │
│NSP: Data Acknowledgment Number                           │
│NSP:    Acknowledge Qualifier         = ACK               │
│NSP:    Message Number Acknowledged = 41                  │
└────────────────────────Frame 31 of 561──────────────────┘
              Use TAB to select windows
┌─┐┌──────┐  ┌──────┐┌─────┐┌───────┐┌──────┐┌──────┐  ┌───────┐
│1││2 Set │  │4 Zoom││5    ││6Disply││7 Prev││8 Next│  │10 New │
│ ││      │  │      ││     ││       ││      ││      │  │       │
│Help││ mark│  │ out ││Menus││options││frame ││frame │  │capture│
└─┘└──────┘  └──────┘└─────┘└───────┘└──────┘└──────┘  └───────┘
```

3-29 Phase IV Intra-Ethernet Packet

a DECnet as an end node but cannot autoconfigure itself. Autoconfiguration is disabled for addresses in the Phase IV compatible address space to avoid problems with the older protocols.

Phase IV Compatibility

DECnet has always been n-1 compatible: A given phase can always coexist with the previous phase. A Phase IV network will coexist within a Phase V routing domain. Coexistence is based on level 2 routing: Phase IV and Phase V intermediate systems do not coexist within a given area. It is possi-

```
┌DETAIL──────────────────────────────────────────────────────────────┐
│DRP:  ----- DECNET Routing Protocol -----                            │
│DRP:                                                                  │
│DRP:  Data Length = 34,  Optional Padding Length = 1                  │
│DRP:  Control Packet Format = 0D                                      │
│DRP:              0... .... = no padding                             │
│DRP:              .000 .... = reserved                               │
│DRP:              .... 110. = Ethernet Endnode Hello Message         │
│DRP:              .... ...1 = Control Packet Format                  │
│DRP:  Control Packet Type = 06                                       │
│DRP:  Version Number  = 02                                           │
│DRP:  ECO Number      = 00                                           │
│DRP:  User ECO Number = 00                                           │
│DRP:  ID of Transmitting Node = 1.42                                 │
│DRP:      Information = 03                                           │
│DRP:          0... .... = reserved                                   │
│DRP:          .0.. .... = not blocking request                       │
│DRP:          ..0. .... = multicast traffic accepted                 │
│DRP:          ...0 .... = verification ok                            │
│DRP:          .... 0... = do not reject                              │
│DRP:          .... .0.. = no verification required                   │
│DRP:          .... ..11 = endnode                                    │
│DRP:  Receive Block Size  = 1484                                     │
│DRP:  Area (reserved)     = 0                                        │
│DRP:  Verification Seed   = 0000000000000000                         │
│DRP:  Neighbor System ID  = 1.40                                     │
│DRP:  Hello timer (seconds) = 15                                     │
│DRP:  MPD (reserved)      = 0                                        │
│DRP:  [1 bytes of Data to test the circuit]                          │
│DRP:                                                                  │
├──────────────────Frame 12 of 561──────────────────────────────────┤
│                  Use TAB to select windows                          │
│ 1      2 Set        4 Zoom  5       6Display 7 Prev 8 Next   10 New │
│ Help     mark         out     Menus  options  frame   frame  capture│
└─────────────────────────────────────────────────────────────────────┘
```

Courtesy of Network General

3-30 Phase IV Ethernet End Node Hello

ble for Phase IV and Phase V end systems to coexist in the same area. The area would run either the LSP or the Phase IV vector routing algorithms.

The basic data transfer mechanism between the two environments is not radically different. Figure 3-28 shows the basic data transfer in a Phase IV environment, consisting of data and hello packets. Figure 3-29 shows the format for the Phase IV data packet. Notice that the addresses include an error report request (or in this case a nonrequest). The packet, although somewhat similar to the ISO 8473 data format, is only applicable to DECnet nodes—nonDECnet nodes cannot read the packet format.

Phase V DECnet nodes are able to read incoming Phase IV packets. This means that two DECnet nodes, assuming they share common applications, will be able to communicate across the area boundaries. A Phase V node,

```
┌DETAIL┐
 DRP:  ----- DECNET Routing Protocol -----
 DRP:
 DRP:  Data length = 136
 DRP:  Control Packet Format = 09
 DRP:               0... .... = no padding
 DRP:               .000 .... = reserved
 DRP:               .... 100. = Level 2 Routing Message
 DRP:               .... ...1 = Control Packet Format
 DRP:  Control Packet Type = 04
 DRP:  Source Node     = 1.22
 DRP:  Reserved field = 0
 DRP:  RTGINFO count = 63
 DRP:  Start Area = 1
 DRP:   Area = 1      Hops = 00    Cost = 0
 DRP:   Area = 2      Hops = 31    Cost = 1023
 DRP:   Area = 3      Hops = 31    Cost = 1023
 DRP:   Area = 4      Hops = 31    Cost = 1023
 DRP:   Area = 5      Hops = 31    Cost = 1023
 DRP:   Area = 6      Hops = 31    Cost = 1023
 DRP:   Area = 7      Hops = 31    Cost = 1023
                 └Frame 25 of 561┘
              Use TAB to select windows
┌1     ┐┌2 Set ┐      ┌4 Zoom┐┌5     ┐┌6Disply┐┌7 Prev┐┌8 Next┐      ┌10 New  ┐
│ Help ││ mark │      │ out  ││Menus ││options││ frame││ frame│      │capture │
└──────┘└──────┘      └──────┘└──────┘└───────┘└──────┘└──────┘      └────────┘
```

Courtesy of Network General

3-31 Phase IV Level 2 Routing Message

for example, could use the Data Access Protocol to access data residing on a Phase IV node.

Within a DECnet Phase IV area, end nodes make their presence known using End Node hello messages (see Fig. 3-30). These messages specify the capabilities of that node (i.e., whether multicast traffic is accepted). The level 1 routers use this information to build their cache of end nodes.

Figure 3-31 shows the message a Phase V intermediate system would receive. It indicates the reachable Phase IV areas that are available using this particular router, and the cost to reach that area. Areas 2 through 7 have costs of 1023, which is equivalent to an infinite cost in Phase IV.

In a typical transition environment, the Phase IV level 2 router will also double as the designated level 1 router. Figure 3-32 shows the Ethernet router hello message which is transmitted periodically to all nodes on the Ethernet. Using this message, the Phase IV end nodes and routers are kept aware of reachable areas. In order for a Phase IV node to communicate with a Phase V node, the Phase V node must be in the Phase IV address space. For example, the area indicator needs to be 63 or less or the maximum area limitation in Phase IV will have been violated.

Phase IV compatibility is useful as a transition aid and to maintain compatibility with Digital products that will not migrate into a Phase V environment. For example, the PDP-11 systems, often used as dedicated controllers

```
┌─DETAIL────────────────────────────────────────────────────────────┐
│ DRP: ----- DECNET Routing Protocol -----                           │
│ DRP:                                                               │
│ DRP: Data Length = 70,  Optional Padding Length = 1               │
│ DRP: Control Packet Format = 0B                                   │
│ DRP:              0... .... = no padding                          │
│ DRP:              .000 .... = reserved                            │
│ DRP:              .... 101. = Ethernet Router Hello Message       │
│ DRP:              .... ...1 = Control Packet Format               │
│ DRP: Control Packet Type = 05                                     │
│ DRP: Version Number  = 02                                         │
│ DRP: ECO Number      = 00                                         │
│ DRP: User ECO Number = 00                                         │
│ DRP: ID of Transmitting Node = 1.41                              │
│ DRP:      Information = 01                                        │
│ DRP:          0... .... = reserved                               │
│ DRP:          .0.. .... = not blocking request                   │
│ DRP:          ..0. .... = multicast traffic accepted             │
│ DRP:          ...0 .... = verification ok                        │
│ DRP:          .... 0... = do not reject                          │
│ DRP:          .... .0.. = no verification required               │
│ DRP:          .... ..01 = level 2 router                         │
│ DRP: Receive Block Size  = 1484                                  │
│ DRP: Router's priority   = 64                                    │
│ DRP: Area (reserved)     = 0                                     │
│ DRP: Hello timer (seconds) = 15                                  │
│ DRP: MPD (reserved)      = 0                                     │
│ DRP: E-List length = 50                                          │
│ DRP: Ethernet Name, reserved = 00000000000000                   │
│ DRP: Router/State length = 42                                   │
│ DRP:                                                            │
│ DRP: Router ID = 1.43                                          │
│ DRP: Priority and State = C0                                   │
│ DRP:          1... .... = State known 2-way                    │
│ DRP:          .100 0000 = Router's priority                    │
│ DRP:                                                            │
│ DRP: Router ID = 1.40                                          │
│ DRP: Priority and State = D0                                   │
│ DRP:          1... .... = State known 2-way                    │
│ DRP:          .101 0000 = Router's priority                    │
│ DRP:                                                            │
│ DRP: Router ID = 1.32                                          │
│ DRP: Priority and State = 80                                   │
│ DRP:          1... .... = State known 2-way                    │
│ DRP:          .000 0000 = Router's priority                    │
│ DRP:                                                            │
│ DRP: Router ID = 1.21                                          │
│ DRP: Priority and State = 80                                   │
│ DRP:          1... .... = State known 2-way                    │
│ DRP:          .000 0000 = Router's priority                    │
│ DRP:                                                            │
│ DRP: Router ID = 1.22                                          │
│ DRP: Priority and State = 80                                   │
│ DRP:          1... .... = State known 2-way                    │
│ DRP:          .000 0000 = Router's priority                    │
│ DRP:                                                            │
│ DRP: Router ID = 1.20                                          │
│ ─────────────────────Frame 1 of 561─────────────────────       │
│              Use TAB to select windows                         │
│ 1        2 Set            4 Zoom  5       6Disply 7 Prev  8 Next      10 Ne │
│ Help     mark             out     Menus   options frame   frame      captur │
└────────────────────────────────────────────────────────────────────┘
```

3-32 Phase IV Ethenet Router Hello

in manufacturing or engineering environments, will not have Phase V support. N-1 compatibility allows an organization to keep those nodes as a Phase IV area and interconnect them to the wider Phase V environment.

Architectural and Performance Parameters

Figure 3-33 shows a variety of architectural parameters in a Phase V environment. The first part of the table is a series of default addresses. Some of these addresses are multicast addresses for things such as all Phase IV end nodes or Phase V end nodes. Other addresses are prefixes and defaults. For example, the Hiord constant is a prefix: A Phase IV node uses this constant to form a 48-bit LAN address. The default area indicator is another default: If a node does not know which area it is in, it will use this number.

Other portions of the table are default values for things like timers. For example, the ESCacheHoldingTime specifies that an end node will maintain a cache entry for 600 seconds before discarding it as too old.

Summary

Figure 3-34 shows a high-level diagram of the routing layer in Phase V that reflects the major components. The subnetwork dependent sublayer handles questions specific to a given subnetwork. Verification of a data link and a neighbor and autoconfiguration of area addresses, for example, vary depending on the broadcast or point-to-point nature of a link.

The subnetwork dependent sublayer also handles the question of dynamically established data links. The routing process only sees a link with a given cost. If it decides to use that link, it sends the packet down to the subnetwork dependent sublayer. That sublayer will, if necessary, activate the dynamic link. When the link has been idle for a specified amount of time, it will clear the dynamic link.

Above the subnetwork dependent sublayer are the four components of the routing process. These four modules work the same way, irrespective of the underlying data links.

The receive process is responsible for reassembling packets that have reached their destination, then distributing packets. Data packets at their final destination go up to the transport user indicated in the selection byte of the network address. Subnetwork-dependent packets (such as hello and XID) go back down to the lower sublayer. If a redirect packet needs to be sent out, it is also sent down.

The forwarding process takes any packet and decides, using the forwarding database, which subnetwork to use. It then hands the packet down to the lower sublayer, which handles the mechanics of getting it ready to send out over the subnetwork.

Parameter	Value	Description
MaxLinkCost	63	Maximum cost for a circuit
MaxPathCost	1023	Maximum cost for complete path
Hiord	AA-00-04-00	Quantity to be prefixed to the 16-bit Phase IV address to form a 48 bit LAN address
AllIVL1Routers	AB-00-00-03-00-00	DNA Phase IV level 1 Routers multicast address
AllIVEndnodes	AB-00-00-04-00-00	DNA Phase IV End Nodes multicast address
AllL2Routers	09-00-2B-02-00-00	All Phase V level 2 Routers multicast address
AllL1Routers	09-00-2B-00-00-05	ISO multicast ID for "all intermediate system network entities."
AllEndnodes	09-00-2B-00-00-04	ISO multicast ID for "all end system network entities."
ProtType	60-03	Protocol type used in Ethernet for DNA Routing Layer
ISO-CLNS	FE	SP used for the ISO Network Layer on 802.3 networks
DNAPrivatePD	8	Discriminator for DNA private protocols
ESISProtocol Identifier	130	Protocol identifier for ES-IS messages (i.e., hello messages)
DefaultArea	49-00-40	Area to use when the real area address is unknown
SingleHop	00-00	Reserved value for the local area portion of the address
EntireIdp	FF-FF	Reserved value for the local area portion of the address
ESCacheHolding Time	600	Holding time for an end node cache entry
SequenceModulus	2E32	32-bit sequence number space used by update process
QueueThreshold	1	If the average queue size exceeds 1 at a router
RoutingInitTimer	6	Wait 6 seconds after initializing a DDCMP circuit before sending a Phase V message
HoldingMultiplier	3	Multiply the hello timer by this number to obtain the holding timer for ES, IS, and point-to-point router-to-router hellos

3-33 Network Layer Architectural Constants

Parameter	Value	Description
ISHoldingMultiplier	10	Multiply the hello timer by 10 to obtain the holding timer for LAN-based router-to-router hellos
MinimumLSP GenerationInterval	30	LSPs are generated no more than once over 30 seconds
PartialSNPInterval	2	Partial sequence number packets are generated no more than once every 2 seconds
WaitingTime	60	Delay for 60 seconds in the *Waiting* state before entering the *On* state. This state is entered if a node is unable to process an incoming LSP
MaxAge	1200	Maximum number of seconds before an LSP is considered to be expired
ZeroAgeLifetime	60	Number of seconds to retain the purge header of an expired LSP
DefaultESHello Timer	600	If the IS does not suggest a value, the ES should use this number as the Current Suggested Hello Timer value
PollESHelloRate	50	The interval in seconds between ES hellos to poll an ES for its configuration
DRISHelloTimer	1	Interval between IS-IS hellos generated by the designated router
Jitter	25	Percentage of jitter to be applied to any periodically geneated PDUs
MaximumArea Addresses	3	Maximum number of area addresses for a single area
PhaseIVMaximum Hops	30	Maximum number of hops to a destination node in a Phase IV area
PhaseIVMaximum Cost	1022	Maximum cost possible in the path to a destination node in a Phase IV area
PhaseIVArea MaximumHops	30	Maximum hops in the path to reach a Phase IV area
PhaseIVArea MaximumCost	1022	Maximum cost possible to reach a Phase IV area
PhaseIVMaximum Visits	63	Maximum number of visits for a packet before the routing layer assumes it is looping
PhaseIVRouting Timer	600	Maximum period to wait before exchanging routing messages on a nonbroadcast circuit

3-33 *(Cont.)* Architectural Constants

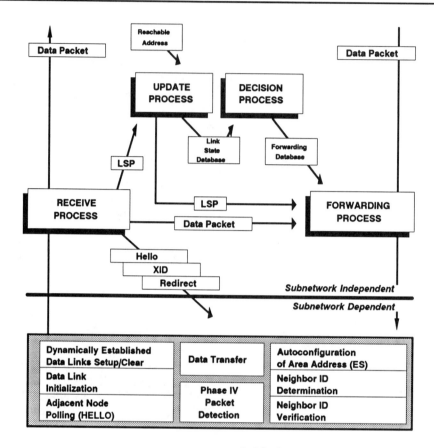

3-34 Basic Routing Layer Components

The two processes that help make the routing decisions are the update and decision processes. The update process is responsible for maintaining the link state database. That information is periodically transmitted through the network using sequence number and LSPs. The decision process uses the link state database plus manually entered reachable addresses and adjacency information to generate a forwarding database. The forwarding database contains, at a given point in time, the lowest cost paths to a given destination or area.

At this point, the network layer provides the basic service intended—a best-effort delivery service between any two nodes in the network. The network layer shields the upper layers from having to know the topology of the network and from having to adapt to changes in the topology. The upper layers can concentrate on direct communication with the destination node and do not have to worry about the mechanics of how to get to that node.

Upper Layers

CHAPTER 4

Upper Layers

The network service provides a computer-to-computer best-effort delivery service. Transmission of a packet is not guaranteed, but the network is able to adapt to changes in the topology of the network and find the best set of transmission paths.

The transport layer uses the delivery service of the network layer and builds on it to provide a user-to-user dialogue. Incoming data from the network service, having reached its final destination, is parceled out by the transport layer to the individual users.

The transport layer provides a stream interface (also known as a virtual connection) that guarantees the data sent by one user are received by the other user in the order received. The transport layer thus provides not only error detection (i.e., lost packets of data) but also error recovery via retransmission of the lost packets.

The session layer takes the virtual circuit service and integrates it into the computer operating system. It lets its users initiate a session, which consists not only of a virtual circuit but of any operating-system dependent functions such as access control. The session control can be considered a bridge between the data-transmission facilities of the network and transport layers and the functional capabilities of specific applications.

What makes DECnet/OSI different from most network architectures is that Digital supports two different types of transport protocols and two different Session Control layers, all sharing the common underlying network and subnetwork layers (see Fig. 4-1).

The Network Services Protocol (NSP) is Digital's traditional, proprietary transport protocol. It is used primarily to communicate with Phase IV nodes, but it can also be used in a Phase V environment. The OSI Transport Protocols consist of three classes of service. The most functional, transport protocol class 4 (TP4) provides essentially the same functionality as NSP. TP4 is used to communicate within a Phase V environment and also provides interoperability to non-Digital OSI environments.

OSI Applications	DNA Applications	
Presentation (Abstract Syntax)		
Presentation (Transfer Syntax)		
OSI Session	DNA Session	
OSI Transport Protocols	Network Services Protocol	
OSI Network Protocols		
	ISO 8473: Data/Error Packets ISO 9542: ES-IS Routing Exchange DEC IS-IS: Dynamic Routing	

4-1 Phase V Dual Protocol Stack

Within a Phase V environment, Digital's proprietary DNA applications will use their own Session Control protocol. The DNA Session Control protocol is heavily integrated with the DNA Naming Service (discussed in Chapter 5) and offers some security services not offered in the OSI Session Control layer.

Quite a few different applications fall in the category of Digital proprietary and thus use the DNA Session Control layer. Many of these, such as the Data Access Protocols (DAP) are discussed later in this book.

Applications like DAP use the DNA Session Control and the OSI TP4 protocols for intra-Phase V communication (see Fig. 4-1). Note that even though a proprietary Session Control layer is being used, the lower layers are often OSI protocols like TP4, the OSI network layer, and data links such as 802.3 Ethernets. NSP is used for communication to Phase IV nodes.

Protocols like DAP are not very useful for communicating in a truly open, heterogeneous environment. For this type of network, Digital conforms to the OSI architecture. Sitting on top of the OSI session layer is the presentation layer, which is split into two sublayers. The transfer syntax specifies issues such as encryption and compression of data. The abstract syntax specifies what types of information are to be transferred (e.g., integers, characters, and constructed data types).

Finally, at the top of the stack, we see a variety of OSI applications. Some provide the equivalent services to Digital proprietary protocols. The Digital DAP protocols, for example, find their equivalence in the File Transfer, Access, and Management (FTAM) service in OSI.

This chapter will discuss the transport through presentation layers of the network. Application layer issues are deferred to later chapters. This chap-

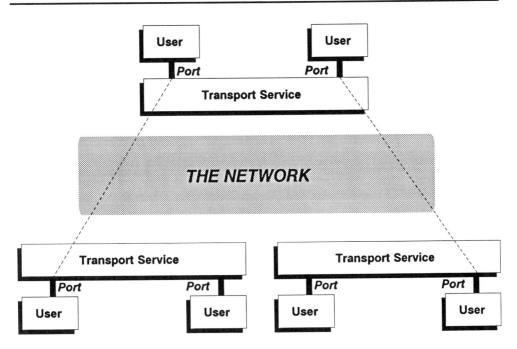

4-2 Transport Layer Virtual Circuits

ter also deals with the concept of protocol towers—combination of the various available protocols that two applications have in common. If two nodes share the same protocol tower—support the same protocols—there is a communication path between them.

Network Services Protocol

The network layer of the stack provided a best-effort delivery service but had no concept of users. All packets of data are just sent up to the transport service. The transport service, in its data header, labels each packet for the port to which it is destined (see Fig. 4-2). In this way, the transport layer provides a virtual circuit between two users of the network.

The transport layer thus allows two programs to communicate. Note that there may be a large number of end users all sharing this virtual circuit. As far as the transport layer is concerned, however, it is providing simple program-to-program communication.

In addition to just delivering the data, the transport layer ensures that all packets are delivered. If a network line goes down, the network layer will adapt its routing tables, but not before losing one or two packets. The job of the transport layer is to detect such lost packets and retransmit them.

The transport layer detects lost and out-of-sequence packets using a sequence number (just as DDCMP did). Note that on many networks this task will be straightforward. If two nodes share the same Ethernet, the job of the transport layer is to deliver packets since it is almost unheard of for the Ethernet to corrupt packets or deliver them out of sequence. In a complicated network, however, the job of the transport layer is more difficult. Complicated topologies may change more often, resulting in lost packets which have to be retransmitted.

NSP uses several strategies to make sure data make it to their destination. First, the user of NSP submits messages of potentially infinite length to NSP. NSP fragments the messages into packets, and sends them down to the network layer. Figure 4-3 shows an example of the NSP data packet format. Notice that the header flags indicate whether this particular packet is the beginning or end of a message. If both flags are set, then the message fits into a single packet.

The NSP header also indicates the destination and source addresses at the transport layer for the message. The NSP packet is itself enclosed in a network layer header, which contains the network layer address of the destination node.

The NSP packet contains, optionally, two acknowledgments. These ACKs are for piggybacking acknowledgments of data received from the other node. Notice that the piggybacked acknowledgments are of two types: data and "other data." The data channel is the normal pipeline for sending data. Some information, such as interrupt messages, may be contained in an other data message, which is required to be a single-packet transmission. Only one other data message may be outstanding at one time.

Figure 4-4 shows an example of an NSP message. The message is a data message, with both the beginning and end of the message in the same packet. The message is segment number 65, and the remote node has been given permission to delay acknowledging. This allows the other end to acknowledge several packets at once, a procedure known as pipelining. The message also acknowledges message number 153 received from the remote node.

Notice that the message contains the indicator "No Process Type Recognized" indicating that the NSP port is not a well-known program such as DAP or another common Digital application. It is also possible for two programs, written by a user or third-party vendor, to use the services of NSP. In this case, the network analyzer is unable to spot which particular program is being used.

If there are no data to send to the other node, it may be necessary to send an acknowledgment by itself. Failing to send the ACK would cause the other node to time out, which would probably lead to an unnecessary retransmission of the packet. Figure 4-5 shows the format of the acknow-

Header Flags		End-of-Message?
		Beginning of Message?
Destination Address		
Source Address		
Acknowledgment Number		Congestion Indicator Bit
		ACK/NACK Bit
Other ACK Number		
Segment Number		Delayed ACK Allowed?
Data		
Notes:		
Both the ACK and other ACK Fields are optional and are indicated by the high bit being set (the segment number always has the high bit clear).		
If bit 4 of the header flags is set, it indicates an expedited message. The expedited data message is always a single segment.		
For the expedited message, the first acknowledgment is for service or expedited, the second is for normal data messages.		

4-3
NSP Data Message

```
┌DETAIL┐
│NSP:  ----- Network Services Protocol -----
 NSP:
 NSP:  Message Identifier = 60
 NSP:         0... .... = Non-extensible field
 NSP:         .110 .... = Begin-End Data Message
 NSP:         .... 00.. = Data Message
 NSP:         .... ..00 = always zero
 NSP:  Type    = 0  (Data Message)
 NSP:  Sub-type = 6  (Begin-End Data Message)
 NSP:  Logical Link Destination = D038
 NSP:  Logical Link Source      = 0490
 NSP:  Data Acknouledgment Number
 NSP:    Acknouledge Qualifier     = ACK
 NSP:    Message Number Acknouledged = 153
 NSP:  Data Segment Number = 65  (delayed ACK ok)
 NSP:  [15 data bytes]
 NSP:
 NSP:  No Process Type Recognized
 NSP:
             ─────Frame 15 of 561─────
             Use TAB to select uindous
 ┌1      ┐┌2 Set ┐    ┌4 Zoom┐┌5     ┐┌6Displyy┐┌7 Prev┐┌8 Next ┐        ┌10 Neu  ┐
 │ Help  ││  mark│    │  out ││ Menus││options ││ frame││ frame │        │capture │
```

4-4 NSP Begin-End Data Message

ledgment message; Figure 4-6 shows a message on the network. Notice that there are three basic types of ACK messages:

- normal data
- other data
- connect acknowledgment

Figure 4-6 shows a normal data acknowledgment being sent on the network. It is possible also to acknowledge an other data message at the same time. Figure 4-7 shows an expedited acknowledgment message.

Connection Initiation

Before a virtual circuit is established, the connection must be properly initiated. This is accomplished with the connect control message (see Fig. 4-8). Notice that the destination address is not specified on a connection initiation. This allows the remote site to dynamically assign a port number. In order to specify a service, the DNA Session Control uses the concept of an object number which is then dynamically mapped to a port number.

The connection initiation message also specifies the type of flow control desired by the initiator. There are three options:

- no flow control
- flow control based on outstanding messages
- flow control based on outstanding segments

The flow control based on outstanding messages is an artifact of older versions of NSP and is now obsolete. When flow control is being used, link service messages are used to give and take away permission to send.

Figure 4-9 shows an example of a connection initiation. The logical link destination is blank and will be filled in by a return connection acknowledgment message. No flow control is specified in the message, and the maximum segment size is 1459 bytes (indicating this is probably an Ethernet).

Figures 4-10 and 4-11 show the format and an example of the disconnection. As with the connection initiation, the disconnect initiation contains user data, in this case a 2-byte code from the session layer indicating the reason.

During normal operation, link service messages (see Fig. 4-12) are periodically transmitted. The two relevant flags are the link service flags and the flow control values.

The flow control value contains a number used to modify the window or number of packets that can be outstanding and unacknowledged. The link service flag indicates how that number is to be interpreted. A value of 0 in the link service flag means that the flow control value in the packet applies

Header Flags		ACK Type Indicator
Destination Address		
Source Address		
Acknowledgment Number		ACK/NACK Bit
Data ACK Number		Congestion Indicator Bit
		ACK/NACK Bit
The Data Acknowledgment message has the data ACK field first with an optional Other-Data ACK field.		
The Other-Data Acknowledgment message has the Other-Data ACK field first, with an optional Data ACK.		
The Connect Acknowledgment message has only the destination address field.		

4-5
NSP Acknowledgment

```
 DETAIL
  NSP:  ----- Network Services Protocol -----
  NSP:
  NSP:  Message Identifier = 04
  NSP:        0... .... = Non-extensible field
  NSP:        .000 .... = Data Acknowledgment Message
  NSP:        .... 01.. = Acknowledgment Message
  NSP:        .... ..00 = always zero
  NSP:  Type    = 1  (Acknowledgment Message)
  NSP:  Sub-type = 0  (Data Acknowledgment Message)
  NSP:  Logical Link Destination = C039
  NSP:  Logical Link Source      = 0491
  NSP:  Data Acknowledgment Number
  NSP:     Acknowledge Qualifier        = ACK
  NSP:     Message Number Acknowledged = 43
  NSP:



                      Frame 17 of 561
                 Use TAB to select windows
  1       2 Set          4 Zoom  5        6Disply 7 Prev 8 Next        10 New
   Help    mark           out    Menus    options  frame  frame        capture
```

Courtesy of Network General

4-6 NSP Data Acknowledgment

```
┌DETAIL────────────────────────────────────────────────────────────┐
│NSP: ───── Network Services Protocol ─────                         │
│NSP:                                                               │
│NSP:                                                               │
│NSP: Message Identifier = 14                                       │
│NSP:        0... .... = Non-extensible field                       │
│NSP:        .001 .... = Other-Data Acknowledgment Message          │
│NSP:        .... 01.. = Acknowledgment Message                     │
│NSP:        .... ..00 = always zero                                │
│NSP: Type     = 1 (Acknowledgment Message)                         │
│NSP: Sub-type = 1 (Other-Data Acknowledgment Message)              │
│NSP: Logical Link Destination = BC27                               │
│NSP: Logical Link Source      = 047B                               │
│NSP: Link Acknowledgment Number                                    │
│NSP:    Acknowledge Qualifier       = ACK                          │
│NSP:    Message Number Acknowledged = 222                          │
│NSP:                                                               │
│                                                                   │
│                                                                   │
│                                                                   │
│                                                                   │
│                                                                   │
│                    ─────Frame 3 of 561─────                       │
│                    Use TAB to select windows                      │
│ ┌1─────┐ ┌2 Set──┐   ┌4 Zoom┐ ┌5   ┐ ┌6Display┐┌7 Prev┐┌8 Next┐   ┌10 New──┐│
│ │ Help │ │ mark  │   │ out  │ │Menus│ │options ││ frame││ frame│   │capture ││
│ └──────┘ └───────┘   └──────┘ └────┘ └────────┘└──────┘└──────┘   └────────┘│
└───────────────────────────────────────────────────────────────────┘
```

Courtesy of Network General

4-7 NSP Other Data Acknowledgement

to the segments of normal data. A value of 1 indicates that the value applies to the other or expedited data channels.

Setting the flow control modification bit in the link service flags is another way to perform flow control. By setting this bit, a node can override flow control by stopping all data from being sent. If a node is temporarily busy, it can send link service messages to other nodes it is communicating with to ask them to stop sending data.

We include one additional message, shown in Figure 4-13, called the no operation (noop) message. It is obsolete and is included in the NSP specification for backward compatibility. The no operation message, needless to say, does not do anything.

Figure 4-14 shows an example of a link service message. A link service message counts as an expedited message and thus is assigned a sequence number (in this case 222). Although the link service flags indicate the flow control value interpretation is for a segment count, there are no segment credits granted to the other node.

Header Flags		Connect Message Indicator
		Retransmitted Connect Bit
Destination Address		0 for Connect Initiate
		Nonzero for Confirm
Source Address		
Service Flags		NSP Version
		Max Segment Size
		Flow control type: Segment count or session control message count
User Data		

4-8 NSP Connect Control Message

```
┌DETAIL────────────────────────────────────────────────┐
│ NSP: ----- Network Services Protocol -----            │
│ NSP:                                                  │
│ NSP:     Message Identifier = 18                      │
│ NSP:           0... .... = Non-extensible field       │
│ NSP:           .001 .... = Connect Initiate Message   │
│ NSP:           .... 10.. = Control Message            │
│ NSP:           .... ..00 = always zero                │
│ NSP:     Type      = 2  (Control Message)             │
│ NSP:     Sub-type = 1  (Connect Initiate Message)     │
│ NSP:     Logical Link Destination = 0000              │
│ NSP:     Logical Link Source      = 0493              │
│ NSP:     Requested Services = 01                      │
│ NSP:           0000 ..0. = always zero                │
│ NSP:           .... 00.. = none                       │
│ NSP:           .... ...1 = always one                 │
│ NSP:     Version Information = 02                     │
│ NSP:           0000 00.. = always zero                │
│ NSP:           .... ..10 = NSP version 4.0            │
│ NSP:     Segment Size (bytes)   = 1459                │
│ NSP:     [18 data bytes]                              │
│                  ─Frame 39 of 561─                    │
│              Use TAB to select windows                 │
│ 1      2 Set     4 Zoom 5        6Disply 7 Prev 8 Next    10 New │
│  Help    mark     out    Menus   options  frame  frame   capture │
└────────────────────────────────────────────────────────┘
```

4-9 NSP Connection Initiation

Header Flags		Disconnect Initiate or Confirm indicator
Destination Address		
Source Address		
Reason		First 2 bytes of Session Control disconnect
User Data		Not present on Confirm message

4-10
NSP Disconnect
Control Messages

```
┌DETAIL┐
 NSP:  ----- Network Services Protocol -----
 NSP:
 NSP:  Message Identifier = 38
 NSP:          0... .... = Non-extensible field
 NSP:          .011 .... = Disconnect Initiate Message
 NSP:          .... 10.. = Control Message
 NSP:          .... ..00 = always zero
 NSP:  Type      = 2 (Control Message)
 NSP:  Sub-type = 3 (Disconnect Initiate Message)
 NSP:  Logical Link Destination = 0493
 NSP:  Logical Link Source      = C03B
 NSP:
 SCP:  ----- Session Control Protocol -----
 SCP:
 SCP:  Reject or Disconnect Reason = 0
 SCP:  User Data length (bytes)   = 0
 SCP:

                  ─Frame 530 of 561─
                  Use TAB to select windows
 ┌1      ┐┌2 Set  ┐    ┌4 Zoom ┐┌5      ┐┌6Display┐┌7 Prev ┐┌8 Next ┐          ┌10 New   ┐
 │ Help  ││ mark  │    │ out   ││ Menus ││options ││ frame ││ frame │          │capture  │
 └───────┘└───────┘    └───────┘└───────┘└────────┘└───────┘└───────┘          └─────────┘
```

4-11 NSP Disconnect Initiation

Header Flags		Link Message Indicator
Destination Address		
Source Address		
Acknowledgment Number		ACK/NACK Bit
Data ACK Number		ACK/NACK Bit
		Congestion Indicator Bit
Segment Number		Expedited and Link share segment numbers
Link Service Flags		Flow Control Value Interpretation
		0: Data segment or message request count
		1: Expedited request count
		Flow Control Modification Bit
		0: No change
		1: Do not send data
		2: Send Data
Flow Control Value		The number of messages that the sender can receive in addition to those previously requested by similar link service message; number may be negative

4-12
NSP Link Service
Message

Header Flags		No Operation Indicator
Any Data		

4-13
NSP No Operation
Message

```
 ┌DETAIL
 │NSP:  ----- Network Services Protocol -----
 │NSP:
 │NSP:  Message Identifier = 10
 │NSP:         0... .... = Non-extensible field
 │NSP:         .001 .... = Link Service Message
 │NSP:         .... 00.. = Data Message
 │NSP:         .... ..00 = always zero
 │NSP:  Type     = 0  (Data Message)
 │NSP:  Sub-type = 1  (Link Service Message)
 │NSP:  Logical Link Destination = 047B
 │NSP:  Logical Link Source      = BC27
 │NSP:  Link Acknowledgment Number
 │NSP:     Acknowledge Qualifier      = ACK
 │NSP:     Message Number Acknowledged = 101
 │NSP:  Link Segment Number = 222
 │NSP:  Link Service Flags = 00
 │NSP:         .... 00.. = data/message request count
 │NSP:         .... ..00 = no change
 │NSP:  Message Credit = 0
 │NSP:
 │                    Frame 2 of 561
 │                 Use TAB to select windows
 │ 1         2 Set        4 Zoom  5        6Display 7 Prev 8 Next      10 New
 │   Help      mark         out     Menus  options  frame  frame      capture
```

4-14 NSP Link Service Message

OSI TP Classes

The OSI transport layer is broken up into five classes of operation, each giving a different class of service. Of these five classes, Digital supports three:

• TP0 provides minimal features.
• TP2 provides multiplexing of multiple users over a single underlying network link.
• TP4 provides both error detection and recovery.

TP classes 1 and 3 are basically nonexistent, so nonsupport is not really an issue. All of the original five TP classes were designed to operate over a connection-oriented network service, with extensions for connectionless network services. Digital only provides the connectionless network service.

Basic TP0 and TP2 are provided simply as a means of connecting to non-Digital environments, primarily with the use of X.25 as the underlying subnetwork. Since X.25 is a connection-oriented subnetwork, provision of a connection-oriented network service is not difficult.

In the more general networking environment, Digital provides a variant of TP4, known as TP4 bis, designed to use an underlying connectionless network service. A typical computing environment for Digital-to-Digital communication thus uses TP4 bis as the basic protocol.

We can break the functions of the OSI transport protocol into elements of procedure, each signifying a particular function of the transport layer (see Fig. 4-15). Notice that all five classes assign a transport layer virtual connection to an underlying network connection—in TP4 bis this step is not necessary. Notice that all classes do provide the basic function of transfer of data, segmentation, and reassembly (not to mention connection establishment).

Concatenation and separation allow several upper layer segments to be put into a single transport protocol data unit (TPDU) before being submitted to the underlying network service provider. TP0 does not provide this service nor does it provide most of the other elements of procedure.

Notice that in TP4 we see much better error detection and recovery mechanisms. TP4, for example, uses a checksum to check the integrity of the data. In other service classes, we assume a reliable lower level, such as a connection-oriented network service based on X.25. In the other service classes, the upper-layer users are responsible for ensuring their own data integrity.

In TP4 we also see that data are retained until acknowledged. If for some reason the data are negatively acknowledged (or a timer runs out), the data can be retransmitted without notifying the upper-layer user. Once the upper-layer user has submitted data to the transport service, it can be assured that the data will be delivered, barring catastrophic errors such as all links failing or the destination computer blowing up.

Figure 4-16 shows the basic format of the transport layer message. The TPDU code selects either a normal data message or an expedited data message. For classes TP0 and TP1, since only one user can use the virtual circuit, there is no need for a destination user address. The sequence number is used to number this particular message.

Figure 4-17 shows the data acknowledgment message. In the previous data packet, we saw that credits were always 0. Credits in the TP protocols are granted using the ACK message. The credit indicates how many more messages may be sent and unacknowledged. Notice the extension credit field used for extended sequence numbering (allowing more messages to be outstanding).

In the TP4 class of service, the parameter section at the end of the packet includes flow control information. This information has a lower window edge (the lowest sequence number where all messages are acknowledged) and the node's view of what the next sequence number and the current credit are. These last two pieces of information allow the remote and local transport entity to perform "reality checks" on each other.

Figure 4-18 shows an example of typical TP4 traffic. First, two data packets are sent; then, the remote node sends back two acknowledgments. On

Transport Layer Element of Procedure	Transport Class				
	TP0	TP1	TP2	TP3	TP4
Assignment to network connection					
TPDU transfer					
Segmenting and reassembling					
Concatenation and separation					
Connection establishment					
Connection refusal					
Normal release - implicit					
Normal release - explicit					
Error release					
Association of TPDU with connection					
TPDU numbering - normal			M1	M	M
TPDU numbering - extended			O1	O	O
Expedited data transfer (4)		M	1		
Reassignment after failure					3
Retention until ACK of TPDU		M5			
Resynchronization					3
Multiplexing and demultiplexing			2		
Explicit flow control (with)			M		
Explicit flow control (without)			O		
Checksum (use of)					M
Checksum (nonuse of)					O
Frozen references					
Retransmission on timeout					
Resequencing					
Inactivity control					
Treatment of protocol errors					
Splitting and recombining					
Source: ISO/IEC 8073: 1988 (E) (22-23)					

KEY:	
	Not applicable
	Required in class
M	Implementation mandatory, use optional
O	Implementation optional, use optional
1	Not applicable to TP2 when explicit flow control not used
2	Multiplexing may not work well if explicit flow control not used
3	Function provided in TP4 using different element
4	M for TP1 using network normal services; optional if network provides expedited
5	M for TP1; required for TP3 and TP4 unless network provides confirmed delivery, then optional for TP1 and not applicable to other classes

4-15 ISO TP Elements of Procedure

Length Indicator		
TPDU Code + Credits		Code = 1111 or 1100
Destination Reference		Not present on TP0 and 1
Sequence Number and EOT Bit		EOT: Last fragment
Parameter Code		Checksum if used
Parameter Length		
Parameter Value		
User Data		< Max TPDU - Header
Credits always 0 on both Expedited and Normal data messages. Maximum data 16 octets on expedited data message.		

4-16
ISO TP Data Messages

Length Indicator		
TPDU Code + Credits		Code = 0110 or 0010
Destination Reference		
Sequence Number		Next sequence number expected
Credit		For extended format; not present for expedited ACK
Parameter Code		
Parameter Length		
Parameter Value		
Parameters		
Checksum		
Subsequence number for TP4 to ensure that ACKs are processed in correct order		
Flow control information for TP4; contains lower window edge, remote subsequence number, remote credit. Allows remote node to be sure of state of local transport entity		

4-17
ISO TP Data
Acknowledgment

```
SUMMARY—Delta T—DST————SRC—
M   1              Bridge00E10E←Sun    0173C5   ISO_TP Data D=0009      NS=12 EOT
    2    0.9019    Bridge00E10E←Sun    0173C5   ISO_TP Data D=0009      NS=12 EOT
    3    0.0111    Sun    0173C5←Bridge00E10E   ISO_TP Ack  D=5F97 NR=13 CDT=9
    4    3.8587    Sun    0173C5←Bridge00E10E   ISO_TP Ack  D=5F97 NR=13 CDT=10
    5    0.8278    Sun    0173C5←Bridge00E10E   ISO_TP Data D=5F97      NS=15 EOT
    6    0.0034    Bridge00E10E←Sun    0173C5   ISO_TP Ack  D=0009 NR=16 CDT=32
    7    0.0367    Bridge00E10E←Sun    0173C5   UTP  C Not echo Next X array
    8    0.0846    Sun    0173C5←Bridge00E10E   ISO_TP Ack  D=5F97 NR=14 CDT=10
    9    3.1559    ISO End Stns←Bridge00FA00     ISO_IP Routing Exchange ESH PDU,

DETAIL
  ISO_TP: ----- ISO Transport Layer -----
  ISO_TP:
  ISO_TP: Header length = 9
  ISO_TP: TPDU type = 6 (Ack )
  ISO_TP: Destination reference = 5F97
  ISO_TP: Next expected sequence number = 13
  ISO_TP: Credit value = 9
  ISO_TP:

                       —Frame 3 of 260—
                      Use TAB to select windows
 1         2 Set            4 Zoom  5          6Disply 7 Prev  8 Next             10 New
 Help      mark             in      Menus      options frame   frame             capture
```

4-18   ISO TP4 Traffic

the first ACK, the credit value is 9; on the second ACK the credit has increased to 10, allowing the first node to have more packets outstanding.

Following the two ACK messages, the node labeled Sun sends out a data message. Notice that in the ACK coming back from the node labeled bridge the credit value is 32, which is much higher than the credit value of 10 for traffic flowing the other way. Two nodes can maintain different credit windows, depending on their processing power and their view of congestion on the network.

Figure 4-19 shows the TP connection request and confirmation message formats. As in the NSP protocol, the destination address is left blank on a connection request and is filled in by the confirmation message. This message also allows the users to select the class of service and to determine whether normal or extended format should be used for sequence numbers.

Of particular interest is the wide variety of parameters that can be included in these messages. Although many implementations of the TP protocols ignore most parameters, the parameters do show the potential power of the protocols and how they will, in the future, be able to provide sophisticated negotiation of the parameters of a virtual connection. Five parameters are particularly interesting in this regard:

Length Indicator		
TPDU Code + Credits		CR Code = 1110 or 1101
Destination Reference		Zero on request
Source Reference		
Class and Flags		Classes TP0-4
		Normal or Extended for TP2-4
		Explicit flow control for TP2
Parameter Code		Identifier of calling or called TSAP
		Proposed maximum TPDU size (default 128 octets)
		Version number (default of 1)
		Protection parameters (user defined)
		Checksum (only for TP4 preferred class)
		Use of network expedited in TP1
		Use of receipt confirmation in TP1
		Use of 16/32 bit checksum for TP4
		Use of transport expedited data service
		Alternative protcol classes
		Maximum time to acknowledge indicator (TP4 only)
		Throughput negotiation
		Residual error rate
		Priority
		Transit delay
Parameter Length		
Parameter Value		

4-19
ISO TP Connection
Messages

- Protection parameters are used for security negotiation.
- Throughput negotiation allows two users to negotiate an acceptable level of data throughput.
- The residual error rate negotiates an acceptable level of uncorrected errors.
- Priority indicates the priority of service needed.
- Transit delay indicates the acceptable delay in transit for a given piece of data.

Quality of service parameters at the transport layer are only meaningful if the underlying network service and subnetworks are able to provide the service desired. The transport layer will simply pass the quality of service request down to the lower-layer service provider. As we saw in Chapter 3, the initial release of Digital's network layer ignores most of these types of parameters. As a result, the transport layer also ignores this type of negotiation.

Figures 4-20 and 4-21 show a typical connection request sequence. In Figure 4-20, we see the connection request, followed by a confirmation, followed by a simple data/ACK sequence. Notice that the 13 credits extended by the node labeled DG (probably a Data General computer) are fairly liberal compared to the 1 credit extended by the Ungerman-Bass computer.

In Figure 4-21 we see a more detailed view of the connection request. The user has left the destination reference blank, as required. We also see that protocol class 4 has been requested, with normal sequence numbers. The message also indicates the maximum TPDU size of 1024 bytes, which corresponds to a typical block of data off a disk drive. Notice also that the user of the transport service (the transport service access point) is indicated in the options. We can assume that the TSAP "DGC01" is the name of the application using the underlying service.

Figure 4-21 also shows additional options. In this case, the connection request indicates that the 16-bit checksum can be omitted. The other node, in the connection confirm, will need to agree with this.

Figure 4-22 shows the format of the disconnect message. In contrast to the NSP protocols, where only 2 bytes of session control data are allowed, TP permits 63 bytes or less. It also indicates a reason code (some of the possible reasons are shown) and an opportunity to include more information on the disconnection reason.

Figure 4-23 shows two more TP messages. The reject message is a negative acknowledgment and is used when a particular message received has an error or when an expected sequence number did not arrive and a timer expired. The error message is used when an invalid message is received. Typically, either the checksum or the offending part of the protocol data unit is echoed back. One hopes this message only shows up during debugging sessions.

```
 SUMMARY  Delta T   DST         SRC
   18     0.0062  DG    010400+U-B   38F200   ISO_TP Connection request D=0000
   19     0.0126  U-B   38F200+DG    010400   ISO_TP Connection confirm D=0002
   20     0.0079  DG    010400+U-B   38F200   ISO_TP Ack   D=0005 NR=0 CDT=1
   21     0.0064  DG    010400+U-B   38F200   ISO_TP Data  D=0005      NS=0 EOT
   22     0.0093  U-B   38F200+DG    010400   ISO_TP Ack   D=0002 NR=1 CDT=13
   23     0.1188  U-B   38F200+DG    010400   ISO_TP Data  D=0002      NS=0 EOT
   24     0.0103  DG    010400+U-B   38F200   ISO_TP Ack   D=0005 NR=1 CDT=1
   25     0.0009  DG    010400+U-B   38F200   ISO_TP Ack   D=0005 NR=1 CDT=1
   26     0.0069  DG    010400+U-B   38F200   ISO_TP Data  D=0005      NS=1 EOT

 DETAIL
  ISO_TP: ----- ISO Transport Layer -----
  ISO_TP:
  ISO_TP: Header length = 33
  ISO_TP: TPDU type = E (Connection request)
  ISO_TP: Destination reference = 0000
  ISO_TP:      Source reference = 0002
  ISO_TP: Class/options = 40
  ISO_TP:     0100 .... = Protocol class 4
  ISO_TP:     .... ..0. = Use normal formats in all classes
                         Frame 18 of 93
                       Use TAB to select windows
  1        2 Set       4 Zoom   5        6Disply 7 Prev  8 Next           10 New
   Help     mark        in      Menus   options  frame   frame          capture
```

4-20 ISO TP4 Connect Request Sequence

```
 DETAIL
  ISO_TP: ----- ISO Transport Layer -----
  ISO_TP:
  ISO_TP: Header length = 33
  ISO_TP: TPDU type = E (Connection request)
  ISO_TP: Destination reference = 0000
  ISO_TP:      Source reference = 0002
  ISO_TP: Class/options = 40
  ISO_TP:     0100 .... = Protocol class 4
  ISO_TP:     .... ..0. = Use normal formats in all classes
  ISO_TP:     .... ...0 = Use explicit flow control in class 2
  ISO_TP: Initial credit allocation = 1
  ISO_TP: Protocol version number: 1
  ISO_TP: Maximum TPDU size = 1024 bytes
  ISO_TP: Destination TSAP: "DGC01"
  ISO_TP:      Source TSAP: "DGC01"
  ISO_TP: Additional options = 02
  ISO_TP:          .... 0... = No use of network expedited in class 1
  ISO_TP:          .... .0.. = Use explicit AK variant in class 1
  ISO_TP:          .... ..1. = Omit 16-bit checksum in class 4
  ISO_TP:          .... ...0 = No use of expedited data transfer
  ISO_TP: Header checksum = 3B10
                         Frame 18 of 93
                       Use TAB to select windows
  1        2 Set       4 Zoom   5        6Disply 7 Prev  8 Next           10 New
   Help     mark        out     Menus   options  frame   frame          capture
```

4-21 ISO TP4 Connect Request Message

Length Indicator		
TPDU Code + Credits		Code = 1000 or 1100
Destination Reference		
Source Reference		
Reason Code		Reason not specified
		Congestion at TSAP
		Session entity not attached to TSAP
		Address unknown
		For classes TP1 and TP4:
		Normal disconnect initiated by session entity
		Remote transport entity congestion at connect request time
		Connection negotiation failed
		Duplicated source reference detected for same pair of NSAPs
		Mismatched references
		Protocol error
		Connection request refused on this network connection
		Header or parameter length invalid
Parameter Code		More info or checksum
Parameter Length		
Parameter Value		
User Data		Less than 64 octets

4-22
ISO TP Disconnect
Message

Session Layer and Towers

From the physical through the transport layers, DECnet/OSI presents a unified protocol stack. Although there may be multiple options at different layers (i.e., different physical media or transport protocols), the options combine together to provide a single, integrated network.

Length Indicator		
TPDU Code + Credits		Code = 0101 Reject message
Destination Reference		
Sequence Number		Next sequence nunmber expected
Credit		For extended format
Length Indicator		
TPDU Code + Credits		Code = 0111 Error message
Destination Reference		
Reject Cause Number		
Parameter Code		Echo of invalid TPDU or checksum
Parameter Length		
Parameter Value		

4-23
ISO TP Exception
Messages

At the session layer, this unity is destroyed and DECnet/OSI becomes two separate networks: DECnet and OSI. The DECnet Session Control layer supports the Digital proprietary upper-layer protocols, such as the Data Access Protocol. The OSI session layer module supports the OSI-compatible upper-layer protocols, starting with the presentation, the application support protocols (ACSE, ROSE), and finally the Application Entities such as the X.500 directory or the FTAM file access protocols.

The role of the session layer, for either protocol stack, is to integrate the transport service into the operating system on which it is running. At a minimum, this means providing a method for starting a virtual circuit (a transport entity) and assigning it to a particular upper-layer application.

The session layer can thus be thought of as the visible portion of the network. The user of the session layer service requests a session, sends data, then releases the session.

Some session layer services are more sophisticated than the establishment and release of the session. For example, the DECnet session service allows the user to request a remote service by name. The Session Control layer, with the cooperation of the DNA Naming Service, translates the logical name into a network address.

Other types of services at the session layer are access control, maintenance of the local node in the network-wide namespace, and a session recovery mechanism. Which services belong at the session layer and which are part of the upper layers is a matter of philosophy.

The two session layers examined in this chapter, DECnet and OSI, are just two of the session layer services operating in a Digital network. The LAT protocols, for example, also have a session layer component, as does the System Communication Architecture used in VAX Clusters.

DNA Session Control Service

The DECnet Session Control layer provides five major functions for users:

- manages the transport connections on behalf of users
- enforces access control policies
- uses the naming service to map object names to protocols and address
- given a set of protocols that form different paths to a remote object, chooses one of them and attempt a connection
- maintains the set of possible paths in the network-wide namespace

The session control module in DECnet is made up of three functional components:

- connection control
- address resolution
- address selection

The connection control component is responsible for system-dependent functions related to transport connections. For example, the transport layer can establish a connection (virtual circuit), but it is the Session Control layer's decision whether or not that connection should be permitted.

In addition to value-added functions (like accepting and rejecting sessions), the session layer is the interface into the transport layer services of sending and receiving data, as well as the mechanics of establishing and terminating the virtual circuit. By providing a unified interface, the user can deal with one service provider—the session layer—instead of issuing calls to different service providers (transport, session, and possibly data link) for different kinds of services.

The value-added services of the connection control component can be split into two major functions. First, connection control allows an end user to be identified. This function is system dependent, but it basically consists of assigning user names or other identifying information to the user.

The second value-added function is to validate the end user, again using some system-dependent function. In a VMS environment, this validation takes two forms. In the first form, a password is passed in with the connection request, which is compared with the local rights database. The second form is the proxy login which lets a remote user from a particular node have rights on the local node without a password. Proxy logins are based on an assumption that the remote node has properly validated the user and this is not a masquerade.

The advantage of the proxy login scheme is that a password does not have to be sent over the network. The disadvantage is that once a user compromises security on one node, he or she has access to other computers on the network. Note that this might also be true in a password-based scheme since many users store passwords in files or use the same password on all nodes.

Figures 4-24 and 4-25 show typical session-level traffic. In Figure 4-24, the first message is a session control protocol connect message. The destination is an object (indicating that this is the Phase IV version of the session control protocol). The destination object 17 is a File Access Listener, which is a process on the target node that uses the Data Access Protocol. Notice that the source object is a normal user, in this case an interactive user of the MS-DOS operating system trying to get files off of a VAX-based file server.

Figure 4-25 shows more details of another connection request. In this case the destination object is 42, indicating that the destination process is the virtual terminal service. The source, once again, is a general user process (in this case the Digital Command Language session of an interactive user).

Note that this particular message includes a user data field, the username of the requestor, a password, and an account for accounting purposes. Also note that all of these fields are blank. Since this particular connection is being used for a demonstration the system has allowed a fairly loose access control policy.

Address Resolution

The address resolution component maintains the mapping between a node name and a set of possible addresses. When communicating with a node, it is possible that there are several different paths. For example, a node may have multiple Ethernet adapters. Running on the adapters could be Phase IV and V routing protocols. The Phase V routing protocol has the option of using several different transport layers.

A combination of protocols that can be used to communicate with a node is known as a protocol tower. A simple protocol tower would be

- Phase V routing
- Transport protocol Class IV
- DNA Session Control layer

That same node may also have an alternative tower:

- Phase V routing

```
SUMMARY—Delta T——DST————SRC—
M    1              DECnet00FF04←DECnet000104  SCP CONN  D=17 (FAL)  S=_LLA4995
     7    0.2008    DECnet00FF04←DECnet000104  DAP OS=MS-DOS FILSYS=MS-DOS
     8    0.0088    DECnet000104←DECnet00FF04  DAP OS=MS-DOS FILSYS=MS-DOS
     9    0.0360    DECnet00FF04←DECnet000104  DAP (File Attr) Open existing fi
    12    0.1329    DECnet000104←DECnet00FF04  DAP (File Attr) (Created/Updated
    15    0.0604    DECnet00FF04←DECnet000104  DAP Connect
    17    0.0114    DECnet000104←DECnet00FF04  DAP (Ack)
    21    0.0663    DECnet00FF04←DECnet000104  DAP Read
    24    0.2166    DECnet000104←DECnet00FF04  DAP Data, 91 bytes (more...)

DETAIL—
SCP:   ----- Session Control Protocol -----
SCP:
SCP:   Destination Name:
SCP:      Name Format Type = 0
SCP:      Object Type      = 17  (File Access FAL/DAP-Version 4 and later)
SCP:   Source Name:
SCP:      Name Format Type = 2
SCP:      Object Type      = 0  (General Task, User Process)
SCP:      Group Code       = 0000
                            —Frame 1 of 26—
                       Use TAB to select windows
1         2 Set              4 Zoom  5         6Disply 7 Prev  8 Next            10 New
Help      mark               in      Menus    options  frame   frame            capture
```

4-24 DNA Phase IV Session Control

```
DETAIL
SCP:      Name Format Type = 0
SCP:      Object Type      = 42  (CTERM/FOUND Host Terminal Handler-Version 2
SCP:   Source Name:
SCP:      Name Format Type = 2
SCP:      Object Type      = 0  (General Task, User Process)
SCP:      Group Code       = 0030
SCP:      User Code        = 0000
SCP:      Descriptor Length = 4
SCP:      Descriptor       = "DEMO"
SCP:         Menu Version = 03
SCP:         0... .... = non-extensible field
SCP:         .00. .... = version 1.0
SCP:         ...0 00.. = reserved
SCP:         .... ..1. = USRDATA field included
SCP:         .... ...1 = RQSTRID, PASSWRD and ACCOUNT fields included
SCP:   Source User Identification  = ""
SCP:   Access Verification Password = ""
SCP:   Account Data Length          = 0
SCP:   End User Connect Data Length = 0
SCP:
                            —Frame 39 of 561—
                       Use TAB to select windows
1         2 Set              4 Zoom  5         6Disply 7 Prev  8 Next            10 New
Help      mark               out     Menus    options  frame   frame            capture
```

4-25 Phase IV Access Control Information

- Network Services Protocol
- DNA Session Control

Note that either of these towers could be used to set up a connection with this node. The two towers make up this node's tower set. In addition to the name of the protocol, the tower includes the address to be used. For the Phase V routing layer, this would be the network address. For the transport class, the address would be the transport selector.

The address resolution component is thus responsible for maintaining a mapping between a logical node name and the network towers that are available. The address resolution component will:

- Maintain the local tower.
- Compute and cache the paths available through the tower set.
- Update the namespace attribute for DNA$Towers so remote nodes can retrieve the local nodes tower set.
- Create and destroy naming service soft links used to provide a backward translation from the address to a node name.
- Map incoming connection requests from a network address into a node name.

The node name is important for several reasons. First, users do not want to have to remember network addresses. Aside from convenience, though, is the fact that security in a Digital environment is based on usernames and node names. A node may have several network addresses and many protocol towers. Getting a single node name simplifies a lookup of proxy logins, permissible connections, and other security-related decisions.

An example of a tower set follows:

```
{{{  DNA$ProtID$FAL },
  {  DNA$ProtID$SessCtlv3    "17=" },
  {  DNA$ProtID$ISOTransportv1 '010203040506'H },
  {  DNA$ProtID$Routingv3  37-1234:2060:08-00-2B-05-45-1C-42}
},

  {{  DNA$ProtID$FAL },
  {  DNA$ProtID$SessCtlv3    "17=" },
  {  DNA$ProtID$NSP },
  {  DNA$ProtID$Routingv3  37-1234:2060:08-00-2B-05-45-1C-42}
}}
```

The basic tower maintained by the session layer goes from the network layer up to the session layer—handling the problem of multiple network addresses and multiple transport layer protocols. It is also possible to have towers that start at the session layer and go up—different combinations of application stacks. The user application can request that the DNA Session Control service maintain the upper-layer tower in the namespace.

When a user (i.e., DNA DAP) wishes to provide services, it passes in a valid DNS name and a set of higher-layer towers, starting at the session layer. The address resolution mechanism will store this information in the tower maintenance database. Whenever a new or changed entry is detected, the address resolution component will combine the upper towers with the local session towers to derive a set of possible communication paths. It then compares the derived set with the towers already stored in the namespace and makes any necessary adjustments.

Note that it is possible that an upper tower will start with a different session control service: such as OSI. The DNA session control service only maintains DNA-based towers; it leaves the others in the namespace. This means that, theoretically at least, OSI-based services can register themselves, along with their addresses, in the DNA Naming service.

Before a user application can submit a tower to the session control service for maintenance, it must create a valid naming service name with access control on the DNA$Towers attribute set to allow session control to change it. It then submits the name of the tower to the session control service.

The address resolution component thus maintains name to tower correspondences for itself (the node) as well as upper layers that reside on the node. What the user has done is initialize a "towerette" and let the Session Control layer fill in the bottom layers. Once the Session Control layer has found the possible protocols in common between two nodes wishing to communicate, the node will cache this information.

To compute the path, the requesting object will pass to session control the name of the destination object and the requesting object's upper-layer towers. The address resolution will then build two towers: one for the local requesting object and another for the remote destination object. The two towers are then compared by forming the cartesian product and looking for the matches. The result is a tower that contains a protocol ID, the destination address, and the source address at each layer.

Address Selection

Given the set of possible protocol sequences, the address selection module will choose one. It will first order the protocol sequences in a system-dependent fashion. An example of the ordering would be to give priority to TP4 over NSP for a transport selection. Another ordering policy would be to select the first protocol that the naming service retrieves.

Once a set is retrieved and ordered, the protocol sequence on the top of the list is tried. If, for some reason, the connection fails, the address selection module will keep on trying until the list of protocol sequences is exhausted.

Phase IV of DNA uses a six-character node name. The address selection module in Phase V keeps a local alias database that translates these six-char-

Call	Description
UserNameToAddress	Map name to protocol sequence; option allows bypass of cache
KeepMeHere	Requests session control to maintain the DNA$Towers attribute for the object
RemoveFromHere	Tells session control to stop maintaining the local tower
EnumerateLocalTowers	List available lower towers
RequestConnection	Allows explicit selection of protocols or the specification of a name
ReceiveConnectionRequest	Opens a port and waits fora matching request
IncomingPoll	How the application receives the calling node name, password, user name, account, or alias
AcceptConnection	Accepts request; allows 16 bytes of user data to be sent back with the acceptance
RejectConnection	Rejects request; allows 16 bytes of user data to be sent back with the rejection
Send/ReceiveData	Buffering of data is a system-dependent problem
Disconnect Connection	Session Control will try and see if the transport layer still has unacknowledged data
Abort Connection	Allows a 2-byte disconnect code and 16 bytes of user data
Port Status	Returns transport PDU size and confidence in network (true or false)
Module Status	Given a protocol ID returns a status of on or off

4-26 DNA Session Control Interface

acter node names into a DNS full name. Any time the Session Control layer finds a "short" name, it first looks in the alias database. If it cannot find it, it assumes that this must be a short DNS full name.

Services

The session layer services offered to the user are summarized in Figure 4-26. The majority of the services are oriented around the maintenance of the tower. For example, an application can issue the KeepMeHere call, which indicates to the Session Control layer that it is responsible for maintaining an upper-layer tower in the namespace. The session layer will in turn issue calls to the naming service to update the address information for that application.

User Disconnect
Remote shut down
Unrecognized application
Application too busy
Aborted by management
User abort
No session resources
Bad user (access control reject)
Bad account
Timeout (application did not respond)

4-27
Session Control
Disconnect Reasons

Other calls enable an application to establish itself as a service provider. An application can open a port to the session layer, then periodically poll for incoming requests. A poll does not accept a session—the application is allowed to examine the data from the poll, then issues a reject or accept call.

For interactive login, the acceptance or rejection will be performed by the operating system interactive login process. For other users, each application will enforce the access control policies. A remote procedure call program, for example, would accept and reject procedure execution instructions on a call-by-call or session basis.

Termination of a session can be accomplished either gracefully or abruptly. The disconnection request is graceful in that it will first check with the transport layer to make sure all data sent were received and acknowledged at the remote end. The abort connection request immediately terminates the session.

With either the disconnect or abort request, a 2-byte code can be sent explaining the reason for termination. Figure 4-27 shows a few of the possible reasons for termination of the request. Programs can also come up with their own reasons.

OSI Session Layer

The OSI session layer is similar in function to the DNA Session Control layer—it provides a means for a session to be established and discontinued. In contrast to the DNA Session Control layer, however, the OSI service does not offer access control or name resolution services. Both security and naming are higher-level services in the OSI model. As a consequence, the OSI session layer is in some ways simpler than the DECnet service. The OSI session layer does, however, provide an additional service in the form of a higher level of flow control.

```
┌─Delta─T──DST────────SRC─────────────────────────────────────────┐
│         Sun    0035CF←Intrln0061B1   ISO_SS Connect              │
│ 0.0249  Intrln0061B1←Sun    0035CF   ISO_SS Accept              │
│ 0.0127  Sun    0035CF←Intrln0061B1   ISO_SS Give Tokens, Activity Start │
│ 0.0082  Sun    0035CF←Intrln0061B1   ISO_SS Give Tokens, Data Transfer (3 fra │
│ 0.0110  Sun    0035CF←Intrln0061B1   ISO_SS Give Tokens, Activity End │
│ 0.0889  Intrln0061B1←Sun    0035CF   ISO_SS Prepare            │
│ 0.0065  Intrln0061B1←Sun    0035CF   ISO_SS Please Tokens, Major Sync Ack │
│ 0.2577  Sun    0035CF←Intrln0061B1   ISO_SS Finish             │
│ 0.0188  Intrln0061B1←Sun    0035CF   ISO_SS Disconnect         │
│20.5285  Intrln0061B1←Sun    0035CF   ISO_SS Connect            │
│ 0.0746  Sun    0035CF←Intrln0061B1   ISO_SS Accept             │
│ 0.0342  Intrln0061B1←Sun    0035CF   ISO_SS Give Tokens, Activity Start │
│ 0.0457  Intrln0061B1←Sun    0035CF   ISO_SS Give Tokens, Data Transfer │
│ 0.0041  Intrln0061B1←Sun    0035CF   ISO_SS Give Tokens, Activity End │
│ 0.0663  Sun    0035CF←Intrln0061B1   ISO_SS Prepare            │
│ 0.0066  Sun    0035CF←Intrln0061B1   ISO_SS Please Tokens, Major Sync Ack │
│ 0.0923  Intrln0061B1←Sun    0035CF   ISO_SS Give Tokens, Activity Start │
│ 0.0084  Intrln0061B1←Sun    0035CF   ISO_SS Give Tokens, Data Transfer │
│ 0.0041  Intrln0061B1←Sun    0035CF   ISO_SS Give Tokens, Activity End │
│ 0.1059  Sun    0035CF←Intrln0061B1   ISO_SS Prepare            │
└─────────────────────────────────────────────────────────────────┘
               Use TAB to select windows
┌─┐       ┌2 Set┐    ┌4 Zoom┐ ┌5    ┐ ┌6Display┐┌7 Prev┐┌8 Next┐      ┌10 New┐
│1│       │     │    │      │ │     │ │       ││      ││      │      │      │
│Help│    │mark │    │ out  │ │Menus│ │options││frame ││frame │      │capture│
└─┘       └─────┘    └──────┘ └─────┘ └───────┘└──────┘└──────┘      └──────┘
```

4-28 ISO Session Layer Traffic

Figure 4-28 shows a basic session layer session. Notice that the first two messages are a connect request and accept. After that, however, there is a variety of give and accept tokens messages. Tokens are a way of controlling the dialogue between two nodes.

In Figure 4-28 we only see the session layer traffic. There is also a variety of lower-layer traffic that has been filtered out. For example, messages at the session layer are sent down to the transport layer, which uses independent ACK messages to make sure data packets reached their destination. The session layer view of the traffic takes the issues of acknowledgment for granted.

Figure 4-29 shows the basic session layer connect message. This connect message specifies that multiple session PDUs cannot be put together into a single message being sent down to the transport layer.

The connect message also includes a token setting item. The possessor of a token is the only side able to engage in a particular activity. This figure shows four tokens. The data token governs which side is able to send data. The activity tokens are a form of checkpoint used in the case of recovery operations. The release token indicates which side of the dialogue is able to release the session.

Finally, there are session user requirements. These indicate which of the session layer capabilities are needed for this particular session. Exceptions,

```
┌DETAIL┐
│ISO_SS: ----- ISO Session Layer -----
│ISO_SS:
│ISO_SS: SPDU type = 13 (Connect)
│ISO_SS: Length of SPDU parameter field = 83
│ISO_SS: -- Connection identifier parameter group (length = 27)
│ISO_SS: Calling SS-user reference = 0700
│ISO_SS: Common reference = (1711)880726145404-0700
│ISO_SS: -- Connect/Accept item parameter group (length = 9)
│ISO_SS: Protocol options = 00
│ISO_SS:        .... ...0 = Not able to receive extended concatenated SPDUs
│ISO_SS: Version number = 1
│ISO_SS: Token setting item = 00
│ISO_SS:        00.. .... = Release token: requestor's side
│ISO_SS:        ..00 .... = Major/activity token: requestor's side
│ISO_SS:        .... 00.. = Synchronize-minor token: requestor's side
│ISO_SS:        .... ..00 = Data token: requestor's side
│ISO_SS: Session user requirements = 0249
│ISO_SS:        .... 0... .... .... = No symmetric synchronize
│ISO_SS:        .... .0.. .... .... = No typed data
│ISO_SS:        .... ..1. .... .... = Exceptions
│ISO_SS:        .... ...0 .... .... = No capability data
│ISO_SS:        .... .... 0... .... = No negotiated release
│ISO_SS:        .... .... .1.. .... = Activity management
│ISO_SS:        .... .... ..0. .... = No resynchronize
│ISO_SS:        .... .... ...0 .... = No major synchronize
│ISO_SS:        .... .... .... 1... = Minor synchronize
│ISO_SS:        .... .... .... .0.. = No expedited data
│ISO_SS:        .... .... .... ..0. = No duplex
│ISO_SS:        .... .... .... ...1 = Half-duplex
│ISO_SS:
│ISO_PR: ----- ISO Presentation Layer -----
│ISO_PR:
│ISO_PR: PPDU type = Connect Presentation (length = indefinite)
│ISO_PR: Mode selector = 0 (X410-1984 mode)
│ISO_PR: Checkpoint size = 5
│ISO_PR: Window size = 6
│ISO_PR: Dialogue mode = 0 (Monologue)
│ISO_PR: Application protocol = 1 (P1)
└─────────────────Frame 4 of 171─────────────────
                Use TAB to select windows
┌1       ┌2 Set     ┌4 Zoom ┌5        ┌6Disply ┌7 Prev  ┌8 Next  ┌10 New
│ Help   │ mark     │ out   │ Menus   │options │ frame  │ frame  │capture
```

4-29 ISO Session Layer Connect Message

for example, allow special messages to be sent regardless of the tokens. Activity management is the checkpointing operation governed by tokens. Half-duplex indicates only one side can send data at a time, governed by the data token.

Following the session layer connect message in Figure 4-29 is the presentation layer connection information. By including several layers of connection information in one packet, a great deal of initial overhead for connection establishment can be avoided. In this case, the application driving both the session and presentation requests is the X.400 message delivery service. Figures 4-30 through 4-32 show the concept of tokens and activity management in action. We can break a session down into a series of activities. Periodically within the activity, there are major breaking points. For example, a file access regime could be an activity. Access to a particular file would be a major break in activity, known as a major sync point.

There can also be minor breaks, as in the case of the successful transfer of several blocks of data. These are known as minor sync points. Activities, major sync points, and minor sync points allow two applications to structure a session into a series of manageable units. If there is a need to abort the session, the two applications, if they agree on where a sync point occurred, are able to recover later.

Figure 4-30 shows some typical traffic. The node labeled "Intrln" sends a give tokens message followed by an activity start indicator. Notice that several session layer activities are concatenated together. The activity includes an identification field for future reference.

After the activity start message, there are three frames of data (possibly transmitted by additional transport-layer messages) followed by an activity end message. The target node, labeled "Sun" responds with a prepare message that indicates that the other node should prepare for a major sync acknowledgment (see Fig. 3-31). The major sync acknowledgment follows. The purpose of these messages is to allow both nodes to make sure they agree as to when the major sync point exists. In the case of a recovery operation, they will both know which data preceded and which data followed the major sync point.

Figure 4-32 shows the use of the minor sync point. In addition to the give tokens message there are please token messages. These allow a node to request that the other node relinquish its tokens.

Synchronization points are used in tandem with the resynchronization services in OSI. The abandon service says that all prior data should be abandoned and a new synchronization should be applied. The restart service allows nodes to go back to any point after the last major synchronization. In other words, a major sync point indicates that both nodes agree the data are (subject to an abandonment) safe.

OSI Upper Layers

In the DNA portion of the stack, we saw that the applications rest directly on top of the Session Control layer. This means that applications have to agree on the proper way to structure data—an issue handled in the presentation layer of OSI. In the DNA stack, the presentation layer is null because the network is DEC-centric: Digital applications know what data look like because the universe is fairly small.

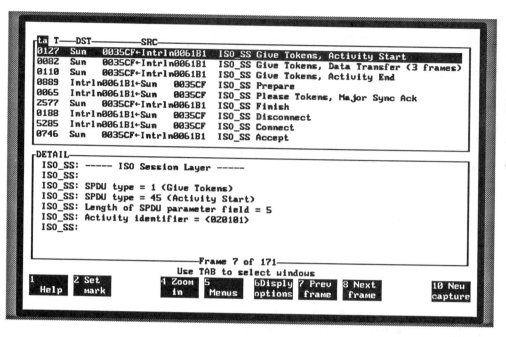

4-30 ISO Give Tokens Message

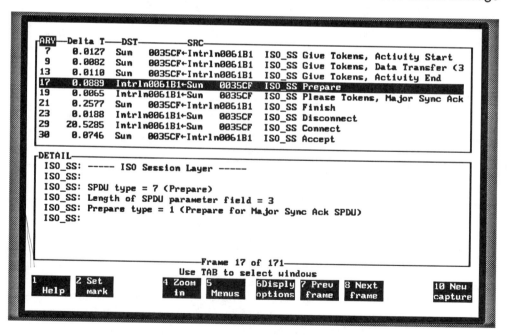

4-31 Preparation for Major Sync Point

```
 ta  T——DST————SRC——
0121   Sun    0035CF←Intrln0061B1   ISO_SS Give Tokens, Activity Start
0427   Sun    0035CF←Intrln0061B1   ISO_SS Give Tokens, Data Transfer (6 frames)
0230   Sun    0035CF←Intrln0061B1   ISO_SS Give Tokens, Minor Sync Point
0048   Sun    0035CF←Intrln0061B1   ISO_SS Give Tokens, Data Transfer (6 frames)
0234   Sun    0035CF←Intrln0061B1   ISO_SS Give Tokens, Minor Sync Point
0051   Sun    0035CF←Intrln0061B1   ISO_SS Give Tokens, Data Transfer
0015   Sun    0035CF←Intrln0061B1   ISO_SS Give Tokens, Activity End
0802   Intrln0061B1←Sun   0035CF    ISO_SS Please Tokens, Minor Sync Ack
0385   Intrln0061B1←Sun   0035CF    ISO_SS Please Tokens, Minor Sync Ack

┌DETAIL─
  ISO_SS: ----- ISO Session Layer -----
  ISO_SS:
  ISO_SS: SPDU type = 1 (Give Tokens)
  ISO_SS: SPDU type = 49 (Minor Sync Point)
  ISO_SS: Length of SPDU parameter field = 3
  ISO_SS: Serial number = "2"
  ISO_SS:

                    ──Frame 132 of 171──
                   Use TAB to select windows
  1          2 Set        4 Zoom   5         6Disply  7 Prev   8 Next         10 New
   Help       mark         in       Menus    options   frame    frame         capture
```

Courtesy of Network General

4-32 Minor Sync Point Give Tokens Message

In a general OSI environment, we cannot make that assumption. There needs to be a way to allow two applications to agree on how information is to be represented. In OSI, we split this presentation layer function up into two sublayers (see Fig. 4-33).

The concept of an abstract syntax is an agreement on what data types, simple and constructed, are going to be used. Agreement on these data types means that applications can then concentrate on the semantics of a data exchange. For example, two messaging services can agree that the message header data type is constructed of a series of basic data types (typically, a series of time stamps, addresses, and character fields). Then, when an application wants to send a message, the application can simply indicate that a message header will follow. The target application can concentrate on the functionality of processing the message header, leaving the encoding and decoding to the presentation layer.

The abstract syntax thus deals in constructed and simple data types. How that information is actually represented for a given transfer is the function of the lower sublayer. The transfer syntax deals with the issues of compression, encryption, and other functions that affect the sending of data in a particular session.

By the time we get to the presentation layer, we have a very high level of service in the OSI network. The transport layer deals with the actual deliv-

Application Service Element	Application Service Element
Remote Operations Service Element	Committment, Concurrency, Recovery
Application Control Service Element	
Presentation Abstract Syntax	
Presentation Transfer Syntax	
OSI Session Layer	

4-33
OSI Upper Layers

ery of data, the session layer provides synchronization, and the presentation layer allows the user to send data as meaningful records that make sense to the application.

The application layer of the OSI network adds a few support services before we see actual services such as X.400. These support services are known as application service elements. The basic application service element is the Association Control Service Element (ACSE), which is the way that two OSI applications form an association with each other. Advanced versions of ACSE even allow switching of application contexts: Two applications could begin by sending messages, then move to FTAM-based data transfer within the context of a single session.

Other service elements include the commitment, concurrency, and recovery service (CCR). CCR provides the same basic service as the session layer synchronization service but over multiple nodes. CCR thus allows an application to make sure resources are available on several nodes and the operations are actually performed. CCR is useful in distributed applications such as distributed databases.

The last basic support element is the Remote Operations Service Element (ROSE). ROSE, similar in function to the Remote Procedure Call (discussed in Chapter 6), allows an application to request that particular operations be performed on its behalf.

On top of all these application service elements are the functional service elements, such as X.400, FTAM, or the virtual terminal service. The power of OSI lies in the structure at the application and presentation layer allowing rich, functional applications to be constructed.

Figure 4-34 shows an example of an OSI connection request. The first line is the tail end of the session layer connection request. The session layer user data are the presentation header. Note that several different presentation contexts are specified, each one consisting of an abstract and a transfer syntax. The use of multiple presentation contexts allows two applications to switch rapidly.

Following the presentation layer header is the ACSE association request. The request specifies an application context name and the name of the desired application (its "title"). That's it. ACSE is simply a way for two applications to get set up.

Finding the AP title and other such information is the job of the X.500 directory services. We search the directory services for a node that offers a particular type of service, which would then return a network address and an AP title. A connection request is then made to that node.

Figure 4-35 shows an example of the Abstract Syntax Notation used to define and send data elements. At the presentation layer, the command is to select a presentation context. Following that is the ASN.1 encoding of the data (the 1 indicates this is the first, and so far only, method for specifying abstract syntaxes). The ASN.1 definition consists of a constructed data type. The first element of the set is an integer, followed by another constructed data type, which is a sequence of an integer followed by a time.

Summary

Up to the network layer, we saw a single network in DECnet/OSI Phase V. In this chapter we saw there are in fact two different networks sharing the services of two different transport layers.

The OSI network uses the traditional OSI stack, starting with the Transport Protocol, moving up to the session layer, and then the presentation and application layer elements. This stack is used for OSI applications such as FTAM and X.400.

The DECnet side of the stack uses the TP4 transport protocol and also supports NSP as a way of interacting with Phase IV domains. The DNA Session Control layer, through the use of protocol towers, is able to select the appropriate combination of protocols.

Note that protocol towers could be used in OSI, but applications would need to be written that communicated with the DNA Naming Service, extracted the tower set, and chose the appropriate tower. In the DECnet side, the Session Control layer handles all these functions.

The Session Control layer, in addition to name resolution, handles housekeeping. An application registers itself with the session layer, which is responsible for maintaining the higher-level tower set.

```
┌─DETAIL────────────────────────────────────────────────────────────────┐
│ ISO_SS:      .... ....  .... ...0 = No half-duplex                      │
│ ISO_SS:                                                                 │
│ ISO_PR: ----- ISO Presentation Layer -----                             │
│ ISO_PR:                                                                 │
│ ISO_PR: PPDU type = Connect Presentation (length = 73)                 │
│ ISO_PR: Mode selector = 1 (Normal mode)                                │
│ ISO_PR: Presentation context identifier = 1                            │
│ ISO_PR:  Abstract syntax name = {1.17.1.1.1} (?)                       │
│ ISO_PR:  Transfer syntax name = {1.0.8825} (ISO standard.8825)         │
│ ISO_PR: Presentation context identifier = 3                            │
│ ISO_PR:  Abstract syntax name = {2.2.1.0.1} (ACSE)                     │
│ ISO_PR:  Transfer syntax name = {2.1.1} (ASN.1)                        │
│ ISO_PR: Next presentation context identifier = 3                       │
│ ISO_PR:                                                                 │
│ ACSE: ----- ISO ACSE Association Control Service Element -----         │
│ ACSE:                                                                   │
│ ACSE: APDU type = Associate request (length = 18)                      │
│ ACSE: Application context name = {1.17.1.1.2} (?)                      │
│ ACSE: Called AP title = {1.17.4.0.8}                                   │
│ ACSE:                                                                   │
│                         ─Frame 10 of 203─                              │
│                      Use TAB to select windows                         │
└────────────────────────────────────────────────────────────────────────┘
```

| 1 Help | 2 Set mark | | 4 Zoom out | 5 Menus | 6 Display options | 7 Prev frame | 8 Next frame | | 10 New capture |

4-34 ISO Presentation and ACSE

```
┌─DETAIL────────────────────────────────────────────────────────────────┐
│ ISO_SS: ----- ISO Session Layer -----                                  │
│ ISO_SS:                                                                 │
│ ISO_SS: SPDU type = 1 (Give Tokens)                                    │
│ ISO_SS: SPDU type = 1 (Data Transfer)                                  │
│ ISO_SS: Length of SPDU parameter field = 3                             │
│ ISO_SS: Enclosure item = 03                                            │
│ ISO_SS:      .... ..1. = End of SSDU                                   │
│ ISO_SS:      .... ...1 = Beginning of SSDU                             │
│ ISO_SS:                                                                 │
│ ISO_PR: ----- ISO Presentation Layer -----                             │
│ ISO_PR:                                                                 │
│ ISO_PR: Next presentation context identifier = 1                       │
│ ISO_PR:                                                                 │
│ ASN.1: ----- Abstract Syntax Notation One -----                        │
│ ASN.1:                                                                  │
│ ASN.1:  1.1  Context-Specific Constructed [2], Length=23               │
│ ASN.1:  2.1    INTEGER, Length=1, Value = "1"                          │
│ ASN.1:  2.2    SEQUENCE [of], Length=18                                │
│ ASN.1:  3.1      INTEGER, Length=1, Value = "0"                        │
│ ASN.1:  3.2      UTCTime, Length=13, Value = "09 Oct 1988  16:40:13"   │
│                         ─Frame 21 of 203─                              │
│                      Use TAB to select windows                         │
└────────────────────────────────────────────────────────────────────────┘
```

| 1 Help | 2 Set mark | | 4 Zoom out | 5 Menus | 6 Display options | 7 Prev frame | 8 Next frame | | 10 New capture |

4-35 ISO Presentation Layer Context

The session layer in DECnet also handles access control functions, a function operating at higher layers in OSI. The DECnet access control policies are centered around either a proxy login or a simple password-based scheme. There is no reason why this could not be extended to support public or private key authentication methods in the future.

At this point, we have two fairly powerful platforms for the provision of distributed applications. Before looking at the applications, however, we will look some more at the underlying infrastructure on the DECnet side of the protocol stack. Things like time synchronization services, terminal-host protocols, and remote procedure calls are used to supplement the session control service. We will also look in some depth at how names are maintained on the network. We will then look at a few examples of applications written for both of these network platforms.

Names

CHAPTER 5

Names

Names are used at many different levels of the network. The data link layer uses a 48-bit unique ID to identify stations on an Ethernet. The network layer uses a 20-byte unique ID, often encapsulating the data link address into the network layer address. Unique 20-byte addresses are suitable for programs such as the network layer of a protocol stack, but they pose problems for human beings: The address may be unique, but it is difficult to remember. Names provide a higher-level, more intuitive form of addressing.

A naming service takes human-readable names and resolves them into a series of attributes, such as a network address or protocol tower. This is one of the more complex tasks in the network. Complexity is provided by the need to enforce uniqueness in the namespace, to allow the namespace to function efficiently in a large network, and to take into account the constraints introduced in supporting the quirky nature of human names and matching these names to the rigid formats used by network protocols.

Names exist at four different levels (see Fig. 5-1). The names we have been dealing with up to this point have been the bottom two layers: network addresses and routing information. We have seen it is desirable to separate the network address of a node from the paths used to reach that address. Since paths change dynamically, we have the network layer translate a network address into the reachable paths at a particular moment, shielding higher layers from the necessity of knowing routing information.

Just as a particular network address may have many reachable paths, a particular node may have multiple towers. A common cause is multiple protocol stacks: A Phase V node may have addresses for DNA Phase IV, DNA Phase V, TCP/IP, and generic OSI (not to mention a VAX Cluster address and possibly even an SNA network address for IBM mainframes).

A unique name allows a node to be referred to by upper-layer programs in the same fashion, no matter what the network address. A unique name in the network also lets us continue to refer to the services offered by the

Descriptive Names	X.500
Primitive Names	DNA Naming Service
Addressing	ISO Addresses
Routing Information	IS-IS Exchanges

5-1
Levels of
Naming Services

same name if it is moved to another computer. Instead of focusing on processors, we can focus on service providers.

Not only do we want unique names for nodes, we need names for programs and users. If a user has a unique name, we can move that user from one computer to another. The naming service will inform a program (e.g., an electronic mail program attempting to deliver a message) of the current location of that particular user.

The service provided by Digital's DNA Naming Service (DNS) is known as a primitive naming service. Given prior knowledge of the unique name of an object (e.g., a user, program, or node), the naming service will return an attribute of that object, typically the current network address of that object.

Another level of naming service is known as a descriptive naming service. Its purpose is to resolve attributes into names. One can think of the primitive name service as a white pages function and the descriptive service as a yellow pages function. For example, we might want to find all user names where the attribute "organization" is equal to "Digital" and the attribute "organizational affiliation" is equal to "Public Relations Engineer."

Digital's DNS focuses strictly on primitive name translation. The higher-level descriptive service is provided by an international standard known as X.500, after the CCITT committee that formulated the standard. X.500 is also an OSI standard.

This chapter starts with a detailed discussion of Digital's DNS. It goes on to discuss X.500, its major components, and the relationship to the primitive naming service. Finally, it discusses the question of the relationship of security services and naming services.

Purpose of the DNA Naming Service

One of the major functions of DNS is to provide a node name to network address translation. The primary user of the service is thus the DNA Session Control layer (see Fig. 5-2). The session control service contains an address resolution component, which uses the services of the DNS Clerk. The clerk, in turn, queries the naming service for a name-to-address translation.

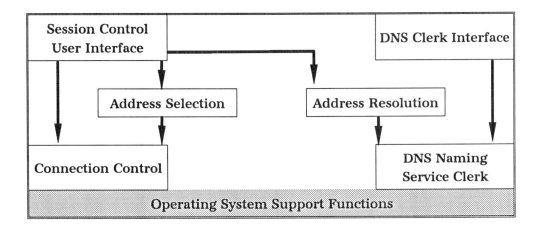

5-2 Relationship of DNS and Session Layer

There are other users of the naming service as well. The Distributed File Service (DFS) allows a user to access files without knowing their location. When a user requests a file, DFS will query the naming service to find the current location of the file.

It is important to realize that name-to-address translation is not the only function of the naming service. We will see that the security services will use DNS for storing authentication information. An object has many attributes; the network address is just one.

Structure of the Namespace

A namespace is a set of unique names. In DNS, the namespace is distributed on several name servers, each one managing one or more clearinghouses. The clearinghouse is the actual data; the name server is the software used to access the data in a controlled fashion.

Figure 5-3 shows the components of a DNS namespace. The namespace is structured as a tree containing directories. A node in the directory has one of three child entries:

- object entry
- child pointer to another directory
- soft link

Object entries have a name and a set of attributes. The most prominent attribute is the network address—the current location of the object. We will soon examine a variety of other attributes used for management of the namespace.

5-3 Structure of the Namespace

The soft link is a pointer that allows the namespace to be viewed as a directed graph instead of as a pure tree. A soft link is the equivalent of an alias. Although soft links allow the namespace to appear as a general mesh structure, it is still really a tree. Each directory thus has only one parent and is not a child of one of its descendants.

DNA Naming Server Operations by Replica Type			
Operation	Replica Type		
	Master	Secondary	Read Only
Lookup	Y	Y	Y
Create Entry	Y	Y	N
Delete Entry	Y	Y	N
Update Entry	Y	Y	N
Skulk Directory	Y	Y	N
Create/Delete Directory	Y	N	N

5-4 Naming Service Replicas

The namespace is a partitioned, partially replicated database. A partition of the namespace is a clearinghouse—a collection of directories. A clearinghouse also has a name, which is very tightly controlled since one must always be able to find the clearinghouse, or the naming service becomes useless.

Replicas allow copies of a directory to be stored in multiple clearinghouses. There are three kinds of replicas:

- master
- secondary
- read only

Figure 5-4 shows the different kinds of operations that can be performed on the different types of replicas. Notice that the master replica is the only place a child directory can be created. Other objects can be created on a secondary replica. The read-only replica is for lookup operations. It is important to note that the user does not see any of these issues; the DNS clerk interface shields the replica type from the user. The clerk, in cooperation with name servers, will find the appropriate type of replica for the operation being performed.

Replication is a loose consistency guarantee. You may get different answers at different times or locations because updates are not fully propagated. Periodically, an operation known as a skulk is performed and brings all the replicas into synchronization.

It is possible that update operations will occur simultaneously on different replicas. To resolve conflicts, an update is always time stamped, and the latest one always wins. The time service is thus an important part of the naming service infrastructure. Updates have the following properties:

- Updates are total—every update is applied irrespective of the history of past updates.

- Updates are idempotent—if you apply an update several times, the result is the same.
- Updates are commutative—no matter which order the updates are applied the latest one always wins and the result is the same.

DNS guarantees the integrity of the namespace subject to the above update rules. At any one time, updates may not be totally propagated through the namespace and the servers may give different answers to different people. Over time, however, the namespace will converge to a common view to all users.

Names and Attributes

A name is a complete path specification starting from the root, consisting of the concatenation of the names of each of the objects in the path. Each of the objects has a name known as a simple name. The concatenation of names is known as a full name. Name servers only operate on full names, although many systems will have a local nickname processor.

It is up to each network administrator to decide how to structure the namespace. Presumably, the root would be the name of the organization. The next level might be individual divisions. The next might be the category of names, followed by instances. For example, the node Xenophobe in the Digital PR group might have the following DNS name:

DigitalPR.NODES.XENOPHOBE

"DigitalPR" is the name of a directory; NODE is a subdirectory; and the full name above is an object (or possibly a soft link to another name). Other organizations might structure their namespace on a geographical basis, on the assumption that geography is a more stable label for an object (i.e., a person) than either organizational hierarchy or function.

In addition to the set of simple names, the full name includes the Namespace Creation Time Stamp (NSCTS), which is the unique identifier for this namespace. The use of the NSCTS as part of the full name allows the merging of namespaces in the future. Note that people will almost always use the namespace nickname instead of the NSCTS.

Full names have two properties:

- absoluteness
- referential transparency

Absoluteness means the full name will completely identify one object. Referential transparency means that a given full name always refers to the same object, no matter which client submitted the request (subject to the question of update propagation delays).

Names can be referred to in internal or external format. Internal format is used across the client interface. External format is used for human beings. Programs should use the internal format as the external format is subject to nickname translation and other potential problems.

The external format is a namespace nickname plus a sequence of simple names. The $ in a simple name is reserved for Digital use. Uppercase and lowercase can be mixed—they are preserved for presentation purposes but do not affect the lookup operation.

There is also a quoted name syntax, which allows additional characters to be used. For example, if you are importing names that make use of the period (i.e., DOS file names) you might want a period as part of a simple name.

The last form is the binary simple name, which consists of "%X" followed by a series of hex characters. Note that a binary simple name never matches a regular or quoted simple name even if they would encode the same. A final rule for external forms of names is that if they start with a leading separator (e.g., a period) then all default nickname processing is suspended.

Wildcards can be used on external names. The * matches zero to n characters; the ? matches 1 character. The ... (ellipsis) matches a terminal subtree (all parts of the space below). Thus,

> *...

matches all entries.

Internal Names

The name server only works on internal names. This consists of the NSCTS plus a sequence of simple names. The simple name, in turn, is a flag octet plus a counted string. Internal names are treated as opaque by programs. A null internal name is equivalent to the root of the tree.

There are some arbitrary size limits for names. The user should expect the limits to go up. A single simple name has a permanent limitation of 255 octets, including flag and count fields. The arbitrary limit is on the full name size; it is currently set at 402 octets including the NSCTS and all other characters.

Attributes

Attributes can be single valued or set valued. Sets contains no duplicates but have no ordering. Three operations are available on set-valued attributes:

- Redundant insert: If the value is not present, insert it. Otherwise ignore the operation, but do not return an error.

- Redundant delete: Delete if present, otherwise ignore but do not return an error.
- Full lookup of all values.

Attributes can be global or class specific. Global attributes apply to all objects.

An individual attribute value is limited to 4000 octets. Because of the loose update methods used in the naming server, it is impossible to limit the size of a set—everybody could be adding a member at the same time.

The naming service maintains a tree consisting of objects. Each of these objects contains a set of attributes. Some attributes are user created; others are system defined. Figure 5-5 shows some architecturally defined attributes used in the naming service.

The first category of attributes is present on all objects. The creation time stamp shows when the object was created, and the update time stamp shows when this particular version of the object was last updated. A time stamp is used in the skulking process to resolve multiple updates on different replicas. The third attribute, the access control set, is discussed later.

Clearinghouse objects contain a variety of attributes used to manage the naming service. For example, the last address attribute is used whenever a clearinghouse initializes itself to see if it has moved. Other attributes, such as the clearinghouse state and directory version, allow the name server software to perform consistency checks.

Predefined Objects

Three objects are predefined:

- DNS$Group
- DNS$Clearinghouse
- DNA$Principal

The group object has two class-specific attributes. The DNS$Members is a list of members in the group. It contains two fields—a Boolean and a full name. The Boolean indicates whether the name is in turn another group. The second attribute is the DNS$GroupRevoke, which is a timeout factor. It indicates how long a user should cache the result that a member X is a member of this group.

The clearinghouse object is a special class of object that is never modified by clients. Associated with this class of object is either a DNS$Address (a Phase IV Address) or a Phase V protocol tower (DNA$Towers). The last predefined object is the DNA$Principal. This is the name of a principal user for the purpose of authenticating clients.

Attribute	Set/Single	Access	Scope	Description
DNS$CTS	Single	R		Creation Time Stamp (UID)
DNS$UTS	Single	R	All	Update Time Stamp
DNS$ACS	Set	RW		Access Control Set
DNS$CHName	Set			Name
DNS$CHCTS	Single			Unique ID
DNS$CHLast Address	Single			Phase IV address or Phase V tower, used when a clearinghouse initializes to see if it has moved
DNS$UpPointers	Set			Pointers to replicas of directories closer to root; stored as tower or Phase IV address
DNS$CHState	Single		Clearinghouse	New, On, or Dying
DNS$CH Directories	Set	N/A		Full name plus CTS of each directory replica
DNS$ACS				Note: default and nopropagate are meaningless here
DNS$NSNickname				Nickname of namespace
DNS$NSCTS				Unique ID of namespace
DNS$Directory Version	Single			Current version of DNS (V2.0)
DNS$ReplicaState				New Directory, New Replica, On, Dying, Dying Directory, Dying Replica, Dead
DNS$Replica Type				Master, Secondary, Read only
DNS$LastSkulk				
DNS$LastUpdate				
DNS$RingPointer	Single		Replica	During a skulk contains the CTS of the next clearinghouse in the ring
DNS$Epoch				ID of an incarnation of a ring; used to recover from hard failures of replicas that prevent a skulk from finishing
DNS$Replica Version				Allows graceful upgrading
DNS$Class	Single	RC		Object Class
DNS$ClassVersion	Single	RW	Object	Version within Class
DNS$ObjectUID	Single	RWD		Object UID

Attribute	Set/ Single	Access	Scope	Description
DNS$Address	Set	RWD	Object/ CH	Address (DNA$Tower for Phase V)
DNS$Replicas	Set	R	Dir./ Child Pointer	
DNS$AllUpTo	Single	R	Directory	Last skulk
DNS$ Convergence	Single	RW		Priority for replica convergence (Low, Medium, High)
DNS$InCHName	Single	RWD		Boolean indicating if directory of descendants may store clearinghouse names
DNS$Parent Pointer	Set	R		Single value CTS of Parent
DNS$Directory Version	Single	R		Version of DNS to which this directory applies
DNS$UpgradeTo	Single	RWD		Tells skulker to upgrade to new version
DNS$ChildCTS	Single	CW	Child Pointer	CTS of child directory
DNS$LinkTarget	Single	RW	Soft Link	Full Name
DNS$Link Timeout	Single	RW		When to check validity of link
Access: Read, Write, Delete, Create/Write (Write only when created)				

5-5 *(Cont.)* Global Attributes

Name Server Protocols

The user of the name server uses the clerk interface. The clerk, in turn, communicates its request to servers (see Fig. 5-6). The clerk is present in every DNA Phase V node. Servers are located throughout the network, although not on every node. To inform clerks about the presence of servers, a solicitation and advertisement protocol is used. Once clerks find servers, they use the clerk-server protocol to communicate. A third protocol is the

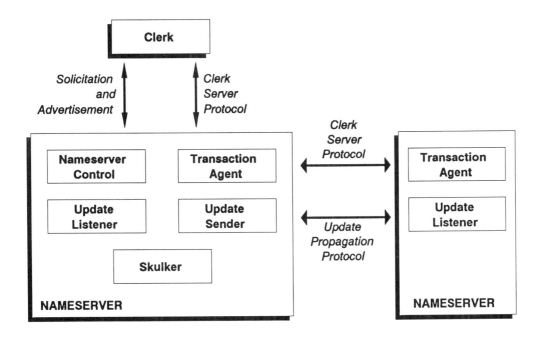

5-6 Naming Service Components

update propagation protocol, used between name servers to keep replicas in synchronization.

The name server contains four functional modules:

- Name server control contains the management interface and handles the solicitation advertisement protocol.
- Transaction Agent handles the clerk server protocol and uses the directory maintenance protocol to coordinate directory operations.
- Update Sender propagates high-priority changes.
- Update Listener responds to the update sender.

The update sender and listener are also responsible for making sure that clearinghouses can find each other.

Protocols

The operations presented to the user are shown in Figure 5-7. The operations in the client interface are then turned into messages between clerks and servers (or between multiple servers).

The naming service can operate as either a direct client of the data link or as a client of the session control interface using a virtual circuit. If a clerk is contacting a server on the local data link, the datagram service

Attributes	Enumerate Attributes
	Read Attribute
	Modify Attribute
	Test Attribute
Objects	Create Object
	Enumerate Objects
	Delete Object
Directories	Create Directory
	Add Replica
	Remove Replica
	Delete Directory
	Enumerate Children
	Skulk
	Allow Clearinghouses
	Disallow Clearinghouses
	New Epoch
Soft Links	Create Link
	Delete Link
	Enumerate Links
	Resolve Name
Utilities	Test Group
	Convert Full to Internal
	Convert Full to External
	Convert Simple to Internal
	Convert Simple to External

5-7
Naming Service
Clerk Interface

would be used. If the server is in a wide-area environment, the virtual circuit is used.

Figure 5-8 shows the format of the message header for request response exchanges in both of the environments. Notice that in a virtual circuit environment, there is no need for a sequence number since the underlying session and transport services will deliver infinite-length messages.

All queries to the name service are request/response messages. Each request will receive zero or one responses. A request is never retransmitted by the clerk, although it might be retransmitted by the underlying virtual circuit provider.

In addition to the request/response messages, there are solicitation and advertisement messages. The solicitation is used by a clerk that has just initialized and is attempting to find a server. The advertisement message is used by servers to indicate their presence on the network. The advertise-

Request/Response Messages		
Datagram		**Virtual Circuit**
Protocol Version		
Transaction ID		Transaction ID
Sequence Number		
Total Length		
Message Type		Message Type
Operation		Operation
Clearinghouse CTS		Clearinghouse CTS
Rest of Message		Rest of Message
Solicit/Advertisement Messages		
Advertise		Solicit
Protocol Version		Protocol Version
Solicit Indicator		Advertisement Indicator
		NSCTS
		NS Nick Name
		Clearinghouse Count
		Clearinghouse
		Clearinghouse

5-8

Basic Naming Service
Message Format

ment includes the unique ID of the namespace, as well as a list of clearing-houses currently active.

Once a server has been found, the clerk is responsible for taking full names as input from clients and finding selected attributes. It is possible that a particular server will not have the name desired. Most queries sent in by clerks, as well as the responses from servers, contain a progress record to help in this situation (see Fig. 5-9).

The progress record is used to convey hints to clerks on which clearing-houses might contain information on the desired name. The record contains the unresolved (original) name, plus the resolved name after translation of soft links. It also includes a timeout indication for any soft link information.

Figures 5-10 through 5-14 show some typical message exchanges between clerks and servers. Figure 5-10, for example, is the enumerate attributes exchange. The request contains a progress record (which might have been the result of a prior search) and an indicator of the maximum size of a valid response. The response contains a list of attribute names and values and a context name. The context name is used when there are more attribute

Flags		Done
		Up
		Linked
		Hit Link
		Ignore State
Timeout		Timeout for soft links
Unresolved Name		
Resolved Name		
Clearinghouse List		Hints for subsequent calls

5-9
Naming Service
Progress Record

Enumerate Attributes Request		
Progress Record		
Entry Type		Normal Name
		External Quoted Name
		External Binary Name
		Name with Wildcard
		Name with Ellipsis
Context		Simple Name for Repeats
Maximum Size		Size of Response
Enumerate Attributes Response		
Progress Record		
Number of Entries		Beginning of Result Set
Attribute Name		
Attribute Value		
Attribute Name		
Attribute Value		
Optional Context Name		For Subsequent Calls
Whole Set Indicator		Boolean

5-10
DNS Enumerate
Attributes Exchange

Read Attributes Request		
Progress Record		
Entry Type		Normal Name
		External Quoted Name
		External Binary Name
		Name with Wildcard
		Name with Ellipsis
Context		Timestamp for Repeats
Maybe More		Boolean
Attribute		Simple Name
Maximum Size		Size of Response
Read Attributes Response		
Progress Record		
Number of Entries		Beginning of Result Set
Attribute Name		
Attribute Value		
Attribute Name		
Attribute Value		
Whole Set Indicator		Boolean

5-11
DNS Read Attribute
Exchange

Modify Attributes Request		
Progress Record		
Entry Type		Normal Name
		External Quoted Name
		External Binary Name
		Name with Wildcard
		Name with Ellipsis
Operation		Present or Absent
Attribute		
Time Stamp		
Value		
DNS Modify Attributes Response		
Progress Record		

5-12
DNS Modify
Attributes Exchange

Create Object Request	
Progress Record	
Class	
Class Version	
Create Object Response	
Progress Record	
Time Stamp	
Time of Actual Creation	

5-13
DNS Create
Object Exchange

Enumerate Objects Request		
Progress Record		
Wildcard		Simple Name
Class		Class Name
Context		Simple Name
Maximum Size		
Return Class		Return Class with Objects?
Enumerate Objects Response		
Progress Record		
Result Set		Last Entry is Context
Whole Set?		
Returned Class?		

5-14
DNS Enumerate
Objects Request

values than can fit into the maximum size specified. Subsequent requests will contain this context name, which will be used to continue the process. Context indicators are used to get around the DNS constraint that one request must have only one response.

Operation of the Clerk

The clerk has six functions:

- discover available namespaces and set on one as the default
- send out requests and receive responses
- communicate with one or more servers
- maintain credentials needed by client for authentication
- walk the directory tree on one or more servers to resolve client requests
- maintain a cache

Contacting Name Servers

To establish communication with a server, the clerk has to perform four operations:

- select a likely clearinghouse
- locate its name server
- establish communication
- authenticate the client to directory and vice versa

Given a particular directory lookup request, the clerk must make a random stab at deciding which clearinghouse is the most likely. This random stab can be aided by a cache or through the use of the solicitation and advertisement process.

The best way is to start with a cached replica set for the parent directory. The replica set has all the clearinghouses that contain the information needed. Some of these clearinghouses cannot perform the desired operation and can be discarded. Some clearinghouses may not give the accuracy that the client specified in the confidence argument to the call. If any clearinghouses are left after taking out the ones that will not work, one is chosen. Otherwise, the clerk will have to walk the tree.

Once a potential clearinghouse is identified, the clerk needs the network address of the relevant name server. This address may be cached from a recent communication attempt or cached from listening to advertisements. There is also an address hint in the replica set, or the clerk can perform a lookup on the name of the server. Once a set of possible network addresses is found, one is picked randomly.

To increase efficiency, the DNS architecture specifies several suggested, but optional, optimizations. First, existing virtual circuits can be used. Instead of terminating a circuit after each request, the circuit is kept up. It is possible that the name server will sever the connection to reduce overhead.

A second optimization is to use cached name server entries that have had prior success rather than those that are untried. If there is a cache of recent failures, those should be avoided. Finally, close name servers should be tried over ones that are far away. This means that a server on the local LAN should be tried over those multiple hops away. Note that this optimization requires the routing layer to inform the clerk of the "distance" of a location.

Once the network address is selected, the clerk uses either a datagram or a virtual circuit service to establish communication. The client call includes authentication and addressing information.

Walking the Tree

If a clerk initializes with no cache, it may have no idea which clearinghouse to use. In this case, the clerk is forced to walk the tree, following pointers through the namespace. Given the address of one clearinghouse, it is possible to query the UpPointer attribute of that clearinghouse, looking for another clearinghouse closer to the root. Once at the root, the client can then walk back down.

When a name server gets a request from a client, it will begin performing the request. Periodically, it may return progress records, which indicate that another clearinghouse can provide further guidance.

The progress record has two functions. First, it gives the clerk a new list of clearinghouses to try. Second, it encodes information for subsequent clearinghouses to help guide their search. A progress record has eight fields:

- Unresolved name; the portion of the original full name that is yet unresolved.
- Resolved name.
- Clearinghouse list.
- Linked; a Boolean set to true the first time a name server follows a soft link.
- HitLink; a Boolean set to true when the name server hits a soft link. It is then returned to the clerk so it can check for loops in soft links.
- Timeout; a timer parameter for soft link caching.
- Up; set to true if the clerk wants the name server to find the root or chain up the tree
- Ignore state; set to true by the clerk if it wants the name server to ignore the state of a directory or a replica. Used for low confidence setting.

A clerk can use a progress record to formulate a second search. Passing the record back and forth also alleviates looped searches because nodes can keep track of soft links found and clearinghouses visited.

Clerk Bootstrapping

When a clerk initializes, it begins by using the solicitation and advertising protocol if the clerk is on a LAN. If the clerk is on a WAN, a manual address for a server (plus the NSCTS of default namespace) must be added. It is possible that a name server might have to send out multiple advertisements if the data will not all fit into one packet. A clerk can solicit this information but only either within the LAN or the area. The parameter solicitation distance parameter sets the limit of the solicitation.

When a clerk initializes, it must wait at least several seconds before sending a solicitation. This wait keeps excessive solicitations off of the network. After the set period of time (SolicitHold), it then waits a random period of time. This jitter prevents all workstations from flooding the LAN at the same time in case of a power failure. This random period of time, which prevents synchronized multicasts, has a mean of 3 seconds.

Clerks and Caches

Each clerk maintains two types of caches:

- The global cache is used by all clients of the clerk.
- The client cache is specific to each client.

The global cache contains three types of information. First, there is a mapping of a clearinghouse name to the clearinghouse time stamp and address. Second, there is a mapping of directory names to the clearinghouses where the replicas are stored. Third, there is the status of name servers. Information in the name server status table includes the network address and possibly other implementation-dependent information such as the time of last contact, the status of the virtual circuit, the last failure, and the distance of the server.

The client-specific caches include information such as attributes of an entry, mapping of soft links to full names, and group membership. The client caches may actually be a single cache, as long as a client is not able to browse another client's cache.

Name Server

The name server is the software system that manipulates the state of the clearinghouse. The clearinghouse is the file or database where names are stored and where the structure of the namespace is maintained. We can divide the discussion of the name server into five pieces:

- the structure and content of the clearinghouse
- the name server clerk, which provides a superset of the client clerk functions
- the transaction agent, which retrieves and modifies entries in the namespace
- the update sender/listener, which is responsible for convergence of replicas (including skulking)
- the name server control module, which manages the server and handles the solicitation and advertisement process

Structure and Content of the Clearinghouse

Each clearinghouse is a separate database. It is possible for multiple name servers to access some clearinghouse (as in the case of a VAX Cluster), but consistency and atomicity are not specified.

A clearinghouse contains six types of information:

- clearinghouse global information
- directories
- objects
- child pointers
- soft links
- namespace-wide information

The clearinghouse global information is stored in a pseudodirectory which bears the same Creation Time Stamp (CTS) as the clearinghouse. The pseudodirectory allows the clearinghouse to be named, and its attributes manipulated. Thus, to find a clearinghouse, we simply send in the name, and get back the CTS. Namespace-wide information is used when the clearinghouse stores a directory that was the root of a namespace that has since been merged.

Name Server Clerk

The name server clerk provides a superset of the functions of the normal client clerk. Examples of the new operations are the ability to combine replicas, to link up new replicas with others, and to copy an update from one replica to another.

The name server clerk is used by the transaction agent and the update sender to manipulate other clearinghouses, thus maintaining the consistency of the namespace.

Transaction Agent Module

The transaction agent module has three responsibilities:

- processing clerk transactions from clients
- reading and writing to the clearinghouse
- communicating with other transaction agents at other name servers to synchronize updates

The transaction module uses two protocols. The clerk-server protocol is used to communicate with clerks; the directory maintenance protocol is used to synchronize the state of parent and child clearinghouses when directories and replicas are created and destroyed. The transaction agent is multithreaded. That is, it must be able to handle multiple outstanding requests.

When the transaction agent receives a request, it must first determine if the clearinghouse is available. If it is, it finds the requested entry in the clearinghouse (or returns a progress record). Additionally, the transaction agent must authenticate the client access to the directory.

A special type of transaction is used to manipulate a directory. To create a directory, the clerk must contact the transaction agent that controls the clearinghouse that has the master replica for the new directory. Note that the master replica for a directory is not necessarily in the same clearinghouse that has the master replica for the directory's parent.

The simplest case of creating a new directory is when the parent and the child are both on the same node as the transaction agent. The agent first creates the new directory, with a state of "newDirectory" and a pointer to the purported parent. Then, the agent goes to the parent directory and, if it exists, creates a pointer to the child. Next, the agent goes back to the child and sets the "parentPointer" to the actual name (resolving any soft links necessary). Finally, the agent skulks the new directory. This gets the ACS from the parents, sets the state to on, and sets the directory to operational.

To create a replica, a similar process is followed. First, the CTS and resolved full name of the directory are gotten from another replica. Second, a check is done to make sure the local clearinghouse does not already have this replica. Next, the replica is created, with a state of "newReplica." A temporary ACS is then borrowed that has at least enough permissions to allow a subsequent skulk to work. If the new replica is a secondary replica, the epoch and ring pointers are set up. A read-only does not need this, and the master is the original directory.

Next, the transaction agent uses the clerk to send a request to the transaction agent, which has the master replica to modify the replica set to include the new replica's clearinghouse. Then, a skulk is initiated to turn the replica on. Finally, an attempt is made to modify the child pointers of the parent directory. If this does not work, it can be done later.

Update Propagation

The update sender and listener together ensure that replicas of a directory converge to a consistent state in a reasonable period of time once updates cease. Although convergence is guaranteed under normal operation, network partitions or nonfunctioning servers may prevent (or delay) this.

There are two basic ways to update replicas:

- skulks
- propagation

Skulks have the potential for being expensive. In fact, continually running a skulk is prohibitive, so propagation is used to supplement the process.

The skulker is run periodically but is considered by the DNS architect to be the "central critical algorithm for maintaining the structure of the namespace." Skulks are done on a per-directory basis. This is because the directory is the unit of replication (not the clearinghouse), and the skulk is responsible for maintaining the consistency among replicas. It is possible

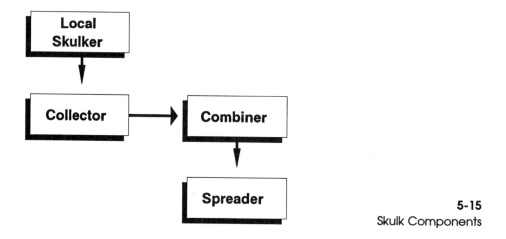

5-15
Skulk Components

to have several skulks running in parallel. If multiple skulks are initiated on the same directory, all but one will self-abort due to an inability to form a ring.

A skulk can be initiated in three ways. First, a client can explicitly start the skulk. Second, it can be run on demand by a transaction agent, as in the case of creating a directory. Third, and most typical, a skulk is run periodically by a name server as a background process. The frequency of skulks is determined by the DNS$Convergence attribute for a particular directory.

If a skulk fails repeatedly, this is evidence of corruption in the name-space. The most probable reasons are that one of the name servers is not running or the clearinghouse is off line. More obscure reasons are also possible, such as the clearinghouse being destroyed or a major skew in the clocks.

Epochs are a way of forcing all old skulks to fail. When a clearinghouse becomes permanently unavailable, it is possible that a skulk will be unable to finish. The new epoch reconstructs the entire replica set, resynchronizes all copies and recovers as much of the original state as possible. A new epoch is used when a master or secondary is destroyed, or when it is necessary to change the master replica to a new location.

The skulker process is aided by two other processes—the collector and the spreader (see Fig. 5-15). The collector follows the ring of replica pointers for a current epoch. It collects all updates, then uses the combine process to merge them. The spreader then takes the combined update and sends them out.

The propagator is used for high-priority updates that cannot wait for a skulk. Although the specification for the propagator is "instant" updates, the architecture recommends that various techniques be used to delay the updates; for example, updates can be batched. Connections can be cached, and the updates can be implemented in order of clearinghouse instead of time received. The propagator can also wait and see if a skulk is about to start. If so, there is no need to propagate the updates since the skulker will bring all replicas up to date.

The Clearinghouse Background Process

The clearinghouse background process runs periodically and is responsible for the following:

- recovering clearinghouse resources from dead replicas
- recovering clearinghouse resources from absent attribute values older than DSN$AllUpTo
- initiating skulks
- checking directory parent pointers and updating child pointers
- rebuilding the UpPointers set for the clearinghouse
- upgrading local replicas when new versions begin running

Solicitation and Advertisement

A name server will advertise its services under two circumstances. First, if the periodic advertisement timer expires. Second, if a solicitation message is received. When a solicitation is received, the name server checks to see whether the solicitation is local to the LAN or comes from the same DNA area. It then multicasts the answer to either the LAN or the whole area. Note that replies to solicitations are subject to a jitter adjustment to prevent synchronized multicasts.

The following are the timers specified for advertisement in the naming service:

Distance	Root Clearinghouse (minutes)	Nonroot Clearinghouse (minutes)
LAN	5	5
To area	10	10
To whole net	20	never

Note that advertisements to the area or the whole network need a multicast capability. In the case of Phase V, we have no WAN multicast.

Security in the Naming Service

Security in the name server is provided in two ways. First, there are an access control provision and internal consistency guarantees to prevent the unauthorized disclosure, introduction, modification, or destruction of names. Second, the name server is an integral part of any authentication service. The authentication service is a set of attributes that are part of object names. In version 2 (current version) DNS uses authentication based on either passwords or proxy logins.

Access control is provided by the name server. In DNS, security is placed in the hands of the object owners. This is discretionary access control. A service that DNS does not provide is nondiscretionary—centralized decisions through a security officer. In DNS, it is up to each object owner.

Discretionary controls are provided through an access control set. The access control set (ACS) attribute is applied to every object entry, directory entry, soft link, and clearinghouse. An access control set is made up of a set of access control entries. The entries consist of a name (person) and access rights. The name can be an individual or a group; the group may in turn contain other groups.

To process security, each name server includes a reference monitor function. The reference monitor takes into consideration four pieces of information:

- the ACS of the referenced object
- the name of the principal requesting access
- whether the principal was authenticated
- the operation the principal wants to perform

Access Control Sets

An access control entry has three fields (see Fig. 5-16):

- principal
- options
- access rights

The principal is one of three names. First, it can be an individual user name, which is represented as a DNS full name. Second, it can be an implicit group, represented as a wildcarded full name. Third, it can be an explicit group.

The first flag in the options field contains an indication if the principal name is really a group. The second flag is the default flag: If this particular object is a directory, the default flag indicates that this particular ACE should be propagated to the ACS of any child created. Note that when the ACE is replicated in the child entry, the default flag is not set on that entry. A third flag is the nopropagate flag. It indicates that the ACE should not be inserted in a child directory. Otherwise, the default is to propagate. The fourth flag is the unauthenticated flag which lets the reference monitor at-

Flags		Unauthenticated
		Default
		No Propogate
		Group
Rights		Read
		Write
		Delete
		Test
		Control
Identifier		Group or Principal

5-16
Naming Service
Access Control Entry

tempt to match the requesting user to the principal field, even if that user has not been authenticated.

The access rights for an ACE include read, write, delete, test, and control. The test access right allows the user to test a value but not necessarily read it, as in the case of comparing an incoming password with one stored in the clearinghouse. The control right allows the user to modify the access control set.

To process the access control set, the access control entries are partitioned into individual, implicit groups, and explicit groups. Each one of these partitions is processed separately, starting with the individual.

The reference monitor takes the desired operation for the user and attempts to find permission in one of the access control entries. As soon as a match is found the reference monitor is given those rights.

To blacklist a user, put the individual name in with a null rights list. Note that a blacklist does not work with a group since a user may be in many different groups. The reference monitor processes all groups until the desired rights are conferred or there are no ACEs left.

Implicit groups are always processed before explicit groups. This is because membership in an implicit group can always be determined locally: The group is a wildcarded name. An explicit group, on the other hand, may require network processing. Since the members of a group are full names, it is possible that a lookup on a member of a group will require a query to another clearinghouse.

Creation and Propagation of Access Control Sets

If the new entry is an object, the parent ACS is scanned for any access control entries with the default flag set. Those ACEs are copied into the child ACS but with the default flag turned off. If the new entry is a directory, the parent is scanned for any access control entries without the no-propagate flag. Next, go to the ACS in the new entry and look for an ACE

Constant	Value
Simple Name Max	255 octets
Full Name Max	402 octets
Attrib Name Max	31 octets
Max Attribute	4000 octets
Class Size	31 octets
Update Packet Max	16K octets
NSAdvertisement	09-00-2B-02-01-00
NSSolicitation	09-00-2B-02-01-01
NamingService	80-3C
	08-00-2B-80-3C
MajorVer	2
MaxDatagramSize	1400
MinDatagramSize	256
BkgdSkulk	24 hours
NSMaxsize	16K octets
TSSkew	5 minutes
Source: DNS Functional Specification	

5-17
Naming Service
Architectural Values

containing the principal that created the object. This object, if present, if modified to full rights; you can always control your own object. Note that if the principal is not authenticated, the noauthenticate flag is set. If the ACE does not exist for the principal, it is created.

Other Reference Information

Figure 5-17 shows some architectural definitions in the current version (version 2) of the naming service. Figure 5-18 shows the possible errors returned by the naming service interface.

X.500

X.500 is the CCITT equivalent of ISO standard 9594. The CCITT and ISO versions are nearly identical. X.500 is used to communicate information between, with, or about objects. These objects can be application entities, people, terminals, distribution lists, or any other OSI or user-defined objects. Note that X.500 is not a general-purpose relational DBMS. Convergence over time for updates is acceptable. An implementation that favors queries over updates is also acceptable.

X.500 does not give different answers based on the location of the user. In this sense, it would not be appropriate to use X.500 as a means for get-

Error	Number	Description
Invalid Arguement	1	For example
Invalid Name	2	badly-formed name
No Local Resources	3	Function cannot be performed at this time
No Communication	4	No response from target resource
Access Violation	5	Caller does not have access rights
Cannot Authenticate	6	Authentication failed
Conflicting Arguements	7	Protocol violation
Timeout Not Done	8	Operation did not complete in time allotted and no modifications were made
Timeout Maybe Done	9	Timeout, but modifications may have been made to namespace
Entry Exists	11	Creation of entry not possible
Unknown Entry	12	Entry does not exist in namespace
Not Implemented	14	Optional function not available
Invalide Update	15	Attribute cannot be directly modified
Unknown Clearinghouse	16	
Not A Replica	17	Clearinghouse does not have replica of this directory
Already Replica	18	Clearinghouse has a replica of this directory
Crucial Replica	19	May not remove this replica
Not Empty	20	Delete on nonempty directory failed
Not Linked	21	Supplied name was not a soft link
Possible Cycle	22	Possible cycle followed in follwing soft links or groups
Dangling Link	23	Soft link does not point to entry
Not a Group	24	Group operation requested on an object that is not a group
Clearinghouse Down	25	Clearinghouse exists but not available
Bad Epoch	26	Wrong epoch encountered while skulking
Bad Clock	27	Update contained invalid time stamp
Data Corruption	28	Clearinghouse may be corrupted
Wrong Attribute Type	29	Type mismatch in access to an attribute
More Than One Replica	30	Attempt to delete directory with multiple replicas failed
Cannot Put Here	31	Attempt to create a directory in a clearinghouse that cannot store it

5-18 Naming Service Errors

Error	Number	Description
Old Skulk	32	Skulk in progress encountered a newer skulk in progress and aborted
Untrusted Clearinghouse	33	Access violation encountered by a clearinghouse accessing another clearinghouse on behalf of a client
Version Skew	34	Attempt to add replica of a directory on a clearinghouse running an older version of the naming service
Wrong State	102	Entity cannot perform the operation in its current state
Bad Nickname	103	Proposed nickname already in use by anothe name space
Not Root	105	Operation must be performed at the root master replica of the namespace
Not Clearinghouse Directory	106	May not store a clearinghouse in this directory
Root Lost	107	Connectivity with the root of the namespace may have been lost

5-18 *(Cont.)*   Naming Service Errors

ting routing or other directional information. With the exception of access rights and unpropagated updates, a query will always give the same answer regardless of location.

The basic distributed database, the Directory Information Base, consists of a series of objects. Objects have attributes and attribute values. The objects are arranged in a tree, known as the Directory Information Tree (DIT) (see Fig. 5-19).

As in the case of the Digital Naming Service, a full name can be derived from an object's location in the tree. In X.500, this full name is known as a distinguished name (distinguished referring to the name's uniqueness and not to the social status of the object). Also analogous to the Digital Naming Service is the alias entry, equivalent to the DNS soft link.

To keep the directory consistent, there is a schema for the directory. The schema defines constraints on the directory usage, such as constraining attribute values to a certain range for an attribute type. Other schema entries constrain the types of attributes an object class can have.

A variety of important considerations are not covered in the 1988 version of the directory. Specifically, ways to replicate the directory information base are not considered. Additionally, management of the schema, access control, and knowledge information are not covered.

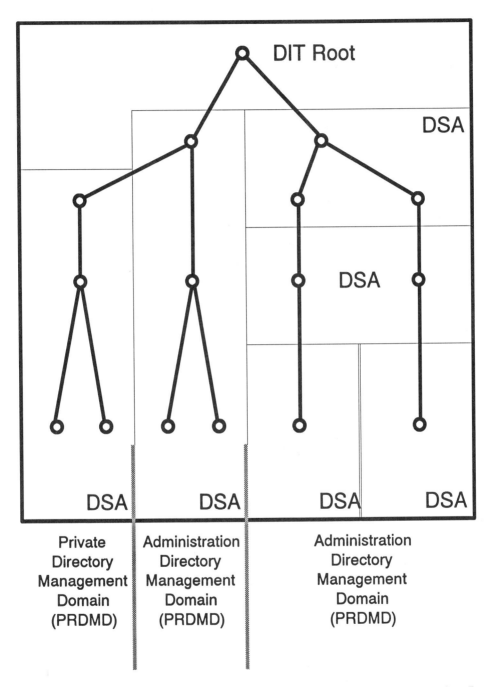

5-19 X.500 Direction Information Tree

X.500 allows the directory system agent to deny service based on a variety of considerations, including the

* amount of time a search would take
* size of the results
* scope of the search
* priority of the request

It is also possible for the DSA to require validation, such as a digital signature, on a request.

The basic directory search operations include

* read one or more attributes of an entry
* compare a supplied value with an attribute value
* list the immediate subordinates of an object
* search the directory information tree for objects that satisfy some filter
* abandon an outstanding interrogation

It is also possible to modify the directory by adding, removing, or modifying an entry. The user can also modify a relative distinguished name.

The directory is divided into directory management domains. At the top of the tree are public domains, known as administration directory management domains. At the bottom of the tree are privately run directory management domains (DMDs). A DMD consists of at least one directory system agent and zero or more directory user agents.

X.500 Components

The X.500 architecture specifies two components. The directory user agent (DUA) is equivalent to the DNS clerk. The directory system agent (DSA) is the equivalent to the name server in DNS (see Fig. 5-20).

The outcome of a request by the DUA can be a result, an error, or a referral. Referrals direct the DUA to another DSA. The DUA can specify either chaining, where the DUA contacts another DUA on behalf of the user, or referrals where the DSA retains control of the search but requests a hint from the DSA. It is possible that the DSA will refuse to chain the request, thereby returning an error message (and presumably a referral).

The interaction between the DUA and the DSA is not really specified in the X.500 standards. It is possible that a DUA will always interact with the "home" DSA. A more sophisticated DUA might have several queries outstanding to different DSAs.

The two protocols defined in X.500 are the Directory Access Protocol (DAP) and the Directory System Protocol (DSP). DAP is used for user agents to communicate with system agents. The system protocol is used with system agents. Both protocols are built on top of the Remote Operations (ROSE) protocols defined in X.219.

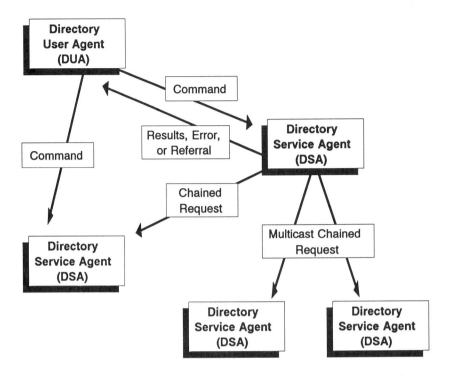

5-20 X.500 Service Components

Several patterns of usage are envisioned for X.500. The basic operation is the lookup: Given a name, an alias, or the value of an attribute, read the values of other attributes. Other patterns might be browsing the directory (subject to access control) or a yellow pages application. A yellow pages application would be a filter based on some attribute, such as the business category attribute defined in X.520. Another pattern of operations would be a group validation which would answer questions such as "Is a particular user in a group?" and "Who are the members of a distribution list?" Finally, X.500 might be used for authentication. The directory could hold passwords, public key certificates, digital signatures, or other forms of authentication information.

Directory Schema

The directory schema contains four types of information:

- Directory Information Tree (DIT) structure
- object class definitions
- attribute type definitions
- attribute syntax definitions

The DIT structure rules identify which objects may be subobjects of a particular object. In other words, this part of the schema defines the valid subordinate and superior classes for an object. The object class definitions identify what the mandatory and optional attributes are for a particular object. It also identifies if an object is a subclass of another object. Two special object classes are top (at the top of the tree) and alias.

The attribute syntax rules use ASN.1 data type definitions (see Fig. 5-21). It also allows the specification of matching rules for values, based on equality, substrings, or ordering. An example of an ordering rule is that the value must be greater than zero.

Not all names are required to be user friendly, since not all names will be used directly by the user. If they are however, the names should be designed so a person can guess the name. To design a name that can be guessed, several rules are specified in the X.500 standards. One of the most important naming rules is to avoid imposing artificial constraints to remove natural ambiguities. An example is a common last name. Instead of changing a common last name to Smith2 (hard to guess), use another attribute (such as location) to distinguish common names. For example, use "John Smith in Chicago" or "John Smith in Marketing." In addition, a good user interface should be able to handle common abbreviations and variations in spelling. This of course requires an X.500 implementation intelligent enough to vary the queries.

Figure 5-22 shows how the attribute types can be organized into a directory information tree. Countries, localities, and organizations are at the root of the tree. Either localities or organizations will eventually point to a name or a group of names. It is also possible to have organizational people (e.g., a vice president), devices (a computer), or a program (i.e., the directory itself) as part of an organization.

Access Control in X.500

Access control is a matter outside of the X.500 standard, but some guidelines are provided. First, access control can be provided at different levels:

- the entire tree
- an individual object
- an attribute
- a select instance of an attribute value

For a particular level, different access categories are defined, including detect, compare, read, modify, add/delete attributes, and add/change object names.

Each service request has a set of common arguments:

Labeling Attribute types	Organizational Attribute Types
Common Name	Organization Name
Surname	Organizational Unit Name
Serial Number	Title
Geographical Attribute Types	Relational Attribute Types
Country Name	Object Owner
Locality Name	Role Occupant
State or Province Name	See Also
Street Address	Preference Attribute Types
Postal Addressing Attribute Types	Preferred Delivery Method
Postal Address or Code	Explanatory Attribute Types
Post Office Box	Description
Physical Delivery Office Name	Search Guide
Telecommunications Attribute Types	Business Category
Telephone Number	Security Attribute Types
Telex Number	User Password
Teletex Terminal Identifier	User Certificate
Facsimile Telephone Number	CA Certificate
X.121 Address	Authority Revocation List
International ISDN Number	Certificate Revocation List
Reigistered Telegram Address	Cross Certificate Pair
Telegram Destination Indicator	System Attribute Types
OSI Application Attribute Types	Object Class
Presentation Address	Aliased Object Name
Supported Application Context	Knowledge Information

5-21 Selected X.500 Attribute Types

- service controls (empty as default)
- security parameters (empty as default)
- requestor name (optional)
- aliased RDNs
- extensions
- operation progress

The operation progress record is used when a DSA must resubmit a query to another DUA. The aliased RDN indicator is used much like the DNS progress record to show the resolution of aliases.

Service controls are used by the DSA to control the type of search that will be carried out on the user's behalf. These controls include:

- prefer chaining
- chaining prohibited
- local scope only
- do not use copied information
- do not dereference aliases

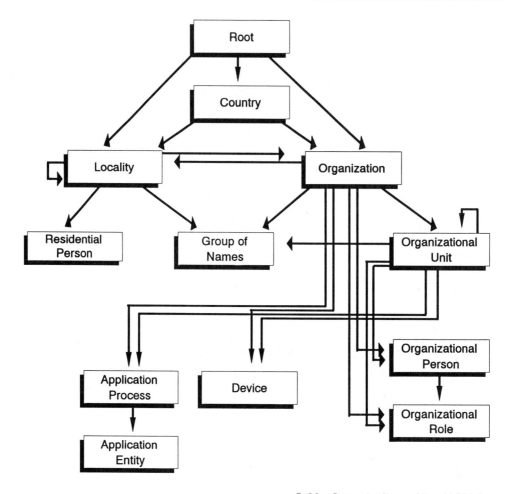

5-22 Organization of the X.500 Tree

- priority (low, medium, high)
- time limit for the search
- size limit for results
- scope of referral (limited to the management domain or to the country)

In addition to service controls, a search request will also add an entry information selection that specifies all attributes, one attribute, or selected attributes, plus the desired name and a filter. Filters are based on a particular attribute value, matching on equality, a substring, whether value is present, or an approximate match (based on a locally defined algorithm such as soundex).

Resolving requests

There are three ways to get information:

- chaining
- multicasting
- referrals

Multicasting is a special form of chaining where we can send the same request to several places. A referral contains a knowledge reference, which is an indication of which DSA might be able to resolve a particular request.

When a DSA cannot resolve a request, it will usually chain, unless the request said do not chain or there is some administrative reason not to chain. If the DSA cannot chain, it will provide a referral.

Every entry in the DIB is administered by a single DSA. There is no reason, however, why other DSAs cannot make a copy of the entry and cache it. It is possible for the DUA to specify that copies are not to be used. The answer to a query will specify if it is from a copy. The specific methods used to control caching and replication are not defined in X.500: There are no equivalents to the skulking and update policies of the naming service.

A particular DSA has two kinds of information: directory information and knowledge information. Knowledge information resolves the naming context information held by a particular DSA. A part of the tree is known as a naming context. The context has a context prefix (the tree from the root to the beginning of the context). A naming context is the context prefix and a collection of knowledge references.

You need to keep at least the superior references, internal references, and subordinate references. It is possible you will also keep nonsubordinate references (known as cross-references). The first-level DSAs (those near the root) are responsible for knowing about all other first-level DSAs. The lower-level DSAs need to have a reference to the path to the first-level DSA.

Security

X.509 defines an authentication method based on the public key cryptosystem developed by Rivest, Shamir, and Adleman. (Technically, X.509 puts the RSA cryptosystem into an appendix, but it is widely accepted as the method to provide authentication services).

The X.509 standard defines four types of information:

- authentication information held by the directory
- how to get authentication information
- how the information is formed and placed in the directory
- three ways applications might use this information

Authentication comes in two forms. The simple, or weak, authentication is a simple password exchange. Password-based exchanges are subject to human-engineering problems: People are somehow tricked into giving away their password, or somebody observes the password on the network. A more advanced form of authentication is cryptographically formed credentials, known as strong authentication. Credentials are formed offline, then placed in the directory. The X.509 standard uses RSA technology as an example of a public key method. Other public key methods could also be used.

For a strong authentication method, each user has three attributes:

- a unique name
- a secret key
- a public key

The goal is to find out if the user really has the secret key, given a name and public key.

To get a user's public key, you must first have the public key of the certification authority (CA). When you communicate with the CA it produces a certificate. To open the certificate, we use the public key of the CA. Hidden inside that certificate is the public key of the user. If the service provider has the CA's public key, the public key of the user can be found.

A certificate is based on the following:

- the user's full name
- the user's public key
- a certificate serial number
- an identifier of the algorithm used
- the time validity of the certificate

The certification authority maintains a variety of different kinds of certificates:

- Forward certificates are the keys of this CA as encoded by other certification authorities.
- Reverse certificates are the keys of other CAs as encoded by others.
- Certificates for users.

The forward and reverse certificates allow a certification path to be set up. In this case, you can eventually get the public key for a user maintained by another CA.

Once the public key of a user is obtained, we attempt to authenticate it: The user sends a digital signature, encrypted with the user's digital signature. A one-way hash (decryption) algorithm is applied to the digital signature, then compared to the results obtained using the public key of the user. If the results match, the user had the proper secret key and is presumed to be the valid user.

How the key data are generated is an issue beyond the scope of the X.509 standard. A user might generate his or her own key pair, or a CA might generate it. Things like smart cards are a possible repository for the key pair. The smart card would itself be secured by a Personal Identification Number (PIN).

DASS

DASS is Digital's distributed authentication security service. DASS is based on public key technology, and has three components:

- key generation
- a certification authority
- authentication routines

DASS is part of a longer-range program from Digital known as the Digital Distributed System Security Architecture (DSSA). The architecture covers:

- user and system authentication
- mandatory and discretionary security
- secure initialization and loading
- delegation of authority

The security architecture is not meant to address top-secret, multilevel security requirements in the military. It instead addresses commercial grade requirements. The architecture makes extensive use of encryption.

Summary

The DNA Naming Service is a key component of DECnet/OSI Phase V. The naming service is a replicated, distributed database with a loose consistency guarantee.

A prime user is the DNA Session Control layer, which uses the naming service to resolve full names into the network address or tower set of the node. Other naming service users are electronic mail systems, security systems, and remote procedure call mechanisms.

DNS is a primitive naming service which takes a full name and resolves it into one or more attributes. X.500 is a descriptive service which starts with a few attributes and returns one or more names. DNS could be used to form the infrastructure for a descriptive name service.

Security is integrally linked with naming services. Public key cryptography systems use the naming service as a repository for public keys. Making the public keys generally available allows a user to engage in authenticated communications with a wide user base.

Support Protocols

CHAPTER 6

Support Protocols

The DNA Naming Service is one thing that distinguishes the DNA side of the protocol stack from the OSI side. As we saw, the Digital naming service, which provides a distributed, replicated, primitive service, offers a service significantly different from X.500.

Digital calls this strategy "adding value" to international standards. Rather than wait for a complete standard, Digital goes ahead and develops its own proprietary standards. The naming service is one example, but we will see several others such as the Local Area Transport protocols, and their network management strategy.

There can be no argument that many of these services are valuable in a network. Purists maintain that using proprietary protocols violates the spirit of open systems and OSI. Digital marketing managers maintain that they are simply filling in holes until the international standards mature. In some cases, particularly the naming service, Digital has used other forums such as the Open Software Foundation to try and make their approach acceptable to a wider audience.

Whatever the merits of the two points of view, we see that there are a number of such holes Digital has filled. These supplementary protocols operate only on the DNA side of the protocol stack, further distinguishing the Digital-to-Digital functionality in the network from the services available in a truly heterogeneous environment. Needless to say, this gives Digital salespeople features to sell that their competition does not have. On the other hand, salespeople from other companies can argue that taking advantage of the added functionality locks the customer into Digital. They are probably both right.

In this chapter we look at three sets of supplementary protocols. First, we look at the time service. The time service allows many different computers to synchronize their clocks within a degree of precision and error factors. We saw in Chapter 5 that the naming service skulk process de-

6-1 DNA Support Protocols

pends heavily on an accurate update time stamp to coordinate distributed updates. We will see other instances in which an accurate clock is vital.

Next, we look at the remote procedure call (RPC) mechanism. As part of the Open Software Foundation, Digital has adopted the Hewlett-Packard/Apollo RPC protocols as a way of telling remote computers to perform a particular task. The RPC performs functions equivalent to the OSI presentation layer and the OSI Remote Operations Service (ROSE).

Finally, we look at a specialized, low-level protocol called the Maintenance Operations Protocol (MOP). MOP, a direct user of the data link, extends a system's console across a data link. This simple task is actually quite powerful, allowing a node to boot across the network. Specialized gateways and servers, as well as diskless workstations, all use MOP as the way of obtaining their operating system from another node.

The time service, the naming service, and the remote procedure call all operate at either the Session Control layer or as direct clients of the data link layer (see Fig. 6-1). Being a direct client of the data link layer makes sense for two nodes on a local Ethernet, which do not need the extra overhead of routing or other upper-layer functions.

In a wide-area environment, or one with multiple subnetworks, it does not make sense to bypass the upper-layer functions. Routing, transport level reassembly and error recovery, and sessions all become valuable functions in a WAN environment. In this case, services like RPC and the time protocol are able to establish a DECnet session for communication. Note that none of these services uses the OSI session layer, making these services unavailable to native OSI applications.

MOP is different in that it does not use the Session Control layer. MOP is an extremely primitive protocol, intended to be simple enough to be implemented in Read-Only Memory (ROM) in a processor. When a diskless node initializes, it is running the MOP protocols and broadcasts an appeal for help. Another node will respond and force-feed it the operating system. Until the operating system is resident, the node is not really running DECnet, but only the MOP component.

Need for Synchronized Time

On one computer, an inaccurate clock is not really a problem. All users get the same inaccurate reading, and the temporal ordering of their operations is maintained—an operation performed before another gets an earlier time stamp. In a network, it is quite possible that clocks have different readings. If a database such as the Naming Service, is being updated by two different users, an accurate update time is vital.

When two clocks have different readings, it known as skew. In all probability, both times are wrong. The difference between two local clocks is skew, whereas the difference between a clock and "correct" time is an inaccuracy.

Correct time is measured with respect to Universal Coordinated Time (UTC), which is maintained by the BIH (International Time Bureau). From UTC, we can derive political derivations such as Pacific Standard time. We can represent a political derivation as the UTC plus a Time Differential Factor (TDF).

There are two other factors, aside from skew and inaccuracy, that can affect the representation of time. One is drift, which is an increasing inaccuracy of a clock over time. The other is resolution, the ability of a clock to measure time in increasingly granular chunks.

At the level of a computer clock, measuring time in microseconds or milliseconds, it is unlikely we will have perfectly accurate time. The clock will be inaccurate, will be skewed with respect to other clocks, will drift, and will probably not have enough resolution to time stamp all operations oc-

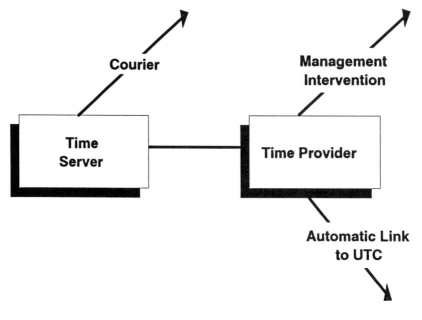

6-2 Time Protocol

curring on a processor. The time service, within the constraints of inaccuracy and other problems, attempts to provide the best possible representation of time in a distributed computing environment. Typically, some computer (or computers) on the network has a time provider—a clock that is considered accurate (see Fig. 6-2). That provider can be an automatic link to UTC, or can be set by management. Setting a clock by management (known as the "wristwatch protocol") will not provide the accuracy of an automatic link.

The time protocol is a way of taking the time provider's information and distributing it to the rest of the network. The process that makes the information available is a time server. It is possible that a time server does not have a direct time provider and instead uses a courier protocol to get and adjust another computer's time. Figure 6-3 shows a typical network configuration. As with the naming service, we have servers and clerks. Typically, every node will have a clerk component. A few computers will be considered to be servers.

If there are enough computers on the same LAN, clerks will use datagram-based services to retrieve the time from each of the servers. The union of these times will become the local version of time. If there are not enough local servers available, a node can use the global servers, using the Session Control layer to set up a virtual circuit. Once again, several different servers are consulted by the clerk to derive a union of time.

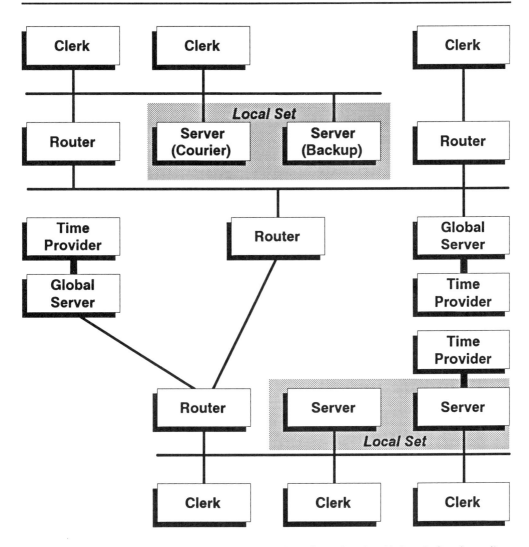

6-3 Time Service Network Configuration

The courier in Figure 6-3 is a local server that makes use of the global server as a time provider. In any case, sets of servers always try to synchronize their clocks with each other on a periodic basis.

Deciding what the time is on a server is not necessarily an easy matter. If we could get an instant reading it would be no problem, but the network introduces propagation delay, and individual nodes take time to process network packets. Figure 6-4 shows the process a node goes through to find the time from another node. First, the clerk reads the local clock and prepares a request to go on the network. That request has a preparation delay

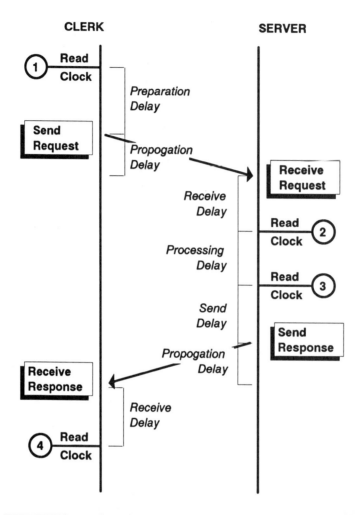

6-4 Time Service Message Exchange

and once sent, a propagation delay. At the server, the packet is again delayed while it is decoded. Once the packet reaches the time service, the server makes note of what time the packet arrived. At this point, there may be an additional delay, so the server waits until the response is just about ready to send and makes another note of the time.

Once again, the packet has a sending delay and a propagation delay on the network. Once received back at the clerk, there is a further delay while the packet is copied into buffers and decoded by lower layers. When the clerk gets the packet, it once again takes note of the time.

The problem for the clerk is to find out what the time really was (at least according to this one server) when the original packet was sent out. The bottom of Figure 6-4 shows the formula to decide what the time really was when the packet was sent and thus by how much the local clock should be adjusted.

In addition to the "real" time, the clerk maintains an error factor. Instead of a point in time, we represent time as a range. By consulting several servers, the clerk takes the union of these different times to represent the local time. The formula used in the Digital time service can throw out one of the server's responses if they are too far out of the range.

To find a server, most nodes wait for a time server advertisement (see Fig. 6-5). The advertisement, sent out periodically, includes the network ID of the server and the role as a courier. The courier role indicates whether the node is a courier and, if so, whether it is the active or backup courier for a local set of servers. The message then includes the data link and network IDs of any other servers known at the time.

If there is no advertisement before a clerk needs the information, the clerk can multicast a solicit servers request (see Fig. 6-6), which generates a response similar to the advertisement (see Fig. 6-7). Notice that all of these messages include 4 bytes of version information, allowing graceful updates to the time protocol in the future. A clerk can find out which versions of the protocol a particular server supports (see Fig. 6-8).

Advertisements and requests are multicast only within the breadth of a subnetwork. To find out global servers, a node would use the DNA Naming Service. The naming service would return the network address of any global servers. A node that is not on a broadcast-type subnetwork (e.g., Ethernet) would use the naming service as a way of finding the location of servers.

The actual time request and response messages are shown in Figures 6-9 and 6-10. The request is simple, including a message ID as a way of correlating incoming responses. The response includes the server time (when the packet was first read) and the processing delay (when the response was sent back out).

Version		4 Bytes (Major and Minor)
Message Type		Type = 5
Message ID		ID of request
Network ID		Sending Node
Courier Role		No, Active, Backup
Count		Number of servers
Data Link ID		
Network ID		
Courier Role		
Data Link ID		
Network ID		
Role		

6-5
Time Server
Advertisement

Version		4 Bytes (Major and Minor)
Message Type		Type = 3
Message ID		ID of request

6-6
Time Solicit
Servers Request

Version		4 Bytes (Major and Minor)
Message Type		Type = 4
Message ID		ID of request
Count		Number of servers
Data Link ID		
Network ID		
Courier Role		No, Active, Backup
Data Link ID		
Network ID		

6-7
Time Solicit
Servers Response

Version		4 Bytes (Major and Minor)
Message Type		Type = 6
Message ID		ID of request

6-8
Time Supported
Version Message

Version		4 Bytes (Major and Minor)
Message Type		Type = 1
Message ID		64 Bits

6-9
Time Request Message

Version		4 Bytes (Major and Minor)
Message Type		Type = 2
Message ID		ID of request
Pad Count		
Pad Data		Implementation specific
Server Time		
Processing Delay		
Epoch		For server coordination

6-10
Time Response Message

The time response message also includes an epoch. As with the naming service, the epoch is used to allow groups of servers to coordinate their activities. In the time service, the epoch allows several different domains of time to run concurrently. Over time, the different domains are gradually merged into a unified time domain.

Unique Identifications

A time stamp is a way of identifying an operation uniquely over time. It does not, however, uniquely identify an operation over space—the union of possible computers on the network. For many operations, both a time stamp and a unique ID are necessary.

The unique ID is unique across both time and space. Note that a time stamp is also needed. Although the current version of the Digital unique ID architecture preserves temporal ordering (because it incorporates a time stamp), there is no guarantee this will hold in the future. The unique ID architecture document cautions developers that in the future there may be large random numbers used for unique IDs.

A unique ID consists of the following pieces of information:

- 48-bit system ID
- UTC
- UTC Specifier to allow multiple UIDs to be generated in one clock tick

- clock sequence value (to guard against a nonmonotonic resetting of clock value)
- version number for UID architecture

The unique ID has a total size of 128 bits. This unique ID from Digital is basically interoperable with the UUID used in the Hewlett-Packard/Apollo Network Computing Services. This interoperability is important because the remote procedure call mechanism may operate in both DECnet and Hewlett-Packard/Apollo networking environments.

Remote Procedure Calls

In a single-machine environment, programs are structured as a set of procedures (see Fig. 6-11). A procedure calls another, passing in some arguments and receiving back some information. The information received back can be a simple status indicator that the procedure executed properly or could be complex information as in the case of a database query.

A remote procedure call mechanism extends this paradigm to work in a network-based environment (see Fig. 6-12). The trick is to furnish a program on the local computer that emulates the called procedure. This program, called the client stub, masks the network-resident aspects of the communication from the main program. A client stub, using network calls, will communicate the call to a server on the network, sending in the arguments. The called procedure, like the calling procedure, should be unaware of the network operations and uses a server stub that emulates the calling procedure.

This simple paradigm allows program developers to concentrate on the functionality of their programs, then later deploy their programs in a distributed network of clients and servers. A well-developed remote procedure mechanism works on numerous computing platforms and over a variety of networks.

Digital has chosen the Hewlett-Packard/Apollo RPC mechanism as the basis for DECnet remote procedure calls. The Hewlett-Packard mechanism was extended in cooperation with Digital to support DECnet and the DNA Naming Service. In addition, the Digital implementation uses the Digital multithread architecture, which allows a single server process to keep multiple threads of execution going, one for each of the requesting procedures.

Most of the protocols examined in this book, such as LAT, the name server, and network management, use a remote operations method of clients communicating requests to servers. All of these different protocols have in effect implemented their own remote procedure call mechanism. It is likely that all of these protocols will eventually migrate to the common RPC platform.

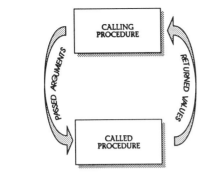

6-11
Single-Machine
Procedure Call

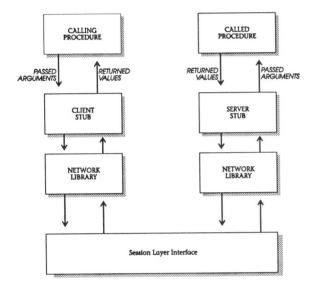

6-12
Network-Based
Remote Procedure
Call

The RPC mechanism handles many tasks that are handled in the OSI environment by the presentation layer. The RPC bind message (see Fig. 6-13) sets up an association between a client and a server. The main work being done in this bind message is to specify how data are to be represented.

In the RPC mechanism, an interface is a set of operations packaged together. The interface is uniquely identified by a UID (known as a UUID in the Hewlett-Packard terminology). The interface, in addition to operation definitions, includes a definition of how data are to be represented. The RPC bind message takes each of these data representations (known as ab-

Version Number		Current = 5
Packet Type		
Flags		First Fragment
		Last Fragment
		Pending Alert at Sender
		Async Alerts Disabled
		Authentication, Integrity, or Privacy
		Authenticate
		Fault: Guaranteed Call Problem
		Did Not Execute
		Maybe Semantics
		Maybe Semantics Requested
Body Data Representation Label		Data format for integers, char, and floating point.
Fragment Body Length		
Header Padding		
Max Transmit Size		
Max Receive Size		
Association Group ID		
Number of Items		Number of Context Elements
Context ID		ID of First Context
Number of Transfer Items		
Number of Transfer Syntaxes		
Abstract Syntax UUID		Set to Interface UUID
Abstract Syntax Version		
Transfer Syntax UUID		Data Representation UUID
Transfer Syntax Version		
Transfer Syntax UUID		
Transfer Syntax Version		
Pad		Only if Authentication Trailer
Authentication Type		
Authentication Length		
Credentials		

stract syntaxes) and assigns one or more transfer syntaxes to it for the purpose of transmitting information on the network.

In addition to the data representation, the bind message has two other sections: authentication and flags for different operation methods. The authentication is not actually specified in the RPC mechanism. Various types of authentication can be supported and it is up to the client and the server to support a particular kind mutually. As Digital moves toward public key-based authentication, we can expect that to be one of the types supported.

The flags allow a bind message to have multiple fragments, which is useful in a LAN-based environment. For a virtual circuit interface, the fragmentation is not necessary since the session and lower layers take care of fragmentation and reassembly of messages.

The pending alert flag is used when a client has multiple threads of execution, all talking to a server. A particular thread may be blocked because it is waiting for the server to complete. Another thread, when sending a message, sets the pending alert flag to notify the server it is blocking execution. Presumably, the well-behaved server will do something to move the blocked thread forward. The asynchronous alerts flag indicates whether status messages are desired.

The authentication flags provide optional hooks for authentication, message integrity, and privacy services. The actual values for all three types of integrity mechanisms are not specified in the RPC architecture but depend on the underlying network environment. For example, Digital uses a "weak" (password-based) authentication scheme at the session layer. The RPC mechanism would use that.

The "did not execute" flag is only meaningful on an error (fault) message. This flag indicates there is a guarantee the indicated call did not execute. Otherwise, there is a possibility that the call did execute, and the client is responsible for figuring out what really happened.

The last flag indicates that maybe call semantics are requested. Normally, a call is explicitly acknowledged by the server. With maybe semantics, the server does not have to acknowledge the request, and there is no guarantee the server has received the packet.

Figure 6-14 shows the bind accept message. As with the bind request, the flags are present. A body data representation label enables the client to read the rest of the packet. The accept message includes a maximum receive and transmit size for requests and responses. It also includes a secondary address. When a server receives a request, it may start up a new process to handle this particular set of calls.

For each of the contexts specified in the bind request, the accept message also includes which transfer syntax was chosen. Finally, there is an interface hint. The meaning of the hint is up to the server, and the hint is

Version Number		Current = 5
Packet Type		
Flags		
Body Data Representation Label		Data format for integers, char, and floating point
Fragment Body Length		
Header Padding		
Max Transmit Size		
Max Receive Size		
Association Group ID		
Secondary Address		For Process Incarnation
Pad		
Number of Items		Number of Context Elements
Context ID		ID of First Context
Result		Accept or Reject
Transfer Syntax Choosen		Set to Interface UUID
Interface Hint		Server Choosen Number
Context ID		
Result		
Transfer Syntax Choosen		
Interface Hint		
Pad		Only if Authentication Trailer
Authentication Type		
Authentication Length		
Credentials		

Note: The Alter Context Response is identical to the Bind Response message, just as the Alter Context Request is identical to the Bind message. The alter messages are used to pick a new interface or version.

6-14
RPC Bind Accept

provided to allow a server to identify the meaning of a particular call quickly. A typical use of a hint is a handle—a pairing of a server process and a particular remote user.

The packet also allows an authentication trailer. This trailer, as in a bind request message, is optional. Figure 6-15 shows that a third leg is also possible for the authentication process. Again, it is up to the underlying network to provide an authentication model to be used by the RPC mechanism.

The bind request and bind accept messages have a variant, known as alter context messages. These messages allow a particular client and server to switch the interface they are using. For example, the association may start out using a database interface—a series of operations supporting different SQL calls. The association may wish to switch after that to an electronic mail interface supporting the transmission and posting of messages.

Instead of a bind accept message, it is possible that the server may send back a bind reject (see Fig. 6-16). Note that the bind reject, like all messages, has an optional authentication trailer. In a high-security environment, it may be necessary to authenticate every message to prevent some other node from masquerading as the target of a call.

The reject message includes a variety of reasons for rejecting a bind; for example, the server could be too busy to service the call. It is possible that authentication failed, in which case the well-designed server returns "not specified" as the reason for the reject.

Figures 6-17 and 6-18 show the format of the RPC request and response. Notice that the request keeps a pending alert count to notify the server how many alerts it has outstanding. It also includes an allocation hint, useful in telling the other side of a dialogue how much space a particular operation might take. The message also has a call identifier, which will be used to identify the incoming response. Remember that a client may have several calls outstanding at once. The particular operation needed is specified by interface and object UIDs plus any data passed in by the stub.

The response contains the call identifier plus the returned data. It also includes a runtime fault code, equivalent to a return status message in a single-machine environment.

In addition to the request and response messages, there is a wide variety of status messages (see Fig. 6-19). A client can "ping" a server to find out the status of a particular message. There are also explicit acknowledgments available for responses and quit messages. Finally, there are the working and no call answers to the ping message used by the server to indicate the current status of a call.

This discussion of the RPC mechanism is a brief introduction to a complex subject. In addition to the Hewlett-Packard/Apollo mechanism, there is another model used by Sun Microsystems and Netwise that forms the basis

Version Number		Current = 5
Packet Type		
Flags		
Body Data Representation Label		Data format for integers, char, and floating point.
Fragment Body Length		
Pad		
Authentication Type		
Authentication Length		
Credentials		

Note: RPC Shutdown message has an identical format and is used by the server to request the client to terminate the connection. The remote alert (i.e., "quit") and orphaned (sender aborting) requests are also identical.

6-15
RPC Third Leg
Authentication

Version Number		Current = 5
Packet Type		
Flags		
Body Data Representation Label		Data format for integers, char, and floating point
Fragment Body Length		
Rejection Reason		Not specified
		Temporary Congestion
		Local Limit Exceeded
		Version unsupported
Pad		Only if Authentication Trailer
Authentication Type		
Authentication Length		
Credentials		

6-16
RPC Bind Reject

Version Number		Current = 5
Packet Type		
Flags		
Body Data Representation Label		Data format for integers
Fragment Body Length		
Presentation Context ID		
Pending Alert Count		
Call Identifier		
Allocation Hint		That is, buffer space to allocate
Interface Version		
Object UID		
Interface UID		
Operation Number		
Interface Hint		That is, which interface in server
Pad		
Stub Data		
Authentication Trailer		Optional

6-17
RPC Request

Version Number		Current = 5
Packet Type		
Flags		
Body Data Representation Label		Data format for integers, char, and floating point
Fragment Body Length		
Presentation Context ID		
Pending Alert Count		
Call Identifier		
Allocation Hint		i.e., buffer space to allocate
Runtime Fault Code		Zero if no fault
Stub Data		
Authentication Trailer		Optional
Note: RPC Fault message has an identical format, but with a different packet type flag.		

6-18
RPC Response

Ping		Status of outstanding request
Ack		Explicit ACK of response
Fack		Explicit ACK of response fragment
Quack		Server ACK of client quit
Working		Server processing request
Nocall		Server is not processing request and has no record

6-19
RPC Status Messages

for the Open Network Computing model (ONC), Novell networks, and several other environments.

Maintenance Operations Protocol

The maintenance operations protocol is a direct user of the data link. Typically, MOP uses the Ethernet data link, but it can also work over point-to-point links such as HDLC or DDCMP (typically running in maintenance mode). MOP provides three levels of functionality:

- tests the communications link
- acts as a remote console
- uploads and downloads to remote system memory

The main use of MOP is as a remote booting protocol, but it is also used by network management products as a way of managing remote systems.

The three functions operate in increasing levels of complexity: One has to be operating before the next will operate successfully. The system console function allows low-level control of a system across the subnetwork. The manager can perform the following functions:

- identify the processor
- read data link counters
- issue a boot command

Note that this is not a secure protocol: it is extremely low level. There is an ID parameter, but it just prevents a system from receiving the wrong operating system. Presumably, if security is an issue, data link encryption would be used.

MOP Memory Load with Transfer Address		
Message Code		Code = 0
Load Number		For multisegment loads
Load Address		Load address (physical)
Image Data		
Transfer Address		Transfer address for image.
Notes:		
Code = 2 is a simple memory load (no transfer address)		
Transfer address is optional; image data also optional		
MOP Request Memory Dump Message		
Message Code		Code = 4
Memory Address		Starting Address
Count		Number of Units
MOP Request Program Message		
Message Code		Code = 8
Device Type		
Protocol Version		Current version = 4
Program Type		0 - Secondary loader
		1 - Tertiary loader
		2 - System image
		3 - Management image
		4 - CMIP script
Software ID		
Processor		Front End or System
Other Information		

6-20
MOP Messages

Figure 6-20 shows a summary of MOP messages. The loop message allows the MOP module to test the link by performing a loopback operation. The read counters message returns the counters being kept by the underlying data link.

After the low-level loop and counters messages, we see the console commands. These two messages allow a remote process to submit commands as if they were on the local console of a device. Many operations, such as

MOP Request Memory Load Message		
Message Code		Code = 10
Load Number		From previous request.
Error		Success or Failure

MOP Request Dump Service Message		
Message Code		Code = 12
Device Type		
Protocol Version		Current Version = 4
Memory Size		
Bits		For backward compatability
Other Information		Data Link Buffer Size

MOP Memory Dump Data Message		
Message Code		Code = 14
Memory Address		
Image Data		

MOP Parameter Load with Transfer Address Message		
Message Code		Code = 20
Load Number		
Parameter Type		0 - End Marker
		6 - Host System Time
Parameter Length		
Parameter Value		
Parameter Type		
Parameter Length		
Parameter Value		
Transfer Address		

MOP Dump Complete Message		
Message Code		Code = 1

MOP Assistance Volunteer Message		
Message Code		Code = 3

MOP Loop Messages		
Message Code		24 - Loop Request
		26 - Loop Reply
Loop Request Number		
Data		

6-20 *(Cont.)*
MOP Messages

MOP Boot Remote Console Message		
Message Code		Code = 6
Verification Code		4 or 8 Bytes
Processor		Which Processor to Boot?
Control Flags		Use requestor as server?
Device ID		
System Software Length		Normal or maintenance?
System Software Name		
Script Software ID		CMIP Scripts
MOP ID Remote Console Messages		
Message Code		5 - Request ID
		7 - Response
Reserved		
Receipt Number		Identifies requests
Other Info Type		1 - MOP Version
		2 - Functions Supported
		3 - Current Console User
		4 - Console Reservation Timer
		5 - Console Command Size
		6 - Console Response Size
		7 - Hardware Address
		9 - Node ID
		10 - System Time
		11 - Node Name
		100 - Communication Device
		200 - Software Running Now
		300 - System Processor

6-20 *(Cont.)*
MOP Messages

	400 - Data Link Protocol	
	401 - Data Link Buffer Size	
	Other Info Length	
Other Info Value		
Other Info Type		
Other Info Length		
Other Info Value		

MOP Counters Messages		
Message Code		9 - Request Counters
		11 - Response
Receipt Number		
Counters		Data Link Specific

MOP Console Reservation Messages		
Message Code		13 - Reserve Console
		15 - Release
Verification Code		Only for Reservation

MOP Console Command Message		
Message Code		Code = 17
Control Flags		Insert Break?
Command Data		Optional

MOP Console Response Message		
Message Code		Code = 19
Control Flags		Command or Response Lost
Command Data		Optional

6-20 *(Cont.)*
MOP Messages

the boot command, must be done on the console of a device. The console commands thus form the basis for other operations such as remote booting.

Next is the console reservation command, allowing a network management device to "reserve" the console for future use. The same message has a release option. Notice the verification code—this is a password-like mechanism. It does not provide security, but is used so a node does not mistakenly attach itself to the wrong remote console.

The remote ID message allows a manager to identify a remote operation. Different parameters can be used to identify which version of MOP and which functions are supported. Other options support things like reserva-

Courtesy of Network General

```
┌DETAIL──────────────────────────────────────────────────────────────┐
│ MOP:  ----- Maintenance Operation Remote Console Protocol -----     │
│ MOP:                                                                │
│ MOP:  Data length = 28                                              │
│ MOP:  Code = 7  (System ID)                                         │
│ MOP:  Reserved      = 0                                             │
│ MOP:  Receipt Number = 0                                           │
│ MOP:                                                                │
│ MOP:  Information Length =  3, Type = 1 (Maintenance Version)       │
│ MOP:     Version Number  = 03                                       │
│ MOP:     ECO Number      = 00                                       │
│ MOP:     User ECO Number = 00                                       │
│ MOP:                                                                │
│ MOP:  Information Length =  2, Type = 2 (Functions)                 │
│ MOP:     Functions Mask (byte 0)  = 00                              │
│ MOP:                     0... .... = not console carrier reservation│
│ MOP:                     .0.. .... = not data link counters         │
│ MOP:                     ..0. .... = not console carrier            │
│ MOP:                     ...0 .... = not boot                       │
│ MOP:                     .... 0... = not multi-block loader         │
│ MOP:                     .... .0.. = not primary loader             │
│ MOP:                     .... ..0. = not dump                       │
│ MOP:                     .... ...0 = not loop                       │
│ MOP:     Functions Mask (byte 1)  = 00                              │
│ MOP:                     0000 0000 = unused bits                    │
│ MOP:                                                                │
│ MOP:  Information Length =  6, Type = 7 (Hardware Address)          │
│ MOP:     Hardware Address = AA0003012280                            │
│ MOP:                                                                │
│ MOP:  Information Length =  1, Type = 100 (Communication Device)    │
│ MOP:     Communication Device = CNA                                 │
│ MOP:                                                                │
└────────────────────Frame 72 of 153─────────────────────────────────┘
                     Use TAB to select windows
 ┌1      ┐┌2 Set ┐    ┌4 Zoom┐┌5     ┐┌6Display┐┌7 Prev┐┌8 Next┐      ┌10 New  ┐
 │ Help  ││  mark│    │  out ││ Menus││options ││ frame││ frame│      │capture │
 └───────┘└──────┘    └──────┘└──────┘└────────┘└──────┘└──────┘      └────────┘
```

6-21 MOP Remote Console

tion timers for reservation request and the types of systems and communication devices being used.

Figure 6-21 shows an example of the remote ID message. The message shows that version 3 of MOP is being used and many of the MOP functions are not supported. It does allow a node to attach itself as the console, but this particular implementation does not support booting other nodes on the

Category	Attribute	Note
MOP Module	Version Number	
	Supported Functions	
	Current State	
Operation Subentity	Operation	Operation being performed
	Address	Data link address of client system
	Client	Client Name
Client Module	Circuit to Use	Default Value = ""
	Addresses	LAN Addresses to Use
	Secondary Loader	File specification of local file for client.
	Tertiary Loader	
	System Image	
	Diagnostic Image	
	Management Image	
	Script File	CMIP Initialization Script
	Phase IV Host Name	
	Phase IV Host Address	
	Phase IV Client Name	
	Phase IV Client Address	
	Dump File	Where to put upline dumps.
	Dump Address	Memory address
	Dump Count	Number of memory units to allocate.
	Verification	Verification string in boot message.

6-22 MOP Management Attributes

network. The message also includes a hardware address and the type of communication device being used.

One special type of console command is the boot command. This message tells a remote node to reboot itself. It indicates which management (CMIP) scripts to use during the boot process and whether to boot in normal or maintenance mode. It also allows the requestor to furnish the operating system to be used during the boot process.

A boot command is one way to specify that a boot operation should be done. Another way is to do it when a node initializes. At that time, the node will broadcast an appeal for help. A node on the subnetwork will then volunteer assistance.

The actual boot process consists of loading into memory at the requesting node. Another version of this is to have a node dump data from memory used for diagnostics. Next, we have the memory load message, indicating

Category	Attribute	Note
Circuit Subentity Module	Simple Name	
	Circuit Type	
	Link Name	Data link service access point
	Retransmit Timer	Default 4 seconds
	UID	
	Create Time	
	Functions	Functions enabled on this circuit
	Load Requests Done	
	Unknown Load Clients	
	Failed Load Requests	
	Dump Requests Done	
	Unknown Clients	
	Failed Dump Requests	

6-22 MOP Management Attributes *(Cont.)*

the node is ready to accept data. The data message is used to transfer loaded data into memory.

To specify what information is needed, the request program message is used. Typically, the remote booting process starts with a very primitive primary loader. This program then loads the secondary loader, followed by a tertiary loader. At this point, the node is almost operational and loads the operating system in. Instead of loading the normal operating system, it is possible to load a management image. The CMIP script, the network management initialization script, is used to set network management parameters such as maximum data packet sizes or retransmission timers.

As with other DNA modules, MOP keeps a variety of different kinds of management information. Figure 6-22 shows the kinds of information kept. For each MOP client, for example, the MOP module keeps information such as which circuit to use, the names of files to use, and any host names and addresses.

For each circuit (subnetwork link), there are the name of the link, the retransmit timer, and a varieties of other counters. This information is presented to show, as in the case of the chart of DDCMP management information, the variety of different counters and parameters available in the DECnet environment. The final chapter of this book on network management will show how this information is made available to the network manager.

CHAPTER 7

LAT

LAT

In previous chapters we examined three different network architectures. The two main architectures, DECnet and OSI, used a common infrastructure up to the transport layer. At the session layer, they split into two separate architectures, each with its own applications.

The third architecture was the Maintenance Operations Protocol. Although MOP is technically part of DECnet, it is a direct user of the data link layer and can operate without the rest of DECnet. An extremely simple protocol consisting of one layer and a set number of messages, MOP is used for downline loading an operating system from a remote node.

In this chapter we examine two additional architectures. We will briefly look at the VAX Cluster, which is used to take a disk drive and make it available to multiple computers simultaneously while preserving the integrity of the data.

We will devote the rest of the chapter to the Local Area Transport (LAT). LAT, like MOP a direct user of the Ethernet, is a protocol intended for a terminal server or other workstation such as a PC to make use of the services of a host.

Figure 7-1 shows a typical Digital configuration. Three workstations and two terminal servers, a work group, share a single Ethernet. A second Ethernet has several minicomputers acting as servers. The two Ethernets are bridged together to form a single extended LAN.

On the backbone system we see three VAX minicomputers. The VAX systems are also connected to a second type of network, the VAX Cluster. The VAX Cluster uses a 70 Mbps data link called the CI Bus to connect minicomputers to Hierarchical Storage Controllers (HSC)—a specialized server for attaching disk drives.

In addition to the CI Bus, the VAX Cluster protocols could be direct users of the Ethernet but at an order-of-magnitude slower speed. Digital is also enhancing the VAX cluster architecture to use FDDI-based backbones. No

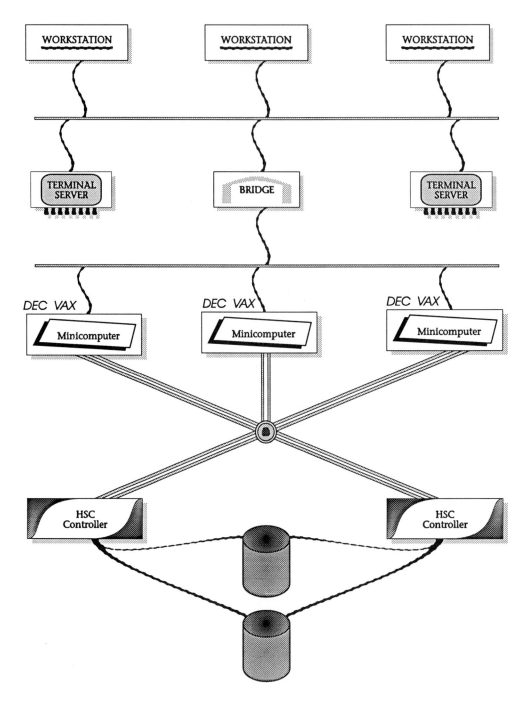

7-1 DEC Network Configuration

matter what the subnetwork, the cluster architecture does the same thing—allows several minicomputers to share a single disk drive.

The HSC controllers are each connected to two disk drives. The two disk drives are in turn dual ported to multiple controllers, providing fault tolerance. The data are shadowed—that is, written simultaneously on two different disk drives in case of failures.

A distributed lock manager running on the VAX systems is used to coordinate access to the data on the HSC controllers. The combination of remote access to data and the lock manager plus a few incidental services form the VAX Cluster.

To the user, each of the different VAX systems looks the same—they all have the same data. Whether a workstation or a terminal user, it does not care which of the systems they log on.

The purpose of LAT was originally to solve the problem of which of the cluster computers to log onto. Since they all provide the same data, the user only wants to log onto the computer that is providing the best service at the time. Needless to say, the question of trying to connect to many different hosts has a broader applicability than just to the VAX Cluster, allowing LAT to be used in many other situations besides clusters.

LAT has since been extended to solve other problems. In addition to load balancing, LAT allows a single virtual circuit to be maintained between a terminal server and a host, multiplexing data from several users. This multiplexing feature means less of the subnetwork bandwidth is being used.

The multiplexing aspect of LAT makes it ideal as a platform for the X Windows System and X Windows terminals. An X Windows terminal is a device dedicated to providing X Windows services to the user. The operating systems and applications all reside on servers on the network.

X, by its nature, consists of many asynchronous events. Things like mouse movements, window resizing, and mouse clicks can happen at any time. The X terminal is responsible for packaging these events and sending them to the relevant application, which decides how to interpret the events.

LAT allows several events to be packaged in a single packet and sent over the network, saving network bandwidth, as well as host processing power. If each event gets a separate packet, each packet generates a CPU interrupt. Combining the events allows the host to deal with them all at once.

LAT assumes a LAN-like data link with a very low probability of problems. Things like datagram duplication, excessive delay, bandwidth saturation, and misdelivery are low or very low probability events. Low probability is less than one per hour. Very low is less than one per a very long time (e.g., a year).

LAT requires the following functionality of the data link:

- IEEE 802.2 Type 1 operation
- Multicasting capability

- Specification of source and destination addresses, protocol ID, or type indicator
- 48-bit addresses

Examples of data links that meet these requirements are FDDI and CSMA/CD (Ethernet). Currently, only CSMA/CD is used for the LAT protocols (although FDDI may act as the backbone to bridge two Ethernets together).

LAT is an asymetric master–slave model. This makes the operation of the slave/host simple. LAT assumes an environment where it is a minor client of the LAN: The LAT throughput needed should be much less than the bandwidth of the LAN on which it runs.

There are several important nongoals of LAT:

- no general-purpose transport services
- no security beyond what the LAN provides
- fault-tolerance provided by the underlying LAN

The last nongoal, fault-tolerance, is provided in a minimal respect. LAT allows the use of multiple LAN adapters (and hence multiple LANs). The LAT protocols will try alternative paths in the case of a failure.

The basic characteristic of LAT is that it is timer based: Messages are exchanged periodically based on the timer value. The second characteristic is that messages provide multiplexing: Data from multiple sessions can all share a single message.

LAT divides functionality into masters and slaves. The typical implementation, however, can support both master and slave operation. A terminal server, for example, is typically run in master mode—the user on the terminal wishes to use a program on a host. Occasionally, the host is the master, as when an application wishes to use a printer or modem on the terminal server.

It is possible for a single port on a terminal server to be engaged in several simultaneous sessions. It is up to the particular implementation to decide how to interleave the data. Typically, the user has a hot-key to switch between sessions. The operative question is what happens to data that would have gone on the screen: is it buffered or lost?

There are two main layers in LAT, with an additional sublayer (see Fig. 7-2). The virtual circuit layer maintains a virtual circuit between a master and a slave. It provides the error-free sequential message streams found in other transport layer providers. The session layer is the data transport interface to the user. Its function is to multiplex one or more user sessions onto the underlying shared virtual circuits.

In addition to the virtual circuit and session layers, there are two additional services: the LAT directory service and the slot sublayer. The LAT directory service is responsible for managing service names and ratings.

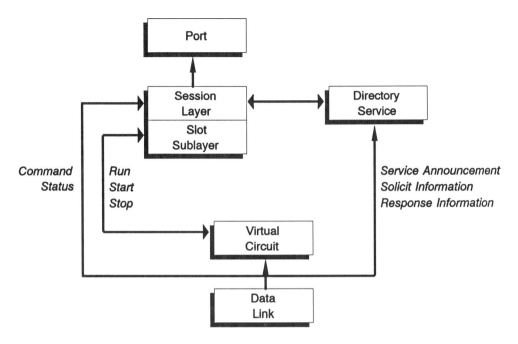

7-2 LAT Component Structure

Names are used to identify LAT resources. LAT provides a directory service that helps translate names to a particular entity (not to be confused with the separate DNA Naming Service in Chapter 5). LAT supports three types of named entities:

- ports
- nodes
- services

A rating is used by the session layer to balance the number of sessions across a set of nodes: If more than one node offers the same service, the session layer is able to pick the one with the best service rating at the time a session is initialized.

This load balancing balances new sessions, not existing sessions. If we initialize a session on a node with a good rating and service subsequently degrades, LAT will not move to a better node. In addition, load balancing is not based on the amount of traffic going to each node; it is based on whatever service rating is broadcast by a particular node.

The LAT directory service operates in two modes:

- In announcement mode the services and their ratings are periodically multicast.
- In solicitation mode an explicit request/response polling is performed.

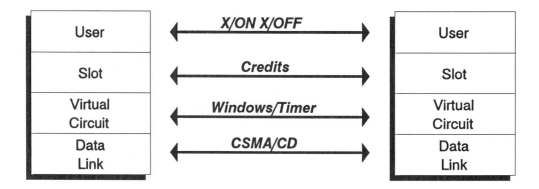

Levels of LAT Flow Control

Announcements are used by masters to construct and update a local cache of services and their ratings. Solicitation is used when a user requests a service not in the cache or when a node intializes. Solicitation may also be used by low-functionality implementations (slave only) that do not wish the burden of listening to periodic announcements.

Flow Control in LAT

The terminal user is a particularly slow user in comparison to other network components, hosts, and servers. Flow control is thus quite important in LAT to avoid large amounts of data from overflowing buffers or saturating devices. Flow control in LAT is provided at several different levels (see Fig. 7-3).

At the lowest level, the underlying Ethernet provides flow control among different users through the CSMA/CD protocols. Too many terminal servers (or any device for that matter) causes excess collisions. As long as we have an appropriate number of nodes, the CSMA/CD protocols arbitrate use of the medium.

The virtual circuit layer arbitrates the flow of data between two nodes. Windows and timers, identical to the TP4 and NSP transport layer functions, make sure the number of packets reaching a device do not overwhelm the buffers.

At the session layer, we see the same token-like mechanism used in the OSI session layer. Here they are called credits. A user or program may only submit a slot of data when it has a credit. If an application is busy, it withholds credits from the user.

At the highest level is the X/ON and X/OFF mechanism. If a user sees too much data, the user can hit the control/s sequence to freeze the screen. This will eventually fill the user's buffers, which will cause the session layer to withhold further credits from its peer.

Virtual Circuit Layer

The virtual circuit layer provides an interface to its user, the slot sublayer. It provides the following services:

- start-up and shutdown of circuits
- reports to the slot layer on circuit quality
- delivery of messages in sequence to the slot sublayer
- verification that messages are addressed to known circuits
- pipelined transmission of messages or a ping-pong acknowledgment
- optional caching of out-of-sequence received messages

Pipelined transmission uses a window-based flow control method. The virtual circuit layer uses data link addresses provided by the LAT directory services.

Normally, the virtual circuit component on the master sends messages to the slave based on a timer. The slave responds to the message with a message of its own. Under a few circumstances, it is possible for a slave to send unsolicited messages.

Virtual circuit overhead is minimized because there is only one circuit for a particular master–slave pairing, instead of one for each application–user pairing. Further, messages are exchanged on a regular, periodic basis. Polling and frequent interrupts are both minimized. Another efficiency mechanism is that both virtual circuit control and user data can share a single message.

The virtual circuit message is an eight-octet header consisting of the circuit ID and sequencing information. This is followed by a series of slots. Each slot has a 4-byte slot header and data (see Fig. 7-4).

We can see in the header that in addition to the sequence numbers (and piggybacked acknowledgment) there are several flags. The flags, in addition to identifying the message type, indicate whether the master or the slave sent the message. The response requested flag, discussed in more detail later, indicates that a slave has more data to send and therefore wants the master to send it another message. Remember that the slave can only send data in response to a master's message.

The virtual circuit layer has three types of messages. The start and stop messages are used for setup and tear down. The run message is used to convey state and session data. It is possible for a particular master–slave combination have multiple virtual circuits. If so, a circuit name is used to distinguish them.

The start message is shown in Figure 7-5. Before the first session can be initialized between two nodes, the virtual circuit layer has to initialize the underlying circuit. The start message never carries data slots (these belong in the run messages). It does, however, contain a variety of pieces of data

Message Type Flag		0: Run Message
		1: Start Message
		2: Stop Message
Master Flag		Set on messages from master.
Response Requested Flag		
Number of Slots		
Destination Circuit ID		
Source Circuit ID		
Message Sequence Number		
Message ACK Number		

7-4
LAT Virtual Circuit
Layer Header

used to negotiate the parameters for a session. The master initially sends the start message, then the slave responds with its own message.

The maximum sessions parameter is an example of a negotiated parameter. Each session requires CPU resources. In addition, too many sessions competing for an underlying virtual circuit means each session only gets a limited number of slot transmission opportunities. Limiting the number of sessions on one virtual circuit is a fairness mechanism.

The master circuit timer indicates how often the master will send a message (and thus how often the slave will have to respond). A typical value for this timer is 80 ms. If the extended Ethernet uses wide-area bridges, 80 ms may not be enough time for a packet to be sent and a response received before the timers expire. In a wide-area environment, the manager may set the timer up to its maximum of 200 ms. This degrades throughput, however.

The actual data in LAT is sent using the run message (see Fig. 7-6). The run message contains, in addition to message sequence numbers, zero or more slots. Zero slots would be used in the case of a tickler packet to keep a circuit alive in times of inactivity. Each slot contains data for a different session. Slots are required to use an even number of bytes, and are padded if they have an uneven number of bytes. The slot header contains a destination and source ID, the slot length, and credits.

Once the last session on a virtual circuit is gone, the virtual circuit is dismantled using the stop message (see Fig. 7-7). The stop message includes a reason indicator but no data slots. In addition to orderly termination, a stop message might be sent in the case of abnormalities, such as excessive network problems or protocol errors (i.e., an unknown session ID is received in a slot).

Header Flags		Message Type = 1
Number of Slots		Always 0
Destination Circuit ID		Nonzero from slave
Source Circuit ID		Non-zero always
Message Sequence Number		
Message Ack Number		
Receive PDU Size		
Protocol Version		6
Protocol ECO		0
Maximum Sessions		Lowest wins
Max Window Size		Number of PDUs
Master Circuit Timer		In 10-ms intervals
Keep Alive Timer		0 means no ticklers sent
Retransmit Limit		In seconds before aborting
Product Type		
Product Major Version		
Product Minor Version		
Slave Name Length		
Slave Node Name		
Master Name Length		
Master Node Name		
Node Description Length		
Node Description		
Node UID		
Node ID		
Parameter Code		None defined
Parameter Length		
Parameter Data		

7-5
LAT Virtual Circuit
Start Message

For each circuit, the virtual circuit layer keeps a virtual circuit block (see Fig. 7-8). The block is used to keep track of information such as the current sequence number and the value of timers. In addition to the timers, the virtual circuit block keeps two important flags. The data waiting flag (DWF) is set by the slot sublayer whenever it has slots that are ready to be packaged. The response requested flag (RRF) is set by the slave to indicate to

Header Flags	Message Type = 0
Number of Slots	
Destination Circuit ID	
Source Circuit ID	
Message Sequence Number	
Message ACK Number	
Destination Session ID	
Source Session ID	
Slot Length	
Slot Type and Credits	
Slot-Specific Data	
Pad	If Slot length is odd
Destination Session ID	
Source Session ID	
Slot Length	
Slot Type and Credits	
Slot-Specific Data	
Pad	

7-6
LAT Virtual Circuit
Run Message

the master that it has data to send. The two flags interact to force the transmission of virtual circuit messages.

The Data Waiting Flag

The data waiting flag is a circuit layer flag. It indicates user data from the slot sublayer is available for encapsulation. The master sets the data waiting flag whenever it receives a message from the slave with the RRF flag set (even if the message is out of sequence). The master also sets this flag if it has data waiting to send. The DWF flag is cleared whenever there are no more slot sublayer buffers. The slave also sets the flag if it has data from the slot sublayer. Note that the slave will never receive a message from the master with the RRF flag set.

If slots arrive faster than the virtual circuit message transfer, the data waiting flag is always set. Otherwise, at some point the circuit becomes

Header Flags		Message Type = 2
Number of Slots		Always 0
Destination Circuit ID		
Source Circuit ID		0
Message Sequence Number		
Message ACK Number		
Disconnect Reason Number		0 means no reason
Reason Length		
Reason Text		

7-7
LAT Virtual Circuit
Stop Message

idle. When the data waiting flag is set on the master, it stuffs as many slots as it can fit into a message and passes it off to the data link layer. It does this until the data waiting flag is clear, there are no transmit buffers, or the maximum window size is achieved.

Balancing the Circuit

Normally the LAT operates in unbalanced mode: The master sends messages every time the circuit timer expires; the slave immediately acknowledges. Note that the master always sends; this allows the slave to send any data it has. Since the slave in normal, unbalanced mode cannot send data on its own, it uses the acknowledgment to send data.

If there are no data to send, however, unbalanced mode is a waste of resources. If the slave sees it has no data to send, that it has acknowledged everything from the master, it will send a balancing message. This puts the circuit into balanced mode and no more data goes across the link.

In balanced mode, either node can send. This means that if the slave gets data, it can send unsolicited messages up to the current window size. It is possible for the slave to send several balancing messages in a row without the data waiting flag ever becoming set.

When a balancing message is sent out, it usually does not have to be acknowledged. This outstanding message, however, takes up queue space on the slave. To get the resources freed, the slave can set the response requested flag. This forces an acknowledgment from the master, thus freeing up resources on the slave. The slave sets the RRF flag in three cases:

- The free buffer queue is empty, and a response is needed to free up resources.
- The maximum window size is about to be reached.

Circuit Name	
Node Block Reference	Pointer to node block for destination
Path Block Reference	Last path over which a message was sent
Master Flag Bit	When set indicates this node is the master
Response Request Flag	Response requested from the other node: set by slave
Remote Circuit ID	Reference to the destination address's circuit block
Local Circuit ID	
Next Transmit	Next sequence number (modulo 256)
Last ACK	Last sequence number received
Data Waiting Flag	Usage depends on whether master or slave
Low Transmit	Lowest unacked message transmitted
High Transmit	Highest unacked message transmitted
Slave Retransmit Timer	Set when a message is sent with a response requested flag; if expires, all unacked messages are resent
Circuit Timer	Master only; used for sending new messages not for unacked prior messages
Master Retransmit Timer	Used for retransmission of unacked messages
Circuit Lost Timer	Initialized to the retransmit limit. Used to decide when to give up a circuit due to no acknowledgments after the retransmit limit.
Virtual Circuit Quality	Acceptable or unacceptable
Transmit Buffer Free Queue	Number of buffers
Unacked Transmit Queue	List of unacked messages
Maximum Window Size	Default 1; number of unacknowledged messages possible
Current Window Size	
Receive List	Messages awaiting delivery because out of sequence

7-8 Virtual Circuit Block

- The data waiting flag is set; another message is needed from the master to send the slave slots.

Timers

The master uses the master circuit timer to control the retransmission policy. It is possible for the slave in its LAT directory service messages to give an advertised circuit timer. The master can, if it wishes, use this.

Retransmit timers always set to value of 1 second. When a timer expires, the master will initiate a path test. If necessary, it will also select another path then retransmit the message at the head of the unacknowledged queue.

The keep alive timer ensures that a virtual circuit is operational when there are no slots to transmit. When the keep alive timer expires on the master, the data waiting flag is set, forcing a run message to the slave.

If the circuit lost timer expires, it is up to the session layer to decide what to do. For example, the session layer may stop the virtual circuit and tell the user or it may report the quality problem to the user and let it decide.

LAT Traffic

Figures 7-9 and 7-10 show LAT data on an Ethernet. Figure 7-9 shows the simple nature of LAT, consisting of a series of data messages once the circuit is up and running. The summary portion of Figure 7-9 shows the virtual circuit header. The message is a run (data) message, and the slave has not set the response requested flag. The message contains only a single data slot.

Figure 7-10 shows both the virtual circuit and slot layers of a LAT packet. Notice there are sequence numbers for both sides of the conversation. The single slot includes 8 bytes of data, but no credits are being transmitted.

Session Layer and Slot Sublayer

The slot sublayer is transparent to the user. It is responsible for session state transitions, flow control and buffer management, and multiplexing. When the session layer has data to send to its peer, it submits the data to the slot sublayer. The slot sublayer, in turn, buffers the slot until the virtual circuit layer is ready for it.

The session layer is the interface to the LAT service. It allows the user to

- establish and terminate a session
- do data transfer
- interface to the LAT directory service

Session establishment in LAT is based on names. We assume the user knows the name, either a priori or through the LAT directory service. Once a name is found, the session layer will use the LAT directory service to find the node with the best service rating. A slave in LAT cannot initiate a session, but it can send out a connection solicitation.

The session layer provides the user with three channels of communications:

- data A
- data B
- attention

```
SUMMARY──Delta T──DST────────SRC────
M    1                DECnet0032D0←DEC    059DF4  LAT C Data D=3D01 S=7C02 NR=9C N
     2    0.0024  DEC    059DF4←DECnet0032D0  LAT R Data D=7C02 S=3D01 NR=C9 N
     3    0.0033  DEC    059DF4←DECnet0032D0  LAT R Data D=7C02 S=3D01 NR=C9 N
     4    0.0742  DECnet0032D0←DEC    059DF4  LAT C Data D=3D01 S=7C02 NR=9E N
     5    0.0019  DEC    059DF4←DECnet0032D0  LAT R Data D=7C02 S=3D01 NR=CA N
     6    0.0033  DEC    059DF4←DECnet0032D0  LAT R Data D=7C02 S=3D01 NR=CA N
     7    0.0745  DECnet0032D0←DEC    059DF4  LAT C Data D=3D01 S=7C02 NR=A0 N
     8    0.0017  DEC    059DF4←DECnet0032D0  LAT R Data D=7C02 S=3D01 NR=CB N
     9    0.0782  DECnet0032D0←DEC    059DF4  LAT C Data D=3D01 S=7C02 NR=A1 N
┌DETAIL──────────────────────────────────────────────────────────
 LAT:  ───── Local Area Transport ─────
 LAT:
 LAT:  Flags and type = 02
 LAT:      0000 00.. = Data message
 LAT:      .... ..1. = To host
 LAT:      .... ...0 = No response requested
 LAT:  Number of entries = 1
 LAT:    Destination link ID = 3D01
 LAT:        Source link ID = 7C02
                    ──Frame 1 of 10──
                Use TAB to select windows
┌───┐┌─────┐      ┌─────┐┌─────┐┌───────┐┌──────┐┌──────┐      ┌───────┐
│1  ││2 Set│      │4 Zoom││5    ││6Disply││7 Prev││8 Next│      │10 New │
│Help││ mark│      │  in  ││Menus││options││frame ││frame │      │capture│
└───┘└─────┘      └─────┘└─────┘└───────┘└──────┘└──────┘      └───────┘
```

7-9 LAT Traffic

```
┌DETAIL────────────────────────────────────────────────────────────
 LAT:  ───── Local Area Transport ─────
 LAT:
 LAT:  Flags and type = 02
 LAT:      0000 00.. = Data message
 LAT:      .... ..1. = To host
 LAT:      .... ...0 = No response requested
 LAT:  Number of entries = 1
 LAT:    Destination link ID = 3D01
 LAT:        Source link ID = 7C02
 LAT:        Sequence number = C9
 LAT:  Acknowlegement number = 9C
 LAT:
 LAT:  ───── Local Area Transport Data to Host (Entry 0) ─────
 LAT:
 LAT:  Destination sublink ID = 01
 LAT:        Source sublink ID = 21
 LAT:  Data length = 8
 LAT:  Type and credit = 00
 LAT:      0000 .... = Data
 LAT:      .... 0000 = 0 Credits
                    ──Frame 1 of 10──
                Use TAB to select windows
┌───┐┌─────┐      ┌─────┐┌─────┐┌───────┐┌──────┐┌──────┐      ┌───────┐
│1  ││2 Set│      │4 Zoom││5    ││6Disply││7 Prev││8 Next│      │10 New │
│Help││ mark│      │  out ││Menus││options││frame ││frame │      │capture│
└───┘└─────┘      └─────┘└─────┘└───────┘└──────┘└──────┘      └───────┘
```

7-10 LAT Slots

Both data A and B are flow controlled. Typically, data A would have regular data and data B would have status and control information. The attention channel is not flow controlled and is only for small amounts of information.

The actual use of the different slots is up to the user programs. LAT defines service classes that contain the semantics of the information in the different slots (e.g., the fact that a control/Y is an interrupt instead of a redisplay).

Figure 7-11 shows the format of the three different data slots. Notice that all three have an identical format, with the constraint that credits are ignored on the attention slot.

Session Level Flow Control

Flow control at the virtual circuit layer was based on a window scheme and acknowledgment timers. At the session layer, it is based on credits. A user cannot send unless it has a credit—the session interface will reject the attempt. If it is rejected, it is up to the local port to implement some flow control policy. For example, the terminal port could beep the terminal, thus signaling the user that data are being thrown away.

Up to 15 credits may be extended at any time. As soon as slot data are given to the user, the credit should be returned. The credits ensure that if more than one user has data to send over a single virtual circuit, the slots are fairly allocated. A typical way to provide fairness is to limit each session to one slot. This guarantees each session one slot in the outgoing message. Just before the message is submitted to the virtual circuit layer, any additional slots are added. The additional slots are on a sort of standby basis.

Two other mechanisms are used to ensure fairness. First, when a circuit transmit buffer becomes available, loading of slots starts at different sessions. This prevents a session from being permanently frozen out when there are many sessions sharing a circuit. Second, the slot size is limited. This causes credits to be used up faster, allowing more sessions to be accommodated.

Within a virtual circuit message, the attention slots always go first, followed by the data slots. Note that the data slots are phase-locked: within a particular session data A and data B appear in the order the user submitted them. If we get an illegal slot (a gross violation), we terminate the whole virtual circuit and all sessions that use it.

Other Slot Types

Figure 7-12 shows the start slot used to set up a session between two ports. This slot, contained in the virtual circuit run message, is sent after a virtual

Data A Slot		
Destination Session ID		
Source Session ID		
Slot Length		
Slot Type and Credits		Slot Type = 0
Slot Data		Up to 256 bytes
Pad		
Data B Slot		
Destination Session ID		
Source Session ID		
Slot Length		
Slot Type and Credits		Slot Type = 10
Slot Data		Up to 256 bytes
Pad		
Attention Slot		
Destination Session ID		
Source Session ID		
Slot Length		
Slot Type (No Credits)		Slot Type = 11
Slot Data		Up to 256 bytes
Pad		

7-11
LAT Data Slots

circuit has been initialized. The start slot contains a series of names for the desired service and the user. It also contains the minimum size for a data buffer and attention buffer, as well as the connection solicitation ID. The connection solicitation process, used to reserve a service, will be examined in more detail later.

The other two slot types are shown in Figure 7-13. The reject slot is used to reject a session. The stop slot is used for orderly termination of a session. Both use a reason code to indicate why a session was terminated.

Once the session is established, each session has a session control block, maintained at each of the two nodes communicating. The block (see Fig. 7-14) keeps track of local and remote credits. It also contains flags indicating if there are data ready to send and if there is an attention buffer. By consulting the session control block, a node is able to decide whether that

Destination Session ID		
Source Session ID		
Slot Length		
Slot Type and Credits		Slot Type = 9
Service Class		
Min Data Buffer Size		
Connect Solicitation ID		
Min Attention Buffer Size		
Service Name Length		
Object Service Name		
Object Port Name Length		
Object Port Name		
Object Service PW Length		
Object Service Password		
Subject Port Length		
Subject Port Name		

7-12

LAT Start Slot

particular session needs to send data and, if so, the maximum size allowed for transmission.

Service Classes

Service classes extend the functionality of LAT by defining the semantics within a data B and attention slot. Two service classes have been defined. Service class 1 is for interactive terminals; class 2 is for loopback and testing.

The service class information is contained in the start slot. It is up to the slave node's session layer to deliver the connection request to the appropriate subsystem. The question of the service class is transparent to both the virtual circuit and the session layers. This concept is equivalent to the object in the Phase IV Session Control layer—an indicator of the type of application that should receive this particular session request.

Reject Slot		
Destination Session ID		
Source Session ID		
Slot Length		
Slot Type & Reason Number		Slot Type = 12
Supplemental Status Information		
Status		
Pad		

Stop Slot		
Destination Session ID		
Source Session ID		
Slot Length		
Slot Type & Reason Number		Slot Type = 13
Supplemental Status Information		
Status		
Pad		

Slot Reason Codes
Service in Use
No Such Service
Unknown Reason
Service Disabled
User Requested
Service Not Offered by Port
Node Shutdown
Unknown Port
Illegal Slot Received
Invalid Password
Invalid Service Class
Entry Not in Queue
Insufficient Resources
Immediate Access Rejected
Access Denied
Corrupted Solicit Request

7-13
LAT Utility Slots

Remote Session Name	
Local Session Name	
Remote Session ID	
Local Session ID	
Remote Credits	
Local Credits	
Data Ready Flag	
Receive Buffer Queue	
Transmit Buffer Queue	
Attention Buffer Ready	Semaphore indicating if any attention buffers are available; user can supply more
Maximum Attention Buffer Size	Maximum that remote node can handle; parameter is set in the start slot at the beginning of the session
Maximum Data Buffer Size	For remote node

7-14 Session Block

Service Class 1

We can think of an interactive terminal session on a terminal server as having three databases:

- the local physical port characteristics
- the remote physical and status characteristics
- the current status attributes

Examples of the physical port characteristics include the receive and transmit speed, the parity type, the frame size, whether a bell is sent on discard of data and the presence of modem control. Status information includes things like errors (framing, parity, overrun) and the status of the session (are data passed through?). All changes to this type of information are done through the use of the data B channel. The service class 1 has extended the data B to include two subtypes: the set and report slots.

To indicate which type of subslot is being used, bits 5 and 6 of the control flags in the slot header are used. Bit 5 set is a set slot, bit 6 set is a report slot.

In addition to the data B slot extension, the service class extension includes a definition of the attention slot. If bit 5 is set in the attention slot header, it indicates the node should abort processing the current data A or data B slot, flush all receive queues, and return any credits. If bit 4 is set in the attention slot header, it indicates a modem poll. The current DCE and DTE states should be sent in an attention slot.

The start slot has been enhanced with a set of flags that show which DCE and DTE circuits are being used, if this is a modem-controlled device, if dial up access is permitted, and other relevant communication information.

Directory Access Control

Each named object in LAT (ports, nodes, services) has an optional access control list as part of the LAT directory service. When a request is made to the LAT directory service, the user supplies an identifier list (IDL). The requestor's IDL is compared with the object's access control list (ACL). Each list consists of a set of up to 256 groups. Each item in the list is a group number. The ACL or IDL is up to 256 bits long, each bit represents a group. If the bit is 0, the group is missing; if the bit is 1, it is present in the list.

The access control process is not a security mechanism. Instead, it is a way of partitioning services and other resources among different groups. This way, a user in one group has no need to see services intended for another group.

As an example, assume there are two work groups of users sharing a large LAN. Some resources are specifically intended for each of the work groups. Others are LAN-wide resources. Each service is then put into one of these three categories. A particular user is a member of two groups in the ID list: the LAN-wide group and one of the two work groups. This partitioning means that when a user requests a directory listing, the user does not have to see irrelevant resources in the listing.

A service is always the object of a request, not the initiator. It therefore only has an ACL. A node or a port, on the other hand, may be both the object and the requestor. It may therefore have both an ACL and an IDL. The port list must be a subset of the node's list since access control will first be tested at the node level for establishment of the virtual circuit.

Figure 7-15 shows which type of list is included in which LAT message. In a start slot, the user includes an IDL. The session service will compare the IDL with the target service's ACL to see if there is a match. The other message types shown in Figure 7-15 are used in the connection solicitation and advertisement process to filter out illegal or unnecessary requests for a particular user or service.

Lists are used to filter directories as well as provide access control to services. For example, a master node will ignore a solicit information or service announcement from slaves belonging to other groups.

Connection Solicitation

An interactive terminal is one with a human being behind it. Another kind of terminal on a terminal server is the application terminal. This one has

Message	Type of List
Response Information	ACL
Service Announcement	ACL
Solicit Information	IDL
Command	IDL
Start Slot	IDL

7-15

Use of ACLs and IDLs

an application driving it. A typical example is the printer. When an application terminal is being used on a terminal server, the roles of the host and the terminal server are reversed: The terminal server becomes the slave and the host becomes the master (see Fig. 7-16).

Under normal circumstances, only the master can solicit a connection. The mechanism in this section describes how the slave can let the master know it wishes to start a session. Related to session solicitation is the concept of queuing for services.

To see how the concepts are related we can look at a typical scenario. The master tries to access a service on the slave. The service is in use and is thus unavailable. LAT allows the request to be queued. When the resource becomes available again, it is up to the slave to let the master know that it can attempt to start a session again.

When a request for a resource is submitted, it will be either accepted, rejected, or queued. Every request submitted by a master contains a request ID. If the request is queued, a request ID is put into the queue. Along with the request ID, the object (slave) returns a queue entry identifier.

The requestor can then do one of three things: It can wait until the object becomes available. It can request queue information, either for this particular entry or for the whole queue. It can cancel the entry.

The process of solicitation and queuing is managed by the command and status messages. These messages are composed directly by the session layer. Instead of being put into a slot, they are submitted directly to the virtual circuit layer where they are sent as datagrams. This makes sense since there may not be a virtual circuit in existence to the target node (and in any case, if there were, slots would not work since they must be identified with a session).

The command message is used to solicit a connection (see Fig. 7-17). Solicitation can begin with either the slave or master. For the first exchange, it would typically be sent by a master, requesting access to a queued service. The object would send back the request ID along with the entry ID (the position in the queue). Note that command and status messages are simply for queue information and the availability of services. To start the service,

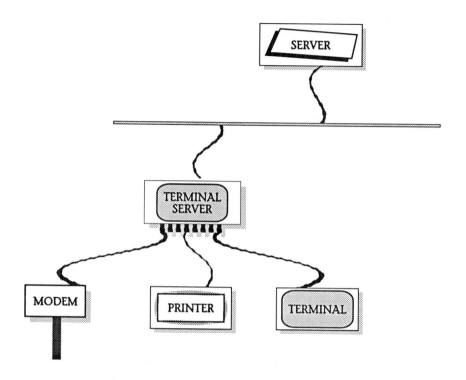

7-16 Reverse LAT

we will still need start and stop slots (with the associated virtual circuit messages underneath).

A typical exchange might be as follows:

- Master requests service (command).
- Slave returns entry ID (status).
- Master requests status (command).
- Slave returns status (status).
- Slave informs node service is available (status).
- Master sends start message to start session.

Queuing for services can be on a service basis or on a particular port.

Note that the requestor is able to examine the whole queue; there is no access control to prevent the user from seeing who the other queue members are. Deleting an entry can only be done by the requesting node (or the local network management).

When a status command is returned, it contains the position of the request within the queue. These are approximate positions; in the time it

Header Flags		Message Type = 12
Protocol Format		802.3, Ethernet, Both
High Protocol Version		LAT Version
Low Protocol Version		
Current Protocol Version		6
Current Protocol ECO		
Receive PDU Size		
Request Identifier		To correlate replies
Entry Identifier		From previous command
Command Type		0: solicit non-queued access
		1: Solicit queued access
		2: Cancel queue entry
		3: Send single entry
		4: Send status of queue
		5: Send multiple
Command Modifier		0: send periodically
		1: if depth changes
Object Node Name Length		
Object Node Name		
Subject Groups Length		
Subject Groups		
Subject Node Name Length		
Subject Node Name		
Node UID		16 byte node UID
Node ID		6 byte (IEEE) ID
Subject Port Name Length		
Subject Port Name		
Subject Description Length		
Subject Description		
Object Service Name Length		
Object Service Name		
Object Port Name Length		
Object Port Name		
Parameter Code		0: End of List
		1: Service Class
Parameter Length		
Parameter Value		

7-17
LAT Connection
Solicitation Command

takes the message to be processed, sent, and received the queue could have changed.

If a node sends multiple status messages, the subject of the request may return all status information in a single status message. The requesting node must be prepared to filter the entries. If the subject node returns more status information than is requested; the requesting node must again be prepared to filter.

Part of the command message includes two status request indicators. The user can request a status message be sent

- periodically
- whenever the queue depth changes

The command and status process maintains five timers:

- The multiple status timer is the gap between individual status messages so they are not bunched close together.
- The status report timer indicates how long to wait in between periodic status messages.
- The response timer is how to wait before retransmitting a message to which there is no answer.
- Command retry timer indicates how long to wait before giving up on retransmission attempts and giving up the connection request.
- Status retry timer indicates how a service will keep a resource available after sending the status message to the requestor.

Figure 7-18 shows the format of the status response message. Note that there may be several different entries in a status message. It is up to the requesting node to filter out those entries in which it is not interested.

LAT Directory Service

The session layer translates a service name request into a node name that provides that service. The virtual circuit layer will then use the LAT directory service to translate that node name into a 48-bit data link address.

The LAT directory service is based on a multicast capability, which is responsive to LAN topology changes. The LAT directory service uses three types of messages:

- The service announcement is multicast by slave nodes.
- The solicit information message is either multicast or physically addressed.
- The response information message is physically addressed to the master that did the solicitation.

Header Flags		Message Type = 13	
Protocol Format		802.3, Ethernet, Both	
High Protocol Version		LAT Version	
Low Protocol Version			
Current Version			
Current Protocol ECO			
Receive PDU Size			
Status Report Timer		For retransmissions	
Number of Entries			
Node UID		16 byte node UID	
Node ID		6 byte (IEEE) ID	
Subject Node Name Length			
Subject Node Name			
Pad			
Entry Length		Length of this entry	
Entry Status		0: No additional information	
		1: Request already queued	
		2: Entry accepted	
		3: Periodic status not available	
		4: Queue-depth status not available	
		7: Solicitation rejected	
Entry Error		Reject reason	
Request Identifier			
Entry Identifier			
Elapsed Queue Time			
Minimum Queue Position			
Maximum Position			
Object Service Name Length			
Object Service Name			
Object Port Name Length			
Object Port Name			
Subject Description Length			
Subject Description			
Pad			
Parameter Code			
Parameter Length			
Parameter			

7-18
LAT Status Message

It is possible for an LAT implementation not to support the LAT directory service and to enter all information manually. Needless to say, this means the dynamic load balancing does not work, and we cannot really tell if a service is even working. The solicitation and response are for nodes which do not listen to multicasts—slaves and dumb masters.

Service Ratings

Each instance of a service offered on a node gets a service rating. Remember, a particular service can be offered on different nodes. Thus, each node–service pair gets its own rating. A rating can range from 0 to 255. A rating of 0 means the node is highly likely to reject sessions, a rating of 255 means the node is highly likely to accept sessions.

It is up to each node to decide what the semantics of a node mean and how to assign ratings. Ratings can be static (i.e., 0 when service is gone, 255 when it is up) or dynamic. An example of a dynamic rating is on the VMS operating system, where the service rating includes factors such as the CPU type, the number of login slots, and the amount of idle CPU time.

Multilink nodes and the LAT directory service

The LAT directory service will detect the set of different data link addresses a node uses. It then recommends to other LAT components which of several available working paths to use. The LAT directory service also tests data link paths when they fail.

Note that this is not a routing protocol: The Cartesian product of all data link station addresses forms the set of available paths between two nodes. Each of these is treated as a point-to-point, equal-cost link. Paths are then chosen on a round-robin basis.

When to use a new path depends on which component is transmitting. The circuit layer will select a new path every time the circuit timer or retransmit timer expires. The session layer will select a new path whenever a connection solicitation is transmitted.

If a component suspects a path is not functioning, it will tell the LAT directory service. The LAT directory service will eliminate its use by other LAT components and then test the path.

Advertisement

A slave will advertise its state in three circumstances:

- on initialization
- on expiration of the periodic slave multicast timer
- on shutdown

During the periodic multicasts, the advertisement includes a message incarnation field (see Fig. 7-19). If any information has changed, the message incarnation field is incremented, and the bits in the change fields flag are set. At shutdown, a node will try to send at least two messages, with the shutting down status set in the node status field.

When a master receives an advertisement, it first compares the incoming access control list to the ID list on the node. If there is a match, the message is added to the cache. If the message is from a new node, a new node entry is created. The source address and the address of the local LAN controller are added as the first possible address path. When subsequent messages are received, the message incarnation field is checked to see if there have been any changes.

If the cache is limited in size or if there is no cache, the solicit information message asks for information on a node or on a service (see Fig. 7-20). The solicitation can be physically addressed if the node and path are known or can be multicast out of all of the node's LAN ports. The solicitation includes a solicitation identifier, used for correlating incoming responses. The response timer indicates how long a node will wait. The solicitation also includes the name of a target node and the name of the desired service. Either of these names might be blank.

The response to the solicitation includes information on the node and optional information on one or all services. It is possible that a node may get multiple solicitations if there are multiple paths. The node should respond to each one separately; the requestor will use the multiple responses to build a list of working paths.

Each solicitation has an identifier. This ID is used on all copies of the solicitation and is used by the requestor to correlate incoming responses. Figure 7-21 shows the format of the solicitation response. Note that when a solicitation is sent to a multicast address, it is possible that several nodes will attempt to respond. To prevent excess collisions on the LAN medium (or deafness at the requesting node), each responder will delay a random period of time, known as jitter.

A solicitation can include a null or nonnull node name. It can also include a null or nonnull service name. Finally, it can be multicast or physically addressed. Whether a node should answer or not is shown in Figure 7-22.

Directory Caches

Caches are typically limited in size. If necessary, the cache entries are eliminated in the following order:

- Eliminate those that have definitely timed out: The circuit retransmit limit was reached on an active virtual circuit.

Header Flags		Message Type = 10
Protocol Format		802.3, Ethernet, Both
High Protocol Version		LAT Version
Low Protocol Version		
Current Version		6
Current Protocol ECO		
Receive PDU Size		
Message Incarnation Number		Indicates changes
Change Flags		0: Node group codes
		1: Node description
		2: Service names
		3: Service ratings
		4: Service descriptions
		5: Service classes
		6: Node UID or ID
		7: Other parameters
Master Circuit Timer		
Node Multicast Timer		
Node Status		Will accept sessions?
Node Groups		
Node Name Length		
Node Name		
Node UID		
Node ID		
Node Description Length		
Node Description		
Service Name Count		
Service Rating		
Service Name Length		
Service Name		
Service Name Description Length		
Service Name Description		
Service Rating		
Service Name Length		
Service Name		
Service Name Description Length		
Service Name Description		
Node Service Length		
Node Service Classes		Classes supported

Header Flags		Message Type = 15
Protocol Format		802.3, Ethernet, Both
High Protocol Version		LAT Version
Low Protocol Version		
Current Protocol Version		6
Current Protocol ECO		
Receive PDU Size		
Solicit Identifier		
Response Timer		Time node will wait
Destination Node Name Length		
Destination Node Name		
Source Groups Length		Maximum Value of 32
Source Node Groups		
Source Node Name Length		
Source Node Name		
Node UID		
Node ID		
Service Name Length		
Service Name		Specific Service Name
Parameters		None defined

7-20
LAT Solicitation
Message

- Eliminate those that may have timed out: No service announcement has been reached for more than five times the slave multicast interval.
- Eliminate those nodes that indicate they are shutting down.
- Eliminate reachable nodes that have no virtual circuits currently operating.

If after purging all this the cache is still full, the node should ignore LAT directory service messages. Note that if a virtual circuit is connected, cache information must be maintained for that node.

Header Flags		Message Type = 15
Protocol Format		802.3, Ethernet, Both
High Protocol Version		LAT Version
Low Protocol Version		
Current Protocol Version		6
Current Protocol ECO		
Receive PDU Size		
Solicit Identifier		
Response Status		Does node offer service?
Source Node Status		Slave, Master, Disabled?
Node Multicast Timer		
Destination Node Name Length		
Destination Node Name		
Source Groups Length		Maximum value of 32
Source Node Groups		
Source Node Name Length		
Source Node Name		
Node UID		
Node ID		
Source Description Length		
Source Node Description		
Service Count		

7-21
LAT Solicitation
Response

Summary

LAT is a direct user of the Ethernet service and is thus limited to the boundaries of an Ethernet or extended Ethernet. LAT is composed of two types of nodes: the master and the slave. The slave is typically a general-purpose host; the master is a terminal server, an X Windows Terminal, or a workstation with the LAT protocols (i.e., a PC running DECnet/DOS).

Object Name	Node Name	Multicast Address	Physical Address
Null	Null	Any node may respond; services optional	Must respond with node; services optional
	Nonnull	Named node must respond; services optional	Respond if node name correct; services optional
Nonnull	Null	Respond if you offer service	Respond with node information and either the service or a not-offered indication
	Nonnull	Must respond with information or error message (service not offered)	If node name is correct respond to service

7-22 Responses to Solicitations

A slave has a series of applications, known as services in LAT. Each service is named and includes a service rating and multiple nodes can provide the same service. The LAT directory service on a master node keeps track of available services, and logs the user onto the service provider with the best service rating at the time.

LAT is timer based; a master will periodically send a message with zero or more slots. The periodic message exchange and multiplexing of multiple sessions into a single message is important for a host, reducing the number of interrupts and eliminating the need to poll different users. LAT thus places a good part of the load of a terminal session on the master, freeing up host resources.

Data

CHAPTER 8

Data

In earlier chapters, we concentrated on issues concerning the network infrastructure including the presentation of data, session establishment, transport circuits, and name resolution. None of these services, however, is of direct use to the user. With LAT, we saw something closer to the application a user would see. LAT provided the infrastructure that allowed a communications program on a terminal server to send and receive data from a host. Even there, however, the actual semantics of the application-level operations were avoided.

In this chapter, we move to the application layer and begin examining some of the services available to the user. Even here, many of the services are not directly seen by the user. For file access, for example, a user sees the operating system interface, known as a command processor. The command processor in turn issues commands to the file system, which then uses the network-based file services.

Although the application layer is at the top of the network protocol stack, it is at the bottom portion of the user's protocol stack. The user sees operating systems, file systems, windowing systems, word processors, and a variety of different native services. Most of these services ultimately use the network applications, which in turn use the underlying layers of the network. You can think of this process as peeling an infinitely layered onion. This chapter looks at one particular form of network application—access to data located on a remote computer. The goal of this service is to make the disk drive on a remote computer appear locally attached. There are a variety of different ways to accomplish this task.

Figure 8-1 shows different file access protocols arranged by the degree to which they integrate different systems. The most integrated system (in a Digital computing environment, at least) is the symmetric multiprocessor (SMP). This is a single computer with several different processors. All the different CPUs are able to access a single pool of shared memory. The local lock manager and a single CPU scheduling processor arbitrate which CPU

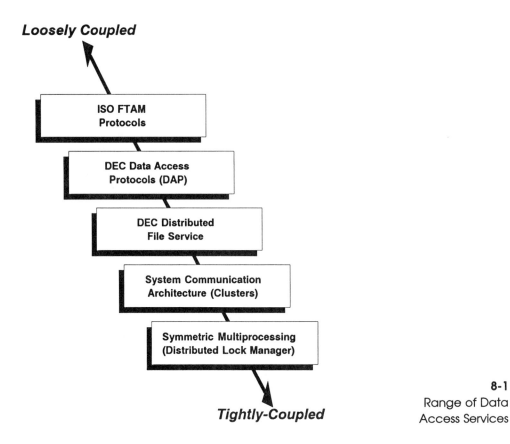

Loosely Coupled

ISO FTAM
Protocols

DEC Data Access
Protocols (DAP)

DEC Distributed
File Service

System Communication
Architecture (Clusters)

Symmetric Multiprocessing
(Distributed Lock Manager)

Tightly-Coupled

8-1
Range of Data
Access Services

will access, and thus process, which portion memory at a given time. As long as a system has several different users or a single program broken up into several processes, the symmetric multiprocessing capability looks like a single CPU with shared memory.

The VAX cluster, which uses the System Communication Architecture, provides a slightly looser degree of integration. In the VAX Cluster, each CPU has its own memory. Memory is not shared among processors unless a particular system is an SMP system, but appears as a single processor as far as the VAX Cluster is concerned.

To share information in memory, the VAX Cluster protocols are used to exchange packets of information. One of the exchanges made is for distributed lock management. Here, all of the systems communicate with each other before granting a user access to a portion of the file system.

Once the lock is granted, a CPU sends a VAX Cluster message down to the HSC controller asking for a certain block of the disk. The HSC, using the

Mass Storage Control Protocol (MSCP), provides the service of delivering blocks of data. What the blocks mean and how they are arranged into files is up to the computer to interpret.

The VAX Cluster is an example of a disk service: The remote computer does not interpret the data on the disk drive. A higher level of service is the file service. The information on a disk is structured as a series of files.

The Distributed File Service (DFS) is an example of a file service used strictly within VAX computers that use the VMS operating system. With DFS, a remote computer can deliver files to a local computer, making them appear as if they were locally mounted.

Within a file, a file service does not interpret the data. A file is simply one or more blocks of data. It is up to the file system on the requesting computer to interpret how those blocks are broken up into records or some other form of structure. The highest level of service is when the remote computer breaks a file up into records, pages, indexes, and other ways of structuring a file. In this record service, most of the load is placed on the server. When the client gets data, they have been interpreted already and can be fed directly into a program. Digital's Data Access Protocol is an example of a Digital record-based network protocol. With DAP, users can perform operations such as asking a remote computer to search a file for all records meeting particular search criteria, and then sort the information before sending it back over the network.

DAP works fine in DECnet implementations, but it lacks generality for a truly open systems environment. The OSI File Access, Transfer, and Management (FTAM) provides a similar record service to DAP but does so as an OSI application instead of a DECnet application. FTAM is one of the fundamental OSI services used to connect a wide variety of different systems.

File systems provide a basic level of data interchange in a distributed environment. The problem with file access, however, is that the programmer must provide the code to break the file into the underlying fields. A database system provides an even higher level of abstraction than the file system. With a relational database system, the programmer can begin dealing with the semantic content of the data, asking the remote server to process queries that have a variety of complicated conditions.

Asking the remote server to do the bulk of the processing allows the database server to be a highly optimized server. The database server can be a very powerful system, with large amounts of main memory and disk space. Workstations are able to access that data without using an inordinate amount of local processing power. This means the workstation can be optimized for the semantics of the user interface—how data should be presented and displayed—instead of the brute-force sorting and filtering of data from a large database.

Data Access Protocol

We begin our discussion of remote access to data with DAP for historical reasons. DAP was the original remote data access mechanism in DECnet and still maintains a large installed base of users and programs. As we will see, the DAP capabilities closely parallel the file system capabilities in Digital's VMS operating system, making a remote VMS-based VAX appear just like a local one.

The VMS operating system provides a variety of services to the user. The interactive user sees the Digital Command Language (DCL), a command line processor. There are also programmatic interfaces to the operating system used for programming languages. When either a program or a DCL user needs access to data, calls are issued to the Record Management Services (RMS). RMS in turn insulates the user from all different types of data access. When RMS receives a call, it examines the "device" name being accessed. Based on a lookup table, it then hands the request to a device driver.

The usual device driver is the local device driver: a combination of software and hardware that sends a command over the peripheral bus to access the hardware that makes up the disk drive. For network-based access, RMS hands the request off to a set of Network File Access Routines (see Fig. 8-2). Typically, these routines will send a request down through DECnet to a process called a File Access Listener (FAL). The FAL is a DAP-speaking process whose function is to negotiate the file system on a remote node and get the desired data. The FAL looks to that remote system like a user.

Once the data are retrieved by the FAL, the FAL packages the information in a set of DAP packets and sends them down to DECnet. DECnet sends the data back over the network and hands them up to the Network File Access Routines; the information then goes up to the user.

The power of this model is considerable. A programmer can use a logical file name in a program. At runtime, that logical name is translated to a particular device. A program can begin by using a local disk drive. Later, the logical name can be changed to point to a remote disk drive. This means that without recompiling or changing a program, a user can access both local and remote data.

The FAL model of remote data access can even be used to access foreign file systems. For example, the Digital Data Transfer Facility (DTF) uses the DAP protocols to access data on an IBM mainframe (see Fig. 8-3). A special application-layer protocol is sandwiched between the DECnet Session Control layer and DAP. This Gateway Access Protocol (GAP) sets up a session to the System Network Architecture (SNA) Gateway, a specialized server on the network. The gateway, in turn, sets up an SNA session onto the IBM mainframe. At the mainframe, the program is an implementation of the FAL for the MVS operating system.

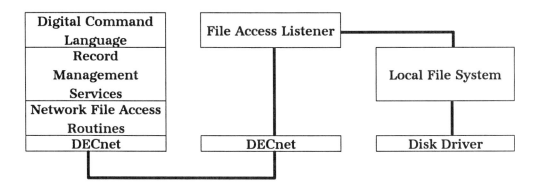

8-2 DAP Process Structure

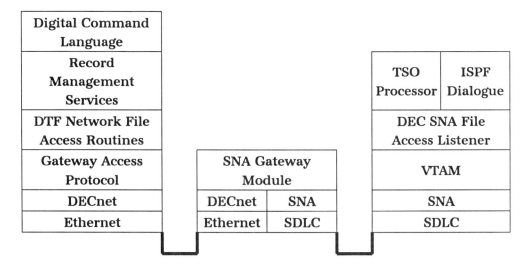

8-3 DEC Data Transfer Facility

The actual user of the FAL on the IBM can be one of three different sources. The remote DECnet user can use DTF to access IBM-based data transparently, just as the user would access DECnet or local data. In addition, the IBM-based user can use an interactive MVS Time Sharing Option (MVS/TSO) command processor or a menu-based ISPF Dialogue (a series of forms) to access data in the Digital environment.

All of this access, both internal to the DECnet and foreign environments, is subject to the security constraints in both environments. The FAL runs as a user process and is thus subject to access control and authentication requirements. In the IBM environment, the user must be registered with an access system such as Top Secret or the Access Control Facility (ACF). In the Digital environment, access information must be explicitly passed with the request or must be present in the form of a proxy login on the remote system.

DAP Files

DAP was designed initially to work on PDP systems, followed by VAX systems running the VMS operating system. Since then, DAP has been ported to run on Unix and DOS operating systems plus a few others, such IBM's MVS and the Apple Macintosh. Despite the recent ports, the reader will see a definite VMS orientation in the protocol.

DAP supports a variety of different file organizations (see Fig. 8-4). The basic file types are fixed-length, variable-length, and stream formats. In a stream format, the file is a string of data, and the application must provide any internal structure. Stream formats closely parallel the file system on Unix operating systems.

Within a record-oriented file, there can be additional structure imposed, known as an extended file type. In FORTRAN carriage control, for example, the first byte is used to indicate things like formfeeds. In the print file carriage control format, 4 bytes contain both prefix and postfix information.

The data inside of the file can be of three different formats:

- ASCII text
- EBCDIC
- image

Image data is a simple bit string transmitted with the low-order bit of the low-order byte first. For all three data types, DAP also offers a compression option to eliminate duplicates (see Fig. 8-5).

When compression is used to eliminate duplication, normal data are preceded by a byte that indicates how long the normal data string is. If the high bit is set to 0, it indicates that they are normal data. If the high bit is set to 1, it indicates that duplicates will follow. For nulls, the two high bits are 1 and 0, followed by a 6-bit count, allowing up to 64 nulls to be represented as a single byte of data. Other characters can also be compressed but not quite as efficiently. The high bits are set to 110, followed by 5 bits of a repetition count, allowing up to 32 characters to be represented by 2 bytes of data.

DAP message exchange

DAP can operate in several different modes, allowing different levels of functionality. A primitive implementation of DAP, for example, can offer only the file transfer mode that allows an entire file to be sent across the

DAP-Supported File Types	
Basic File Types	
Fixed-Length Records	Maximum Record Size (MRS) field contains length.
Variable-Length Records	MRS field contains maximum length.
Variable-Length with Fixed-control format records	Normal variable-length records with a control field. The field is immediately before the data. Length of the control field is in the Fixed Part Size (FSZ) field
Stream Format	Variable length with Line Feed
Stream-Carriage Return	Carriage return is record terminator.
Stream-Line Feed	Line Feed is record terminator.
Extended File Types	
FORTRAN Carriage Control	First byte contains a FORTRAN carriage control character.
COBOL Carriage Control	First byte contains a COBOL carriage control character.
Print File Carriage Control	First 4 bytes contain prefix and postfix carriage control information.
Implied LF/CR Carriage Control	Each record has implied leading line feed and trailing carriage return.
Embedded and "None" Carriage Control	Carriage control embedded in data if present.
Line Sequenced ASCII	Line sequence is imbedded in fixed data portion.
MACY11	Format for storing PDP-11 binary data on TOPS file system.

8-4 DAP File Types

Noncompressed characters	High bit 0
	7-bit count
	String
Nulls	High bits 10
	6-bit count
Repetitions	High bits 110
	5-bit repetition count
	Repeated character

8-5
DAP Data
Compression

network. All data are sent in a continuous stream with explicit acknowledgment at the end of file (EOF).

Four other modes provide a more sophisticated access to a file:

- Random Access Mode. Access on per-record or block basis. DAP operates in request/response mode for random access.

- Record Data Access Mode. Allows access based on the relative record number, record file address, virtual block number, string key, or byte offset.
- Block Data Access. Access data based on 512-byte blocks.
- Stream Data Access. File is a continuous stream and any structure is provided by the using application.

A DAP session consists of a single logical link for each remote file access. The same logical link can be used for different files if there is no overlap. There is no multiplexing of multiple files within a single link. If a program wishes to perform such an operation, it would set up a separate DAP session for each simultaneous file access.

All DAP files share a common message header (see Fig. 8-6). This message header is embedded inside of a DECnet Session Control header (i.e., it does not work with OSI-based stacks). The node accessing the file always initiates the DAP session. Each exchange is a session-level transmit request and receive request. A session begins with the creation of a link, followed by an exchange of configuration messages (see Fig. 8-7). The configuration messages set up the lowest common denominator of services offered and desired between the two nodes.

Following the configuration exchange, a node sends an access message, indicating which file and the type of access desired. The FAL will typically send an attribute message showing more information on the file desired and an acknowledgment that the file is available.

The requesting node then sends a control message. The control message establishes the data stream and is followed by a series of data messages. The remote FAL uses the service of its operating system to get data, then packages them up in DAP data messages. At the end of the data, a status message is sent indicating an EOF. The access complete message and a response terminate the session.

Figure 8-8 shows a more sophisticated session involving the use of wildcards. Following the beginning configuration exchange, the requesting node sends an access message containing a wildcard. The result is a series of different messages indicating the volume and directory being sent.

Following this information, the name of the first file is sent back, along with an attributes and acknowledgment message. The node then has the option of using a control message to reserve the file and get the data. Following the data and the EOF message, the requesting node closes the file.

Then the next file is sent, along with the attributes. Notice that the requesting node, not desiring this file, immediately sends an access complete message. If there were more files in the wildcard specification, we would see this process repeat several more times.

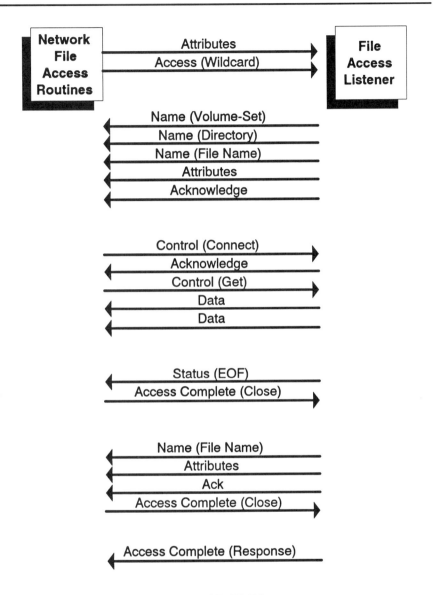

Source: DAP Specification, Version 7.2, PP. 52-53

8-8 DAP Wildcard Sequential File Access

Many VAX systems have a "default" area used for general public files. Anybody on the network is able to access these files. Take the example of a programmer wishing to compile programs, a very CPU-intensive function. If the system on which a programmer is working is slow, the programmer looks for a machine with a default DAP area on the network. The programmer sends the source code to the default area using a DAP copy command. Then the programmer sends a command file that takes the source code and compiles it. The programmer then retrieves the resulting object code, deletes any trash lying around, and goes to lunch. The attributes message is used to specify the attributes of a file or the attributes needed. A bitmap is used to indicate which attribute fields are present (see Fig. 8-11). The data type field indicates not only the basic data type (ASCII, EBCDIC, or image) but also such options as compression or sensitive data. The record format indicates how an individual record looks, and the record attributes indicate information such as FORTRAN carriage control.

The rest of the fields indicate a variety of different parameters available on a file. For example, the allocation quantity shows the total amount of allocated space for a file. The device characteristics allow a system mailbox, a tape drive, or some other device to act as a file.

Once attributes are established, the access message is used to access a file (see Fig. 8-12). Based on the access message, the FAL can obtain necessary locks from the local file manager and open the file. Notice that one access type is the submit/execute used for remote execution of command files. The access message also includes a file specification, an access code (for which type of access), a sharing code (for which type of mutual access is allowed), and any extended attributes required. Extended attributes provide information such as the data and time a file was created.

Figure 8-13 shows an example of attributes and access messages being sent to an FAL. Notice that both of these messages are in the same network packet. This concatenation of upper-layer functions into a single session-layer packet is useful for conserving bandwidth and providing higher throughput. The attributes message indicates that a sequential file will be sent in the basic ASCII format, consisting of 8 bits per byte. The access message indicates that a file called "ncphelp.bin" has been opened, and will subsequently be retrieved. The requesting node is also indicating that it wishes to see a main attributes message, a data and time message, and the full name of the file. No password is specified for this access, so presumably the file is a public file or a mechanism like proxy login was used.

The control message (see Fig 8-14) is used to begin the data transfer after the access message opens the file. The DAP control message includes a variety of different functions, many of which are only used in specialized circumstances. The basic control message starts a data stream. During that process, other control messages can be sent that change the type of access or specify the keys used for searching a file.

Figure 8-15 shows a basic file access operation. The message in the detail portion of the screen is a control message with the get record or block op-

Message Type		Type = 1
Maximum Buffer Size		0 = Unlimited
Operating System Type		Includes DOS, VMS, Ultrix
File System Type		
Version Numbers		5 Bytes
System Capabilities		72 Generic Capabilities Defined
Partial Listing of Capabilities		
ALLOCATION extended attributes message		Append to file access supported
Blocking of DAP messages in response		Change in file attributes on close
Change of file attributes on rename		Command file submission and/or execution
Continue/retry after error		DATE-TIME extended attributes message
Default file specification		Direct file organization
Directory list operation as part of access		Display of file attributes via Control (display) messages
Establish data streams		File checksum option
File deletion		File name and type of access
File rename operation		Go/Nogo option in Access message
Initial file allocation		KEY DEFINITION extended attributes message
Manual file extension		Modified attributes returned on create
Multi-keyed indexed file supported		Multiple Data streams
NAME message		Non 8-bit aligned data
PROTECTION extended attributes message		Random access by record file address (RFA)
Random access by virtual block number (VBN)		Random access by key
Random access by relative record number (RRN)		Relative file organization
Segmented DAP messages		Sequential file organization
Sequential file transfer		Sequential record access

Capabilities *(Cont.)*	
SUMMARY extended attributes message	Supports Block I/O access modes
Supports colllating table message	Supports command file submission
Supports only octal file version numbers	Supports spooling
Supports stream file access mode to any file	Supports stream file acess to stream files
Switching record access mode supported	Switching between record and block modes
Three-part NAME message bit	2-byte length field
Unrestricted blocking of DAP messages	Use of Bit Count field
Use of BLKCNT in CONTROL message	Warning status message
Wildcard operations	

8-9 *(Cont.)* DAP Configuration Message

```
DETAIL
DAP: ----- Data Access Protocol -----
DAP:
DAP:
DAP:  Code = 1  (Configuration)
DAP:  Buffer Size         = 1460
DAP:  Operating System Type = MS-DOS
DAP:  File System Version   = MS-DOS
DAP:  DAP Version Number              = 7
DAP:  DAP ECO Number                  = 0
DAP:  DAP User Number                 = 0
DAP:  DAP Software Version Number     = 1
DAP:  DAP User Software Version Number = 0
DAP:  Generic System Capabilities:
DAP:     Sequential file organization
DAP:     Sequential file transfer
DAP:     Append to file access
DAP:     Command file submission and/or execution as in Access Message
DAP:     Blocking of DAP messages up to response
DAP:     Use of 2 byte operand length in DAP message header
DAP:     Directory list
DAP:     Date and Time Extended Attributes Message
DAP:     Spooling, specified by bit 20 of FOP field
DAP:     Command file submission, specified by bit 21 of FOP field
DAP:     File deletion, specified by bit 22 of FOP field
DAP:     Wildcard operation
DAP:     Name message
DAP:
                        Frame 7 of 26
                   Use TAB to select windows
 1          2 Set              4 Zoom  5        6Display 7 Prev  8 Next          10 New
  Help       mark               out     Menus    option: frame   frame          capture
```

8-10 DAP Configuration Message

Message Type		Type = 2
Fields Bitmap		Specifies which fields present
Data Type		ASCII, EBCDIC, Image, Compressed, Sensitive, Executable, Privileged
File Organization		
Record Format		Fixed, Variable, Stream
Record Attributes		Example: Carriage Control
Physical Block Size		Default 512 Bytes
Maximum Record Size		Actual size for fixed records
Allocation Quantity		File size
Bucket Size in Blocks		
Fixed Part Size		For variable records
Max Record Number		For relative files only
Run-Time System Environment		Used for emulation
Extension Size		In blocks
File Access Options		Example: Rewind on Close
Bits Per Byte Stored		Transfer always 8 bits
Device Characteristics		Examples: Mounted, mailbox
Spooling Device Chars		Intermediate device
Longest Record Length		
Highest Virtual Block Number		Highest allocated
EOF Virtual Block Number		
First Free Byte		In EOF block
Starting Logical Block Number		For contiguous files.

8-11
DAP Basic Attributes
Message

tion specified. Notice that the next message shows that 91 bytes of data were actually sent.

Figures 8-16 through 8-20 show a variety of other DAP messages. The DAP data message specifies the record number and some data. The record or block number is useful if packets must be reassembled by the application program. The continue transfer message specifies what to do if there has been an error.

Message Type		Type = 3
Type of Access		Open, Create, Rename, Erase, Directory List, Submit/Execute
Access Options Flags		I/O Errors nonfatal
		Modify attributes on create
		16-bit file checksum
		Go/NoGo: Allows accessor to Resume or Skip each step
File Specification		Up to 255 bytes
File Access Code		Put, Get, Delete, Update, Truncate, Block, Switching
Sharing Access Code		
Display		Extended attributes required
Password		Up to 40 characters

8-12
DAP Access Message

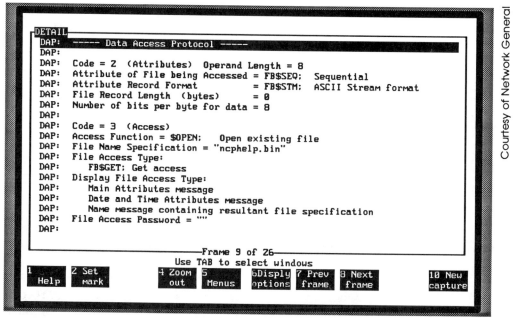

Courtesy of Network General

8-13 DAP Attributes and Access Messages

Message Type		Type = 4
Control Function		
Control Options		Bitmap plus included fields
Display		Extended attributes to return
Block Count		Maximum size of data message
User Size Field		Number of bytes in stream mode
Control Functions		
Get record or block		Extend file
Update current record		Release specific lock
Delete current record		Rewind file
Truncate at current position		Put record/Write block
Release all record locks		Connect: Initiate data stream
Flush buffers		Find record
Display - return attributes		Space forward X blocks
Space backward X blocks		Checkpoint
Restart get from checkpoint		Restart put from checkpoint
Control Options		
Change access type		Key Value
Key Reference Number		Processing Options Bitmap
Processing Options		
Position to EOF		Fast delete
Disable auto unlocking		Read ahead
Write behind		Key is ≥
Key is >		Do not lock record
Use read-only lock		Read despite lock

8-14
DAP Control
Message

When an error does occur, the status message (see Fig. 8-19) is used to signal the error. For example, a write operation might fail because a disk drive is full. The continue transfer message (see Fig 8-17) allows the requestor to try again, skip this particular operation, or abort the entire data transfer.

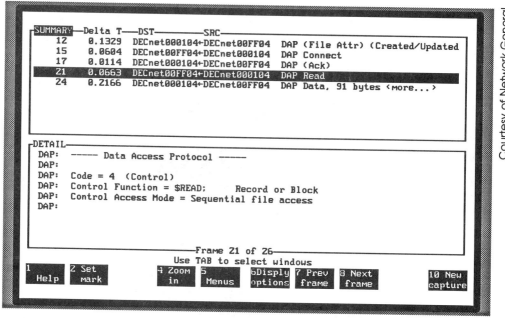

```
┌SUMMARY──Delta T──DST────────SRC────
│   12   0.1329  DECnet000104←DECnet00FF04  DAP (File Attr) (Created/Updated
│   15   0.0604  DECnet00FF04←DECnet000104  DAP Connect
│   17   0.0114  DECnet000104←DECnet00FF04  DAP (Ack)
│   21   0.0663  DECnet00FF04←DECnet000104  DAP Read
│   24   0.2166  DECnet000104←DECnet00FF04  DAP Data, 91 bytes <more...>
│
│
│
┌DETAIL─────────────────────────
│DAP:  ───── Data Access Protocol ─────
│DAP:
│DAP:  Code = 4 (Control)
│DAP:  Control Function = $READ;    Record or Block
│DAP:  Control Access Mode = Sequential file access
│DAP:
│
│                    ──Frame 21 of 26──
│                   Use TAB to select windows
┌1     ┐ ┌2 Set ┐        ┌4 Zoom┐ ┌5     ┐ ┌6Disply┐ ┌7 Prev┐ ┌8 Next┐        ┌10 New ┐
│ Help │ │ mark │        │  in  │ │ Menus│ │options│ │ frame│ │ frame│        │capture│
└──────┘ └──────┘        └──────┘ └──────┘ └───────┘ └──────┘ └──────┘        └───────┘
```

8-15 DAP Control Message

Message Type		Type = 8
Record Number		Record or block number
Data		

8-16
DAP Data Message

Message Type		Type = 5
Continue Function		Try again
		Skip and continue
		Abort transfer
		Resume (unsuspend)
		Terminate processing

8-17
DAP Continue Transfer Message

Message Type		Type = 6

8-18
DAP Acknowledgment

Message Type		Type = 9
Status Code		4-byte Macro Code
		12-byte specific status code
Record File Address		Record or block number
Record Number		Relative record number
Secondary Status Code		Ex: RMS Device Error Codes

8-19
DAP Status Message

Message Type		Type = 7
Completion Function		Close file and all data streams
		Response (ACK)
		Reset: Restore file to previous
		End of this stream
		Begin Change Attributes
		Skip - Go to next file
		End Change Attributes
		Terminate, Reset DAP State
File Access Options		For Wildcard Functions
File Checksum		Only on Close Function

8-20
DAP Access
Complete Message

Message Type		Type = 15
Name Type Code		Full file specification
		File name
		Directory name
		Volume/structure name
		Default file specification
Name		

8-21
DAP Name Message

Extended Attributes Messages

The basic attributes message is useful for specifying information like record sizes that is used in all transfers. Other information, however, is only needed infrequently. Rather than send all this information at once, DAP specifies a series of extended attributes messages to contain this supplemental information.

Figures 8-21 and 8-22 show two examples of these messages. The name message allows a node to specify the full file specification (useful when a wildcard is originally used to request a file) as well as information like the current directory or volume. The default file specification shows where in the directory tree default file access will be performed.

The date and time attributes message (Fig. 8-22) shows the date and time a particular file has been created, updated, or deleted. The revision number shows the VMS orientation of the DAP protocols. VMS, unlike many operating systems, labels each file with a revision number. In a typical user session, the last three revisions of a file are kept online. If a new revision is created, the earliest one is deleted. The choice of how many revisions to keep online is a local management decision—many system managers impose no default limit, letting users manage their own files within the limits of their disk quota.

Keeping multiple revisions is useful as an online archiving technique. Not all operating systems have this capability and would thus omit the field. The fields bitmap allows unneeded information to be kept off the network.

Figure 8-23 shows an example of extended attribute messages. First, a regular attribute message is sent, indicating this is an ASCII file, with 34 blocks allocated and 34 blocks used. Then, the date time message indicates when the file was last created and updated. The name message gives the current directory path and name of the file.

One of the important functions of DAP, particularly when used between VMS systems, is to allow random file access. The key definition message (see Fig. 8-24) is used to inform a requesting node what the key definitions of a file are. The option flag indicates whether duplicates are allowed and the programmer is able to change the key definitions. The fill fields show the target percentage that each area of the file will be filled (allowing for adding new data without allocating new areas or reorganizing the index).

Not all of the fields allowed in this message would be found in a single message. A typical indexed file, for example, would include from one to eight position/size pairs for the key definition. A hashed file (another type of file organization) would have the hash algorithm value.

The allocation attributes message is used to extend a file (see Fig. 8-25). Before large amounts of data can be added, particularly on an indexed file, new space must be allocated. This message indicates how much space is

Message Type		Type = 13
Fields Bitmap		
Date/Time Created		
Date/Time Updated		
Date/Time Deleted		
Revision Number		
Date/Time Backed Up		
Physical Creation Time		Date/Time on this device
Last Accessed Date/Time		

8-22
DAP Date-Time
Message

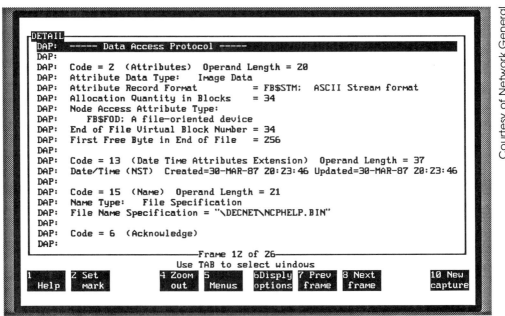

8-23 DAP Attribute Extensions Message

Courtesy of Network General

Message Type		Type = 10
Fields Bitmap		
Key Option Flag		Duplicates allowed
		Allow keys to change
		Null key character defined
Data Bucket Fill		
Index Bucket Fill		
Number of Segments		No. of POS/SIZ Pairs (Eight Max)
Position of Key (Offset)		
Size of Key		
Position of Key (Offset)		
Size of Key		
Reference Indicator		Key of reference indicator
Reference Name		Name of Key of Reference
Null Character Value		
Index Area Number		
Lowest Level Index Area		
Data Level Area Number		
Data Type of Key		
Root VBN		Virtual Block Number for Key
Hash Algorithm Value		
First Data Bucket VBN		
Data Bucket Size		
Index Bucket Size		
Level of Root Bucket		
Total Key Size		
Minimum Record Length		
Collating Table ID		
Size of Collating Table		

8-24
DAP Key
Definition Message

Message Type		Type = 11
Fields Bitmap		Relative Volume Number
Alignment Options		Cylinder boundary, logical block number, near file
Allocation Options		Contiguous required or best try
Reserved field		
Space to Allocate		
Area ID		For index references
Bucket Size for This Area		
Default Extend Quantity		For automatic extends

8-25

DAP Allocation Message

needed and if the space has special requirements, like keeping all of the data blocks contiguous.

The summary attributes extension message (see Fig. 8-26) is useful when a user wants to know how a file is indexed but does not need all the detailed parameter information. A user may wish to get a directory listing, for example, that indicates which files are indexed and how many keys are in them. The network file access routines would send an access message indicating that the summary attributes extension message should be returned along with the name of each file.

The protection attributes message (see Fig. 8-27) is another example of a VMS-centric type of message. Protection on the VMS operating system is organized around four classifications of users:

- system
- owner
- group
- world

System users have special privileged accounts. The owner is usually the username that originally created the file. Certain users will be in the same group as the owner, and everybody outside of the group is considered the world. For each of these four categories, there is a variety of capabilities that can be granted.

DAP file protections are enforced (or subverted) by the operating system itself. For example, one could deny the system read access to a file. This does not mean the system cannot read a file, only that it would use its special privileges to bypass the protection scheme. The one probable result

Message Type	Type = 12
Fields Bitmap	
Number of Keys in File	
Number of Areas in File	
Number of Record Descriptors	

8-26
DAP Summary
Extension Message

Message Type	Type = 14	
Fields Bitmap		
Owner		
Owner Access Bitmap	0: Deny read access	
	1: Deny write access	
	2: Deny execute access	
	3: Deny delete access	
	4: Deny append access	
	5: Deny directory list access	
	6: Deny update access	
	7: Deny change protection	
	8: Deny extend	
System Access Bitmap		
Group Access Bitmap		
World Access Bitmap		

8-27
DAP Protection
Message

of denying the system read access is that the file will not be backed up, since backup is an automatic program that typically skips over any problem files.

The last attributes extension message is the collating table (see Fig. 8-28). A collating table is used to indicate how a file is to be sorted when indexed retrievals are to be performed. For very large collating tables, it is possible to include a sequence number so the message can be sent in pieces. If a large collating table is in use, it indicates a complex sort is needed for the data. Anytime that a large, multikeyed operation is consistently going over the network, it might be wise to investigate an alternative model, such as a network-based relational database management system (DBMS). The

Message Type		Type = 17
Fields Bitmap		
Collating Table ID		As specified in preceding key definition message
Collating Table Size		
Sequence Number		For large collating tables
Table Format Version Number		
Data		

8-28
DAP Collating
Table Message

DBMS, with its sophisticated query optimizer, is able to perform the different operations to sort data in the proper order efficiently.

Distributed File System

Whereas DAP provides record-level access among different operating systems, the Distributed File System is limited to VMS-based systems and is meant to operate in a single LAN-based environment. Because DFS is optimized for the LAN and because it provides a lower level of structure (files instead of records), it operates approximately 10 times faster than DAP.

The purpose of the DFS is to make a remote directory appear as if it were locally mounted. DAP allows remote file access but only if the user knows where the file is located. With DFS, the access is transparent. The difference between the two is the degree of transparency: With DAP you have to explicitly reference the node on which the file exists (possibly using wildcards), whereas with DFS the remote node becomes transparent.

The advantage of a distributed file system is that if a file system moves, all that is needed is to reregister the system with the naming service. The user command, mount access point name, does not change. DAP and FTAM provide temporary access to a particular file. The file system is more permanent—it provides access to a file for a longer time.

A server makes a file system available to clients using the DFS Control Program (DFSCP) register command. The register command lets the DNA Naming Service know that a particular file system is available on this server node using an access point name. The access point name is then used by the client to mount the file system. The mount command makes a pseudodevice that appears on the local file system as a file structured device. This pseudodevice will then forward requests to the DFS server. Proxy logins are used for authentication and authorization.

Figure 8-29 shows the structure of the connection once a file system has been mounted. The application (i.e., the Digital Command Language) com-

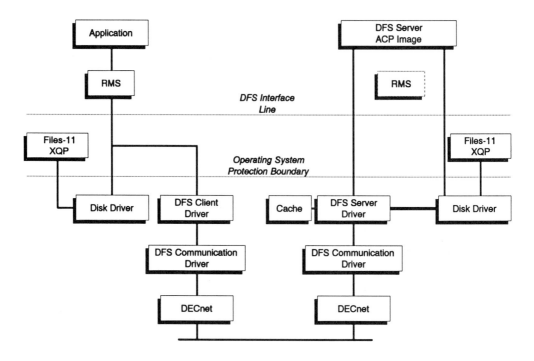

Source: Digital Technical Journal, No. 9, P. 25

8-29 DEC DFS Structure

municates with the Record Management Services. RMS in turn parcels out requests to the appropriate driver.

For DFS-based access, the DFS client driver is used. This driver, in turn, uses the DFS communication driver, which is a request/response protocol. This communication driver would presumably be replaced by a remote procedure call mechanism. The RPC-like communication driver then uses the service of a DECnet session.

The files-11 XQP shown in Figure 8-29 is an artifact of the VMS operating system. In VMS, QIO (data access) requests go down to the disk driver. The disk driver separates out two kinds of requests. Read and write operations go straight down to the device. Control operations (open, close, extend, truncate) go up to the files-11 XQP, a subroutine library that runs in the user application context. Thus, open and close operations are subject to security because they run in the user context, whereas read and write operations (which always follow a previous open operation) run in the much quicker operating system confines. The server runs a single asynchronous control process (ACP) that provides services to multiple users. Since proxy logins are used to maintain security, the files-11 XQP is available to perform the appropriate open and close operations. Once the context is established, the server driver is able to use driver context to requeue operations to the disk driver without causing a VMS rescheduling operation.

The server allocates a nonpaged pool in memory for caching. Each open file gets some of these blocks. The caching uses a combination of read-ahead and least recently used methods. A block will stay in cache after a file close.

DFS does not assure that writes are performed. The client needs to re-read the data to make sure the operation worked properly. After communication fails on a connection, the access point remains mounted. Each user access to a file will result in a connection retry. When a connection is lost, the server will close all open files. DFS does not provide automatic fallback to another cluster member in the case of a node failure.

Studies show that DFS is fairly fast. For example, compilation on a remote node only takes 125 percent of the time it would on a local node. Compilation is CPU intensive: File access is only a small part of the access. Of course, if the results of the compilation need to be transferred back to the home system, that adds additional overhead.

The PC

Digital's VMS Services for MS-DOS are based on Microsoft Networks/Open-NET Architecture (MS-NET). Three services are provided: a file server, a disk server, and a print server. The disk server uses an area of the VMS disk formatted for DOS, and is used for downline loading.

File services use the Server Message Block (SMB) protocol, which is in turn built on top of NetBIOS, a session-layer protocol. NetBIOS, in turn, uses NSP to set up the virtual circuit on DECnet (see Fig. 8-30). The VMS file server is responsible for mapping incoming SMB calls into the VMS file system. The file server is DECnet object 64—a single detached process. It is multithreaded, allowing multiple user's of a single process.

Since VMS and DOS have different file systems, the file server must do several kinds of mapping. File names in VMS are longer, but DOS has a larger legal character set. For illegal VMS characters used in DOS, the file server maps the character into _XX, where XX is the hex character. Long file names on VMS are not shown to the DOS client. The DOS hidden, system, and archive attributes are not available in VMS. The VMS system creates an application access control list entry in the access control list.

To simplify client access and to provide default profiles, a user requests services by naming a service name—an ASCII text string of 1–25 characters. The file server maintains service names in a file server database. A service has the following attributes:

```
┌─────────────┐        ┌─────────────┐
│ Application │        │ Management  │
│             │        │  Utilities  │
└─────────────┘        └─────────────┘
      ▲                       ▲
      │                       │
┌─────────────┐        ┌─────────────┐   SMB      ┌─────────────┐
│    DOS      │◄──────►│  Redirector │◄─Protocol─►│  VMS File   │
│             │    ▲   │             │            │   Server    │
└─────────────┘    │   └─────────────┘            └─────────────┘
          ▲────────┘          ▲                          ▲
          │                   │                          │
┌─────────────┐        ┌─────────────┐  NetBIOS   ┌─────────────┐
│    BIOS     │        │  NetBIOS    │◄─Protocol─►│  NetBIOS    │
│             │        │  Emulator   │            │  Emulator   │
└─────────────┘        └─────────────┘            └─────────────┘
                              ▲                          ▲
                              │                          │
                       ┌─────────────┐   NSP      ┌─────────────┐
                       │ DECnet/DOS  │◄─Protocol─►│ DECnet/VAX  │
                       └─────────────┘            └─────────────┘
                              ▲                          ▲
                              │                          │
                       ┌─────────────┐  Ethernet  ┌─────────────┐
                       │    Data     │◄─or DDCMP─►│    Data     │
                       │    Link     │            │    Link     │
                       └─────────────┘            └─────────────┘
```

Source: Digital Technical Journal, No. 9, P. 45

8-30 DEC PCSA Architecture

- root directory (entry point)
- service type (system, application) that defines the level of security protection
- default RMS protection mask
- RMS file types (stream, or 512-byte fixed-length sequential)
- VMS print queue to use
- form to use on the printer

Access to a service is based on an access control list.

Authentication

The Session Control layer of DECnet will authenticate a user, but does not
pass authentication information up to the application. This presents a
problem, since the VMS file server is multithreaded. What Digital did to
provide authentication was to extend the SMB TREE command, which in-

cludes a password field. Digital then encoded the user name into the service name field. Instead of just a service name, the field reads:

service%username

The server uses this information to authenticate the user, using the rights-list database and the User Authentication File (UAF). Note that this scheme has some potential pitfalls such as when an application wants to keep data in a shared area.

Each service is one of three types: system, application, or user. The system and application services allow all users to read and update all files in the area. The user-level security is on a per-user basis, using standard VMS access control facilities.

Locking and the Disk Server

MS-NET and DOS allow byte range locking, which is very different from the RMS scheme based on records. Therefore, the VMS file server maintains its own lock manager. This lock manager, in turn, uses the service of the VMS lock manager, taking out a private, exclusive lock on a file. In a clustered environment, this means multiple VMS file servers can be running. A particular file is only available to one of those file servers. If another server gets a request for that file, it uses the cluster services to determine who is acting as the lock manager for the file, then uses DECnet virtual circuits to route request to that lock master.

Access to the disk service is based on three Digital protocols. First, MOP is used to bring the initial module to the PC. This module then uses the second protocol, the Local Area System Transport (LAST), to load the second module. The third protocol, the Local Area Disk Driver (LAD) then loads the control program. The control program then loads the operating system. The disk server is used for remote booting. Only one user can use the disk at once (whereas the file server allows multiple users).

FTAM

The OSI File Transfer, Access, and Management (FTAM) protocols are similar in scope to DAP, although FTAM has been provided to connect a wider variety of file systems. As such FTAM provides a general model from which implementations will pick a specific subset. This subsetting of the protocol is important—two implementations will not necessarily interconnect at full functionality if they do not support the same subsets of the protocol (or cannot negotiate the same subset).

The general FTAM filestore model is of a single file, divided into a series of data units. A data unit consists of nodes structured in a tree. Attached to a node are zero or more data units. In a traditional file system, a node is a file and the data units are the data inside of the file. In FTAM, the model is based on a single file (there is no concept of multiple files inside a directory). In the FTAM model, a data unit is a record, page, block, or any other unit of structure inside a file.

We can model most file structures within this general model. A sequential text file, for example, consists of a single node under the root node, accompanied by a series of data units, one per record. A binary file consists of one node and one data unit.

Hierarchical file organizations, such as the Btree or the Indexed Sequential Access Method (ISAM), can be modeled as a multilevel tree. To lend some order to this potentially infinite tree, the FTAM model takes data units and structures them into file access data units (FADUs). A FADU is a portion of the tree down to the leaf nodes. Thus, the entire file can be considered a single FADU, just as lower-level portions can be a FADU.

The FADU model of operation makes it easy to structure operations on the virtual file. Remember that actual operations on the file are performed by a local file operation. All that is needed by the FTAM protocols is an ability to communicate what operation needs to be done.

An FTAM session consists of a series of nested regimes. These regimes have certain operations that can be performed. An association regime, for example, is necessary before a file can be selected. Next, a file is opened, followed by any transfer operations. Notice that access is sequential: FTAM, like DAP, does not provide an asynchronous model of file processing.

The general FTAM model is broken up into functional modules, called service classes. Service classes structure the capabilities of the protocol into subsets. Document types structure the general filestore model into specific subsets.

Service classes are levels of capabilities within the protocol and are negotiated by the two ends of a connection at connect time. FTAM has five service classes specified:

- File access allows access and manipulation at the record level.
- File transfer of whole files or parts of files.
- File management: reading and changing file attributes.
- File transfer and management includes creation and deletion of files.
- Unconstrained allows negotiation on the basis of available functional units instead of service classes.

Functional units are a more granular way of dividing up the capabilities of the protocol. Within a particular class of service, there are mandatory and optional functional units. You can always negotiate for optional functional units within a class of service. The unconstrained service class is one with no mandatory functional units. The following are the ten basic functional units defined in FTAM:

- Kernel: basic file services for establishment of a connection
- Read
- Write
- File access: locating and manipulating FADUs within a file
- Limited file management: file creation and deletion, reading of attributes
- Enhanced file management: changing file attributes
- Grouping of operations so regimes can be efficiently established
- Recovery: re-creation of select or open regimes
- Restart data transfer
- FADU locking

Whereas the functional units and service classes deal with the services available in the protocol, document types limit what types of data may be contained in a virtual file being exchanged in an FTAM regime. Individual users may register their own file types with the proper authorities, specifying the structure of the data units and FADUs within the virtual filestore model.

In addition to user-defined document types, the ISO has defined five basic document types:

- FTAM-1: unstructured text files
- FTAM-2: sequential text files
- FTAM-3: unstructured binary files
- FTAM-4: sequential binary
- FTAM-5: simple hierarchical

The FTAM model is based on a single file. Most operating systems have more than one file, structured as a directory. A standard developed by the National Institute of Standards and Technology (NIST, formerly known as the National Bureau of Standards) provides a supplemental document type, that treats files in a directory as a special type of file. The user can retrieve this special file, then move on to individual files.

Figure 8-31 shows an example of a typical FTAM session. Notice that the first thing that happens is an OSI transport protocol virtual circuit is established and the connection request and confirm packets are acknowledged.

Once the circuit is initialized, the FTAM initialize message is sent, presumably embedded within OSI ACSE, Presentation, and Session Layer initialize messages. It is possible to have the session layer reuse an existing transport layer connection, in which case there is no need to reinitialize. Once the FTAM association is in place, the requesting node sends a series of operations, structured together as a single group of operations. First, a file is created, then the file is opened in "replace, extend" mode. Replace, extend mode is used in FTAM document types 1 and 3; insert mode is used for document type 2.

```
 -Delta T--DST---------SRC---
    2.0497  DECnet004E13←DECnet00A911  ISO_TP Connection request D=0000 S=F600
    0.0698  DECnet00A911←DECnet004E13  ISO_TP Connection confirm D=F600 S=A400
    0.0052  DECnet004E13←DECnet00A911  ISO_TP Ack  D=A400 NR=0 CDT=4
    0.0097  DECnet00A911←DECnet004E13  ISO_TP Ack  D=F600 NR=0 CDT=4
    0.0210  DECnet004E13←DECnet00A911  FTAM C Initialize
    0.1360  DECnet00A911←DECnet004E13  ISO_TP Ack  D=F600 NR=1 CDT=4
    5.6895  DECnet00A911←DECnet004E13  FTAM R Initialize
    0.1892  DECnet004E13←DECnet00A911  ISO_TP Ack  D=A400 NR=1 CDT=4
    0.2088  DECnet004E13←DECnet00A911  FTAM C Begin Group
                                       FTAM C Create SUCCESSFUL_FTAM_TEST.TXT A
                                       FTAM C Open Mode=Replace,Extend
                                       FTAM C End Group
    0.0078  DECnet00A911←DECnet004E13  ISO_TP Ack  D=F600 NR=2 CDT=4
    0.4420  DECnet00A911←DECnet004E13  FTAM R Begin Group
                                       FTAM R Create SYS$COMMON:[OSIT$DEFAULT]S
                                       FTAM R Open Document=Unstructured binary
                                       FTAM R End Group
    0.0036  DECnet004E13←DECnet00A911  ISO_TP Ack  D=A400 NR=2 CDT=4
    0.1632  DECnet004E13←DECnet00A911  FTAM C Write Operation=Extend
    0.1956  DECnet00A911←DECnet004E13  ISO_TP Ack  D=F600 NR=3 CDT=4

                       Use TAB to select windows
 1        2 Set        4 Zoom  5          6Disply 7 Prev  8 Next        10 New
   Help     mark         out     Menus     options  frame   frame       capture
```

8-31 FTAM Session

Next, the other node sends a message back acknowledging each of the operations. Notice that the file name returned is the full name that has been translated into an open on the unstructured binary document type. The first node then goes back and extends its file.

Figure 3-32 shows the FTAM initialize request in more detail. Notice that the service is being established based on functional units. The node has requested write, limited file management, and grouping. Attribute groups signify which file attributes are negotiated for a session.

The FTAM quality of service is used to indicate whether recovery is needed on this operation. The recovery and underlying checkpointing can make the session significantly slower: therefore if the application does not need it, recovery is often avoided.

The initialize request also indicates that two document types may be used—the unstructured and sequential text document types. It is up to each side to know what the document types mean in their real file systems and how they are interpreted by the application.

Figure 8-33 shows more detail on the operation to close and deselect a file. Notice that in between each of the FTAM commands there is a presentation layer header that indicates which of the possible presentation context identifiers applies to the upcoming command. Figure 8-34 shows a session with a data transfer operation. First a file is created, and the file extended.

```
┌DETAIL──────────────────────────────────────────────────────────────────────
│ FTAM: ───── ISO FTAM File transfer, access and management ─────
│ FTAM:
│ FTAM: FPDU type = Initialize request (length = 41)
│ FTAM: Functional units = 1500
│ FTAM:  ..0. ....  .... .... = No read
│ FTAM:  ...1 ....  .... .... = Write
│ FTAM:  .... 0...  .... .... = No file access
│ FTAM:  .... .1..  .... .... = Limited file management
│ FTAM:  .... ..0.  .... .... = No enhanced file management
│ FTAM:  .... ...1  .... .... = Grouping
│ FTAM:  .... ....  0... .... = No fadu locking
│ FTAM:  .... ....  .0.. .... = No recovery
│ FTAM:  .... ....  ..0. .... = No restart data transfer
│ FTAM: Attribute groups = 8X
│ FTAM:        1... .... = Storage
│ FTAM:        .0.. .... = No security
│ FTAM:        ..0. .... = No private
│ FTAM: FTAM quality of service = 0 (No recovery)
│ FTAM: Document type name = {1.0.8571.5.1} (ISO FTAM unstructured text)
│ FTAM: Document type name = {1.0.8571.5.2} (ISO FTAM sequential text)
└────────────────────────────Frame 6 of 30─────────────────────────────────
                         Use TAB to select windows
┌1─────┐┌2 Set──┐     ┌4 Zoom┐┌5────┐┌6Display┐┌7 Prev┐┌8 Next┐      ┌10 New──┐
│ Help ││ mark  │     │ out  ││Menus││options ││ frame││ frame│      │capture │
└──────┘└───────┘     └──────┘└─────┘└────────┘└──────┘└──────┘      └────────┘
```

8-32 FTAM Initialize Request

```
┌SUMMARY─Delta T──DST─────────SRC─────
│  22    0.0842  DECnet004E13←DECnet00A911   FTAM C Begin Group
│                                            FTAM C Close
│                                            FTAM C Deselect
│                                            FTAM C End Group
│  23    0.1680  DECnet00A911←DECnet004E13   FTAM R Begin Group
│                                            FTAM R Close
│                                            FTAM R Deselect
│                                            FTAM R End Group
│  24    0.0123  DECnet004E13←DECnet00A911   ISO_TP Ack  D=A400 NR=4 CDT=4
└──────────────────────────────────────────────────────────────────────────
┌DETAIL──────────────────────────────────────────────────────────────────────
│ FTAM: ───── ISO FTAM File transfer, access and management ─────
│ FTAM:
│ FTAM: FPDU type = Begin Group request (length = 7)
│ FTAM: Threshold = 2
│ FTAM:
│ ISO_PR: ───── ISO Presentation Layer ─────
│ ISO_PR:
│ ISO_PR: Next presentation context identifier = 1
│ ISO_PR:
└──────────────────────────────Frame 22 of 30──────────────────────────────
                         Use TAB to select windows
┌1─────┐┌2 Set──┐     ┌4 Zoom┐┌5────┐┌6Display┐┌7 Prev┐┌8 Next┐      ┌10 New──┐
│ Help ││ mark  │     │ in   ││Menus││options ││ frame││ frame│      │capture │
└──────┘└───────┘     └──────┘└─────┘└────────┘└──────┘└──────┘      └────────┘
```

8-33 Grouping of FTAM Commands

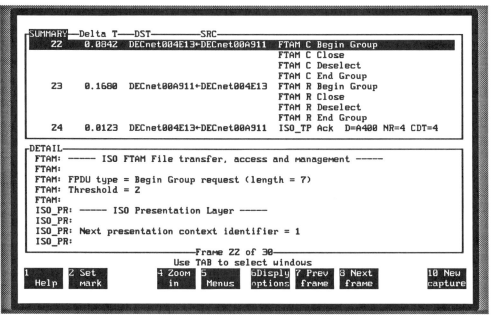

Then, 160 bytes of data are transferred, followed by a data end (the end of the data) and then a transfer end (the end of the transfer regime). Then, the file is closed and deselected, freeing it up for other users.

Figure 8-35 shows another session in which a file is created and opened as an unstructured text document. Ten groups of text data are sent, all included in the same underlying Ethernet packet. This is followed by a data end message and an end of the transfer regime.

One of the aspects of FTAM that makes it useful is the large number of file attributes that have been defined (see Fig. 8-36). Attributes are broken up into four groups, and not all groups must be supported.

The kernel has the basic information on a file, including the name and permitted action. The contents type indicates to what kind of document type (or a more general classification called a constraint set) the file belongs. Just because this information exists, it does not necessarily mean that the operating system will allow it to be divulged to other users.

The storage group includes an account indicator so that charges for access to the file may be directed to the appropriate user. The storage group also indicates size and availability information (i.e., online or on tape), as well as date and time information. The security group is used for a variety of purposes. The access control indicates who may look at the data in the file (or perform other operations such as writing). The legal qualifications indicate information such as copyright that may reflect how the data may be used.

Finally, a group called the private group has a single private attribute. This is where a particular implementation or computing environment would put its historical file attributes or information not supported in FTAM. DEC, for example, might hypothetically put a collating table in this area if there is no document type definition that holds that information. The use of private attributes reduces interoperability and is thus discouraged by open systems advocates.

Digital's FTAM Implementation

Digital's FTAM runs on the ISO protocol stack. DAP runs on the Digital Session Control layer. It appears as if DAP is still the strategic product for internal communication, although, as the cliché says, only time will tell.

Digital's version 2 of their FTAM implementation supports the three basic FTAM document types (unstructured text, sequential text, and unstructured binary) and most of the functional units. Of particular interest is support for file recovery.

Digital's FTAM also includes a DAP-FTAM gateway, allowing DECnet users to access remote OSI systems using the FTAM protocols (see Fig. 8-37). The gateway is essentially an FAL to the Digital user. It then translates the DAP calls into FTAM calls.

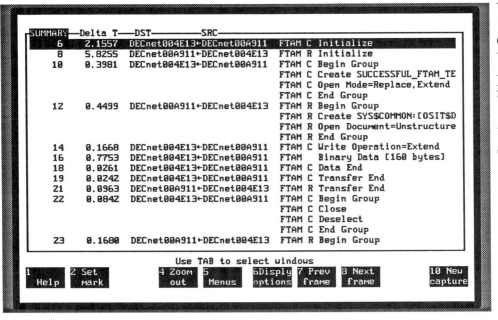

8-34 FTAM Data Transfer Traffic

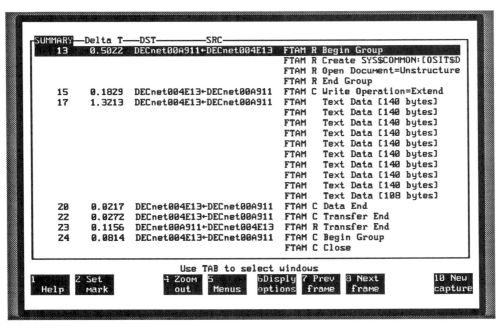

8-35 FTAM Write Operation

Kernel Group	Filename
	Permitted Action
	Contents Type
Storage Group	Storage Account
	Date/Time Attributes
	IDs
	File Availability
	Filesize
	Future Filesize
Security Group	Access Control
	Legal Qualifications
Private Group	Private Attributes

8-36
FTAM Attributes by Group

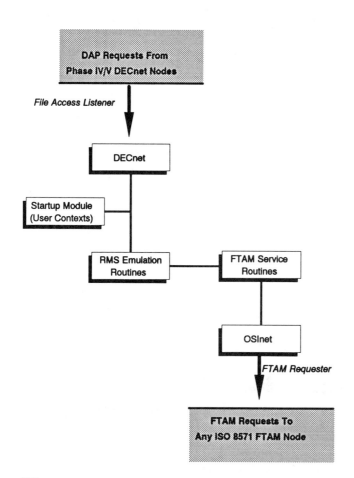

8-37
FTAM-DAP Gateway

To access a remote file, the DCL user uses a special form of the DECnet file specification which embeds access control information and the target node into a single file specification. The gateway allows any DECnet user to access remote OSI files. DECnet and DAP are used up to the gateway, then OSI and FTAM are used. The gateway does have a few limitations: The user must give an exact, complete file specification, and wildcards are not supported.

A DAP-FTAM gateway can be provided because most of the basic DAP calls map quite easily into associated FTAM calls (see Fig. 8-38). The DAP-FTAM gateway provides a transition environment that allows Phase IV nodes to access OSI resources. In a Phase V area, the FTAM application, part of DECnet, is available directly to the user.

TCP/IP-Based Services

A subject not covered extensively in this book is the use of TCP/IP as an alternative to DECnet or OSI services. Both VMS and Ultrix (Digital's Unix) have full support for TCP/IP and the Sun Microsystems-developed enhancements, the Network File System.

The equivalent to DAP and FTAM in the TCP/IP world is the File Transfer Protocol (FTP). Given its age and the wide variety of implementations, FTP is not as rich a protocol as DAP or FTAM. It offers transfer of whole files but does not provide access to the interior structure of files.

A more advanced protocol is Sun's Network File System. NFS is similar in function to Digital's Distributed File System, with the important difference that NFS has been implemented on every major operating system and DFS is only available for VMS. NFS allows a system to mount a remote file system, which is useful in a campus-like environment where the system administrator does not know which workstation (or even which brand of workstation) a given user will be using. NFS allows users to mount "home" files onto any workstation. Little used files, such as help files, can be mounted on all computers but stored on a single help server.

Digital supports NFS on all its platforms, including the VAX Cluster. With the VAX Cluster, the HSC controller can act as a disk server for a large environment of workstations—Digital and non-Digital.

For more information on TCP/IP and NFS, the reader is directed to a companion volume to this book, *Analyzing Sun Networks* (Van Nostrand Reinhold, 1991).

The Relational Database

We now move to the last method of remote data access—the relational database management system, which provides a level of functionality not found

RMS Service	FTAM Service Calls
$CLOSE	F_BEGIN_GROUP
	F_CLOSE
	F_DELETE (if Delete on Close bit set)
	F_DESELECT (if Delete on Close bit not set)
	F_END_GROUP
	F_TERMINATE (if connection not reused)
$CREATE	F_INITIALIZE
	F_BEGIN_GROUP
	F_CREATE
	F_READ_ATTRIB
	F_OPEN
	F_END_GROUP
$ERASE	F_INITIALIZE
	F_BEGIN_GROUP
	F_SELECT
	F_DELETE
	F_END_GROUP
	F_TERMINATE (if connection not reused)
$EXTEND	F_CHANGE_ATTRIBUTE
$FIND	F_LOCATE
$GET	F_READ
	F_GET_INDICATIONS
	F_TRANSFER_END
$OPEN	F_INITIALIZE
	F_BEGIN_GROUP
	F_SELECT
	F_READ_ATTRIB
	F_OPEN
	F_END_GROUP
$PUT	F_WRITE
	F_DATA
	F_DATA_END
	F_TRANSFER_END
$READ	F_READ
	F_GET_INDICATIONS
	F_TRANSFER_END

8-38
DAP-FTAM Mapping

RMS Service	FTAM Service Calls
$RENAME	F_INITIALIZE
	F_BEGIN_GROUP
	F_SELECT
	F_CHANGE_ATTRIB
	F_DESELECT
	F_END_GROUP
	F_TERMINATE
$REWIND	F_LOCATE
$TRUNCATE	F_TRUNCATE (only at beginning of file)
$WRITE	F_WRITE
	F_DATA
	F_DATA_END
	F_TRANSFER_END

8-38 (Cont.)
DAP-FTAM Mapping

in more primitive file systems. Typically, a DBMS uses the underlying file system as a method of storing data, then provides a great deal more functionality.

The biggest piece of functionality is logical access to data. The user sees a series of tables composed of rows and columns. The Structured Query Language (SQL) is used to specify what information, perhaps spanning multiple tables, is needed. The power of this method is that the user does not have to worry about the underlying storage mechanisms. The type of index, the storage structure, and other implementation details are hidden from the user and can be changed over time.

The database manager uses a query optimizer to decide how to get information efficiently in an environment with many tables and complex queries. This specialized query optimizer means that the programmer is freed from worry about the process of getting data and can concentrate on the semantics of how to process the data.

Increasingly, the database management system resides on a network. A program on the workstation issues SQL calls over the network, where they are received by a powerful server tuned to meet the demands of rapid data access. Although Digital has a clearly spelled out strategy for file-based data access, its database strategy is a bit more vague. Digital supports networked access to databases (not to be confused with the network model of database managements systems used in Codasyl). Networked access means the front and back ends are on separate systems. Networked access to relational database systems is provided by Digital using its Rdb database system and the

Digital Standard Relational Interface (DSRI), a network-based programmer's interface.

What Digital does not have (at least at the time that this book went to press) is a distributed database. A distributed database is the ability to treat many different databases as a single logical, distributed database. For example, manufacturing may keep one database, personnel another, and finance yet a third. Often these databases are developed and maintained separately, but queries will often span multiple databases. A distributed database allows the programmer to deal with the different repositories of data as a single whole, rather than work with each separately.

Distributed databases become especially important when updates are involved. One of the jobs of the database manager is to group several operations into a single transaction, guaranteeing that either all or none of the operations are performed. In a distributed environment, it is possible that updates may span several different computers and the DBMS must continue to ensure transaction integrity.

One of the Digital database strategies has been to rely on third-party vendors; for example, Digital has the Rdb database for the VMS operating system, but nothing for Ultrix. Digital therefore uses Ingres as their embedded database for Ultrix.

Summary

Data access protocols such as DAP or FTAM are meant to make the network transparent. As Sun Microsystems put it in a series of advertisements, "the network is the computer."

The goal of transparent access is never totally met, but often the operating system is able to shield the user from the details of remote data access. The record management services on the VMS operating system, for example, makes access to remote files via DAP fairly simple.

The different protocols for data access can be categorized based on the level of service they provide. Disk servers such as the Vax Cluster provide a primitive (and consequently fast) service of access to blocks of data on a disk. DFS provides access to files and blocks within the files. DAP provides the most structured level of service with access to individual records.

DFS and DAP both operate on the DECnet side of the protocol stack. For the OSI side, Digital uses FTAM. Since FTAM and DAP provide similar services, an FTAM-DAP gateway allows the DECnet user access to OSI-based nodes.

The most transparent level of access to data is the distributed relational database system. Instead of worrying about files, location, and other details of physical data access, the programmer is freed to concentrate on logical data access.

Terminals

CHAPTER 9

Terminals

The goal of a network architecture is transparency—the user should not even know the network is there. The computers on the network, and the services they offer, should appear as a simple extension of the user's workstation.

Client-server protocols and data access mechanisms are one way of extending the workstation's reach. There are times, however, when the user needs to attach to another computer as a plain old terminal. The LAT protocols handled the situation of the dumb terminal on a terminal server or by the PC emulating a terminal. Whereas LAT is limited to a single extended LAN, the mechanisms examined in this chapter work across an entire network. The DECnet CTERM protocols use the DNA Session Control layer to connect to other Digital (or DEC-compatible) nodes. The OSI Virtual Terminal Protocol (VTP) lets a user connect to another OSI-based system.

It is worth noting what this chapter does not cover—alternatives to the simple terminal emulation. In most modern networks, users are moving away from protocols like CTERM and toward more advanced capabilities based on network-based windowing environments like the X Windows System. Digital uses X as part of DECwindows.

PostScript, the language used to talk to most modern laser printers, is also used as an imaging system on the graphics screen in DECwindows. PostScript, with its scalable fonts and sophisticated two-dimensional graphics system, is ideal for applications like desktop publishing and graphics editing. For three-dimensional graphics, Digital supports another imaging model, the Programmer's Hierarchical Graphics Control System (PHIGS) or, more specifically, the PHIGS for X implementation known as PEX. PEX allows sophisticated graphics, such as supercomputer-generated visualization of complex models, to be displayed on the workstation screen.

PostScript, X, and PEX are all graphics protocols for the sophisticated workstation communicating with applications on the host. These topics could easily be put into their own book (and indeed have by several authors). This chapter instead concentrates on the lower-level task of simple terminal emulation.

CTERM

We start with the method used to log onto a Digital minicomputer, typically a VAX running either the VMS or Ultrix operating systems. The protocol used to provide this service is known as CTERM, short for the Command Terminal Module, one of the components of the protocol. The goal of the service is to allow a host-based application to treat all terminals, directly attached or network based, the same way. Digital accomplishes this by splitting the terminal device driver into two parts (see Fig. 9-1).

The application, via the operating system, acts as if it is communicating with a locally attached terminal via the services of the terminal class driver. The terminal class driver, based on the terminal ID, sends requests to the actual device driver that controls the asynchronous communications controller to which the terminal is directly attached. This split in functionality between a general class driver and a hardware-specific driver provides a level of transparency between the physical controller and the application. The split has another implication: allowing a PC to dial in as a terminal and then turn into a DECnet node.

As we saw in the subnetworks chapter, asynchronous DDCMP communications can be used as a method of providing DECnet connectivity. Asynchronous DDCMP is an important part of the DECnet/DOS implementation. When a remote PC wishes to use a modem to connect to a VAX, it dials in via a modem. By default, most systems connect the user to the local terminal module instead of to the network DDCMP driver.

The user is then presented with the typical login information, validating the user to that particular VAX. After being validated, the user can switch to a DECnet connection by issuing an escape sequence. The escape sequence, recognized by the device driver, switches the user to the DECnet service provider, and thus makes the PC a member of the DECnet instead of just a terminal.

Emulating a terminal allows the user to do the normal tasks of any interactive user—run programs that reside on the host. Functioning as a DECnet node allows the user to run all the network-based applications, such as DAP, directly from the PC. The two-level driver thus allows an application to be unaware of the local or remote nature of a user. If the user is remote, reads and writes to the terminal are sent to the network driver instead of to the local device driver (see Fig. 9-2).

Figure 9-2 shows that the CTERM protocols are actually two separate protocols. The lower layer, the foundation protocol, allows a physical terminal

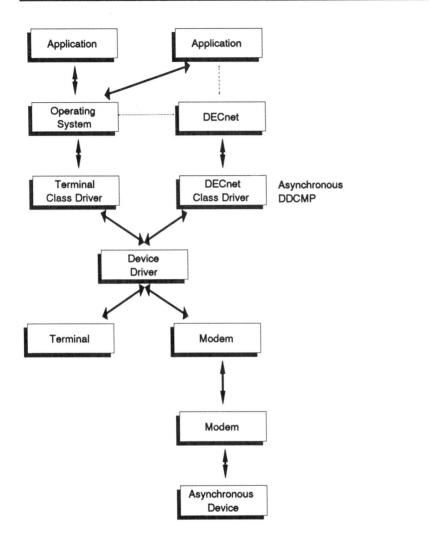

9-1
Multifunction
Device Driver

on a terminal server to send and receive data to a host. The foundation layer allows a variety of value-added upper layers to use this basic data-delivery service. The typical upper-layer module is the command terminal module, which allows a user to emulate a line-oriented, VT-compatible terminal (the VT series is Digital's standard line of dumb terminals). Other modules allow the user to perform forms-oriented operations and to utilize other methods of interacting with a host.

The foundation services thus provide basic data delivery as well as module switching. They also provide a logical terminal module, shielding the

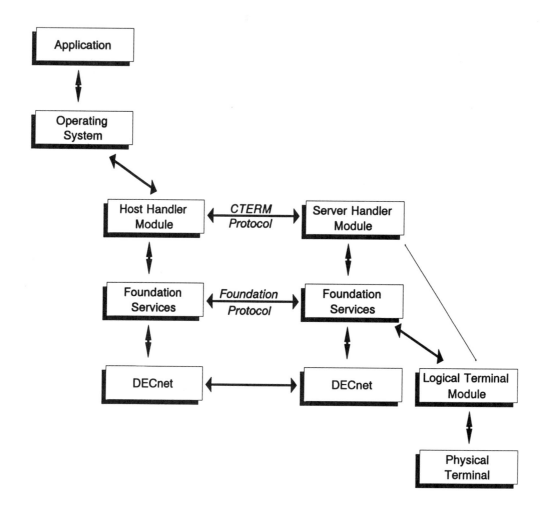

9-2 DEC Foundation and CTERM Protocols

host system from the details of the particular type of terminal. As long as the terminal supports the basic functionality assumed in the logical terminal module, the specific way the functionality is provided (e.g., how a cursor is moved on the screen) is irrelevant.

In addition to reading and writing, the purpose of the protocols is to allow an application to manipulate the various characteristics of the terminal. Figure 9-3 shows a variety of these characteristics. The handler, for example, maintains information that indicates if input should be ignored at that moment, effectively locking the keyboard. It also indicates if normal

Handler-Maintained Characteristics	Foundation-Maintained Counters
Ignore Input	Times Entered Connect State
Character Attributes	Characters Sent
Control/O Pass-Through	Characters Received
Raise Input	Parity Errors
Normal Echo	Overruns
Input Escape Sequence Enable	Framing Errors
Output Escape Sequence Enable	Seconds Since Last Zeroed (16 bit)
Input Count State	**Logical Terminal Characteristics**
Auto Prompt	Mode Writing Allowed?
Error Processing Bit Map	Hardcopy or Video?
Character Attributes Bitmap Flags	Terminal Type
Foundation-Maintained Characteristics	Output Flow Control
	Flow Character Pass-Through?
Input Speed	Output Page Stop?
Output Speed	Input Flow Control?
Physical Character Size (5-8)	Loss Notification?
Bit 8 Cleared?	Line Width
Parity Enable	Page Length
Parity Type	Stop Length
Modem Present?	Fill After Carriage Return?
Auto Baud Detect?	Fill After Line Feed?
Terminal Management Enabled?	Hardware/Software Wrapping?
Switch Mode Character	Hardware/Software Tabs?

9-3 CTERM Characteristics

echo of data is enabled and if certain characters should be passed through to the host (the control/o sequence is a signal that output resulting from a command should be discarded instead of shown on the user's screen).

The raise input characteristic indicates that all lowercase characters are converted to uppercase upon input. This allows communication with primitive host systems that do not support uppercase and lowercase.

The input and output escape sequence flags indicate whether special VT-100 escape sequences are used for input or output. These sequences perform operations like changing video characteristics, positioning the character, and enabling the terminal management mode.

Two bitmaps are provided, one for errors and one for character attributes. The error bitmap indicates what to do when certain types of errors are encountered. For errors such as receiver overruns or parity errors, the character can be ignored or queued for transmission to the host.

The character attributes bitmap specifies, how each character should be handled. The possible handling methods include:

- out-of-band handling
- including it in the input data stream
- altering the output discard state
- echoing control characters
- enabling/disabling special characters

Out-of-band handling bypasses the normal input queue. Altering the output discard state is the control/o toggle. The echo control character indicates whether things like the control/c interrupt should be shown on the screen. The enable/disable indicates whether certain well-known control sequences (like control/s for stop the screen) should be enabled or not.

All of these handler-maintained characteristics operate at the upper, command terminal module, level. A variety of lower-layer characteristics is also maintained by the foundation layer. Some of these are at the logical terminal module; others operate with the physical terminal.

The logical terminal characteristics specify which operations can be handled by the terminal itself and which ones the logical terminal module must perform. For example, a fill after a carriage return is used to delay after a line in the case of a printer that needs to move a carriage back physically. The wrapping characteristic indicates whether the terminal can perform the operation of moving the cursor back to the next line or if the software should handle this. Loss notification indicates if, when the input buffer gets full, the physical terminal or the logical terminal module should notify the user by ringing the bell.

As we can see, the concept of a remote terminal is more than reading and writing data to the screen. The particular mode of operation, in this case the VT-100 specific characteristics, provides a good deal of functionality beyond simple reads and writes.

If the operation were indeed a simple read/write operation, we could have accomplished these tasks simply by using DAP or even using the DNA Session Control layer directly. The functionality provided by CTERM, tailored directly to the interactive terminal user, allows interactive programs to be run effectively in a wide-area environment. In a local-area environment, we will typically see LAT used instead.

Foundation Layer

The basic foundation service has three functions:

- manage the logical connection to a resource in the host (known as a "portal") with a logical terminal
- establish and change the mode
- manage data transfer

Once a DNA Session has been established, the foundation layer performs a bind between the two user processes (see Fig. 9-4). The bind request, sent by the host after it accepts the session, indicates which version of CTERM, which modules, and which specific terminal on the server the host wishes to connect to.

The server (which typically had initiated the session with a DNA Session Control connect message) then responds with a logical terminal ID and the operating system it is running (see Fig. 9-5). Notice that in this protocol, in contrast to LAT, it is the host with the application that is the master in the relationship. The host initiates the session and will control the reading and writing of data.

Once the host is finished, as when the user types "logoff," the host clears the session using the foundation layer unbind message (see Fig. 9-6). The message only has a reason field. The typical reason is number 3, the user unbind request, but it is also possible to have an abrupt termination for a variety of other reasons.

The two other foundation layer messages are shown in Figures 9-7 and 9-8. Figure 9-8 has the mode messages, allowing the user to enter, exit, or confirm a mode. The host can respond with a confirm or no mode message. Typically, the session would begin in command terminal (CTERM) mode, but it then might switch to forms mode for a data-entry operation or some other forms-oriented program such as the ALL-IN-1 office automation software.

After performing the housekeeping of bind and mode messages, most of the session will consist of simple foundation layer data messages. The messages contain either common data or mode control information. Notice that the foundation data message can contain several different data segments, allowing a host to send a screen's worth of data, one line at time. The physical terminal would typically provide an automatic carriage return after each line of data.

A single user may thus transmit multiple pieces of data within a single subnetwork-layer packet. In contrast to LAT, however, a given virtual circuit can only work with one user/application association at once. When there are several users on one server all communicating with the same host, each session is a separate virtual circuit. For this reason, LAT is more efficient within the confines of a single data link. LAT also provides the capa-

Message Type		Message Type = 1
Version Numbers		Version Number
		ECO Number
		Customer Modification
Operating System		
Terminal Communication Protocols Supported		OS-dependent or CTERM
Revision Number		Implementation Dependent
ID		Logical Terminal or Portal
Options Field		High-Availability Host?

9-4
Foundation
Bind Request

Message Type		Message Type = 4
Version Numbers		Version Number (2)
		ECO Number (0)
		Customer Modification (0)
Operating System		
Revision Number		Implementation Dependent
ID		Logical Terminal or Portal
Options Field		Reserved

9-5
Foundation
Bind Accept

Message Type		Message Type = 2
Reason		1 - Incompatible Versions
		2 - No Portal Available
		3 - User Unbind Request
		4 - Terminal Disconnected
		5 - Selected ID In Use
		6 - Selected ID Nonexistant
		7 - Protocol Error Detected

9-6
Foundation
Unbind Message

Enter Mode		Message Type = 5
Mode		DEC or User-Defined (ex: Command Mode)
Exit Mode		Message Type = 6
Confirm Mode		Message Type = 7

9-7
Foundation
Mode Message

Message Type		9: Common Data
		10: Mode Data
Length		
Data		
Length		
Data		

9-8
Foundation Data
Message

bility of naming and advertising services, providing a logical separation between the user and the computer.

Command Terminal Module

The foundation layer allows the host and the server to be separated across the network. The command terminal module adds to this functionality by building more capabilities into the server system. Examples of servers would be a PC acting as a VT-100 terminal, a VAX VMS system with the "SET HOST" command, and a PDP-11/23 acting as a dedicated concentrator.

CTERM provides a variety of functions on the server system, including

- echoing
- type-ahead
- input editing
- output control (i.e., discard output)
- out-of-band input
- quoting (pass in verbatim character using control/v)
- output echo synchronization

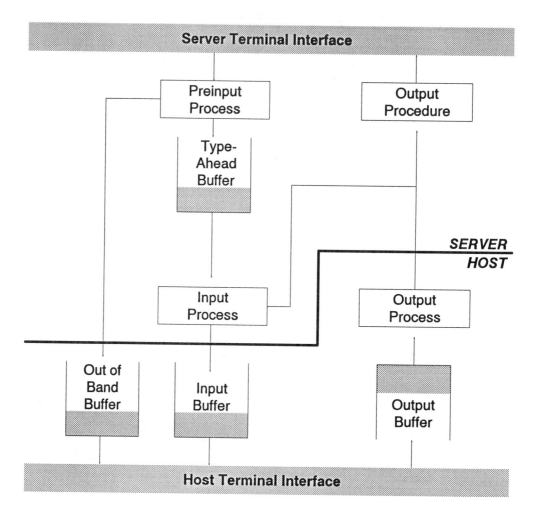

9-9 CTERM Processes on Host and Server

Synchronization ensures that commands and the results are shown in the proper order. This is done by locking one of the data streams at the proper moment.

The CTERM module can be modeled as a set of procedures and buffers (see Fig. 9-9). The preinput process on the server scans incoming keys typed by the user and decides whether they go in the normal buffer or should be sent directly to the host in the out-of-band buffer.

In addition to looking for out-of-band characters, the preinput process performs several other tasks. If control/x processing is enabled and one is received, the process clears the type-ahead buffer. If a read is pending, the control/x is changed to a control/u and placed in the type-ahead buffer. If control/o is enabled, the output-discard state variable is toggled, telling the output process that the user does not wish to see more output.

Normal data go directly into the type-ahead buffer and sit there. Data are moved out of the buffer only when the host issues a read command. If the type-ahead buffer gets full, the terminal will notify the user by ringing a bell.

In addition to guarding data for the host, the input process performs other functions. If escape sequence recognition is enabled, it processes these characters. If input editing is enabled, it looks for characters that affect the command input. The following characters will affect the status of the input buffer:

- delete deletes the last character
- control/w deletes word
- control/u deletes all input on this line
- control/r redisplays the input

Finally, the input process looks for the termination character. When it sees it, the command has been fully composed and the buffer can be handed off to the operating system.

Normal terminator characters are the carriage return or linefeed characters. Other terminators are when no character appears in the type-ahead buffer for a long period of time, when the input process gets an "unread" from the operating system, or when the user enters an input/editing command but the input buffer is empty.

When most data are sent to the host, they are also echoed on the user's screen. The data are thus moved by the input process to the output procedure, which writes the data to the user's screen. In addition to writes from echoing, the screen will also have data from the host, which puts data into an output buffer. The output process then moves that data, using the foundation layer services, to the output process on the user's terminal.

The output process is responsible for two tasks:

- maintaining the output discard state
- sending characters from output buffer to output procedure

The data in the output buffer are a series of characters and flags. The flags are start-of-message (SOM) and end-of-message (EOM). They are put in the output buffer by the host terminal interface write function. Typically, the SOM flag will lock the output procedure. There are two kinds of EOM flags. The first unlocks the output procedure after the last character is processed. The other optionally causes a redisplay of the input buffer.

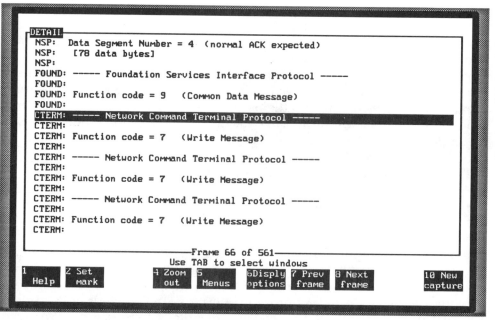

```
┌SUMMARY──Delta T──DST──────────SRC─────
   44                DECnet000B04←DECnet002804   FOUND Bind Request
   46    0.0990      DECnet002804←DECnet000B04   FOUND Bind Accept
   47    0.0093      DECnet000B04←DECnet002804   CTERM Initiate              LEN=2
                                                 CTERM Characteristics       LEN=6
   49    0.0633      DECnet002804←DECnet000B04   CTERM Initiate              LEN=4
   60    1.2263      DECnet000B04←DECnet002804   CTERM Write                 LEN=5
   62    0.1077      DECnet002804←DECnet000B04   CTERM Write Completion       LEN=6
   66    0.2511      DECnet000B04←DECnet002804   CTERM Write                 LEN=6
                                                 CTERM Write                 LEN=5
                                                 CTERM Write                 LEN=5
   68    0.0045      DECnet000B04←DECnet002804   CTERM Start Read            LEN=2
   89    2.4529      DECnet000B04←DECnet002804   CTERM Start Read            LEN=2
  124    1.7244      DECnet002804←DECnet000B04   CTERM Read Data             LEN=1
  131    0.4711      DECnet000B04←DECnet002804   CTERM Start Read            LEN=2
  189    6.2968      DECnet002804←DECnet000B04   CTERM Read Data             LEN=1
  207    3.9448      DECnet000B04←DECnet002804   CTERM Characteristics       LEN=1
  209    2.8650      DECnet000B04←DECnet002804   CTERM Read Characteristics  LEN=6
  211    0.0578      DECnet000B04←DECnet002804   CTERM Characteristics       LEN=1
  212    0.0176      DECnet000B04←DECnet002804   CTERM Start Read            LEN=1
  214    0.1126      DECnet002804←DECnet000B04   CTERM Read Data             LEN=1

                       Use TAB to select windows
┌1     ┌2 Set    ┌4 Zoom ┌5      ┌6Disply┌7 Prev ┌8 Next      ┌10 New
│ Help │  mark   │  out  │ Menus │options│ frame │ frame      │capture
```

9-10   CTERM Traffic

```
┌DETAIL┐
 NSP:   Data Segment Number = 4  (normal ACK expected)
 NSP:   [78 data bytes]
 NSP:
 FOUND: ----- Foundation Services Interface Protocol -----
 FOUND:
 FOUND: Function code = 9  (Common Data Message)
 FOUND:
 CTERM: ----- Network Command Terminal Protocol -----
 CTERM:
 CTERM: Function code = 7  (Write Message)
 CTERM:
 CTERM: ----- Network Command Terminal Protocol -----
 CTERM:
 CTERM: Function code = 7  (Write Message)
 CTERM:
 CTERM: ----- Network Command Terminal Protocol -----
 CTERM:
 CTERM: Function code = 7  (Write Message)
 CTERM:

                       ──Frame 66 of 561──
                       Use TAB to select windows
┌1     ┌2 Set    ┌4 Zoom ┌5      ┌6Disply┌7 Prev ┌8 Next      ┌10 New
│ Help │  mark   │  out  │ Menus │options│ frame │ frame      │capture
```

9-11   CTERM Write Message

The output process basically loops, moving data through the buffer. If the user has XOFF (control/s) enabled, the output process will be unable to move data, which eventually causes the write operation at the host to fail.

CTERM Messages

Figures 9-10 and 9-11 show typical CTERM traffic. In Figure 9-10 we see that the session begins with a bind request and accept. Next, the CTERM mode begins sending a variety of messages to check the characteristics, then performs a series of reads and writes. Figure 9-11 shows a variety of write messages all put in the same foundation layer data message.

The initiate message (see Fig. 9-12) is used to form a binding between the two CTERM modules. It sets the maximum input and output buffer sizes and defines which CTERM messages are supported by a particular implementation.

The start read message (see Fig. 9-13) is sent by the host to start the read process. It is sent when the host is ready to receive data and indicates how long the input buffer on the host is and how much data are currently in that buffer. The timeout factor indicates how long the server has to start the process.

The end of prompt and start of display tell the server input process where the server's prompt is and where the actual data are. This lets the server know how much data came from the user and can be affected by input editing. The termination set indicates which characters can be considered line terminators.

A variety of input flags is defined on this message to control a particular read operation. Underflow handling, for example, defines if a bell should be rung when a user tries to delete characters beyond the beginning of the buffer. The clear type-ahead flag indicates if the type-ahead buffer should be cleared. The terminate on vertical change tells the input process the read should be terminated if there is a change in the vertical position of the cursor while echoing an input character. The terminator echo flag indicates that terminator characters (carriage returns or linefeeds) should be echoed. The nondefault terminator set indicates that a set of terminator characters is specified.

The server will respond to the start read message with a read data message (see Fig. 9-14). The message indicates where in the input buffer the data should be placed and if there has been a change in the horizontal or vertical positions. The flags indicate whether there are more data and, if not, the reason for the termination of the read.

The unread command (see Fig. 9-15) is sent by the host to terminate a current read command if there is one in progress. The unread can be unconditional or can only take effect if there are no data in the input buffers.

Message Type		Message Type = 1
Flags		Not Used
Version Numbers		Version Number
		ECO Number
		Customer Modiification
Software Revision		
Parameter Type		0: Illegal
		1: Max Output Buffer
		2: Max Input Buffer
		3: CTERM Messages Supported
		Others as defined
Parameter Value		
Parameter Type		
Parameter Value		

9-12
CTERM Initiate
Message

In addition to a normal read data message, the server may send an out-of-band data message (see Fig. 9-16). This message does not require the host to initiate the transaction, but may only contain a single character. Repeated out-of-band data messages may be sent by the server (although the host will typically ignore repeated interrupts). Often, an out-of-band data message (such as an input) will result in a message to clear the input buffer of any extraneous data (see Fig. 9-17).

When the host has data to send, it sends a write message (see Fig. 9-18). The message may or may not carry data. The flags indicate if there is a change in the lock handling by the output procedure. The beginning-of-message and end-of-message flags also affect the lock on the output procedure (preventing, usually, the input process from echoing data back while a write operation is in progress).

Prefix and postfix codes allow special characters to be added before or after the data. For example, a certain number of linefeeds might be put in place before or after the data are sent. Alternatively, a character such as a formfeed might be used.

The completion status requested flag indicates that the host would like to know when the write operation is completed. It is possible that the write operation cannot be completed because the user has locked the screen. If so, perhaps the application would like to timeout after a period of time if it does not receive the write complete message (see Fig. 9-19).

		Host ⟹ Server
Message Type		Message Type = 2
Flags		
Input Buffer Length		Total Length
End Of Data		Start of Available Space
Timeout		0 Means Process Now
End Of Prompt		Position in Input Buffer
Start Of Display		Position in Input Buffer
Low Water		Last Char Not Modified
Termination Set		Bit map up to 32 Bytes
Data		
Flags (2 Bytes Total)		
UU: Underflow Handling Definition		
C: Clear Type-Ahead Flag		
F: Formatting Flag: Add LF to CR; Ignore Preloaded LF		
V: Terminate on Vertical Change Flag: Terminate read if change while echoing		
K: Continuation Read Flag: Continuation of previous read?		
II: Raise Input Flag: Convert Alpha to Uppercase		
DDD: Disable Control Definition: Disable some or all control characters		
N: No-echo Flag		
T: Terminator Echo Flag		
Q: Timeout Field Present Flag		
ZZ: Nondefault Terminator Set Flag		
EE: Recognize Input Escape Sequences Flag		

9-13
CTERM Start
Read Message

The write complete message also allows a host to know where the cursor is after the last write operation. Remember that local echoing may have affected the position of the cursor. Knowing this position allows the host to determine if a formfeed or some other control may be necessary.

The read characteristics message (see Fig. 9-20) allows the host to read the characteristics maintained by the server foundation or CTERM modules. This information, previously presented in Figure 9-3, lets the host find out information about the state of a particular terminal.

		Host ← Server
Message Type		Message Type = 3
Flags		
Low Water		Position of last character not modified this read
Vertical Position		Relative change on this read
Horizontal Position		
Termination Position		Number of data characters in buffer
Data		

Flags (1 Byte Total)
T: More data in type-ahead buffer?
C: Completion Code
0: Termination character
1: Valid escape sequence
3: Out-of-band character
4: Input buffer full
5: Timeout
6: Unread
7: Underflow
8: Absentee token
9: Vertical position change
10: Line break
11: Framing error
12: Parity error
13: Receiver overrun

9-14
CTERM Read
Data Message

		Host → Server
Message Type		Message Type = 5
Flags		Unconditional or Only if Buffers Empty

9-15
CTERM Unread
Message

		Host ← Server
Message Type		Message Type = 4
Flags		Output State = Discard?
Character		

9-16
CTERM Out-of-Band
Message

		Host ⇒ Server
Message Type		Message Type = 6
Flags		Empty

9-17
CTERM Clear
Input Message

		Host ® Server
Message Type		Message Type = 7
Flags		
Prefix Value		Newline Count or Character
Postfix Value		Newline Count or Character
Data		Optional
Flags		
UU: Lock Handling Definition (Lock? Unlock? Redisplay?)		
L: Newline Flag (Conditional LF at end of write?)		
D: Set Output Discard Flag (Change to "do not discard"?)		
B: Beginning of Message Flag		
E: End of Message Flag		
PP: Prefix Code (Character or Newline Count?)		
QQ: Postfix Code (Character or Newline Count?)		
S: Completion Status Requested Flag		
T: Transparent Flag (Use Foundation Service transparent services)		

9-18
CTERM Write Message

		Host ⇐ Server
Message Type		Message Type = 8
Flags		Output lost due to user control/o?
Horizontal Position		Relative change since beginning of write
Vertical Position		

9-19
CTERM Write
Complete Message

		Host → Server
Message Type		Message Type = 10
Flags		Empty
Selector		Only present on Character Attributes selector
Subselector		
Selector		
Subselector		

9-20
CTERM Read
Characteristics
Message

		Host ← Server
Message Type		Message Type = 11
Flags		Empty
Selector		
Value		
Selector		
Value		

9-21
CTERM Modify
Characteristics
Message

When a characteristic is modified, either the host or the server can communicate this information with the modify characteristics message (See Fig. 9-21). When the host sends the message it is a command to change a characteristic. When the server sends the command back, it is a notification of the current state.

Both the read and modify messages contain selector and value fields. The selector picks which characteristics are to be modified or reported, and the value is the current or new value.

There are three more messages available that modify the state of the operation. The discard state message (see Fig. 9-22) indicates to the host that the user is not interested in the rest of the output from the previous command and that the output can be safely discarded. The input count/check message (see Fig. 9-23) serves two purposes. First, when the host sends the message, it is an indication to send an input count message. Second, the resulting count shows the total number of characters in the input and type-ahead buffers. Finally, the input state message is sent from the server to the host to show whether the buffer is full or empty (see Fig. 9-24).

		Host ⇐ Server
Message Type		Message Type = 9
Flags		Discard Output?

9-22
CTERM Discard State
Message

		Host ⇐ Server
Message Type		12 - Check Input
		13 - Input Count
Flags		
Count		Not present on check input

9-23
CTERM Input
Count Message

		Host ⇐ Server
Message Type		Message Type = 14
Flags		Buffer count now zero
		Buffer count now nonzero

9-24
CTERM Input
State Message

ISO VTP

In the CTERM protocols we saw a DECcentric method of handling remote virtual terminals. Functions like the control/o keys (discard output) are oriented around asynchronous terminals in general and the VT-100 series in particular. The ISO has a more difficult task of accommodating a variety of different models of terminal interactions, ranging from the IBM-3270 series of synchronous terminals to teletex and videotext terminals.

The OSI Virtual Terminal Protocol is based on an abstract model shared between two communicating processes, known as the virtual terminal space. Within this virtual terminal is a variety of objects. A display object could be a terminal screen or a bell; a control object can be a devices like a joy stick, mouse, or keyboard.

As with the FTAM services, the general model is too broad to be useful and subsets are used in an implementation. Specific models of terminal interaction are registered using terminal profiles. A profile might be an international standard, as in the case of the basic teletex terminal, or vendor specific as in the case of the VT-100 terminal class. At the time this book went to press, Digital had not released details of how it would support VTP, so this discussion is fairly general.

The VTP protocols use the OSI Session Control layer to set up a session with a remote system. The presentation layer and the Association Control

```
┌DETAIL┐
 ISO_SS:       .... ....  ...0 .... = No major synchronize
 ISO_SS:       .... ....  .... 0... = No minor synchronize
 ISO_SS:       .... ....  .... .0.. = No expedited data
 ISO_SS:       .... ....  .... ..1. = Duplex
 ISO_SS:       .... ....  .... ...0 = No half-duplex
 ISO_SS: Calling session selector = PRE
 ISO_SS: Called  session selector = PRE
 ISO_SS:
 ISO_PR: ----- ISO Presentation Layer -----
 ISO_PR:
 ISO_PR: PPDU type = Connect Presentation (length = 102)
 ISO_PR: Mode selector = 1 (Normal mode)
 ISO_PR: Calling presentation selector = <0004>
 ISO_PR: Called presentation selector = <0002>
 ISO_PR: Presentation context identifier = 1
 ISO_PR:  Abstract syntax name = {1.0.9041.2} (VT BASIC)
 ISO_PR:  Transfer syntax name = {2.1.1} (ASN.1)
 ISO_PR: Presentation context identifier = 3
 ISO_PR:  Abstract syntax name = {2.2.1.0.1} (ACSE)
 ISO_PR:  Transfer syntax name = {2.1.1} (ASN.1)
 ISO_PR: Default abstract syntax = {1.0.9041.2} (VT BASIC)
 ISO_PR: Default transfer syntax = {2.1.1} (ASN.1)
 ISO_PR: Next presentation context identifier = 3
 ISO_PR:
 ACSE: ----- ISO ACSE Association Control Service Element -----
 ACSE:
 ACSE: 1.1  Application Constructed [0], Length=26
 ACSE: 2.1   Context-Specific Constructed [1], Length=6
 ACSE: 3.1    OBJECT IDENTIFIER, Length=4, Value = "{1.0.9041.1}"
 ACSE: 2.2   Context-Specific Constructed [30], Length=16
 ACSE: 3.1    Constructed EXTERNAL, Length=14
 ACSE: 4.1     INTEGER, Length=1, Value = "1"
 ACSE: 4.2     Context-Specific Constructed [0], Length=9
 ACSE:
 VTP: ----- ISO VTP Virtual Terminal Protocol -----
 VTP:
 VTP: VTPDU type = Associate request (length = 9)
 VTP: Class = 1 (Basic)
 VTP: Functional units = 08
 VTP:       0... .... = No profile switch
 VTP:       .0.. .... = No multiple interaction negotiation
 VTP:       ..0. .... = No negotiated release
 VTP:       ...0 .... = No urgent data
 VTP:       .... 1... = Destructive break
 VTP:
                  ──Frame 124 of 260──
                  Use TAB to select windows
 ┌─┐    ┌2 Set ┐    ┌4 Zoom┐┌5    ┐   ┌6Disply┐┌7 Prev┐┌8 Next┐      ┌10 New  ┐
 │1│    │      │    │      ││     │   │       ││      ││      │      │        │
 │Help│ │ mark │    │ out  ││Menus│   │options││ frame││ frame│      │capture │
 └─┘    └──────┘    └──────┘└─────┘   └───────┘└──────┘└──────┘      └────────┘
```

9-25 VTP Associate Request

Service Element then set up the association between two applications (see Fig. 9-25). Notice that the session uses a presentation context previously defined for use in the VT model.

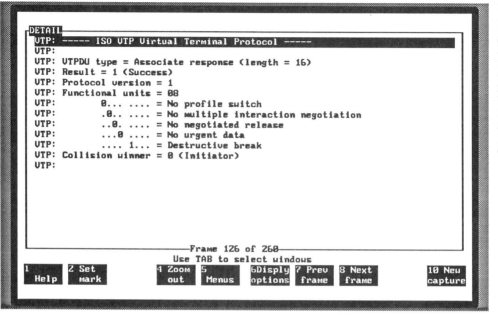

```
┌DETAIL┐
│UTP: ----- ISO UTP Virtual Terminal Protocol -----
│UTP:
│UTP: UTPDU type = Associate response (length = 16)
│UTP: Result = 1 (Success)
│UTP: Protocol version = 1
│UTP: Functional units = 08
│UTP:         0... .... = No profile switch
│UTP:         .0.. .... = No multiple interaction negotiation
│UTP:         ..0. .... = No negotiated release
│UTP:         ...0 .... = No urgent data
│UTP:         .... 1... = Destructive break
│UTP: Collision winner = 0 (Initiator)
│UTP:



                         ─Frame 126 of 260─
                       Use TAB to select windows
┌─────┐┌─────┐  ┌──────┐┌─────┐┌──────┐┌──────┐┌──────┐     ┌───────┐
│1    ││2 Set│  │4 Zoom││5    ││6Displ││7 Prev││8 Next│     │10 New │
│ Help││ mark│  │  out ││Menus││option││ frame││ frame│     │capture│
└─────┘└─────┘  └──────┘└─────┘└──────┘└──────┘└──────┘     └───────┘
```

9-26 ISO VTP Association Response

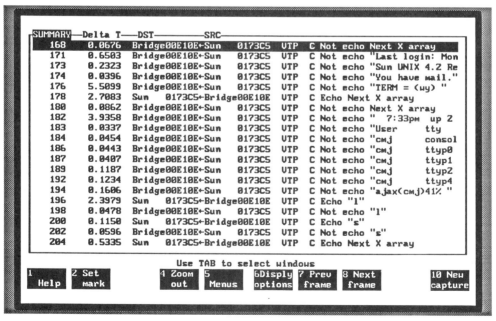

```
┌SUMMARY──Delta T──DST────────SRC─────────────────────────────────────┐
│  168   0.0676  Bridge00E10E←Sun    0173C5  VTP  C Not echo Next X array
│  171   0.6503  Bridge00E10E←Sun    0173C5  VTP  C Not echo "Last login: Mon
│  173   0.2323  Bridge00E10E←Sun    0173C5  VTP  C Not echo "Sun UNIX 4.2 Re
│  174   0.0396  Bridge00E10E←Sun    0173C5  VTP  C Not echo "You have mail."
│  176   5.5099  Bridge00E10E←Sun    0173C5  VTP  C Not echo "TERM = (wy) "
│  178   2.7083  Sun    0173C5←Bridge00E10E  VTP  C Echo Next X array
│  180   0.0862  Bridge00E10E←Sun    0173C5  VTP  C Not echo Next X array
│  182   3.9358  Bridge00E10E←Sun    0173C5  VTP  C Not echo "  7:33PM  up 2
│  183   0.0337  Bridge00E10E←Sun    0173C5  VTP  C Not echo "User      tty
│  184   0.0454  Bridge00E10E←Sun    0173C5  VTP  C Not echo "cmj      consol
│  186   0.0443  Bridge00E10E←Sun    0173C5  VTP  C Not echo "cmj      ttyp0
│  187   0.0407  Bridge00E10E←Sun    0173C5  VTP  C Not echo "cmj      ttyp1
│  189   0.1187  Bridge00E10E←Sun    0173C5  VTP  C Not echo "cmj      ttyp2
│  192   0.1234  Bridge00E10E←Sun    0173C5  VTP  C Not echo "cmj      ttyp4
│  194   0.1606  Bridge00E10E←Sun    0173C5  VTP  C Not echo "ajax(cmj)41% "
│  196   2.3979  Sun    0173C5←Bridge00E10E  VTP  C Echo "l"
│  198   0.0478  Bridge00E10E←Sun    0173C5  VTP  C Not echo "l"
│  200   0.1150  Sun    0173C5←Bridge00E10E  VTP  C Echo "s"
│  202   0.0596  Bridge00E10E←Sun    0173C5  VTP  C Not echo "s"
│  204   0.5335  Sun    0173C5←Bridge00E10E  VTP  C Echo Next X array

                       Use TAB to select windows
┌─────┐┌─────┐  ┌──────┐┌─────┐┌──────┐┌──────┐┌──────┐     ┌───────┐
│1    ││2 Set│  │4 Zoom││5    ││6Displ││7 Prev││8 Next│     │10 New │
│ Help││ mark│  │  out ││Menus││option││ frame││ frame│     │capture│
└─────┘└─────┘  └──────┘└─────┘└──────┘└──────┘└──────┘     └───────┘
```

9-27 ISO VTP Session Traffic

```
┌DETAIL────────────────────────────────────────────────────────┐
│ VTP: ----- ISO VTP Virtual Terminal Protocol -----            │
│ VTP:                                                          │
│ VTP: VTPDU type = Data request (length = indefinite)          │
│ VTP: Not echo, Display name = DISPLAY-OBJECT-1               │
│ VTP:   Text [26 bytes] = "# -----------------------"          │
│ VTP: Not echo, Display name = DISPLAY-OBJECT-1               │
│ VTP:   Next X array                                           │
│ VTP: Not echo, Display name = DISPLAY-OBJECT-1               │
│ VTP:   Text [1 byte] = "#"                                    │
│ VTP: Not echo, Display name = DISPLAY-OBJECT-1               │
│ VTP:   Next X array                                           │
│ VTP: Not echo, Display name = DISPLAY-OBJECT-1               │
│ VTP:   Text [84 bytes] = "#        Termcap source file @(#)termcap.src 1.5 86/│
│ VTP: Not echo, Display name = DISPLAY-OBJECT-1               │
│ VTP:   Next X array                                           │
│ VTP: Not echo, Display name = DISPLAY-OBJECT-1               │
│ VTP:   Text [29 bytes] = "#        Kevin Layer, Berkeley"      │
│ VTP: Not echo, Display name = DISPLAY-OBJECT-1               │
│ VTP:   Next X array                                           │
│ VTP: Not echo, Display name = DISPLAY-OBJECT-1               │
└─────────────────────────Frame 92 of 268──────────────────────┘
                      Use TAB to select windows
┌1       ┐┌2 Set   ┐      ┌4 Zoom ┐┌5     ┐┌6Disply┐┌7 Prev┐┌8 Next┐      ┌10 New   ┐
│  Help  ││  mark  │      │  out  ││ Menus││options││ frame││ frame│      │capture  │
└────────┘└────────┘      └───────┘└──────┘└───────┘└──────┘└──────┘      └─────────┘
```

9-28 ISO VTP Display Objects

The actual VT associate request specifies both basic and extended models of operations. Basic operation is simpler to support. In this particular example, the requestor specifies that no additional functional units shall be used in this session. The response to the associate request is shown in Figure 9-26. The negotiation was a success. If there is a collision of data being sent by the two sides, the initiator is the winner. Functions like profile switching or urgent data have not been selected. A destructive break has been selected.

Figures 9-27 and 9-28 show a typical VTP session. Notice that in Figure 9-27 the session is basically a login by a user onto a workstation running the Sun release of the Unix operating system. The user logs in and is immediately presented with a list of current users. The user then types two keys: l and s. The ls command is the Unix command for listing files.

The not echo version of a write indicates that a particular object does not have to be echoed back by the other side. In the case of a host writing to a client, there is no need to perform an echo. In the case of a client writing to a host, it may or may not want to have information echoed (passwords are usually not echoed back on the user's screen).

Figure 2-28 shows a typical host command with no echo. Since the VTP commands are symmetrical (there is no master and client) it is necessary to

```
┌─DETAIL────────────────────────────────────────────────────────┐
│ VTP: ----- ISO VTP Virtual Terminal Protocol -----             │
│ UTP:                                                           │
│ UTP: UTPDU type = Data request (length = indefinite)          │
│ UTP: Not echo, Display name = DISPLAY-OBJECT-1                 │
│ UTP:   Text [26 bytes] = "# ------------------------"         │
│ UTP: Not echo, Display name = DISPLAY-OBJECT-1                 │
│ UTP:   Next X array                                            │
│ UTP: Not echo, Display name = DISPLAY-OBJECT-1                 │
│ UTP:   Text [1 byte] = "#"                                     │
│ UTP: Not echo, Display name = DISPLAY-OBJECT-1                 │
│ UTP:   Next X array                                            │
│ UTP: Not echo, Display name = DISPLAY-OBJECT-1                 │
│ UTP:   Text [84 bytes] = "#        Termcap source file @(#)termcap.src 1.5 86/ │
│ UTP: Not echo, Display name = DISPLAY-OBJECT-1                 │
│ UTP:   Next X array                                            │
│ UTP: Not echo, Display name = DISPLAY-OBJECT-1                 │
│ UTP:   Text [29 bytes] = "#        Kevin Layer, Berkeley"      │
│ UTP: Not echo, Display name = DISPLAY-OBJECT-1                 │
│ UTP:   Next X array                                            │
│ UTP: Not echo, Display name = DISPLAY-OBJECT-1                 │
│                        Frame 92 of 260                         │
│                   Use TAB to select windows                    │
│ 1        2 Set           4 Zoom  5          6Disply 7 Prev 8 Next      10 New │
│   Help     mark            out     Menus    options  frame   frame    capture│
└────────────────────────────────────────────────────────────────┘
```

Courtesy of Network General

9-28 ISO VTP Display Objects

The actual VT associate request specifies both basic and extended models of operations. Basic operation is simpler to support. In this particular example, the requestor specifies that no additional functional units shall be used in this session. The response to the associate request is shown in Figure 9-26. The negotiation was a success. If there is a collision of data being sent by the two sides, the initiator is the winner. Functions like profile switching or urgent data have not been selected. A destructive break has been selected.

Figures 9-27 and 9-28 show a typical VTP session. Notice that in Figure 9-27 the session is basically a login by a user onto a workstation running the Sun release of the Unix operating system. The user logs in and is immediately presented with a list of current users. The user then types two keys: l and s. The ls command is the Unix command for listing files.

The not echo version of a write indicates that a particular object does not have to be echoed back by the other side. In the case of a host writing to a client, there is no need to perform an echo. In the case of a client writing to a host, it may or may not want to have information echoed (passwords are usually not echoed back on the user's screen).

Figure 2-28 shows a typical host command with no echo. Since the VTP commands are symmetrical (there is no master and client) it is necessary to

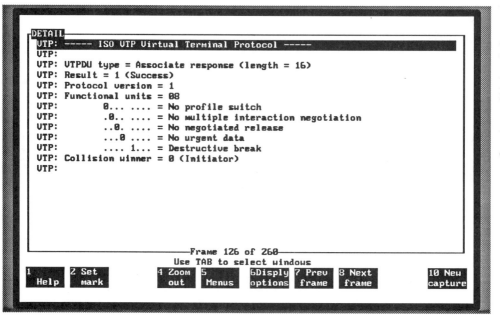

9-26 ISO VTP Association Response

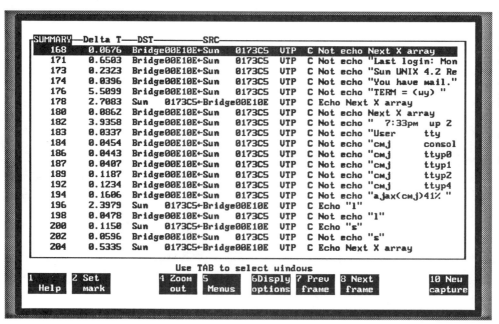

9-27 ISO VTP Session Traffic

specify this information. In the figure, the user is typing a file called the termcap, which lists the capabilities of different kinds of terminals.

Summary

Which model of virtual terminal processing to use depends on the computing environment. All of the models have the same basic aim—making remote applications available.

In a local environment, strictly within a DECnet, the user can take advantage of LAT. LAT is especially useful when multiple users (or a single user with multiple sessions) are communicating with a single host. By multiplexing and by the timer-based protocol, a significant load is taken off the host.

CTERM extends the functionality of LAT by providing virtual terminal services in a wide-area environment. CTERM would be used when a user wishes to log onto a host outside the LAN. Multiple modes and support for a variety of characteristics make CTERM a functional method of communicating to remote Digital hosts.

For a truly heterogeneous environment, the user would pick one of two protocols. VTP is used to communicate with a remote OSI host. In a TCP/IP environment, a similar protocol called Telnet can be used. Both VTP and Telnet have the attribute of being able to support a variety of different terminals, although typically at a fairly low level of functionality. Functions like input editing, for example, are often provided at the host instead of the server.

In a workstation environment, these protocols are rarely used within the confines of the work group. Instead of a line-by-line (or field-by-field display) a windowing environment has more sophisticated graphical cues, including icons, menus, windows, and text in multiple fonts and sizes. For these environments, a system like the X Windows System is necessary.

Even in the workstation environment, however, there is a need to access traditional applications. A workstation, or X Windows Terminal, will thus usually include applications like CTERM or OSI VTP for accessing remote hosts.

Messages

CHAPTER 10

Messages

Remote data access and virtual terminals both allow immediate access to remote systems. For many applications, however, a simple store-and-forward message is more useful. Rather than requiring the immediate attention of all intermediate systems in a path, a store-and-forward transfer allows hosts to perform the tasks when a few cycles are free or to retry a failed transfer at a later time when the network might be less congested.

A messaging system performs a store-and-forward transfer between two applications. The application is a user agent. The store-and-forward transfer is performed by one or more message transfer agents. The basic service of message delivery can be enhanced to offer more sophisticated services such as receipt generation on delivery.

Applications can be traditional email programs. Applications can also be database programs, shareware, document processors, or spreadsheets. Database programs, for example, could use the store-and-forward service to update remote databases or to trigger electronic mail automatically when a certain event occurs. The DECmcc network manager, discussed in Chapter 11, is an example of such a trigger system. When something significant happens on the network, the alert module can be directed to compose mail and send it to a list of relevant users.

In a Digital network, there are actually two messaging systems (see Fig. 10-1). The original messaging system was the mail-11 system, which worked as part of the VMS operating system. The user agent, VMSmail, came bundled with the operating system.

Over time, Digital added another messaging system, known as MAILbus. MAILbus comes with a distributed directory to keep track of names and a user agent that is part of the ALL-IN-1 office automation software.

A third messaging system is X.400. Connecting MAILbus to both mail-11 and X.400 are gateways. X.400, being an OSI application, uses the OSI stack. MAILbus, being a Digital proprietary system, uses the DECnet Session Control layer.

DEC/EDI	ALL-IN-1 Integrated OA Software	ALL-IN-1 MAIL	VMSmail Gateway	VMSmail User Agent
Message Router Message Transport Agent Distributed Directory Service				Mail-11 Protocol
PROFS/SNADS Gateways	Message Router X.400 Gateway	Message Router API (Other Gateways)	DNA Session Control	
SNA Session and Transport Layers	ISO Session and Transport Layers	Other Networks	DNA Transport Layer	

10-1 DEC Messaging Protocols

Digital MAILbus

We start with MAILbus for historical reasons. Digital began developing the MAILbus while X.400 was still in the early stages. After the basic products became available X.400 support was added through the use of a gateway. The components of the MAILbus architecture are shown in Figure 10-2. The Message Router is the message transfer agent, using the services of DECnet to move messages around. Native user agents, as in the case of ALL-IN-1, interact directly with the Message Router.

A user can find the correspondence between a user name and an electronic mail address through the distributed directory. We will see that the distributed directory is also used by gateways as a way of storing address translations.

Gateways are used to connect the native MAILbus architecture to other messaging systems. There are two types of gateways. A user interface gateway accepts delivery of messages and translates them into some native format for the user interface. An example of such a gateway provided by Digital is the one to the older VMSmail system. Digital also sells a toolkit, allowing an application program to interface to the Message Router.

The other type of gateway connects multiple messaging systems. Digital has developed several gateways (see Fig. 10-3). The job of the gateway is to translate message headers and the internal content to conform to the differ-

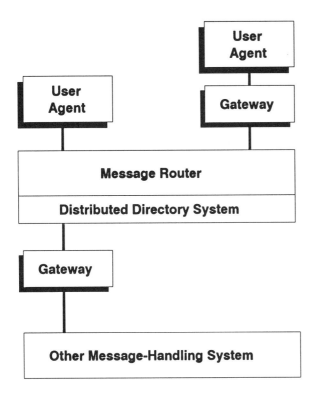

10-2
DEC's MAILbus
Architecture

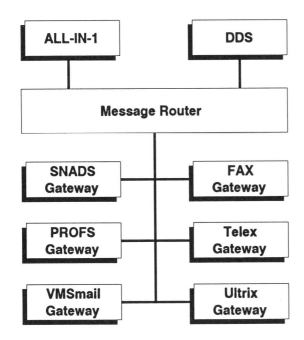

10-3
MAILbus Gateways

315

ent rules. Addresses, possibly stored in the distributed directory, are also converted.

The advantage of this architecture is that a single user interface can communicate with a wide variety of environments. The user can use a single style of interacting with the computer, yet still reach users in other environments.

Two of the important gateways are SNADS and PROFS. SNADS, the SNA Distribution Services, is the message handling system used in large SNA networks, particularly in the DISOSS office automation product. PROFS is the electronic mail system for IBM's VM/CMS operating system.

The Ultrix gateway is also quite useful. It resides on an Ultrix node and interacts with the TCP/IP Simple Mail Transfer Protocol (SMTP). SMTP forms the basis for message exchange in most of the Internet, the loose collection of wide-area networks that includes NSFnet and several other research networks. The Ultrix gateway thus allows DECnet users to have access to a much wider messaging environment.

The fax gateway is a one-way gateway. This software, using a fax card built onto a processor on the network, allows the user to send a mail message in facsimile form. The fax gateway can receive messages but cannot distribute them to individual users. Instead, the gateway prints (or stores) all incoming messages.

Digital also has an X.400 gateway, which allows X.400 nodes to send mail messages to Digital nodes. Although this is not a native X.400 network, it does allow the Digital user, during a transition period, to access a wider X.400 environment. The X.400 capabilities are important because they form the basis for many public national electronic mail networks and for the interconnectivity products of a large number of vendors.

X.400

X.400 structures a collection of message transfer agents and user agents into a management domain—a collection of resources under a single administration (see Fig. 10-4).

A domain maintained by an International Telecommunications Union (ITU) member (or registered private member) is an Administration Management Domain (ADMD). All other domains are Private Management Domains (PRMD).

The PRMD may be connected to multiple ADMDs, but for the purpose of any one message the PRMD is connected to a single ADMD. Routing for a PRMD consists of giving the message to the ADMD. Routing for the ADMD is simple for a directly connected domain. For further routing decisions, the process is outside of the specification, but note that a domain can easily be "directly" connected to another through the use of the OSI Session,

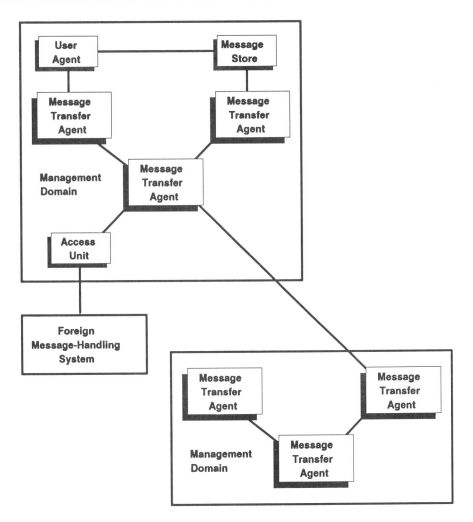

10-4 X.400 Management Domains

Transport, and Network layers. The X.500 directory is used to find the address of a relevant domain.

Figure 10-5 shows the components that make up an X.400 environment. The main components are the user agent and the message transfer agent. The user agent prepares the message and the message transfer agents move messages.

The message store is a staging point that picks up messages from the message transfer system and holds them for the user. The message store appears as a user agent to the message transfer agent: It accepts delivery of messages and holds them for the user. In addition, the user agent can sub-

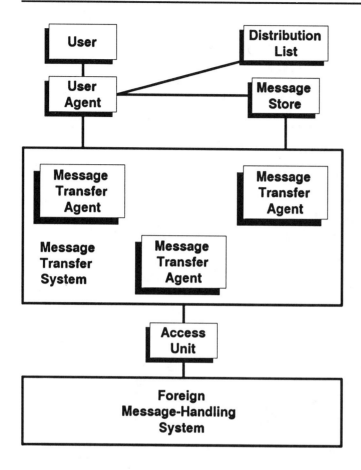

10-5
X.400 Message
Handling Environment

mit messages to the message store, which then hands them off to the message transfer agent. An example of this scenario is a PC (the user agent) and a VAX operating as the post office (the message store). Message stores can be simple stores, as the name implies, but can also include services such as autoforwarding on behalf of a user.

The access unit is a gateway to another message-handling environment. X.400 defines access units for interconnection to telex, postal delivery, and a few other environments. The Digital X.400 gateway is an example of an access unit.

X.400 breaks a message up into three parts (see Fig. 10-6). Each message has a header, put in by the message transfer system. The rest of the message is considered data by the message transfer system. User agents compatible with the Interpersonal Messaging Service (IPMS) are able to add further structure to the message. This layer, similar to an upper-level protocol, also consists of a header and a body.

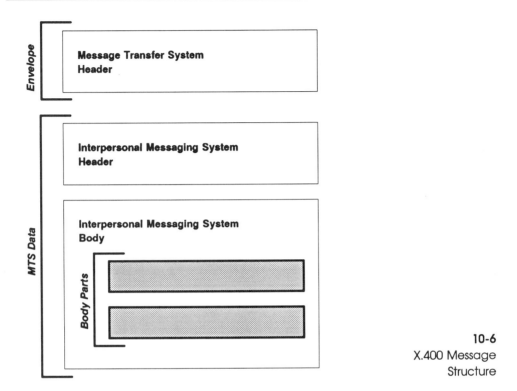

10-6
X.400 Message
Structure

A user agent in X.400 is known by an originator/recipient address (O/R Address). This user could be an individual user or a distribution list. As with network-layer addressing, each user must have a unique address. As with the OSI network addressing standards, a variety of different formats are defined (see Fig. 10-7).

For each of the formats, different elements can be used to identify a user. Some elements are mandatory; others are conditional—their use is up to a particular domain. For the postal address, for example, the country name and postal code are required elements. The name of the physical delivery service is optional—in the United States this information might specify Federal Express, UPS, or even the postal service. In countries with a single delivery service, the field wouldn't be necessary.

IPMS

The Interpersonal Messaging Service (IPMS) is a subclass of user agents. It defines a further structure to a message over that defined by the message transfer system. Instead of arbitrary data, the message is structured as a header and a set of body parts.

Attribute Type	O/R Address Forms			
	Mnemonic	Numeric	Postal	Terminal
General				
Administration Domain Name	M	M	M	C
Common Name	C			
Country Name	M	M	M	C
Network Address				M
Numeric Use Identifier		M		
Organization Name	C			
Organizational Unit Names	C			
Personal Name	C			
Private Domain Name	C	C	C	C
Terminal Identifier				C
Postal Routing				
Physical Delivery Service			C	
Physical Delivery Country Name			M	
Postal Code			M	
Postal Addressing				
Physical Delivery Office Name			C	
Physical Delivery Office Number			C	
Local Postal Attributes			C	
Physical Delivery Organization Name			C	
Physical Delivery Personal Name			C	
Post Office Box Address			C	
Post Restante Address			C	
Street Address			C	
Unformatted Postal Address			C	
Unique Postal Name			C	
Domain-defined	C	C		C
M - Mandatory C - Conditional				

Note: Postal address can be unformatted (all information in one attribute). The unformatted address consists of the *unformatted postal address* attribute. Source: CCITT Data Communications Networks (Blue Book), ITU (Geneva, 1989), Recommendation X.402, p. 121

10-7 X.400 Address Formats

	Access management
	Content type indication
	Converted indication
	Delivery time stamp indication
	IP-message identification
Basic Services	Message identification
	Nondelivery notification
	Original encoded information types indication
	Submission time stamp indication
	Typed body
	User/UA capabilities registration

10-8
X.400 IPMS
Basic Services

The functions provided by the IPMS are known as elements of service. As with the address format, the IPMS includes a variety of different elements. Some elements are considered basic, and are part of every implementation (see Fig. 10-8).

A basic element of service is a content type indication. The content type indication is a field in the IPMS header that indicates what the content looks like—one body part might be a fax image, another might have plain text.

In addition to the structure of the message, the IPMS includes notifications. The message transfer service gives delivery and nondelivery notifications, indicating whether the message was transferred to a user agent. The IPMS adds a further service with receipts and nonreceipts that indicate when the message was read. There are many optional elements defined in the IPMS. If supported, they typically consist of a field in the IPMS header. Figure 10-9 shows the different services offered. The services are categorized as being provided on the origination or reception of a message. For each of these categories, services are further categorized as being essential or additional. An essential element is one that must be provided by the IPMS, but the user does not have to choose it on a particular message. An additional element is one that a particular implementation or management domain may choose not to provide. An example of an additional element is the additional physical rendition, allowing the user to have a copy of the message printed. This is optional on both sides.

The autoforwarded indication is an example of an element that is additional for the message sender: There is no requirement that you be notified if a message you sent was automatically forwarded to another user. On the other hand, this element is considered essential on reception: A user receiv-

Element	Origination	Reception
Additional physical rendition	A	A
Alternate recipient allowed	A	A
Authorizing users indication	A	E
Auto-forwarded indication	A	E
Basic physical rendition	A	E
Blind copy recipient indication	A	E
Body part encryption indication	A	E
Content confidentiality	A	A
Content integrity	A	A
Conversion prohibition	E	E
Conversion prohibition in case of loss of information		N/A
Counter collection	A	E
Counter collection with advice	A	A
Cross-referencing indication	A	E
Deferred delivery	E	N/A
Deferred delivery cancellation	A	N/A
Delivery notification	E	N/A
Delivery via Bureaufax service	A	A
Designation of recipient by directory name	A	N/A
Disclosure of other recipients	A	E
Distribution list expansion indication	N/A	E
Distribution list expansion prohibited	A	A
Express mail service	A	E
Expiry date indication	A	E
Explicit conversion	A	N/A
Forward IP-message indication	A	E
Grade of delivery selection	E	E
Importance indication	A	E
Incomplete copy indication	A	A
Language indication	A	E
Latest delivery designation	A	N/A
Message flow confidentiality	A	N/A
Message origin authentication	A	A
Message security labelling	A	A
Message sequence integrity	A	A
Multidestination delivery	E	N/A
Multipart body	A	E

Element	Origination	Reception
Nonreceipt notification request indication	A	E
Nonrepudiation of delivery	A	A
Nonrepudiation of origin	A	A
Nonrepudiation of submission	A	A
Obsoleting indication	A	E
Ordinary mail	A	E
Originator indication	E	E
Originator requested alternate recipient	A	N/A
Physical delivery notification by MHS	A	A
Physical delivery notification by PDS	A	E
Physical forwarding allowed	A	E
Physical forwarding allowed	A	E
Prevention of non-delivery notification	A	N/A
Primary and copy recipients indication	E	E
Probe	A	N/A
Probe origin authentication	A	A
Proof of delivery	A	A
Proof of submission	A	A
Receipt notification request indication	A	A
Redirection disallowed by originator	A	N/A
Registered mail	A	A
Registered mail to addressee in person	A	A
Reply request indication	A	E
Reply IP-message indication	E	E
Report origin authentication	A	A
Request for forwarding address	A	A
Requested delivery method	E	N/A
Return of content	A	N/A
Sensitivity indication	A	E
Special Delivery	A	E
Stored message deletion	N/A	E
Stored message fetching	N/A	E

10-9 *(Cont.)*
IPMS Optional
Elements

Element	Origination	Reception
Stored message listing	N/A	E
Stored message summary	N/A	E
Subject indication	E	E
Return of undeliverable mail	A	E
Use of distribution list		A
Source: CCITT, Data Communications Networks (Blue Book), ITU (Geneva, 1989) Recommendation X.400		

10-9 *(Cont.)*
IPMS Optional
Elements

Alternate recipient assignment
Hold for delivery
Implicit conversion
Redirection of incoming messages
Restricted delivery
Secure access management
Stored message alert
Stored message autoforward

10-10
X.400 IPMS
Contractual Elements

ing a message should be able to find out if the message was in fact autoforwarded.

Several elements are not available on a per-message basis but must be contracted for (see Fig. 10-10). For example, the message transfer system can hold a message when it receives it and deliver it later. Implicit conversion, redirection, restricted delivery, and services of this sort require additional resources within the message transfer system.

Figures 10-8 through 10-10 show the list of possible IPMS elements in (close to) its entirety, thereby demonstrating the richness of the X.400 messaging environment. Note that not all user interfaces will know what to do with all these elements. The underlying IPMS supports the functions, but the user interface will typically ignore additional elements. For this reason, a user may occasionally examine a message with a plain ASCII editor to see if there are additional elements included but not shown to the user.

Message Transfer Agent

There are three types of objects in the message transfer system:

- messages
- probes
- reports

A probe goes from one user to the message transfer agent that would deliver a message to another user, and is used to test connectivity. A report is an object sent from the message transfer system to a user. Each report concerns a message or probe.

Figures 10-11 and 10-12 show the structure of the message transfer agent modules. Incoming messages are delivered to either the main or report modules, which results in either a message, report, or probe being sent out. The main module provides a variety of different functions. One is splitting, which takes a single message with multiple addressees and splits it into several messages. This occurs when there is a split in routes. One recipient is located in one direction; other users in other directions. Joining is an optional step to join multiple messages headed for the same place. For example, 10 nondelivery messages going from a distribution list to a single address that originated the failed message might be joined.

Name resolution, distribution list expansion, redirection, and conversion are optional services. Nondelivery is an example of a message sent back to a user when a message is discarded, usually because the destination user or domain is unknown. Finally, there is the question of routing—selecting which message transfer agent gets the message next. How information gets routed is up to a specific environment. Presumably, MTAs will use a hierarchical routing system: All unknown messages go to a "root" server, which is connected to other management domains.

Figure 10-13 shows the types of services offered by message transfer agents. Again, they are split up into basic elements (always provided), essential elements (available but not required), and additional elements (optional per implementation). Most of these elements of service are transmitted in the message transfer agent header. For example, a user could specify that an alternative recipient is allowed (or not allowed). Deferred delivery allows a message to be submitted to the message transfer system with the proviso that it not be delivered before a specific time.

The deferred delivery cancellation is an element that shows that not all requests are always granted. A user can send a message with deferred delivery, say a press release announcing DECnet Phase V for VMS. Once the message is sent, it stays in a queue someplace in the message transfer system awaiting delivery. The originator may then decide, perhaps because of technical difficulties, to delay the announcement and sends out a deferred delivery cancellation. There is no guarantee the deferred delivery cancella-

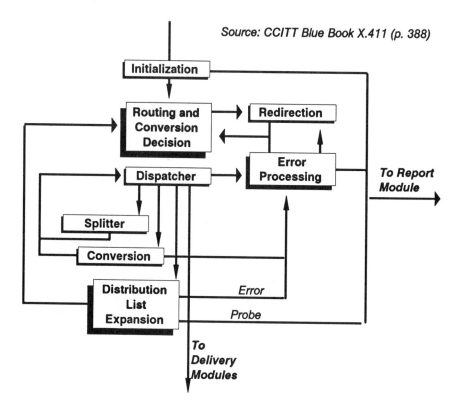

Source: CCITT Blue Book X.411 (p. 388)

10-11 X.400 MTA Main Module

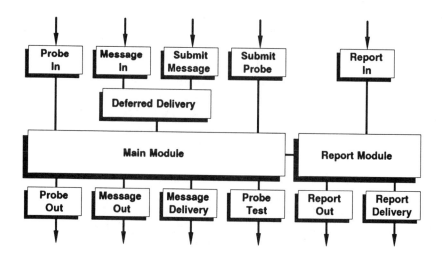

10-12 X.400 MTA Components

		Access management
Basic Elements		Content type indication
		Converted indication
		Delivery time stamp
		Message indication
		Nondelivery notification
		Original encoded information types indication
		Submission time stamp
		User/UA capabilities registration
Essential Elements		Alternate recipient allowed
		Deferred delivery
		Deferred delivery cancellation
		Delivery notification
		Disclosure of other recipients
		Distribution list expansion history indication
		Grade of delivery selection
		Probe
		Requested delivery method
Additional Elements		Alternate recipient assigned
		Content confidentiality
		Content integrity
		Conversion prohibition if information lost
		Designation of recipient by directory name
		Distribution list expansion prohibited

10-13
Messaage Transfer
Service Elements

tion, if issued close to the time of delivery stated on the original message, will catch up with the deferred delivery message in time to cancel the original message.

Figure 10-14 shows a typical X.400 message exchange. First, the presentation-level connection is made and accepted. Next, the session layer activity start is sent. Then, the X.400 P2 protocol is invoked. P2 is a code for the interpersonal messaging service. Notice that this particular message is using the 1984 version of the X.400 protocols.

Figure 10-15 shows the P1 protocol (MTA to MTA) in more depth. This particular message is a delivery report. The message indicates a message identifier (the message Protocol Data Unit ID), as well as the originator of the report. It then has trace information indicating when the message reached different locations.

In the content section is the identification of the original message. The message was sent from the country United States, the administration management domain ATTMail, the private management domain Retix, and

Additional Elements	Explicit conversion
	Hold for delivery
	Implicit conversion
	Latest delivery designation
	Message flow confidentiality
	Message origin authentication
	Message security labelling
	Message sequence integrity
	Multidestination delivery
	Nonrepudiation of origin
	Nonrepudiation of submission
	Originator requested alternate recipient
	Prevention of nondelivery notification
	Probe origin authentication
	Proof of delivery
	Proof of submission
	Redirection disallowed by originator
	Redirection of incoming messages
	Report origin authentication
	Restricted delivery
	Return of content
	Secure access management
	Use of distribution list

Source: CCITT, Data Communications Networks (Blue Book), ITU (Geneva, 1989) Recommendation X.400, pp. 34-5

10-13 *(Cont.)*
MTS Elements

from a particular user ID. The message also indicates that the message was received by a user with the personal name Elena Seifrid and was delivered July 26, 1988.

Figure 10-16 shows the IPMS layered inside of the message transfer protocol. The MTA header includes the originator of the message and the basic information type, IA5text being a basic text message. The content type indicates this is an IPMS message instead of some private protocol.

The message also includes various per-message flags. Notice that the disclose recipients flag is on, allowing each user to know about the other users. No alternative recipient is allowed: if the message cannot be delivered it is dropped.

Next, we see information for the two recipients of the message, including an address and flags indicating basic reports are requested. This is followed by trace information, indicating where the message has been so far. We see that the message appears to have been relayed at least once by a message transfer agent called VAX.

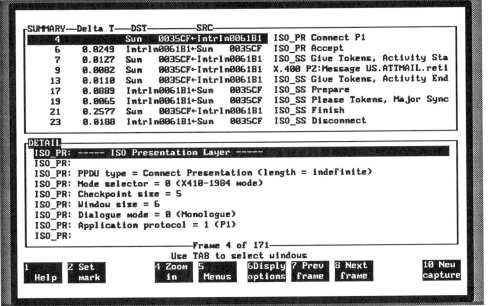

Courtesy of Network General

10-14 X.400 Session Traffic

After all this information, we see the IPMS header. The message has a unique ID, an originator, and two primary recipients. The reply requested flag is set to false. Even if the flag were set to true, there is no way we could have forced our two users to respond. The body of the message, consisting of a single body part, is composed of IA5Text. The message begins "Testing for Andre" and has an additional 1720 bytes.

Distribution Lists

A distribution list is a list of individual O/R addresses or other distribution lists. In addition to its members, a distribution list has several other properties:

- The submit permission says which users and distribution lists can make use of this list.
- The expansion point is the O/R address of the list, the place where it is translated into its constituent members.
- The owner of the list.

Somebody sending mail to a destination does not have to know that the destination address is a distribution list. Remember, however, that message

```
DETAIL
X.400: ----- X.400 Message Transfer Protocol (P1) -----
X.400:
X.400: MPDU type = Delivery Report (length = indefinite)
X.400: Envelope:
X.400:   Report MPDU identifier: /C=US/ADMD=ATTMAIL/PRMD=RETIX/, SUN Tue Jul
X.400:   Originator: /C=US/ADMD=ATTMAIL/PRMD=RETIX/O=VAX/PN=SEIFRID.ELENA.D/
X.400:   Trace information:
X.400:     Global domain identifier: /C=US/ADMD=ATTMAIL/PRMD=RETIX/
X.400:     Arrival = 26 Jul 1988  14:54:43-0700
X.400:     Action = 0 (Relayed)
X.400:   Internal trace info:
X.400:     MTA name = SUN
X.400:     Arrival = 26 Jul 1988  14:54:43-0700
X.400:     Action = 0 (Relayed)
X.400: Content:
X.400:   Original MPDU identifier: /C=US/ADMD=ATTMAIL/PRMD=RETIX/, VAX 880726
X.400:   Intermediate trace information:
X.400:     Global domain identifier: /C=US/ADMD=ATTMAIL/PRMD=RETIX/
X.400:     Arrival = 26 Jul 1988  14:53:58-0800
X.400:     Action = 0 (Relayed)
X.400: Content:
X.400:   Original MPDU identifier: /C=US/ADMD=ATTMAIL/PRMD=RETIX/, VAX 880726
X.400:   Intermediate trace information:
X.400:     Global domain identifier: /C=US/ADMD=ATTMAIL/PRMD=RETIX/
X.400:     Arrival = 26 Jul 1988  14:53:58-0800
X.400:     Action = 0 (Relayed)
X.400:   UA content id = 880726 14:53:53
X.400:   Reported recipient info:
X.400:     Recipient: /C=US/ADMD=ATTMAIL/PRMD=retix/O=sun/PN=seifrid.elena/
X.400:     Extension identifier = 2
X.400:     Per recipient flag = D0
X.400:              1... .... = responsibility flag on
X.400:              .10. .... = confirmed report request
X.400:              ...1 0... = confirmed user report request
X.400:     Intended recipient last trace information:
X.400:       Arrival = 26 Jul 1988  14:54:43-0700
X.400:       Delivery = 26 Jul 1988  14:54:43-0700
X.400:       Type of UA = 1 (Private)
X.400:
--------Frame 41 of 171--------
        Use TAB to select windows
 1        2 Set              4 Zoom  5        6Disply  7 Prev  8 Next              10 New
 Help     mark                out     Menus   options  frame   frame               capture
```

10-15 X.400 Delivery Report

Courtesy of Network General

charges can rapidly mount if one message turns into 100. One option in X.400 is to prohibit distribution list expansion.

The expansion point for a distribution list is a message transfer agent (since the user does not exist). The expansion point will "burst" the message into several pieces, sending them back out the message transfer system (see Fig. 10-17). Any charges for the activity would typically go back to the original user (although it is possible they would be incurred by the owner of the distribution list).

Distribution lists can be nested. When a nested distribution list is expanded, the ID of the parent distribution list, not the originator of the mes-

```
DETAIL
ISO_SS: ----- ISO Session Layer -----
ISO_SS:
ISO_SS: Multi-frame TSDU: frames 9, 11, 12
ISO_SS: SPDU type = 1 (Give Tokens)
ISO_SS: SPDU type = 1 (Data Transfer)
ISO_SS:
X.400: ----- X.400 Message Transfer Protocol (P1) -----
X.400:
X.400: MPDU type = User (length = indefinite)
X.400: Envelope:
X.400:   MPDU identifier: /C=US/ADMD=ATTMAIL/PRMD=RETIX/, VAX 880726 14:53:53
X.400:   Originator: /C=US/ADMD=ATTMAIL/PRMD=RETIX/O=VAX/PN=SEIFRID.ELENA.D/
X.400:   Original encoded information types:
X.400:     Basic information type = A000
X.400:       1... .... .... .... = Undefined
X.400:       .0.. .... .... .... = No tLX
X.400:       ..1. .... .... .... = IA5Text
X.400:       ...0 .... .... .... = No g3Fax
X.400:       .... 0... .... .... = No tIF0
X.400:       .... .0.. .... .... = No tTX
X.400:       .... .0.. .... .... = No tTX
X.400:       .... ..0. .... .... = No videotex
X.400:       .... ...0 .... .... = No voice
X.400:       .... .... 0... .... = No sFD
X.400:       .... .... .0.. .... = No tIF1
X.400:   Content type = 2 (P2)
X.400:   UA content id = 880726 14:53:53
X.400:   Priority = 2 (Urgent)
X.400:   Per message flag = C0
X.400:       1... .... = Disclose recipients
X.400:       .1.. .... = Conversion prohibited
X.400:       ..0. .... = No alternate recipient allowed
X.400:       ...0 .... = No content return request
X.400:   Recipient info:
X.400:     Recipient: /C=US/ADMD=ATTMAIL/PRMD=retix/O=sun/PN=donoghue.barbara/
X.400:     Extension identifier = 1
X.400:     Per recipient flag = A8
X.400:       1... .... = responsibility flag on
X.400:       .01. .... = basic report request
X.400:       ...0 1... = basic user report request
X.400:   Recipient info:
X.400:     Recipient: /C=US/ADMD=ATTMAIL/PRMD=retix/O=sun/PN=seifrid.elena/
X.400:     Extension identifier = 2
X.400:     Per recipient flag = D0
X.400:       1... .... = responsibility flag on
X.400:       .10. .... = confirmed report request
X.400:       ...1 0... = confirmed user report request
X.400:   Trace information:
X.400:     Global domain identifier: /C=US/ADMD=ATTMAIL/PRMD=RETIX/
X.400:     Arrival = 26 Jul 1988  14:53:58-0700
X.400:     Action = 0 (Relayed)
X.400:   Internal trace info:
X.400:     MTA name = VAX
X.400:     Arrival = 26 Jul 1988  14:53:58-0700
X.400:     Action = 0 (Relayed)
X.400:
X.400: ----- X.400 Interpersonal Messaging Protocol (P2) -----
X.400:
X.400: UAPDU type = Interpersonal Message (length = indefinite)
X.400: Heading:
X.400:   IP message id: /C=US/ADMD=ATTMAIL/PRMD=RETIX/O=VAX/PN=SEIFRID.ELENA.
X.400:               880726 14:53:53
X.400:   Originator: /C=US/ADMD=ATTMAIL/PRMD=retix/O=sun/PN=Seifrid.Elena.D/
X.400:   Primary recipient:
X.400:     O/R Descriptor: /C=US/ADMD=ATTMAIL/PRMD=retix/O=sun/PN=donoghue.bar
X.400:     Reply request = FALSE
X.400:   Primary recipient:
X.400:     O/R Descriptor: /C=US/ADMD=ATTMAIL/PRMD=retix/O=sun/PN=seifrid.elen
X.400:   Subject = Test message on Retix X.400 network
X.400: Body:
X.400:   IA5Text = "Testing for Andre...."
X.400:   Unidentified [1720 bytes]
X.400:
```

Frame 9 of 171
Use TAB to select windows

| 1 Help | 2 Set mark | | 1 Zoom out | 5 Menus | 6 Display options | 7 Prev frame | 8 Next frame | | 10 New capture |

10-16 X.400 P1 and P2 Protocols

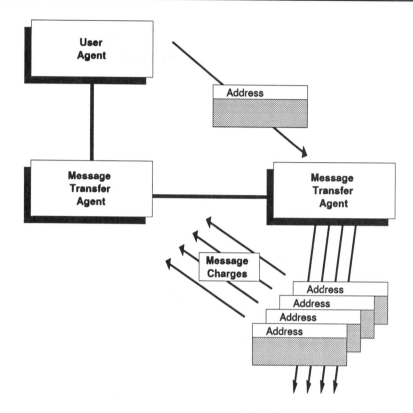

10-17 X.400 Distribution List Expansion

sage, is used to check whether expansion is allowed. A potential problem with distribution lists is recursion. To prevent this, a message includes a chain of the distribution lists used to get it to this point. The expander checks the list to detect any recursion.

Notifications regarding a distribution list can come from the distribution list expansion point (e.g., submit permission denied) or the ultimate destination (e.g., message undeliverable).

Summary

In X.400 we see a rich messaging environment. What makes X.400 so significant is the large number of computer vendors and national telecommunications suppliers who have already implemented the standard. The large number of options available, and the support for access units, message stores, and other capabilities mean that it will be a while before the limits of X.400 are reached. X.400 promises to be one of the foundation services in an OSI environment.

Digital uses the approach that many vendors have in supporting X.400—
an access unit to their native messaging system instead of native X.400 support. The MAILbus architecture is a DECnet application. The X.400
Gateway for the Message Router moves messages out of the MAILbus environment and into X.400.

Management

Management

Management of Phase V conforms to the Enterprise Management Architecture (EMA), a cross-architectural model of how to manage distributed system and its components. As we have seen, DECnet does not operate in a vacuum—other components such as LAT, the extended Ethernet, T-1 and fractional T-1 hardware, all require management.

We can treat a distributed network as a series of hardware and software components. Each of these components is an entity. We structure the entities in a tree to make management easier. For example, in Phase V the top of the tree is the node, and subentities include items such as routing and transport modules. The routing entity will likewise have subentities, such as circuits and adjacencies.

Network management has been broken up by the ISO into a variety of functional areas. These areas include

- configuration management
- fault management
- performance management
- accounting management
- security

Configuration management allows the network manager to install and control a particular module. An example of configuration management is to add manual routing information to the DECnet routing module. Fault management is the detection of faults, their isolation, and, it is hoped, their repair or removal.

Performance management lets the manager tune the network, as in the case of increasing throughput in the transport layer by adjusting maximum window sizes. In LAT, the manager might set the timer on the master to reflect the longer delays in a wide-area extended Ethernet.

Accounting management lets the manager figure out what happened on the network. We might want to know which nodes used the Ethernet, or which users used a particular module, or how many bytes were sent over a particular line.

Three other areas—security, names, and applications—are not strictly network management topics but have a lot of overlap. Security is an issue that is present in all layers of the operational network. Security is also important to prevent unauthorized persons from managing the network. Name management is a question of data administration but quickly impacts the ability of the manager to find managed objects. Management of applications includes database managers, remote file access protocols, or distributed transactions management services, or even an operating system.

Management Model

We begin with the question of local management of an entity. Every entity provides a service interface; that is, the way in which a user of the module takes advantage of its services. The transport module, for example, uses the service interface of the routing module. The routing module, in turn, uses the service interface of the subnetwork modules.

In addition to the service interface, every module presents a local management interface, usually a set of implementation-dependent system calls. The performance of the network management functions is done by a management agent.

Figure 11-1 shows the structure of network management on a single node. The director is the program that performs network management functions. When a management directive is issued, it is done using the local management interface. Since there are several modules, the directive is intercepted by an agent directive dispatcher, which moves the directive to the agent which actually performs the task. Another user of the local management interface is the agent access module; it is a network-accessible module that performs directives on behalf of remote directors.

Figure 11-2 shows the framework for management. We start with the network manager, usually a human being but occasionally a program or batch file. The manager uses a program called the Network Control Language (NCL), which is an example of a director. NCL in turn submits requests to the local management interface, which moves them to the node and its subentities.

A special kind of director is the initialization director, used when the node initializes. This initialization director makes use of scripts, which set initial parameters. This script allows a node and its subentities to have the appropriate parameters set before they begin operation.

In addition to accepting directives, an entity periodically generates reports known as events. These reports, such as error reports or changes in operational status, are sent to sinks where they are logged. The protocol

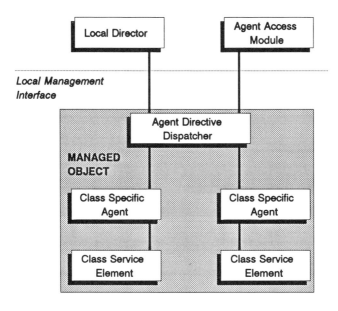

11-1 Agent Operation

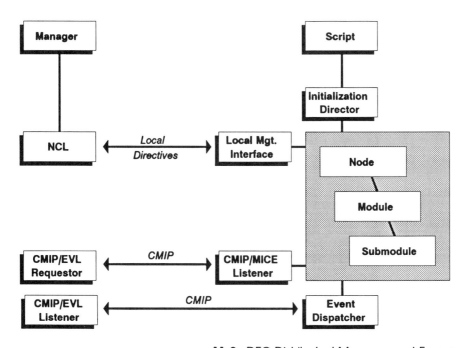

11-2 DEC Distributed Management Framework

used to send reports over the network is the Common Management Information Protocol (CMIP). The event dispatcher on a node uses CMIP to send the event report to a CMIP event logger program known as a listener.

The CMIP event logging protocol is based on Digital's Management Event Notification (MEN) protocol. The other major CMIP protocol is the Management Information Control and Exchange protocol (MICE). The combination of MICE and MEN allows a remote node to define which operations should be performed (including which events are desired), and to receive asynchronous event reports. CMIP is the basis for allowing a remote director to control a Phase V node.

Figure 11-3 shows the structure of a Phase V node. The node's startup/shutdown module is used to set up the initialization director, which in turn feeds the initial management directives into the node. The node structure also includes a name keeper and address module, responsible for maintaining the network address. The CMIP/MICE module receives remote requests for network management.

When a CMIP request is received, the request goes to the agent directive dispatcher, which is responsible for getting the directive to the agent for that particular module. CMIP also uses the functional network modules to communicate requests over the network. CMIP is a user of the DNA Session Control layer. Finally, the UID and time services are used by both network management and functional network modules.

The question of what operations can actually be performed on a module are beyond the scope of the network management architecture. The definition of these tasks is up to the individual module architecture. The network management architecture provides a systematic way for defining these management functions and for making the management functions available in a distributed environment.

The primary way in which a module makes its management capabilities known is through a registry, a central repository of management definitions maintained by Digital. When a Digital architect works out a new module, the definition of the operations and the information maintained by the module are put into the registry that integrates the naming schemes of different modules into a unified namespace.

Particularly important is how an entity fits into the naming scheme. At the top of the namespace are global entities, such as the DNA Phase V node. As in the DNA Naming Service, an entity full name is the concatenation of a set of simple name fragments. For network management purposes, each name fragment has two pieces, a class name and an instance identifier. The class name is required to be unique at least within the child classes and attributes of its parent. Thus a bridge can have a child entity circuit, as can a routing layer. On a Phase V node, we might see two entities, DNA Routing and IP (for the TCP/IP routing layer). Both have child entities named

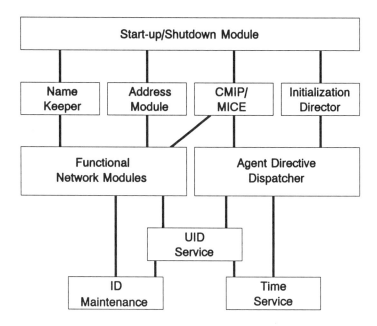

11-3 DEC Network Management Node Structure

"circuit," which may in fact end up with both circuits sharing the same physical hardware.

The instance identifier must also be unique within a particular location in the tree. Thus, two circuits of a routing module must have different names. It is possible to have alternative identifiers for a particular instance, but one is labeled as the primary identifier and shows up in the event reports.

An example of a name is:

Node DigitalPR.XENOPHOBE ROUTING CIRCUIT UNA-0

Node is a global entity, and the node DigitalPR.XENOPHOBE (which happens to be a DNS Full Name) is the instance. Routing is an example of an entity that does not need an instance identifier, since there is by definition only one per node. Finally, we have the circuit subentity class with the identifier UNA-0.

The global entity (of which node is the only one discussed here) has the special characteristic of providing an agent (such as a CMIP listener) so it can be remotely managed. Each global entity has a DNS full name. The global entity is then responsible for distributing incoming directives to its subentities.

In addition to a name, every entity has a series of attributes that are defined. There are three types of attributes:

- identifiers (counters)
- characteristics
- status

The identifiers are attributes such as names and addresses. Characteristics affect the behavior of the entity. Status attributes are used to monitor the behavior of an object.

We can take sets of attributes and put them into attribute groups, such as the groups "summary" (for high-level summary information) or "critical" (for attributes reflecting critical network functions). Attribute groups allow the network manager to refer to collections of information without specifying each individual attribute in the class.

In addition to defining an entity via a name and attributes, the architect defines events and directives. The events contain significant information a network manager may want to see periodically. Once a particular event is described, the manager uses CMIP to specify that he or she is interested in having reports of that event dispatched to a particular event sink.

Directives are the types of commands to which a management entity will respond. Directives are always in response to a command from a director. If an entity feels it should do something, it would send an event report to the director, which would respond, if appropriate, with a directive.

Network Control Language

NCL is an example of a director operating in a command line mode. NCL is a simple user interface. In the DECmcc section, we will see examples of more sophisticated directors, such as graphically oriented windowing applications.

NCL commands are translated into network-based requests, such as CMIP management directives or commands to the DNA Naming Service. Rather than being a network protocol, NCL is thus a specification of how entities, operations, and data are requested by the user and subsequently displayed.

NCL is based on two types of commands. Database commands are used to examine and modify the attributes of an entity. Action commands are used to manipulate the entity itself. The syntax of NCL allows multiple attributes (data maintained by an entity) and arguments (the way an entity performs an action) to be applied to an entity at once. Action commands are a request/response protocol and are always acknowledged.

The initial operation is for the user to type a network management command. The NCL module then performs a lexical parse on the command and separates the letters into white space, comments, command terminators, and tokens. A token is the basic unit of operation on which the parser works.

Next, the parser scans the tokens for any locally stored aliases (such as abbreviations for node names). The parser makes substitutions, then rescans until no more substitutions are made. Finally, the parser makes a syntactical parse, trying to figure what each token means and what the collection of tokens means. The architecture (although not necessarily all of the products) is extensible, allowing the manager to add new entities, attributes, or other operations to the language.

The basic command consists of a verb, an entity, and attributes. The command may optionally have an argument and a prepositional clause. An example of a command is the remove command. To remove an instance of a routing module, the user would type:

    remove node dec.pr.xenophobe routing

Prepositional clauses help to refine the command. An example of a prepositional clause is access control information. Before CMIP (and the target node) will carry out a function, the user must be authenticated. A prepositional clause would carry in the user's account and password information. If proxy logins are being used, this information is not needed and the prepositional clause can be omitted.

Another type of prepositional clause is the entity filter, used to specify which entities are the target; for example,

    show node * with type=endsystem

Node * is a wildcard specification for an entity, here referring to all nodes on the network. The with type clause selects all end systems.

In addition to specifying the format of a command and how it is parsed, NCL defines how the results are to be displayed or how errors are to be shown. The display of a result consists of a header and the data. The header contains the name of the operation, the target entity, any filters, and a time stamp. The data display can be the results of the CMIP, local NCL, or DNS commands.

An example of a command and the resulting display is

```
NCL> SHOW NODE .DigitalENG.Siva ROUTING CIRCUIT UNA-0 ALL -
_NCL> CHARACTERISTICS


    NODE .dec.eng.siva ROUTING CIRCUIT UNA-0
    AT 12-AUG-1987:14:32
    CHARACTERISTICS =
    CREATE TIME = 3-MAR-1987:08:03
    TYPE = ETHERNET
    TEMPLATE NAME =
    LINK NAME =
    HELLO-TIMER = 60
```

```
L1 COST = 20
L2 COST = 20
QUEUE LIMIT = 2
MAX ROUTERS = 32

ROUTER PRIORITY = 64
MANUAL DL BLOCKSIZE = 1024
MULTICAST QUOTA = 4
TRANSIT ACCESS = INTERNAL DNA
EXPLICIT RECEIVE VERIFY = TRUE
MANUAL L2 ONLY = FALSE
MANUAL DESIGNATED ROUTER = 00-00-00-00-00-00
```

An example of an error display is

```
NCL> SET NODE .DigitalENG.Siva ROUTING CIRCUIT UNA-0 -
_NCL> HELLO-TIMER = 60, MULTICAST QUOTA = 4

NODE .dec.eng.siva ROUTING CIRCUIT UNA-0
UID 1987-08-09-17:32:00 120002 AA-00-04-01-AC-DC
AT 12-AUG-1987:14:32
FAILED IN SET OF
 MULTICAST QUOTA
DUE TO
 CONSTRAINT VIOLATION
NCL>
```

CMIP

Whereas NCL defines how commands are entered and displayed, CMIP defines how they are moved across the network. By providing a common definition of network management requests, CMIP allows a director from one vendor to manage an entity from another.

The Digital implementation of CMIP uses the DNA Session Control layer to set up a session between a director (the CMIP requestor) and a managed node (the CMIP listener). Note that the OSI Session Control layer is not being used, which means Digital CMIP may not necessarily interact with other vendors' CMIP implementations. The incompatibility is only at the Session Control layer, since the DNA Session Control layer will then have a choice of OSI TP4 or NSP transport protocols.

The association between the two CMIP-speaking processes is established using the CMIP associate message (see Fig. 11-4). Access control for this session is up to the Session Control layer. The Session Control layer would

DNA Session Control Header		Connection Request
		Connect Accept
		Connect Reject
CMIP Version		5
CMIP ECO		0
Customer ECO		0
CMIP User Data		13 Bytes

11-4
CMIP Associate
Message

Invoke ID		
Linked ID		Optional
Operation Value		Event Report
		Linked Reply
		Get
		Set
		Action
		Add
		Remove
Argument		Operation Dependent

11-5
CMIP Invoke
Operation Message

either use explicit access control (a username and password) or would invoke a proxy login.

Once a session is set up, the CMIP exchange consists of a series of invoke operation messages and their results. The invoke command (see Fig. 11-5) has seven basic types of operations. The event report operation requests that certain events be sent. The linked reply is used to indicate that this command is linked to another one.

The basic CMIP operations are get, set, action, add, and remove. Each entity's management structure is typically worked into those basic five commands. After the command is a set of arguments (see Fig. 11-6) that further specify how the command is to be interpreted. An argument always has an entity class, instance, and (for DEC) the UID of the entity. Then, depending on what type of operation, there is a set of operation-specific arguments. For an event report, for example, the argument specifies what type of event, what time, and any event-specific information. For the set operation, there is synchronization information (to prevent two directors from stepping on each other), an entity filter, and a list of specific attributes.

Entity Class		Common Header
Entity Instance		
Entity UID		
Entity Time		Event Reporting
Event Type		
Event Information		
Entity Filter		Get Operation
Attribute ID List		
Synchronization		Set Operation
Entity Filter		
Attribute List		
Entity Filter		Action Operation
Action Type		
Action Arguement		
Entity Filter		Add Operation
Attribute List		
Entity Filter		Remove Operation
Attribute List		

11-6
CMIP Arguments

Invoke ID		
Operation Value		Link Terminator
		Get Result
		Set Result
		Action Result
		Add Result
		Remove Result
Result		Operation Dependent

11-7
CMIP Return
Result Message

After the operation is performed, the results are put into a return results message (see Fig. 11-7). The result format is dependent on the specific type of operation, but it usually includes at least the resulting entity specification and any attribute values.

If the command cannot be properly executed, the return error message is sent back (see Fig. 11-8). The errors are split into five general classes, with specific numbers assigned within each class of errors. General problems such as protocol errors apply to all operations. Invoke problems such as a

Entity Class		Common Header
Entity Instance		
Entity UID		
Entity Time		Event Reporting
Event Type		
Event Information		
Entity Filter		Get Operation
Attribute ID List		
Synchronization		Set Operation
Entity Filter		
Attribute List		
Entity Filter		Action Operation
Action Type		
Action Arguement		
Entity Filter		Add Operation
Attribute List		
Entity Filter		Remove Operation
Attribute List		

11-6
CMIP Arguments

Invoke ID		
Operation Value		Link Terminator
		Get Result
		Set Result
		Action Result
		Add Result
		Remove Result
Result		Operation Dependent

11-7
CMIP Return
Result Message

After the operation is performed, the results are put into a return results message (see Fig. 11-7). The result format is dependent on the specific type of operation, but it usually includes at least the resulting entity specification and any attribute values.

If the command cannot be properly executed, the return error message is sent back (see Fig. 11-8). The errors are split into five general classes, with specific numbers assigned within each class of errors. General problems such as protocol errors apply to all operations. Invoke problems such as a

DNA Session Control Header		Connection Request
		Connect Accept
		Connect Reject
CMIP Version		5
CMIP ECO		0
Customer ECO		0
CMIP User Data		13 Bytes

11-4
CMIP Associate
Message

Invoke ID		
Linked ID		Optional
Operation Value		Event Report
		Linked Reply
		Get
		Set
		Action
		Add
		Remove
Argument		Operation Dependent

11-5
CMIP Invoke
Operation Message

either use explicit access control (a username and password) or would invoke a proxy login.

Once a session is set up, the CMIP exchange consists of a series of invoke operation messages and their results. The invoke command (see Fig. 11-5) has seven basic types of operations. The event report operation requests that certain events be sent. The linked reply is used to indicate that this command is linked to another one.

The basic CMIP operations are get, set, action, add, and remove. Each entity's management structure is typically worked into those basic five commands. After the command is a set of arguments (see Fig. 11-6) that further specify how the command is to be interpreted. An argument always has an entity class, instance, and (for DEC) the UID of the entity. Then, depending on what type of operation, there is a set of operation-specific arguments. For an event report, for example, the argument specifies what type of event, what time, and any event-specific information. For the set operation, there is synchronization information (to prevent two directors from stepping on each other), an entity filter, and a list of specific attributes.

Invoke ID	
Error Class/Number	
Error Parameter	

Error Classes	
General Problems	Unrecognized Association PDU
	Mistyped Association PDU
	Badly Structured PDU
Invoke Problems	Duplicate Invocation
	Unrecognized Operation
	Mistyped Argument
	Resource Limitation
	Initiator Releasing
	Unrecognized Link ID
	Linked Response Unexpected
	Unexpected Child Operation
Return Result Problems	Unrecognized Invoke ID
	Result Response Unexpected
	Mistyped Result
Return Error Problems	Unrecognized Invoke ID
	Error Response Unexpected
	Unrecognized Error
	Unexpected Error
	Mistyped Parameter

Error Parameters	
Access Denied	Constraint violation
Directive not supported	Read only attribute
Duplicate argument	Duplicate attribute
Required argument omitted	Entity class not supported
Filter invalid for action	Get list error
Invalid argument value	Invalid attribute value
Invalid filter	Invalid operator
Invalid use of wildcard	No resource available
No such action	No such argument
No such attribute ID	No such event type
No such object instance	No such object class
No such reference object	Processing failure
Duplicate object	Write only attribute
Set list error	Synch not supported

11-8
CMIP Return
Error Message

duplicate operation invocation are the result of a request. There can even be problems in returning an error (as in the case of an error report being sent with an unrecognized invocation ID). Following the error number is a series of error parameters that further define the error.

Figures 11-9 and 11-10 show a typical example of a request/result exchange using CMIP. The request and the result share the invocation of ID of 1234. The operation is a get operation, which specifies an entity class and an instance. The entity class is a fully specified example of the class name, resolving down to a particular circuit. The request specifies three attributes—the circuit type, a template name, and a hello time.

The results show that the circuit type is an 802.3 Ethernet circuit, with a hello time of 600 seconds (hello messages are sent every 10 minutes). The template name is used as a method of setting different instances of an entity the same way. The result includes the state of the entity as well as the other requested attributes. A director should be prepared to receive additional attributes in a result on top of those initially requested.

Figures 11-11 and 11-12 show an example of CMIP operating over a TCP/IP-based link (CMIP over TCP/IP is known as CMOT). Again, the get command is being used to get the current status of a module, in this case the transport layer TCP module. The result of the operation shows a variety of different requested counters. The number of passive TCP opened was 46, with no resets and no failed open attempts.

Figure 11-13 shows a typical CMIP session. The session begins with the node Bridge requesting the system ID from another node. The bridge then sends a request for TCP information to three different nodes—another Bridge, an U-B, and one Hewlett-Packard. Next, the node sends a request for the TCP/IP network layer (IP) information.

As can be seen, CMIP allows a network director to request information from several different nodes on the network. The node Bridge could be an automated program that collects periodic information off the network and puts it into a database. The database can then be examined by the manager at a later time.

We will see that DECmcc is an example of such an automated director. The user can submit a request asking for certain information to be collected periodically. DECmcc will store the request and, as each period arrives, send out the proper management directives.

Event Logging

The event logging architecture defines a framework for the definition of how to record, transmit, filter, and process events. The semantics of specific events is up to the individual modules. Event logging uses the CMIP

duplicate operation invocation are the result of a request. There can even be problems in returning an error (as in the case of an error report being sent with an unrecognized invocation ID). Following the error number is a series of error parameters that further define the error.

Figures 11-9 and 11-10 show a typical example of a request/result exchange using CMIP. The request and the result share the invocation of ID of 1234. The operation is a get operation, which specifies an entity class and an instance. The entity class is a fully specified example of the class name, resolving down to a particular circuit. The request specifies three attributes—the circuit type, a template name, and a hello time.

The results show that the circuit type is an 802.3 Ethernet circuit, with a hello time of 600 seconds (hello messages are sent every 10 minutes). The template name is used as a method of setting different instances of an entity the same way. The result includes the state of the entity as well as the other requested attributes. A director should be prepared to receive additional attributes in a result on top of those initially requested.

Figures 11-11 and 11-12 show an example of CMIP operating over a TCP/IP-based link (CMIP over TCP/IP is known as CMOT). Again, the get command is being used to get the current status of a module, in this case the transport layer TCP module. The result of the operation shows a variety of different requested counters. The number of passive TCP opened was 46, with no resets and no failed open attempts.

Figure 11-13 shows a typical CMIP session. The session begins with the node Bridge requesting the system ID from another node. The bridge then sends a request for TCP information to three different nodes—another Bridge, an U-B, and one Hewlett-Packard. Next, the node sends a request for the TCP/IP network layer (IP) information.

As can be seen, CMIP allows a network director to request information from several different nodes on the network. The node Bridge could be an automated program that collects periodic information off the network and puts it into a database. The database can then be examined by the manager at a later time.

We will see that DECmcc is an example of such an automated director. The user can submit a request asking for certain information to be collected periodically. DECmcc will store the request and, as each period arrives, send out the proper management directives.

Event Logging

The event logging architecture defines a framework for the definition of how to record, transmit, filter, and process events. The semantics of specific events is up to the individual modules. Event logging uses the CMIP

Invoke ID	
Error Class/Number	
Error Parameter	

Error Classes		
General Problems	Unrecognized Association PDU	
	Mistyped Association PDU	
	Badly Structured PDU	
Invoke Problems	Duplicate Invocation	
	Unrecognized Operation	
	Mistyped Argument	
	Resource Limitation	
	Initiator Releasing	
	Unrecognized Link ID	
	Linked Response Unexpected	
	Unexpected Child Operation	
Return Result Problems	Unrecognized Invoke ID	
	Result Response Unexpected	
	Mistyped Result	
Return Error Problems	Unrecognized Invoke ID	
	Error Response Unexpected	
	Unrecognized Error	
	Unexpected Error	
	Mistyped Parameter	

Error Parameters	
Access Denied	Constraint violation
Directive not supported	Read only attribute
Duplicate argument	Duplicate attribute
Required argument omitted	Entity class not supported
Filter invalid for action	Get list error
Invalid argument value	Invalid attribute value
Invalid filter	Invalid operator
Invalid use of wildcard	No resource available
No such action	No such argument
No such attribute ID	No such event type
No such object instance	No such object class
No such reference object	Processing failure
Duplicate object	Write only attribute
Set list error	Synch not supported

11-8
CMIP Return
Error Message

Invoke ID		1234
Operation Value		Get
Entity Class		ISO Identified Organization
		ECMA
		DEC
		Distributed-Systems-Management
		Node
		Routing
		Circuit
Entity Instance		Routing: NULL
		Circuit: UNA-0
Attribute ID List		Type
		Template Name
		Hello Time
Source: DNA Phase V CMIP Specification.		

11-9
Example of a CMIP
Request

Invoke ID		1234
Operation Value		Get
Entity Class		ISO Identified Organization
		ECMA
		DEC
		Distributed-Systems-Management
		Node
		Routing
		Circuit
Entity Instance		Routing: NULL
		Circuit: UNA-0
Type		"802.3"
Template Name		""
Hello Time		600
State		On
Source: DNA Phase V CMIP Specification.		

11-10
Example of a CMIP
Result

```
┌DETAIL┐
│CMIP: ───── Common Management Information Protocol ─────
│CMIP:
│CMIP: Remote Operation = 1 (Invoke)
│CMIP: Invoke Id = 133
│CMIP: Operation = 3 (Get command)
│CMIP: Object class = {1.3.6.1.2.2.1.2.4} (tcp)
│CMIP: CMISSync = 0 (Best effort)
│CMIP: Object = 2 (tcpActiveOpens)
│CMIP: Object = 3 (tcpPassiveOpens)
│CMIP: Object = 4 (tcpAttemptFails)
│CMIP: Object = 5 (tcpEstabResets)
│CMIP: Object = 6 (tcpCurrEstab)
│CMIP: Object = 7 (tcpOutSegs)
│CMIP: Object = 8 (tcpRetransSegs)
│CMIP: Object = 9 (tcpInSegs)
│CMIP: Object = 10 (tcpCurrEstabTholdVal)
│CMIP: Object = 11 (tcpCurrEstabDeltaVal)
│CMIP: Object = 12 (tcpRetransSegsTholdVal)
│CMIP: Object = 13 (tcpRetransSegsTholdResetVal)
│CMIP: Object = 16 (tcpEstabEventsEnable)
                      ─Frame 58 of 150─
                    Use TAB to select windows
```

| 1 Help | 2 Set mark | | 4 Zoom out | 5 Menus | 6Display options | 7 Prev frame | 8 Next frame | | 10 New capture |

11-11 CMIP Get Component Message

```
┌DETAIL┐
│CMIP: ───── Common Management Information Protocol ─────
│CMIP:
│CMIP: Remote Operation = 2 (Result)
│CMIP: Invoke Id = 133
│CMIP: Operation = 3 (Get result)
│CMIP: Object class = {1.3.6.1.2.2.1.2.4} (tcp)
│CMIP: Current time = 24 Sep 1988  01:02:30.54
│CMIP:
│CMIP: Object = 2 (tcpActiveOpens)
│CMIP: Value = 1
│CMIP:
│CMIP: Object = 3 (tcpPassiveOpens)
│CMIP: Value = 46
│CMIP:
│CMIP: Object = 4 (tcpAttemptFails)
│CMIP: Value = 0
│CMIP:
│CMIP: Object = 5 (tcpEstabResets)
│CMIP: Value = 0
│CMIP:
                      ─Frame 61 of 150─
                    Use TAB to select windows
```

| 1 Help | 2 Set mark | | 4 Zoom out | 5 Menus | 6Display options | 7 Prev frame | 8 Next frame | | 10 New capture |

11-12 CMIP Get Result

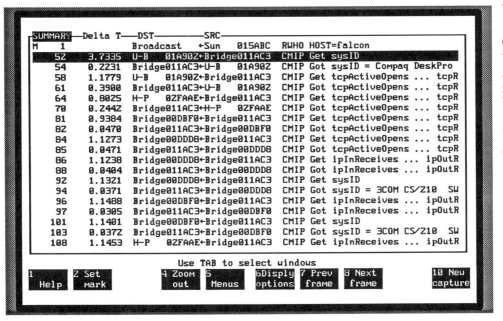

11-13 CMIP Traffic

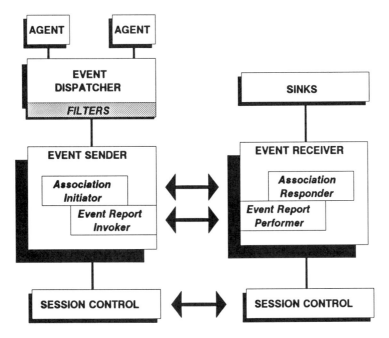

11-14 DEC Event Logging Architecture

protocols (MEN) to get the event from the source to the sink. The components of this architecture (see Fig. 11-14) are

- event sources and sinks
- Phase IV relays
- event dispatcher
- directors

The sink is a named entity that supports the event logging architecture sink interface and CMIP. In other words, the sink specification is layered on top of CMIP. An event stream is a long-lived relationship between a source and a sink. It survives communication, process, and system failures because the network management system monitors the status of sinks and tries to reestablish them in the case of failures.

Each network must have at least one sink (although a null sink would qualify). A hybrid Phase IV/V network must have either a Phase IV sink or a Phase IV event logging relay.

The event dispatcher is a module. As such it has a management agent that uses the MICE protocols to respond to a request. It also has a sink interface to local modules to receive requests and a MEN interface to the network to dispatch events.

Each event is self-describing. The event report includes

- entity name
- time stamp
- UID
- event-specific parameters

A special type of event is the pseudoevent, which is entered into the stream by the event dispatcher or sink. The pseudoevent helps interpret the stream: It represents changes in the logging system. Examples include

- events lost
- change in filter
- enable stream

Pseudoevents are generated at sources and sinks. Any pseudoevent, except the events lost pseudoevent might be lost. Pseudoevents are dispatched to the sink. They come from the sink; they go right back in. An example of an events lost pseudoevent, as displayed in NCL, is

```
Event: EventsLost, from: Node DigitalENG.NAC.LYRE EVD
    at 1987-08-11-18:22:33:04-0500I.02
    Number = 1
    event UID 12345678-9012-B456-8001-08002B033D7A
    entity UID 12345679-9012-B456-8001-08002B033D7A
    stream UID 12345676-9012-B456-8001-08002B033D7A
```

The sink is a generic entity. It could be a system console, a log file, or a flashing red light or siren. It could even be a nose on a Ken Olsen doll that lights up. There are three aspects of the sink that are defined in the architecture:

- communication with the event dispatcher
- local sink filtering
- sink service interface to read event reports

Each event is time stamped. Remember, however, that time in DNA is an interval. The ordering of overlapping time intervals is indeterminate. Within events from a single instance of an entity, it is possible to order events by the midpoints of time stamps. Optionally, if a node issues more than one event in a single clock tick, it can add a sequence number.

Event Filtering

FIltering of events occurs in two places: Each outbound stream at the source has a filter. Additionally, each sink maintains a single filter that applies to all inbound streams.

The filter is set up as a tree, which conforms to the entity hierarchy in Phase V. At each level of the tree, we can pass or block a particular type of event. We might, for example, want to block all events in a given class or to pass events from a specific entity but block all others. Three filters are used to implement this functionality—a specific filter tree, a global filter tree, and a catchall filter. First the specific filter tree is searched. If a value is matched (pass or block) the action is performed. If the value on the tree is ignore, the global tree is searched. Again, we look for an action. Finally, the catchall filter is searched.

The ignore action is a place holder—it maintains the structure of the tree without causing an action. It lets us put a specific entity into that tree, but still have the global action apply.

The filter interface has a test operation, allowing the manager to test a particular event to see if it would pass or block on the trees. There is also a show command to show the tree. For example,

```
block instance = node NAC
               routing circuit QNA-0
               event = adjacency
block instance = node NAC
               routing circuit QNA-O
               event = all
block class = routing circuit
               event = all
block instance = node * routing * circuit * event = all
```

Flow of an Event

An event goes through the following sequence:

- The source entity posts the event to the dispatcher.
- The dispatcher posts the event to all enabled outbound streams.
- The streams filter the event.
- The streams call the CMIP event report sender.
- The CMIP event report receiver gets the event, calls the sink.
- The sink filters the event.
- The sink queues the event.
- The sink client application reads the event.
- The doll's nose lights up.

To maintain compatibility with Phase IV domains, an event may optionally go through a Phase IV relay. The Phase IV relay is an entity on the Phase V node and appears to the Phase IV nodes as a monitor, console, or logging sink. The relay converts Phase IV events to Phase V by encapsulating them.

Phase V is similar to the Phase IV model but with a generic and arbitrary number of sinks (IV only had the three predefined types). Phase V event logging also added filtering at the event dispatcher and the sink, as well as the concepts of pseudoevents.

EMA and DECmcc

The Enterprise Management Architecture defines a model for building extensible management systems (directors) of which DECmcc is one. Management is provided by plug-and-play modules. DECmcc has three pieces (see Fig. 11-15):

- The DECmcc kernel provides the framework routines that allow management modules to exist as different processes on the same or different systems.
- The management information repository contains structured information about entity classes, information about specific entities (entity attribute data) and private information such as historical data, for each of the management modules.
- Management modules provide one of the three types of services: function, presentation, or access.

Examples of presentation modules are DECwindows or the command line interface, known as the Forms and Command Line (FCL) Presentation Module. In addition, presentation modules might include report generators or a 3270 terminal forms interface.

Flow of an Event

An event goes through the following sequence:

- The source entity posts the event to the dispatcher.
- The dispatcher posts the event to all enabled outbound streams.
- The streams filter the event.
- The streams call the CMIP event report sender.
- The CMIP event report receiver gets the event, calls the sink.
- The sink filters the event.
- The sink queues the event.
- The sink client application reads the event.
- The doll's nose lights up.

To maintain compatibility with Phase IV domains, an event may optionally go through a Phase IV relay. The Phase IV relay is an entity on the Phase V node and appears to the Phase IV nodes as a monitor, console, or logging sink. The relay converts Phase IV events to Phase V by encapsulating them.

Phase V is similar to the Phase IV model but with a generic and arbitrary number of sinks (IV only had the three predefined types). Phase V event logging also added filtering at the event dispatcher and the sink, as well as the concepts of pseudoevents.

EMA and DECmcc

The Enterprise Management Architecture defines a model for building extensible management systems (directors) of which DECmcc is one. Management is provided by plug-and-play modules. DECmcc has three pieces (see Fig. 11-15):

- The DECmcc kernel provides the framework routines that allow management modules to exist as different processes on the same or different systems.
- The management information repository contains structured information about entity classes, information about specific entities (entity attribute data) and private information such as historical data, for each of the management modules.
- Management modules provide one of the three types of services: function, presentation, or access.

Examples of presentation modules are DECwindows or the command line interface, known as the Forms and Command Line (FCL) Presentation Module. In addition, presentation modules might include report generators or a 3270 terminal forms interface.

The sink is a generic entity. It could be a system console, a log file, or a flashing red light or siren. It could even be a nose on a Ken Olsen doll that lights up. There are three aspects of the sink that are defined in the architecture:

- communication with the event dispatcher
- local sink filtering
- sink service interface to read event reports

Each event is time stamped. Remember, however, that time in DNA is an interval. The ordering of overlapping time intervals is indeterminate. Within events from a single instance of an entity, it is possible to order events by the midpoints of time stamps. Optionally, if a node issues more than one event in a single clock tick, it can add a sequence number.

Event Filtering

FIltering of events occurs in two places: Each outbound stream at the source has a filter. Additionally, each sink maintains a single filter that applies to all inbound streams.

The filter is set up as a tree, which conforms to the entity hierarchy in Phase V. At each level of the tree, we can pass or block a particular type of event. We might, for example, want to block all events in a given class or to pass events from a specific entity but block all others. Three filters are used to implement this functionality—a specific filter tree, a global filter tree, and a catchall filter. First the specific filter tree is searched. If a value is matched (pass or block) the action is performed. If the value on the tree is ignore, the global tree is searched. Again, we look for an action. Finally, the catchall filter is searched.

The ignore action is a place holder—it maintains the structure of the tree without causing an action. It lets us put a specific entity into that tree, but still have the global action apply.

The filter interface has a test operation, allowing the manager to test a particular event to see if it would pass or block on the trees. There is also a show command to show the tree. For example,

```
block instance = node NAC
                routing circuit QNA-0
                event = adjacency
block instance = node NAC
                routing circuit QNA-O
                event = all
block class = routing circuit
                event = all
block instance = node * routing * circuit * event = all
```

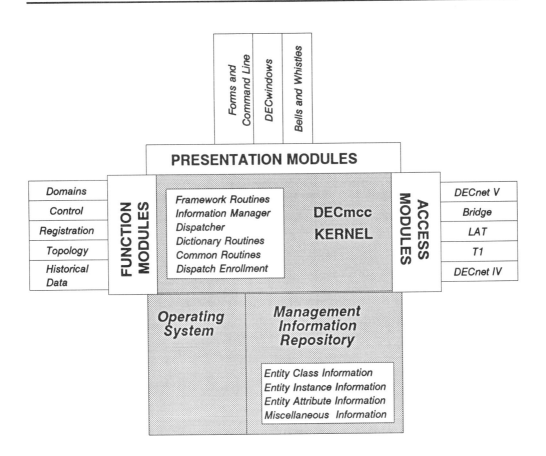

11-15 DECmcc Module Structure

Function modules do things like record historical data, manage network configurations, and generate alarms used to notify users of important events. They take the information received from access modules and add value to that information. Function modules often provide generic functions that apply to a variety of access modules.

Access modules are specific to a management environment, TCP/IP, Ethernet, DECnet, or a voice/data switch. Function modules provide more generic functions like keeping track of historical data, relying on the access modules to get that data.

Four important interfaces are not specified in DECmcc:

- presentation module to the presentation device
- access module to its entities
- kernel to the operating system (i.e., RMS versus Rdb for disk access)
- kernel-to-kernel synchronization for distribution of the DECmcc kernel

DECmcc specifies the interface between a management module and the kernel, which in turn provides access to the operating system and to managed entities and other management modules. DECmcc is extensible. This means that a given management module may or may not be present at any given time. When a management module is added to the system, it is enrolled.

The kernel provides five categories of routines:

- framework routines
- common routines
- information manager and dispatcher
- dictionary routines
- dispatch enrollment

The framework routines are a way of sharing a single kernel among multiple processes. The multithreaded kernel provides efficient operation because blocks of code can be run in parallel in the same virtual address space. This simplifies asynchronous processing.

Three types of framework routines are provided to support the multithreaded environment:

- thread creation and deletion
- interthread synchronization
- interthread communication

The kernel common routines are used for encoding and utility operations such as time conversion.

The information and dispatcher calls are the portion of the kernel that handles the intercomponent procedure calls used to access other management modules. This is provided at two levels. The mcc_call_function services access a value-added service, typically offered by a function module. The mcc_call_access accesses a primitive service, typically offered by an access module (see Fig. 11-16).

The information manager provides access to attribute data in DECmcc and handles the scheduling. The dispatcher does the actual call and handles the results.

The information manager handles most of the scheduling task. For example, if a call refers to historical data, the information manager will try to get the information out of the database before passing the request to the management module. If the time for a request is in the future, the information manager will block the request. If time is a series of distinct time instances, the information manager will break the single call up into a series of distinct calls. This means the management module only sees individual calls.

DECmcc specifies the interface between a management module and the kernel, which in turn provides access to the operating system and to managed entities and other management modules. DECmcc is extensible. This means that a given management module may or may not be present at any given time. When a management module is added to the system, it is enrolled.

The kernel provides five categories of routines:

- framework routines
- common routines
- information manager and dispatcher
- dictionary routines
- dispatch enrollment

The framework routines are a way of sharing a single kernel among multiple processes. The multithreaded kernel provides efficient operation because blocks of code can be run in parallel in the same virtual address space. This simplifies asynchronous processing.

Three types of framework routines are provided to support the multithreaded environment:

- thread creation and deletion
- interthread synchronization
- interthread communication

The kernel common routines are used for encoding and utility operations such as time conversion.

The information and dispatcher calls are the portion of the kernel that handles the intercomponent procedure calls used to access other management modules. This is provided at two levels. The mcc_call_function services access a value-added service, typically offered by a function module. The mcc_call_access accesses a primitive service, typically offered by an access module (see Fig. 11-16).

The information manager provides access to attribute data in DECmcc and handles the scheduling. The dispatcher does the actual call and handles the results.

The information manager handles most of the scheduling task. For example, if a call refers to historical data, the information manager will try to get the information out of the database before passing the request to the management module. If the time for a request is in the future, the information manager will block the request. If time is a series of distinct time instances, the information manager will break the single call up into a series of distinct calls. This means the management module only sees individual calls.

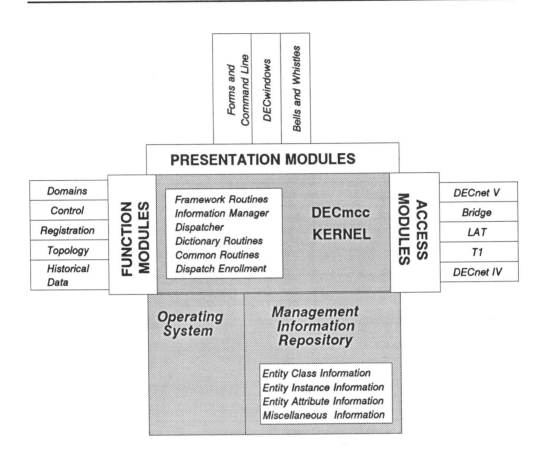

11-15 DECmcc Module Structure

Function modules do things like record historical data, manage network configurations, and generate alarms used to notify users of important events. They take the information received from access modules and add value to that information. Function modules often provide generic functions that apply to a variety of access modules.

Access modules are specific to a management environment, TCP/IP, Ethernet, DECnet, or a voice/data switch. Function modules provide more generic functions like keeping track of historical data, relying on the access modules to get that data.

Four important interfaces are not specified in DECmcc:

- presentation module to the presentation device
- access module to its entities
- kernel to the operating system (i.e., RMS versus Rdb for disk access)
- kernel-to-kernel synchronization for distribution of the DECmcc kernel

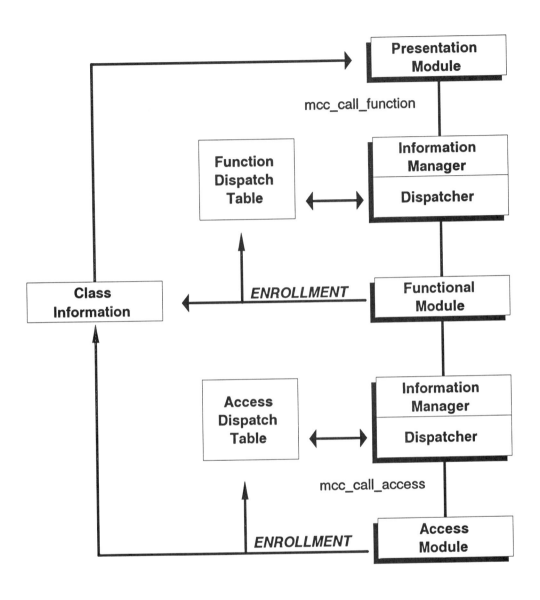

mcc_call (*verb, entity, attribute,*
time_spec, input_params,
input_qualifiers, context_handle,
output_params, timestamp,
output_entity)

11-16 The DECmcc Call Interface

The dispatcher processes the verb, entity, and attribute parameters of a call and chooses the appropriate procedure using a dispatch table. The dispatch table is a registry of which modules are accepting which types of requests. The function dispatch table is first searched by verb and attribute, then by entity. The access dispatch table is optimized for entities: Entities are searched first, then verbs and attributes.

Procedures in two modules cannot call each other directly because they do not know the virtual address of the called procedure nor which module is handling a particular request. The kernel does the dispatching, insulating modules from each other.

Dispatching is based on a verb, entity, attribute tuple (known in the documentation as a <V,E,A> tuple). When a management module enrolls itself, it provides a series of these tuples, along with the associated procedure to call. These tuples might be specified using wildcards. For example, the asterisk (*) specifies all entities in a class, and the trailing ellipsis (...) specifies all subentities in a tree.

Calls are sent down in a request/response scenario. To relate multiple sets of these calls, a context handle is used to inform the mcc_call interface that the present call is related to previous ones. Multiple call sets are used in a variety of instances. For example, the information manager may return multiple time sequences; a management information routine may return information of requests over a range of past times; or, with wildcarding within subentities, multiple access and function modules may handle a single call, returning multiple pieces of information.

<V,E,A> Tuples

Any calls to DECmcc use the same format, which consists of the following components:

- verb
- input_entity
- attribute
- time specifier
- input additional data
- input additional qualifications

The verb, entity, attribute tuple is encoded as a set of internal DECmcc codes. The attribute is only present on nonaction directives such as set or show. The additional data and qualifications are all encoded as indicator, length, value (ILV) sets. The output from the call is

- output parameter
- time stamp
- output entity

There is also a shared (input/output) parameter known as the context handle and a Condition Values Returned (CVR) indicator that shows whether the call had success or failure.

Processing Wildcards

The presentation manager will try to expand global entity wildcards before processing commands. It does this by calling the Domain Function Module. This means a different call would be sent down for, say, database management and network node management.

For lower levels of entity wildcards, the presentation module has the option of calling the configuration function module for a list of all entities that match. If there is no configuration module present, the presentation module can send the request down and let the appropriate function modules handle the request.

When each management module enrolls, it specifies what level of wildcarding it is willing to accept:

- local entity classes
- full global entity instances
- full local entity instances
- partial entity instances

Figure 11-17 shows an example of the processing of a call. The user types in a command using NCL. The Forms and Command Line (FCL) module takes that call and turns it into an mcc_call_function call. The dispatcher, using the function dispatch table, sends the call down to the control function module. The control function module takes the call and formulates it into an mcc_call_access call. Note that the function module, by using the dictionary, could have broken the call up into several access calls, one for each of several different access modules.

In this case, however, the call goes straight to the DECnet Phase IV access module, which uses the Network and Information Control Exchange (NICE) protocol. NICE serves the same purpose in Phase IV that CMIP does in Phase V—the network protocol to allow a remote director to communicate with an entity.

Once the NICE call is formulated, it leaves the boundary of DECmcc and enters the actual network being managed. Presumably, the Phase IV network uses NSP and DNA Session Control to set up a virtual circuit to the managed entity, NODE4. Once the response comes back, the access module sends up the first portion of the response. The returned information includes a context handle that indicates more information is available. The presentation module will make repeated calls with the context handle specified until no more information is available.

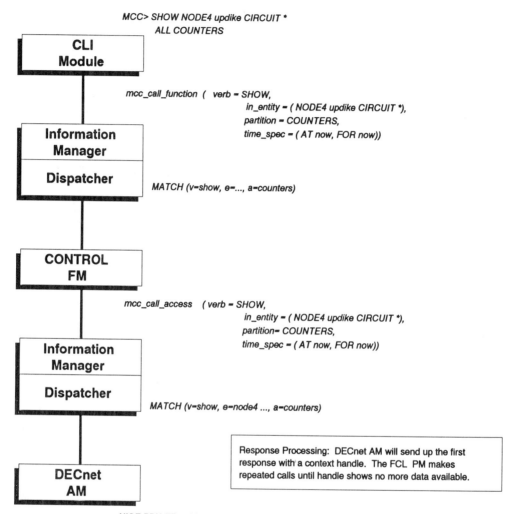

MCC> SHOW NODE4 updike CIRCUIT *
ALL COUNTERS

CLI Module

mcc_call_function (verb = SHOW,
        in_entity = (NODE4 updike CIRCUIT *),
        partition = COUNTERS,
        time_spec = (AT now, FOR now))

Information Manager

Dispatcher

MATCH (v=show, e=..., a=counters)

CONTROL FM

mcc_call_access (verb = SHOW,
        in_entity = (NODE4 updike CIRCUIT *),
        partition= COUNTERS,
        time_spec = (AT now, FOR now))

Information Manager

Dispatcher

MATCH (v=show, e=node4 ..., a=counters)

Response Processing: DECnet AM will send up the first response with a context handle. The FCL PM makes repeated calls until handle shows no more data available.

DECnet AM

NICE PDU ("Read Information Message")

11-17 DECmcc Call Example

Part of the power of DECmcc is the specification of a variety of qualifiers that are part of the call interface. These qualifiers provide a great deal of control over how a particular call gets interpreted.

Qualifiers to a call can be specified by any directive. These qualifiers are handled at one of four levels (see Fig. 11-18):

Qualifier	Category	Handled By			
		Presentation Manager	Information Manager	Dispatcher	Target
As part of the time specification parameter					
AT EVERY	When To Do It		X		
AT START	When To Start		X		
FOR EVERY	Scope Of Interest		X		
FOR START	Scope @Z_TBL_BODY = TABLE TEXT	TABLE TEXT	TABLE TEXT	TABLE TEXT	TABLE TEXT
As Part Of Input Qualifier Parameter					
BY Account/ Password/User	Access Control Filtering				X
VIA PATH	Path Filtering			X	
VIA PORT	Port Filtering				X
Handled By The Presentation Manager					
FROM File	Input Script	X			
FROM Window	Input Window	X			
TO FILE	Output	X			
TO WINDOW	Output	X			
IN DOMAIN	Membership Filtering	X			
Passed In The Input Entity Parameter					
WITH	Entity Filtering	X	X		X

11-18 Qualifiers in the MCC Call Interface

- presentation module
- information manager
- dispatcher
- target module

It is up to each management module to process qualifiers. If a qualifier is not recognized, an error returns. If the qualifier is recognized, the module can process it, return an "unsupported" error, or pass it down the line for another module to process.

An example of a qualifier is the "with" clause:

BRIDGE * WITH STATUS='ON'

"With" is an example of entity filtering, allowing only entities with attributes having certain values to be used. The with entity filter is similar to the CMIP event filtering discussed earlier.

The via path qualifier shows the hops along a path through a hierarchy of management modules. It shows the network port a module should use (i.e., a test of an Ethernet port). The for qualifier is the scope of interest, used to show the time that is needed for a call. There are two variants:

FOR START time
FOR EVERY time UNTIL time

Time specifiers show up in a variety of places in DECmcc, such as the user interface for display, the mcc_call specification, and internally in the management information repository for time stamping data. DECmcc defines two types of time: binary absolute time (BAT) and binary relative time (BRT). The power of the time qualifiers can be seen in this example:

AT EVERY 1:00   (every hour)
    UNTIL 17:00 (until 5 PM)
    START 13:15
    FOR (-0:00)

The qualifier says "give me an instance sample of data starting at 13:15 once an hour until 17:00."

Another variant is:

AT EVERY 1:00   (every hour)
    UNTIL 17:00 (until 5 PM)
    START 13:45
    FOR START (-0:30)
    DURATION :30

This qualifier instructs DECmcc to evaluate the preceding half hour's worth of data starting at 13:45 until 16:45. Note the difference: Scheduling is when to do it, scope of interest is what to bring back.

The at qualifier in the following example says when to start the request, the for following it says how often, once begun, to evaluate the request:

AT START (-0:00) (now)
    FOR EVERY 1:00
    UNTIL 17:00
    START 8:00 DURATION :30

at every 1- (every day)

start (8:00, 17:00)

for start (-0:00)

Notice the ability to have a request started every day. The information manager will ensure that the relevant calls are issued to the access modules to have the call properly performed on a daily basis.

Management Data

DECmcc keeps four types of data in the management information repository:

- entity class data
- entity instance data
- entity attribute data
- miscellaneous

Miscellaneous data are anything a function module chooses to keep in the underlying database. One of the prime examples of miscellaneous data are historical data kept by the Historical Data Recorder (HDR) function module.

Figure 11-19 shows the basic flow of dictionary information in the DECmcc environment. The presentation modules will use entity class information to derive default output formats. The function modules might use entity information to provide services based on known classes at this time. Class information is added when management modules are first enrolled and is not deleted since it is time independent.

Entity instance data include which entities exist and at what times they exist. This information may or not match reality it is the local DECmcc's version of the network. This allows the network manager to look at the configuration if the network is down.

Since entity instance data are time stamped, it allows the manager to look at present, past, and future configurations. It is the responsibility of the function modules to maintain this instance information. Entity attribute data are time stamped, historical data. They are collected by one or more function modules but are available to other management modules.

Miscellaneous information is whatever a module wants to keep. One example is a template of a mail message for use by a function module; another example is a parse table for a presentation module used to decode incoming commands from a human user into the appropriate DECmcc calls.

The dictionary is heavily used by the presentation modules to determine

- validation criteria for input
- translation of input strings into internal ID codes
- determination of presentation names used for input and displays

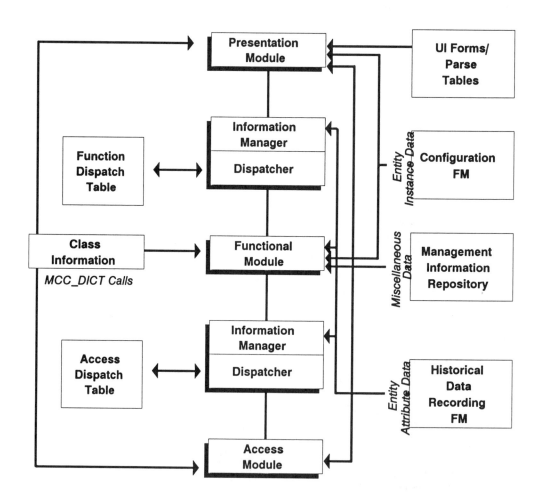

11-19 Flow of Dictionary Information in DECmcc

- determination of the number, data type, prompt string, and default values for arguments passed across the interface
- translation from internal ID codes into presentation formats
- interpretation of status information

Function modules also use the dictionary to

- determine what entity and subentity classes are defined
- determine if an entity class has the attributes on which a function module operates
- help formulate access module calls and to decode replies
- validate incoming requests

Access modules do not really need to use the dictionary, as they already know the structure of the entities they can handle. Remember, the purpose of the access module is to take the incoming calls and translate them into network-specific access calls.

Entity instance data are maintained and accessed by the configuration function module. Entity attribute data are through the HDR Function Module. This module provides an entity attribute polling and storage service.

Miscellaneous information is created through three types of DECmcc calls:

- mcc_rms creates an RMS file
- mcc_qiow begins direct device access
- mcc_mir_create creates a miscellaneous data store managed by the MIR manager (i.e., Ingres or Rdb)

These three examples are for the VMS version of DECmcc. On the Ultrix version, the equivalent native operating systems services can be accessed.

DECmcc Service Routines

DECmcc routines fall into multiple categories, providing different types of support services to the management modules (see Fig. 11-20). Some of these routines are tools that are optionally used by the programmer. An example is the abstract entity specification routines that let the programmer refer to an entity by a "handle." When repeated calls are being made, the entity specification is put into the handle, freeing the programmer from the worry of parsing complex entity specifications.

Other routines, called monitors, provide coordination among different modules. Monitors are two kinds: Mutually exclusive monitors provide access to common resource classes, and thread synchronous monitors provide access to underlying asynchronous services, that is, a way of blocking other threads but not the whole process. Monitors exist for locks, I/O, RMS, thread control, and timers.

For locking, there are four levels of namespaces:

- per process
- per UIC group
- per system
- per cluster

Thread calls let you create and delete a thread. You can also send an alert and test an alert and join threads (synchronize with the completion of one or all of a set of threads).

DECmcc Routines
Abstract Entity Specification (AES) routines allow the programmer to refer to an entity specification by name. They are useful in looking at several different attributes by "walking the tree."
Abstract Handle Specification (AHS) routines allow the programmer to manipulate the context handle. A context handle can be in three different states (first, more, cancel).
ASN.1 Encode/Decode routines allow the programmer to encode and decode based on type length value. It is a way of creating a constructed sequence or set of information.
Abstract Time Specifications allow the programmer to create a "time frame" which has several elements then copy, delete, extract elements, and get the first, last, or next element in a time frame.
Information Manager Routines: MCC_CALL_ACCESS and MCC_CALL_FUNCTION. The dispatcher selects the most specific service from the dispatch services.
DECnet Access routines allow the programmer to set up connections, manage names, read and send messages.
Dictionary routines allow the programmer to query the dictionary. For example, find the DECmcc code assigned to the attribute ROOT ID for a DEBET bridge. Or, given an MCC code, finds the English name. For each class of global entity, the routines provide access to attributes, attribute partitions, directive, and subordinate entities.
Ethernet Access Routines allow the programmer to get and send packets, show available device IDs, request XID to an entity, and perform an 802 loopback.
Enrollment Routines add a management module to the DECmcc runtime environment.
ID Code/Length Value (ILV) routines allow the programmer to build lists, append lists to each other, and perform other list manipulations.
Framework routines create and manipulate threads and monitors.
I/O routines access RMS and QIOW calls (but without the blocking).
Timer routines wait.
MIR routines allow the programmer to create and manage a new private repository, and then read, write, and delete entity data.
Time Conversion Routines are for date arithmetic and to read the current time.

11-20 DECmcc Routines

Module Execution Environment

A management module is a shared image in VMS and a process in Ultrix. This means the code should be reentrant (i.e., counters should not be declared as global variables) and position independent (it will work no matter where it is installed in the virtual address space).

Within the execution environment, threads are used to allow multiple execution paths within a single process. Monitors (semaphores) are then used to synchronize access to resources shared by concurrent threads.

Enrollment and Extensibility

To enroll a management module, four types of information are needed:

- The dispatch table entries: the <V,E,A> types and associated entry points this module is prepared to handle.
- A Management Specification (MS) written using the Management Specification Language (MSL) used to describe the management and service interfaces.
- User presentation information derived from the management specification information. It includes the command line interpreter (CLI) parse table, the command line input output information, window forms, and menu bars.
- Help information to merge into the DECmcc help libraries.

When a management module enrolls, it must provide three routines in addition to the normal functional routines. An initialization routine is called when the management module enrolls. This routine integrates the dispatch tables into the DECmcc dispatch table and maps the management module's shareable image. The PROBE routine is called the first time a user wants the services of this module. It maps the management module into the user address space. The LOG routine is called right after the probe and is used for logging information during debugging.

There are basically six steps to enroll a module (see Fig. 11-21):

- Execute the MSL translator.
- Execute the help file builder.
- Execute the parse table builder.
- Execute the forms builder.
- Merge dispatch tables.
- Map the management module (MM) shareable image into memory.

The translator does two things: First, it merges the management specification information into the dictionary for future use by programs such as the parse table builder. Second, it creates a constant declaration file.

Registration is the process of getting a unique code for information. Typically, you would go to Digital, which would assign/validate codes. If a management module is being sold, registry with Digital assures there is no conflict. If the MM is a unique, private module, registration is advised in that it prevents conflicts with future commercial management modules. In-

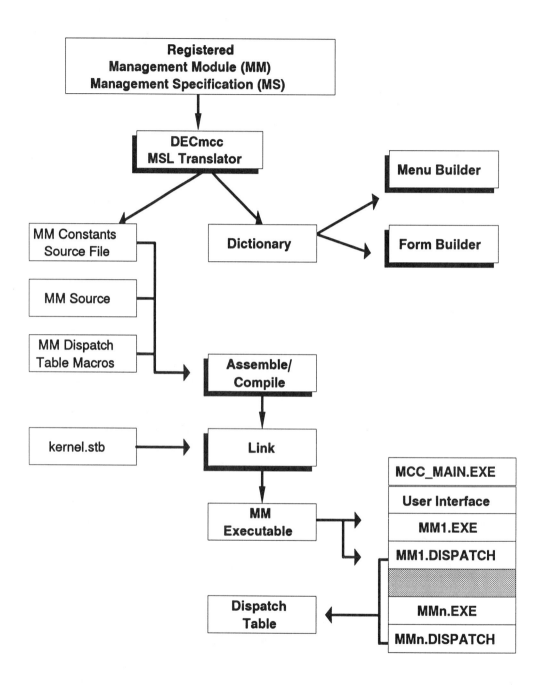

11-21 Creation of a DECmcc Module

formation from the management specification that gets registered includes the following:

- primitive data types
- constructed data types
- entity information: class name and code
- attribute partitions
- directives
- responses to directives
- exceptions to directives
- common exceptions
- arguments
- qualifiers

Figure 11-22 shows a portion of a management specification, taken from the DECmcc manual. The example specification defines an entity with the symbol "NETDEV." Then, the primary identifier, the Phase IV name, Phase IV address, and other identifiers are defined. Next, several attributes of the network are described. First is the send rate, a settable attribute with a default value of 1000 bytes per second.

After the characteristic, settable attributes come the status counters such as the total number of user bytes sent. Following that, an attribute group is defined. Notice that this management specification closely follows the network management architecture of entities, identifiers, attributes, and groups defined in the beginning of this chapter. Directives, exception reports, and other aspects are also defined in the MS language.

The Help System

The automatic help system allows the network manager to find out more about entities, attributes, and other things in a management module. This dynamic help system is important because new management modules may be enrolled at any time. Help information is in one of four categories:

- entity information (provided by the access module)
- function information
- presentation information
- tutorials

Within each category, there are several levels of help information. The basic hierarchy is

- entity
- entity classes
- subordinate entity classes

```
MANAGEMENT SPECIFICATION                          DISPLAY = TRUE,
    EXAMPLE_AM;                                    UNITS = ''Bytes'',
VERSION = T1.0;                                    DEFAULT = NO DEFAULT,
SYMBOL_PREFIX = EXAMPLE_ ;                         SYMBOL = NEDEV_USER_BYTES_RCVD,
GLOBAL ENTITY NETDEV = 100 ;                       CATEGORIES = (CONFIGURATION)
  IDENTIFIERS = (Name, Address),              END ATTRIBUTE User Bytes Received ;
  DYNAMIC = FALSE;                            END ATTRIBUTES; (* COUNTER *)
  SYMBOL = NETDEV,
IDENTIFIER ATTRIBUTES                         ATTRIBUTE GROUP Send and Receive
ATTRIBUTE Name = 01 ; Phase4Name                  Inf = 20 ;
    (* This is the primary identifier *)          ATTRIBUTE-LIST = (Send Rate,
    ACCESS = NONSETTABLE,                          Receive Rate,
    DISPLAY = TRUE,                                User Bytes Sent,
    DEFAULT = NO DEFAULT,                          User Bytes Received),
    SYMBOL = NEDEV_NAME,                           DIRECTIVES-SUPPORTED = (Show),
    CATEGORIES = (CONFIGURATION)                   CATEGORIES = (CONFIGURATION)
END ATTRIBUTE Name;                           END ATTRIBUTE GROUP
ATTRIBUTE Address = 02 : Phase4Address            Send and Receive Inf ;
    ACCESS = NONSETTABLE,                     DIRECTIVE Show = 01 ;
    DISPLAY = TRUE,                               DIRECTIVE-TYPE = EXAMINE,
    DEFAULT = NO DEFAULT,                         DISPLAY = TRUE,
    SYMBOL = NEDEV_ADDRESS,                       SYMBOL = NETDEV_SHOW,
    CATEGORIES = (CONFIGURATION)                  CATEGORIES = (CONFIGURATION),
END ATTRIBUTE Address;                        (* Note: No REQUEST arguments required *)
END ATTRIBUTES; (* Identifier *)              RESPONSE Examine Complete = 1;
CHARACTERISTIC ATTRIBUTES                         SYMBOL = EXAMINE_COMPLETE,
ATTRIBUTE Send Rate = 713 : Unsigned32            ARGUMENT Examine List = 1 : Attrib_List
    ACCESS = SETTABLE,                            DISPLAY = TRUE,
    DISPLAY = TRUE,                               SYMBOL = EXAMINE_LIST
    UNITS = ''Bytes Per Second'',                 END ARGUMENT Examine List;
    DEFAULT = 1000,                           END RESPONSE Examine Complete;
    SYMBOL = NEDEV_SEND_RATE,                 EXCEPTION Unrecognized Argument = 0 :
    CATEGORIES = (CONFIGURATION)                  SYMBOL = UNREC_EXAM_ARG,
END ATTRIBUTE Send Rate;                          ARGUMENT
ATTRIBUTE Receive Rate = 756 : Unsigned32         Exception Class = 0 : ExceptionClass
    ACCESS = SETTABLE,                            DISPLAY = FALSE,
    DISPLAY = TRUE,                               SYMBOL = EXCEPTION_CLASS
    UNITS = ''Bytes Per Second'',                 END ARGUMENT Exception Class;
    DEFAULT = 1000,                           END EXCEPTION Unrecognized Argument;
    SYMBOL = NEDEV_RCV_RATE,                  END DIRECTIVE Show;
    CATEGORIES = (CONFIGURATION)
    END ATTRIBUTE Receive Rate;              DIRECTIVE Set = 2:
END ATTRIBUTES; (* CHARACTERISTIC *)              DIRECTIVE-TYPE = MODIFY,
COUNTER ATTRIBUTES                                DISPLAY = TRUE,
ATTRIBUTE User Bytes Sent = 10 : Counter32        SYMBOL = SET_DIRECTIVE,
    ACCESS = NONSETTABLE,                         CATEGORIES = (CONFIGURATION),
    DISPLAY = TRUE,                               REQUEST
    UNITS = ''Bytes'',                             ARGUMENT Modify List = 1 : Attrib_List
    DEFAULT = NO DEFAULT,                          SYMBOL = SET_MODIFY_LIST
    SYMBOL = NEDEV_USER_BYTES_SENT,                END ARGUMENT Modify List;
    CATEGORIES = (CONFIGURATION)                  END REQUEST ;
END ATTRIBUTE User Bytes Sent ;               RESPONSE Modify Complete = 1;
ATTRIBUTE User Bytes Received = 11 :               SYMBOL = MOD_COMPLETE,
            Counter32                         END RESPONSE Modify Complete;
    ACCESS = NONSETTABLE,                     EXCEPTION Unrecognized Argument = 0 :
```

```
! SOURCE: DECmcc Manual, pp. 186-187
! File: MCC$NETDEV_AM.HELP
WINDOW_TOPICS
ENTITY NETDEV = NETDEV
ENTITY NETDEV CHARACTERISTICS SEND_RATE = NETDEV_CHAR_SR
ENTITY NETDEV CHARACTERISTICS RECEIVE_RATE = NET-
DEV_CHAR_SR
!
ENTITY NETDEV COUNTERS = NETDEV_CNT
ENTITY NETDEV COUNTERS USER_BYTES_RECEIVED = NET-
DEV_CNT_UBR
ENTITY NETDEV COUNTERS USER_BYTES_SENT = NETDEV_CNT_SNT
!
ENTITY NETDEV IDENTIFIERS = NETDEV_IDENT
ENTITY NETDEV IDENTIFIERS NAME = NETDEV_IDENT_NAME
ENTITY NETDEV IDENTIFIERS ADDRSS =  NETDEV_IDENT_ADDRESS
!
ENTITY NETDEV SEND_AND_RECEIVE_INFO = NETDEV_SARI
!
ENTITY NETDEV SET = NETDEV_D_SET
ENTITY NETDEV SHOW = NETDEV_D_SHOW
!
KEY = NETDEV
Network Device help text.
KEY = NETDEV_CHAR
Network Device Characteristics help text.
KEY = NETDEV_CHAR_SR
KEY = NETDEV_CHAR_RR
```

11-23
Help
Specification
Language

```
MCC> HELP

 Additional information available:

 ENTITY  FUNCTION  PRESENTATION  TUTORIAL

Topic? ENTITY

ENTITY

 Entity help text.

 Additional information available:

   NETDEV

ENTITY Subtopic? NETDEV

ENTITY

 NETDEV

   Network Device help text.

 Additional information available:

 CHARACTERISTICS  COUNTERS  INDENTIFIERS
```

11-24
Resulting Help
Text in DECmcc

For each subordinate entity class, there is information on directives, attribute partition, and attribute groups, Under directives there is information on requests, responses, and exceptions, with information for arguments on each.

The presentation tree is similar, including:

- presentation category
- PM module
- UI Feature
- UI Subfeature

Each management module produces a help file under the name mcc_name.help written in the help specification language. Figure 11-23 shows an example from the DECmcc manual of the help specification language. Figure 11-24 shows a sample help session using the topics specified in Figure 11-23.

Modules

DECmcc provides the platform to develop different modules. Several modules have been developed allowing management of a heterogeneous environment from a single platform. Access modules, for example, have been written to manage Phase IV, Phase V, LAN bridges, TCP/IP SNMP, and FDDI.

Of particular interest are the different function modules and presentation modules available. Figures 11-25 through 11-28 show the window-based screens that illustrate a variety of the functions provided in early releases of DECmcc.

Figure 11-25 shows a map of the network topology. Notice the small window has a picture of the domain being managed, the United States. The manager has zoomed in on the Northeast, showing the links coming out of Littleton, Massachusetts. The toolbox has a variety of icons allowing the manager to pick different tools. The domain management tool, already selected, allows the manager to separate a large complex network into different domains.

Figure 11-26 shows a more detailed view of the Massachusetts facility, including a topology map of the network. Notice that miscellaneous MIR information has been used to give names to all the nodes. The network shows that a variety of Ethernet systems is connected together using bridge systems. Notice there are two more domains that could be examined even further—IP-DOMAIN and LKG-C.

Figure 11-27 shows the automatic forms creation capability of DECmcc. The operation SHOW COUNTERS, for example, generates a query that will examine the operation of a bridge. The user clicks on the bridge and the

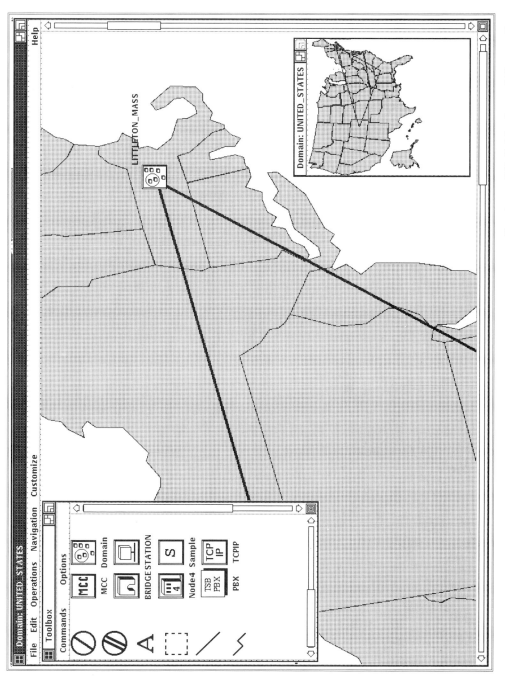

11-25 Map of Northeast Domain

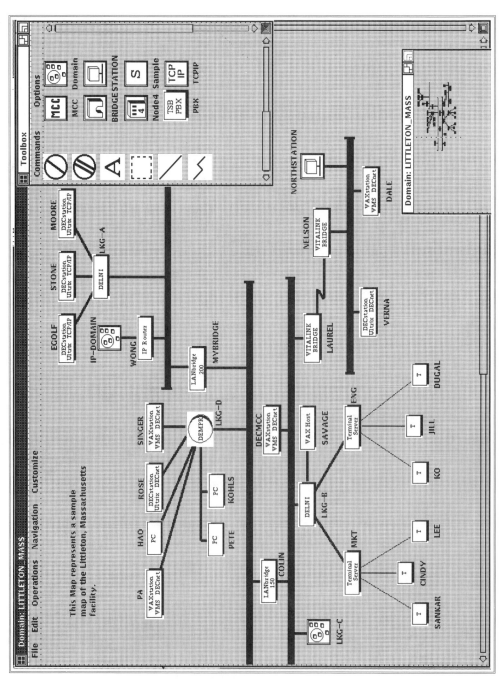

11-26 Map of Massachusetts Domain

Courtesy of Digital Equipment Corporation

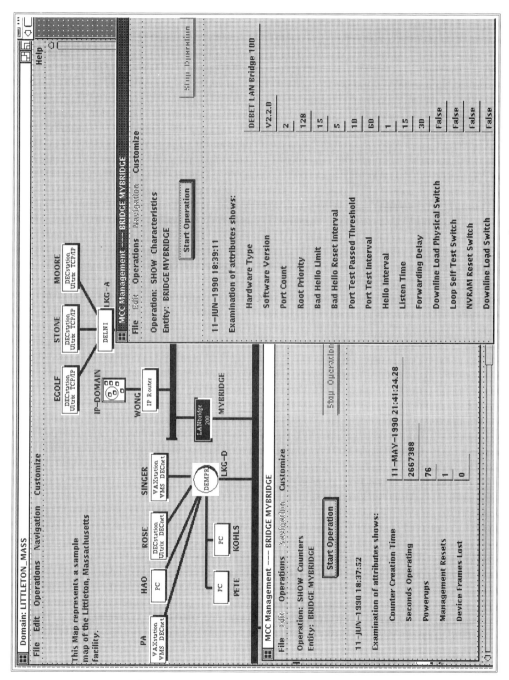

11-27 DECmcc Forms Capability

Courtesy of Digital Equipment Corporation

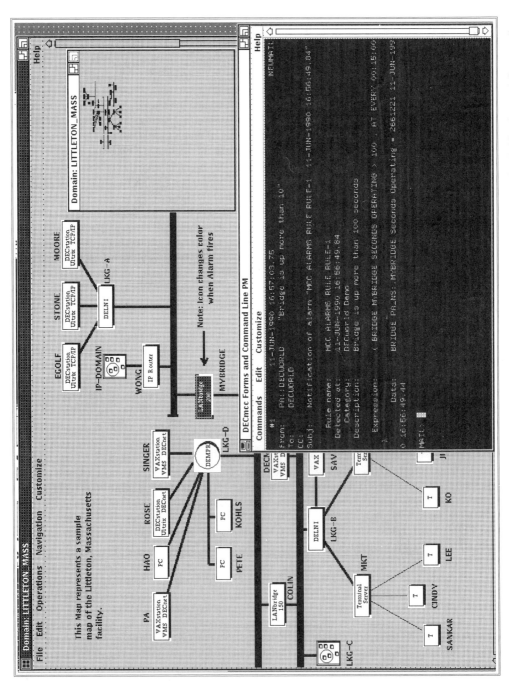

11-28 DECmcc Alert Module

Courtesy of Digital Equipment Corporation

window will open. The different counters available for this bridge are displayed in the window. Next to the show counters window is the show characteristics window. Again, a form is automatically created to show the relevant characteristics. In both windows, the display will be continually updated to show the current version of the data.

What has happened here is that the window-based presentation manager has used the dictionary to find out what the form should look like. When the user hits the start operation button on the form, the presentation module issues a mcc_call_function call, specifying the entity BRIDGE MY-BRIDGE. This is intercepted and eventually turned into an access module call down to the bridge management module.

Figure 11-28 shows an especially powerful function module, the alarms module. The user is able to define the conditions for an alarm. In this case, a rule was defined that said that when a bridge was working successfully, it should trigger an alarm. The alarm did two things. First, it changed the color of the network map. Second, it sent an automatically generated electronic mail message to the network manager. The alarm module could just as easily have used DECtalk, a voice generation system, and a modem to call the network manager at home and give him or her this information.

Summary

Digital's network management architecture has many pieces. The CMIP protocols in OSI are a means of moving management directives and reports around the network. The node architecture defines how modules on a DECnet node will provide management information.

Since network management is more than just DECnet or OSI, Digital provides an architecture for the management director, EMA. EMA, and the resulting implementation of DECmcc, provide management capabilities for multiple network architectures. In fact, DECmcc can be used for system or application management, tasks not usually combined with network management.

The access modules of DECmcc allow remote entities to be managed. The real power, however, is in the functional management capabilities. Allowing historical data records, alarm modules, and WAN topology mapping to work together gives the network manager a wide variety of tools to use. How to use those tools effectively could easily be the subject of another book, so we terminate this book on that thought.

Glossary

Glossary

1003.1	POSIX general definition.
1003.4	POSIX real-time extensions.
1003.6	POSIX security extensions.
1003.7	POSIX system management extensions.
1003.8	POSIX networking extensions.
10BASE2	*10 Mbps/baseband/200 meters.* IEEE standard for thinwire Ethernet.
10BASE5	*10 Mbps/baseband/500 meters.* IEEE standard for thickwire coaxial Ethernet.
10BASET	*10 Mbps/baseband/twisted pair.* IEEE standard for twisted pair Ethernet.
2780/3780	A model of remote batch terminals used in IBM bisynchronous environments. Bisync gateways are often referred to as 2780/3780 emulators.
3+	3Com networking products.
3090	IBM top of the line mainframe, sometimes called Sierra.
3270	A series of terminals used in IBM environments.
3270 Display Stations	Terminals for IBM mainframe computers.

3274 | A cluster controller for IBM equipment, often called a terminal concentrator.

3480 | IBM tape cartridges.

370 architecture | IBM architecture for mainframe computers, including the 3090 processors.

3705 | An IBM communications controller. A PU Type 4 in SNA used to connect token ring networks, cluster controllers, non-IBM SNA gateways, and other devices to a PU Type 5 host.

3725 | *See 3705.*

3Com | A communications company known for Ethernet controllers and PC-based networking equipment. Merged with Bridge Communications.

4.3BSD | *4.3 Berkeley Software Distribution.* The current version of the Berkeley family of Unix products.

4010/4014 | A series of Tektronix graphics terminals. A de facto standard for graphics terminals.

423 | *See EIA-423.* Abbreviation used in DECconnect.

4GL | *See fourth-generation language.*

5250 | IBM terminal used on the System/3X line.

802.2 | IEEE standard for the Logical Link Control.

802.3 | IEEE standard for CSMA/CD (Ethernet) medium access method.

802.4 | IEEE standard for the token bus medium access method.

802.5 | IEEE standard for the token ring medium access method.

80286 | An Intel chip used in the IBM PC/AT and clones. The 80386 is used in new high-end PS/2s and Compaq computers.

80x86 | Family of microprocessors made by Intel used in the PC line. The PC/AT uses the 80286 chip. More modern systems, including the PS/2, use the 32-bit 80386 chip.

9370   Midrange IBM processor.

A   *AT&T Modular Jack.* Abbreviation used in DECconnect.

A Tools   Digital extensions to CDD/Plus to support object-oriented ex-
Integration   tensions to the data dictionary.
Standard

ABM   *See Asynchronous Balanced Mode.*

abstract data type   Concept used in programming and database systems. An
                       abstract data type is a user-defined data type that hides the
                       internal details of its manipulation. For example, date, an
                       abstract data type, is stored internally as an integer but is
                       manipulated   externally   through   date-specific   repre-
                       sentations and operations.

AC   *Access control.* Token ring field that holds the priority and
                       reservation bits for a token or data packet.

access control set   A set of identifiers of objects and their associated rights to
                       some entity (i.e., a node or a file).

access method   A means of accessing information in a file. Btree is an ex-
                       ample of an access method.

access module   An EMA concept. The access module is responsible for the
                       primitive interface to management protocols such as CMIP,
                       which in turn accesses the managed entities. *See also func-
                       tion module and presentation module.*

ACF   *Access Control Facility* Security system for the MVS operat-
                       ing system.

ACK   *Acknowledge.* A network packet acknowledging the receipt
                       of data.

ACL   *Access Control List.* A security feature that allows security
                       on objects to be specified as a list of permitted actions for
                       particular lists of users. Both the VMS operating system
                       and the DNA Naming Service have (different) ACL capabili-
                       ties.

ACP   *Ancillary Control Process. See NETACP.*

ACS   *See Access Control Set.*

ACSE   *Association Control Service Elements.* Core set of facilities in the OSI application layer that allow application entities to form an association.

ACT   *Number of active connectors.* Abbreviation used in DECconnect.

active converter   A device used to convert from one communication signaling interface to another. Digital has an active converter for converting from EIA 232-D to EIA 423-A.

active device   A device with its own power source.

active monitor   A computer on a token ring that acts as the controller for the ring, regulating the token and other performance aspects.

Active Monitor   Packet issued every 3 seconds by the active monitor on a
Present   token ring.

ADDMD   *Administration Directory Management Domain.* An X.500 directory management domain maintained by a public telecommunications entity that is a member of the CCITT.

addressing   The group responsible for assigning addresses within a do-
authority   main.

address space   A collection of addresses that form a unified collection such as an internetwork.

ADMD   *Administration Management Domain.* X.400 message-handling system concept. Countries will typically be an ADMD. They might then delegate management authority to a private management domain (PRMD).

ADT   *See Abstract data type.*

Advanced   Protocol used for peer-to-peer communication in IBM's Sys-
Program-to-Program   tem Network Architecture.
Communication

advertising   The process by which a service makes its presence known on the network. Typically provided through some form of LAN-based multicast.

AES   *Application Environment Specification.* OSF look and feel standards based on the X Windows System.

AFI   *Authority and Format Identifier.* Part of an OSI address that signals what type of address follows the AFI.

AFP   *See AppleTalk Filing Protocol.*

aged packet   A routing layer packet that has exceeded the maximum number of visits.

agent   Network management term for the portion of an entity that responds to management functions.

aggregate   A function in a query language used to perform an operation on several rows of data. Sum is an example of an aggregate.

AHS   *Abstract Handle Specification* Set of DECmcc routines used to establish and manipulate context handles.

AK TPDU   *Acknowledge Transport Protocol Data Unit.* A protocol data unit type in the OSI transport service.

alias   A name that is translated into another name. A DNS soft link is an example of an alias.

ALL-IN-1   Digital's office automation shell, consisting of a menu driver, a mail user interface, a calendar manager, and a file manager.

allocation   Concept used in the transport layer protocols. An allocation is the amount of unacknowledged traffic that may be outstanding at one time.

AM   *See Access Module.*

American National Standards Institute   Private organization that coordinates some United States standards making. Represents the United States in the International Organization for Standardization (ISO).

American Wire Gauge   Standard used to describe the size of a wire.

A-mode	*Asynchronous Mode.* Used in the OSI Virtual Terminal protocols. A model for terminal operation where either side may communicate at any time.
ANSI	*See American National Standards Institute.*
AMP	*See Active Monitor Present.*
annular mark	The mark on an Ethernet coaxial cable that identifies the 2.5-meter separation required for nodes.
ANSI	*See American National Standards Institute.*
API	*See application programming interface.*
APPC	*See Advanced Program-to-Program Communication.*
AppleTalk	Apple's network protocol.
AppleTalk Filing Protocol	The protocol in AppleTalk used for remote access to data.
application	A program that performs functions for a user. Order entry system or word processors are both examples of applications.
Application Control Services	The rules used for application to application interaction in an NAS environment.
application layer	The top layer of the network protocol stack. The application layer is concerned with the semantics of work. For example, getting a certain record from a file by key value on a foreign node is an application layer concern. How to represent that data and how to reach the foreign node are issues for lower layers of the network.
application programming interface	Specification of the calling structure between two programs, usually between a general application program and a specific support service, such as communications support.
application terminal	A LAT object accessed by an application on a slave node. For example, a printer attached to a terminal server would be the application terminal for the print spooler.

architecture

A set of plans that allow different components to work together. A network architecture allows different computers on a network to communicate. An information architecture allows different users to access a variety of data repositories.

ARCNET

Hardware and software data link components manufactured by Datapoint and other companies that allow computers to form a 2.5-Mbps local area network with a star topology.

areas

A DECnet term used in the routing layer. Level 1 routers are used to route within a DECnet area, level 2 routers route between areas. In Phase IV, up to 1023 nodes may be in an area; up to 63 areas may be in a DECnet routing domain. DECnet Phase IV was limited to 63 areas, whereas Phase V has essentially no limits.

ARP

Address resolution protocol. A TCP/IP protocol to translate an IP address into a physical address (i.e., an Ethernet or other subnetwork address).

Arpanet

A Department of Defense sponsored network of military and research organizations. Being replaced by the Defense Data Network.

array

A data structure used in programming.

ASCII

American Standard Code for Information Interchange. A standard character set that assigns an octal sequence to each letter, number, and selected control characters. The other major encoding standard is EBCDIC.

ASN

Abstract syntax notation. The language used in the OSI presentation layer to define complex objects.

ASN.1

Abstract Syntax Notation One. OSI presentation layer protocol.

AST

Asynchronous system trap. A concept used in the VMS lock manager. An AST is a request to be notified when a certain event occurs. In the case of the lock manager, an AST can be set so a process holding a lock on a resource is notified if another process tries to take an incompatible lock on the same resource.

async

> *Asynchronous.* A data transmission method that sends one character at a time. It is contrasted with synchronous methods that send a packet of data and then resynchronize their clocks. Asynchronous also refers to commands, such as in a windowing environment, that may be sent without waiting for a response from the previous command.

asynchronous
balanced mode

> A term used in the IEEE 802.2 standard to refer to a situation where only one side of the connection can send.

asynchronous
communication

> Communication in which every byte is sent individually. Synchronous communication (i.e., X.25 or Ethernet) bunches several pieces of data into a frame or packet.

asynchronous
event

> Events occur asynchronously on a system when you cannot predict which one will happen next.

asynchronous
mode

> FDDI term for data transmission where all requests for service contend for a pool of ring bandwidth.

ATIS

> *See A Tools Integration Standard.*

attenuation

> The level of signal loss, usually expressed in units of decibels.

attenuation
characteristic

> As a signal propagates on a cable, it gets weaker, or attenuates. The attenuation characteristic of the medium is the rate at which it gets weaker.

attribute

> A "perceived property" of some entity that can be read, and maybe modified. Attributes are used in network management as well as in the naming service. An example is the password attribute of the object user. In a relational database, attribute is another name for a column in a table. In a data dictionary or other information model, an attribute is attached to a relationship or entity.

attribute group

> A named collection of attributes.

audit trail

> A record of all actions performed on some entity.

authentication

> The function of verifying the identity of a person or process.

authorization

> Determining if a person or process is able to perform a particular action. Contrast with authentication.

AUTHORIZE	A VMS utility used to add new users and define relevant parameters such as privileges and default login directories.
autobaud	The ability of a modem on the receiving end of a call to detect automatically the speed of transmission used by the calling modem.
AWG	*See American Wire Gauge.*
backbone	A networking term used to refer to a piece of cable used to connect different floors or departments together. Contrasted with a departmental network or work area network.
balun	*balanced/unbalanced.* An adapter between two different pieces of physical media that adjusts for the difference in impedance.
bandwidth	The amount of data that can be moved through a particular communications link. Ethernet has a bandwidth of 10 Mbps.
baseband	Coax cable implementation of Ethernet. Also known as ThickWire.
BASIC	*Beginner's All-purpose Symbolic Instruction Code.* A programming language.
BAT	*See Binary absolute time.*
baud	A term used with older (slow) modems to refer to each modulation of an analog signal. A 300-baud signal modulates 300 times per second. A more accurate term for faster modems is bits per second, since several bits can be carried on one modulation of the signal.
Bayonet nut connector	Connector type used for 10BASE2 (thinwire) coaxial cable. The term bayonet refers to the way the connector slides in and then twists to lock the connection.
BEA	*See broadcast end node adjacency.*
beacon	A token ring packet that signals a serious failure on the ring.
BI bus	*Backplane interconnect.* A peripheral bus used on Digital's 8000 series VAXs. The BI bus operates at a speed of 13.3 Mbps.

big endian
: A computer that stores a multioctet data structure with the lowest addressed octet as being the most significant. *See also endian and little endian.*

BIH
: *International Time Bureau.* The organization responsible for maintaining coordinated universal time (UTC).

binary absolute time
: Time specified as coordinated universal time (UTC), a time differential factor (TDF), and an inaccuracy term. *See also binary relative time.*

binary relative time
: A time system specified by its relationship to its current time.

binary tree
: Often referred to as a Btree. A storage structure with a dynamic index used for environments with frequent updates to data.

BIND
: An SNA term used to establish a session between two logical units.

binding
: Concept used in remote procedure calls. Two remote programs bind with each other by starting a connection then exchanging command requests.

BIOS
: *Basic input/output system.* The MS-DOS library of calls for access to data. Shields the application from the different types of physical disks.

bisync
: A synchronous protocol used in older IBM teleprocessing environments. *See also BSC.*

block
: A unit of I/O on VMS computers. 512 bytes.

blocking call
: A procedure call where the caller halts its own execution until the called procedure finishes.

BNC
: *See Bayonet Nut Connector.* Abbreviation used in DECconnect.

BNF
: *Backus-Naur Form.* A way of representing a language and its elements.

boot nodes
: Used in Local Area Vax Clusters to refer to the node that stores the operating system for other nodes in the cluster.

BOS	*Binary object sequence.* The lowest level of access to a Post-script Interpreter. Higher levels are Postscript programming library calls and ASCII interfaces.
bps	*Bits per second.* Transmission speed on modems, phone lines, and other data communications devices.
BRA	*See broadcast router adjacency.*
bridge	A device used to connect two separate Ethernet networks into one extended Ethernet. Bridges only forward packets between networks destined for the other network. Term used by Novell to denote a computer that accepts packets at the network layer and forwards them to another network.
broadband	An analog medium similar to cable TV. Large bandwidth and very long distances make this medium appropriate for campus settings. Used with various data link protocols including Ethernet and token buses.
broadcast	Sending information to all users of a particular service. An Ethernet broadcast, for example, sends an Ethernet packet to every address on the network.
broadcast end node adjacency	A DNA routing layer concept for an end node reachable over the same subnetwork to which the routing module is connected.
broadcast router adjacency	A router connected to the same broadcast circuit as this node.
brouter	*Bridge/router.* Device that forwards messages between networks at both network and data link levels.
BRT	*See Binary relative time.*
BSC	*Bisynchronous. See bisync.*
BSD	*Berkeley Standard Distribution. See 4.3BSD.*
Btree	*See binary tree.*
bucket	A group of a file's virtual blocks used for I/O transfer.
buffer	A portion of main memory on a computer used to hold data.

bursty traffic

Data communications term referring to an uneven pattern of data transmission.

bus

The part of a computer that connects peripheral devices so that they may communicate with the CPU and memory. IBM's Micro Channel Architecture is an example of a peripheral bus architecture.

CA

See certification authority.

cable patch panel

A device located in the satellite equipment room. Used to connect two sets of wire (i.e., the wire from the satellite to the office and the wire between the satellites).

cached

A piece of information retained in main memory instead of being flushed to disk. Keeping information cached alleviates the need to go to the disk to retrieve the data.

called stub

A piece of code used in an RPC mechanism. The called stub masks the remote nature of the call from the procedure on the RPC server.

capture

The act of removing a token from the ring.

Carrier Sense–Multiple Access/Collision

The methodology used in Ethernet to mediate access to a single physical medium among multiple computers.

Cartesian product

Given two lists of data, the Cartesian product is the set of every possible combination of the two lists.

CATV

Community Antenna TV. The type of cable used in broadband networks.

CC

Connect Confirm. A protocol data unit type in the OSI transport service.

CCA

Conceptual Communication Area. Part of the ISO Virtual Terminal service. The CCA is an abstract area that provides a common view of the virtual terminal between two applications.

CCITT

Comité Consultatif International Télégraphique et Téléphonique. Standards-making body administered by the International Telecommunications Union.

CCR	*Commitment, concurrency, and recovery.* Part of the OSI application service elements that allows the coordination of multiple users access to data on multiple nodes.
CCS	*Common communications support.* A portion of IBM's System Application Architecture (SAA).
CDA	*See Compound Document Architecture.*
CDD	*Common Data Dictionary.* Digital's software that functions as a common repository for data definitions, forms, database schemas, and other parts of an information system. Part of the VAX Information Architecture.
CD-ROM	*Compact Disk—read only memory.* Optical disks that are mastered then can only be read. Used for read only databases.
CDT	*Credit.* A field used for flow control in the OSI transport service.
certification authority	A software process used in X.509 or RSA (public key) authentication schemes. The certification authority maintains the public keys for users. In some architectures the certification entity is off line and public keys would be stored in a name service.
channel	An IBM term referring to a direct high-speed connection into the 370 architecture machine. A "channel attach" device operates at speeds up to 3 Mbps, as opposed to more traditional devices that attach to a communications controller at 56 kbps.
characteristic attribute	A system management concept for an attribute that can be changed or modified by a director, thus affecting the behavior of that entity.
CheaperNet	Another term for ThinWire Ethernet cables.
CI bus	*Computer-room interconnect.* Refers to the 70-Mbps bus and controllers used in the VAX Cluster arrangement. To be contrasted with Local Area VAX Clusters that use a 10-Mbps Ethernet as the transport mechanism.
CICS	*Customer information control system.* An IBM data communications interface used with the MVS operating system.

circuit

A term used in networking that refers to a logical stream of data between two users of the network. A single physical link may have several virtual circuits running on it.

CIT

Computer Integrated Telephony. Digital architecture and products for integrating PBXs into a computer network.

class driver

A term used in VMS. A device driver is used to present data to a particular piece of hardware, for example, a terminal. In VMS, there are two levels of device drivers. The class driver is generic such as a terminal class driver. Underneath the class driver is a physical driver that accepts commands for a specific type of terminal such as a directly connected terminal or a remote terminal session using the LAT protocols. The class driver shields the user of the device from knowing about the particular physical connection used.

clearinghouse

A collection of names such as used in DNS. A user would query the clearinghouse (also known as a name server) to find the location of a particular resource at that time.

CLI

Command line interpreter. Older style of user interface, to be contrasted with graphical or forms interfaces.

client

A module that uses the services of another module. The session layer is a client of the transport layer, for example.

CLNS

Connectionless network service. One of two options for the OSI network layer. *See also CONS.*

Closed User Group

Data communications concept for CCITT (X.25 and ISDN) where only certain users (network addresses) can access a local connection.

cluster

A file system concept. A disk is made up of a series of clusters. The clusters are dynamically allocated to files and directories as needed. Similar to a block.

Cluster

See VAX Cluster.

CMA

See Concert Multithread Architecture.

CMIP

Common Management Information Protocol. OSI network management protocols used in DECnet Phase V.

CMOT

CMIP over TCP/IP. An implementation of the OSI CMIP protocols over TCP/IP instead of OSI. Allows current networks to take advantage of the enhanced capabilities of CMIP without running the entire OSI protocol stack.

CMS

Code Management System or *Conversational Monitor System.* Code Management System is a Digital software product used in the VMS environment as a library for program development. Conversational Monitor System is the user interface on IBM's VM/CMS operating system.

coax

coaxial. A type of cable used for IBM 3270 terminals as well as for baseband and ThinWire Ethernets.

COBOL

Common business-oriented language. One of the first standardized computing languages. See CODASYL.

CODASYL

Conference on Data Systems Languages. The committee that developed COBOL as well as the CODASYL standard for databases using the network model of data management.

Communication and Control Services

NAS concept for the API that allows an application to access communication services on the network.

Compound Document

A document with multiple types of information, such as text, graphics, and voice.

Compound Document Architecture

Digital architecture for the creation, storage, and manipulation of compound documents.

concentrator

A node on an FDDI ring that provides connections to additional stations. Known as a multistation access unit or MAU in 802 token rings.

Concert Multithread Architecture

Digital technology for a portable multithreaded architecture.

concurrency

Multiple users attempting to access the same resource. A lock manager addresses the problem of maintaining the integrity of resources in a concurrent environment.

conferencing

A term used for communication software that allows participants to "post" notes. Contrasts with electronic mail in that participants do not have to be explicitly addressed. Also known as a bulletin board.

confidence

DNA transport layer variable indicating the probability a network connection to the destination is currently working.

connection
manager

A cluster term used to refer to the software component in a VAX Cluster or LAVC that maintains the integrity of the cluster by managing state transitions.

CONS

Connection oriented network service. One of two options for the OSI network layer. *See also CLNS.*

COR

Confirmation of Receipt. From OSI Network Service Definition.

CPP

See cable patch panel.

CR

Connection Request or *carriage return.* A connection request is a protocol data unit type in the OSI transport service.

CRC

See cyclic redundancy check.

credit

A flow control mechanism used in Digital's LAT protocols. A node is allowed to send a packet only if it has a credit available. If not, it must wait for the remote node to send one.

CSMA/CD

See Carrier Sense–Multiple Access/Collision Detect.

CT

Channel transport. An advanced model of Digital's DECnet/SNA Gateway.

CTERM

Command Terminal Protocol. Part of the virtual terminal service in layer 6 of the Digital Network Architecture. An alternative to the CTERM services is the Local Area Transport Architecture (LAT).

CTM

Current transformation matrix. A term used in the Postscript Imaging System to denote the transformation between user space and device space.

CTS

Creation Time Stamp A Digital Naming Service attribute.

CUA

Common user access. The common user interface component of IBM's System Application Architecture. Similar concepts exist with Xerox's Open Look standard and within the DECwindows environment.

CUG	*See Closed User Group.*
cyclic redundancy check	A number derived from a set of data that will be transmitted. By recalculating the CRC at the remote end and comparing it to the value originally transmitted, the receiving node can detect some types of transmission errors.
CVR	*Condition Values Returned* DECmcc term for a status variable.
DA	*Destination address.*
daemon	A Unix term referring to a process that is not connected with a user but performs services, such as a mail daemon. The equivalent VMS term is a detached process.
DAP	*See Data Access Protocol or Directory Access Protocol.*
DARPA	*Defense Advanced Research Projects Agency.* A Department of Defense agency that has helped fund many computer projects including Arpanet, the Berkeley version of Unix and TCP/IP.
DAS	*See Dual Attachment Station.*
DASS	*Distributed Authentication Security Service* Digital security system based on public key technology.
Data Access Protocol	A protocol used in the Digital Network Architecture in layer 6. Provides a rich set of functions used for exchanging data between two nodes of the network. *See also File Access Listener.*
data circuit-terminating equipment	Term used in X.25 networks for the device on the edge of the network that accepts and initiates calls. The DCE is in turn connected to a DTE that communicates with the user.
data country code	An ISO-administered format for unique OSI addresses based on geographic location. The codes are defined in ISO 3166. *See also International Code Designator.*
Data Distributor	A Digital software product for extracting portions of DSRI-compatible databases and replicating this data on another node of the network as an Rdb database.

datagram

A bundle of information exchanged by two units in a network. Datagram usually refers to a best-effort delivery service in a connectionless environment at either the data link or network layers.

DATAPAC

Canadian public packet switched network.

Data terminal equipment

An X.25 term referring to the interface to users' equipment as opposed to the DCE interface to the network.

DB2

An IBM database package based on the relational model and the SQL query language.

DBMS

Database Management System. Software that allows the centralized storage of data with multiple concurrent users, access control, and the use of a high-level data manipulation language such as SQL.

DC

Disconnect Confirm. A protocol data unit type in the OSI transport service.

D-C

Daisy-Chained Faceplate. Abbreviation used in DECconnect.

DCA

Document Content Architecture or *Defense Communications Agency.* Document Content Architecture is an IBM architecture similar in function to Digital's Compound Document Architecture (CDA). The Defense Communication Agency is responsible for the Defense Data Network.

DCC

See Data Country Code.

DCE

See Data circuit-terminating equipment.

DCL

Digital command language. The user interface in the VMS operating system. Similar to the C shell in the Unix operating system.

D-CON

Direct Connect. Abbreviation used in DECconnect.

DDCMP

Digital Data Communications Message Protocol. A data link protocol used in the Digital Network Architecture. Used for point-to-point links between nodes, either synchronous or asynchronous. An alternative data link protocol is Ethernet.

DDFF   *See Digital Document Final Format.*

DDIF   *See Digital Document Interchange Format.*

DDS   *See Distributed Directory Service.*

DDXF   *DISOSS Document Exchange Facility.* A Digital software product that allows transfer of data between Digital and IBM word processing environments. *See also EDE.*

deadlock   A term used in a concurrent environment. If one user holds a lock on a resource and is waiting for another resource to free up and a second user has the reverse situation, it is known as a deadlock. The deadlock must be broken by arbitrarily picking one of the users and releasing its current lock. The deadlock is also known as a deadly embrace.

DEBAM   Model number for the Digital LAN Bridge 200.

DEBET   Model number for the Digital LAN Bridge 100 or 150 used for creating extended Ethernets.

DEBNA   *Digital BI-Bus Network Adaptor.* Abbreviation used in DECconnect. Ethernet controller for the BI-bus.

DEC   *Digital Equipment Corporation.* The company prefers to be known as "Digital."

DECconnect   A Digital cabling architecture used for facilities wiring.

DECdts   *Digital Distributed Time Synchronization Service.*

DECmcc   *Digital Management Control Center.* Digital software that is the implementation of the EMA management architecture.

DECnet   An implementation of the Digital Network Architecture by Digital, as opposed to implementations of DNA by other vendors.

DECnet/DOS   The version of DECnet for the PC-DOS or MS-DOS operating systems.

DECnet Router   A device that routes data between two portions of a DECnet. Could be a general-purpose computer such as a MicroVAX or a dedicated piece of hardware such as the DECSA.

DECOM

A broadband Ethernet modem made by Digital. A DECOM-AA is a dual-cable modem; the DECOM-BA is a single-cable version.

DECrouter 200

A dedicated router with eight asynchronous DDCMP ports and one Ethernet connection.

DECSA

Digital Synchronous Adapter. A general-purpose DECnet Router. The same piece of hardware also forms the basis for X.25 and SNA gateways.

DECserver

Digital terminal servers.

DECtalk

A piece of Digital hardware that can "speak" ASCII files.

DECtdm

Digital database software.

DECUS

Digital Equipment Corporation User Society. Digital user group.

DECwindows

Digital's implementation of the MIT X Window System.

DECwindows Toolkit

A set of utilities (such as default menus) developed by Digital to supplement the basic X services.

DED

See dynamically established data link.

DEFTR

Digital Frequency Translator. Digital's frequency translator for single-channel broadband systems.

DELNI

Digital Local Network Interconnect. "Ethernet in a Can." A multiport transceiver made by Digital.

Delta T

Delta time. Sniffer Analyzer indication of time elapsed between consecutive packets on the network. Contrast to relative time, which is the time that has elapsed since a particular anchor packet was sent.

DELUA

Digital Local Unibus Adapter. An Ethernet controller made by Digital for UNIBUS processors.

DEMPR

Digital Multiport Repeater. A piece of Digital networking hardware that can connect up to eight ThinWire Ethernet segments and optionally connect them to a backbone cable or DELNI.

DEMSA   *Digital MicroServer.* A new generation of routers and gate-
                      ways based on the MicroVAX II architecture as opposed to
                      the PDP-based architecture of the DECSA.

DEMWB   *Digital Metrowave Bridge.* Abbreviation used in DECcon-
                      nect. Ethernet controller for the BI-bus.

DEPCA   *Digital PC Adapter.* Abbreviation used in DECconnect. Eth-
                      ernet Controller.

DEQNA   *Digital Q-Bus Network Adapter.* A Digital Ethernet controller
                      for Q-bus systems.

DEREN   *Digital Repeater/Ethernet.* Digital local repeater or a half of
                      a fiber repeater.

DEREP   *Digital Repeater.* Digital Repeater meant to be used as a
                      half of a fiber repeater and connected to the LAN Bridge
                      100.

DES   *Data Encryption Standard.* One type of encryption scheme.

designated router   A DNA routing concept. A given broadcast circuit (such as
                      an Ethernet) will have a designated router, which is used by
                      end nodes to forward all packets that will need routing deci-
                      sions.

DESNC   *Digital Secure Network Controller.* Digital hardware control-
                      ler to do encryption on an Ethernet. Requires the VAX Key
                      Distribution Center software.

DESPR   *Digital Single Port Repeater.* Abbreviation used in DECcon-
                      nect. Single port ThinWire repeater.

DESTA   *Digital Station Adapter.* Abbreviation used in DECconnect.
                      ThinWire transceiver.

DFM   *Digital Frequency Multiplexor.* A series of Digital products
                      including X.25 asynchronous PADs and multiplexors.

DFS   *Distributed File Service (or System).* A Digital product similar
                      to the Network File System (NFS). Both allow remote files
                      to appear as though they were locally mounted on a work-
                      station, allowing diskless nodes. DFS uses the DNS name
                      server.

DFSCP	*See Distributed File Service Control Program.*
DHCF	*Digital Host Command Facility.* A Digital software product that, in conjunction with IBM's Host Command Facility, allows an IBM terminal user to log onto a Digital network.
DHV11	A synchronous communications board for Q-bus (MicroVAX) systems. Less powerful than the DSV11.
DIA	*Document Interchange Architecture.* An IBM architecture for the interchange of messages. Usually used in conjunction with the Document Content Architecture (DCA). Implemented in a product called DISOSS.
DIB	*See Directory Information Base.*
Digital Document Final Format	CDA subset where a document has been encoded for a specific output device.
Digital Document Interchange Format	CDA specification for documents in revisable format. *See Digital Document Final Format.*
Digital Network Architecture	Digital architectures for networking. DECnet is an implementation of DNA.
Digital Storage Architecture	Digital architecture for mass storage devices and controllers.
Digital Table Interchange Format	Part of CDA. The format for the storage and interchange of table-based information, such as spreadsheets. DDIF and DTIF work together.
directive	DNA network management term for an action to be taken by an entity.
director	The DNA management entity that issues directives. NCP is an example of a director.
Directory Access Protocol	X.500 protocol used for communication between a Directory User Agent and a Directory System Agent.
Directory Information Base	X.500 term for the distributed database used to keep track of application entities, people, terminals, distribution lists, or other objects.

Directory Information Tree	X.500 term for the hierarchical namespace of objects contained in the Directory Information Base.
Directory Management Domain	An administrative group responsible for managing a portion of the directory information base. A directory management domain contains at least one directory system agent and zero or more directory user agents.
Directory System Agent	X.500 term for the software that maintains and provides access to the Directory Information Base.
Directory System Protocol	X.500 protocol used for communication between directory system agents.
Directory User Agent	X.500 term for the software that provides services to the user. The Directory User Agent uses the OSI ROSE protocols to communicate with one or more Directory System Agents.
DIS	*Draft International Standard.* The state before a standard becomes an official international standard. At this point the standard is considered to be technically correct and only minor corrections are anticipated.
DISC	*disconnect.*
DISOSS	*Distributed Office Support System.* An IBM product that serves as a distributed library of documents. *See also DIA and DCA.*
display object	Used in the OSI Virtual Terminal protocols. An abstract object used for communication between two systems. The display object will map to a real object such as a video screen or printer.
distinguished name	An X.500 concept for the unique name of an object derived from its location in the Directory Information Tree.
distributed database	Looks to the user like a single database but is in fact a collection of several different data repositories.
Distributed Directory Service	Part of the MAILbus architecture that allows different forms of addressing to be supported.
Distributed File Service	Digital product to make files on the network appear local. Similar to the Network File System.

Distributed File Service Control Program	The program that implements the Distributed File Service. When a user mounts a foreign file system, he or she is issuing the command to DFSCP.
distributed naming service	Network-based service to allow a user to find the current address of a given resource, such as a printer or file system.
distributed systems management	The family of standards that Digital uses to manage the network. Includes EMA, event logging, and CMIP.
DIT	*See Directory Information Tree.*
DL	*Data Leads.* Abbreviation used in DECconnect. DECserver with no Modem Control.
DLAL	*Dual letter acronym listing. See also MLAL.*
DLC	*Data Link Control.* Sniffer Analyzer notation for data link layer information.
DMA	*Direct memory access.* Allows a device on a computer to access main memory without a CPU interrupt.
DMB32	Digital BI bus-based communications controller.
DMD	*See Directory Management Domain.*
DMF32	Digital UNIBUS-based communications controller.
DML	*Data manipulation language.* A language, such as SQL, used for retrieving and manipulating data in a database system.
DNA	*See Digital Network Architecture.*
DNA Naming Service	A distributed naming service used heavily in DNA Phase V.
DNS	*See DNA Naming Service or Domain Name System.*
domain	An area within which a particular service is performed. In a messaging domain, a message transfer agent for that domain is able to deliver a message.
Domain Name System	TCP/IP service provider that translates names into IP addresses for machines and users.

domain specific part	The portion of the OSI address space that is locally-administered.
DOS	*Digital Operating System.* Microsoft operating system for IBM/PCs.
DOS/VSE	*Digital Operating System/Virtual Storage Extended.* An IBM operating system used on 370 architecture mainframes.
dpi	*Dots per inch.* A measure of the resolution of printers or scanners.
DQS	*Distributed Queuing Service.* A Digital software product that allows print files submitted to a local queue to be automatically sent to a remote queue.
DR	*Disconnect Request.* A protocol data unit type in the OSI transport service.
DRP	*Digital Routing Protocol.*
DSA	*See Digital Storage Architecture or Directory System Agent.*
DSAP	*Destination service access point.* The address for the destination user of a service. A remote IPX process would be considered the DSAP from the point of view of the local data link module.
DSM	*See Distributed systems management.*
DSP	*See Directory System Protocol or domain specific part.*
DSRI	*Digital Standard Relational Interface.* A Digital standard calling sequence for database applications. Allows any DSRI-compatible user interface to access any DSRI-compatible data repository.
DSRVB	Digital terminal server model number.
DSS	*Distributed system services.* A family of Digital software including the Digital Name Service (DNS) and the Distributed File Service (DFS).
DSSA	*Digital Distributed System Security Architecture.* Digital program that includes network security.

DST

Destination address. Sniffer Network Analyzer abbreviation for destination address.

DSV11

A high-performance Q-bus synchronous communications board.

DT

Data. A protocol data unit type in the OSI transport service.

DTE

See Data terminal equipment.

DTF

Data transfer facility. Digital software products that run in both VMS and IBM environments and permit the integration of both types of file systems from within the Digital Command Language.

DTIF

See Digital Table Interchange Format.

DU

Data unit. Part of the OSI File Transfer Access and Management (FTAM) protocols.

DUA

See Directory User Agent.

Dual Attachment Station

FDDI term for a node that is attached to both the primary and secondary fiber optic cables (as opposed to a node that is connected to the ring via a concentrator).

dual porting

Making a disk drive available to two different computers, as in the case of a VAX Cluster.

DUI

Data Unit Identifier. A packet identifier used for reassembly at the network layer.

DWF

data waiting flag An LAT state variable indicating that there are slots at the session layer ready to be sent over a virtual circuit.

dX

Digital software product for transfer of WPS documents into other formats.

dynamically established data link

A DNA Phase V capability to establish a link over connected oriented subnetworks such as ISDN, X.25, X.21, or the public switched telephone network.

E.163

CCITT numbering scheme for public switched telephone networks.

E.164	CCITT standard for numbering in an ISDN environment.
EA	*Expedited Acknowledge.* A protocol data unit type in the OSI transport service.
Easynet	Digital's internal communications network.
EBCDIC	*Extended Binary Coded Decimal Interchange Code.* A character code scheme used in IBM environments. *See also ASCII.*
ECC	*Error-correcting code.* Feature of the Digital Storage Architecture used in error detection. Similar to a CRC.
Echo	A maintenance protocol in XNS. Used to echo information back across the network and thus test the connection.
ECL	*See End Communication Layer.*
ECMA	*European Computer Manufacturers Association.* A leading European standards body.
ECO	*Engineering change order.* Digital term for a minor change to a piece of software. ECOs are more granular and occur between major or minor revisions.
ED	*Expedited Data.* A protocol data unit type in the OSI transport service.
EDE	*Electronic Document Exchange.* A Digital product that allows revisable form document transfer with DISOSS libraries. *See also DDXF.* EDE-W is a similar program for document interchange between Wang and Digital systems.
EDI	*See Electronic Data Interchange.*
EDIFACT	*EDI for Administration, Commerce, and Trade.* Emerging international EDI standard.
EDT	Standard Digital editor on the VMS operating system.
EGP	*Exterior Gateway Protocol.* A means for updating routing tables in the Internet environment.
EIA	*Electronic Industries Association.* Trade association.
EIA-423	Standard interface definition for serial devices.

EJ

Etherjack. Abbreviation used in DECconnect. Terminator for transceiver cable.

Electronic Data
Interchange

A structured form of text exchange used to exchange information such as purchase orders. *See X.12.*

ELK

External Link Interface. A programming library that allows an application to link to a Videotex (VTX) system on a remote DECnet node.

EMA

See Enterprise Management Architecture.

EMACS

An extensible editor developed at M.I.T. based on the LISP programming language.

Email

Electronic mail. Software/networks that allow the exchange of messages between users.

EMS

Enterprice Management Station. An early version of the DECmcc software. Consists of the four packages for SMS (Site Management Station) plus the NMCC/DECnet Monitor.

End
Communication
Layer

The DNA transport layer.

endian

How a computer stores a multi-octet piece of data (i.e., a four-byte integer). See big endian and little endian.

end node

A DECnet term referring to a member of the network that can do everything but route packets through on behalf of other nodes. Ultrix, MS-DOS, and third-party implementations of DECnet are all end nodes.

end system

OSI term for a nonrouting node. Equivalent to end node.

ENSDU

Expedited Network Service Data Unit. From OSI Network Service Definition.

Enterprise
Management
Architecture

A Digital architecture for network management user interfaces that can work with multiple displays and protocols. DECmcc is the implementation of this architecture.

entity

DNA network management term for a manageable piece of a distributed system.

EOF	*End of file.* A mark that tells the file system that it has reached the end of a file.
EOM	*End of message.* A mark put into network traffic to indicate logical boundaries on a stream interface.
epoch	Term used in the DNA Naming Service. Epochs control the replication of directories. After a disaster, a new epoch is declared preventing previously initiated skulks from interfering with the reconstruction of the directories.
ER	*Error.* A protocol data unit type in the OSI transport service.
ERCO	*Entry rules control object.* Provides validation checks for the OSI virtual terminal service in field mode.
Error	XNS protocol used to report errors across a network.
ES	*See End system.*
ES-IS	*End system to intermediate system.* ISO 9542 routing exchange protocol. Includes end and intermediate system hello messages.
ESH PDU	*End System Hello PDU.* From OSI Network Service Definition.
Ethernet	A data link protocol jointly developed by Intel, Xerox, and Digital and subsequently adopted by the IEEE as a standard. Several upper-layer protocols, including DECnet, TCP/IP, and XNS, use the Ethernet as an underlying transport mechanism. Ethernet is to be contrasted with other data link protocols such as the token ring, DDCMP, and SDLC.
Ethernet controller	A device controller that gives the computer access to the Ethernet services. Typically, the CSMA/CD protocols are built into the controller so the CPU does not have to worry about the details of the protocol.
Ethernet Version 2.0	The second version of the original specification for Ethernet, which differs slightly from the IEEE 802.3 standard.
ETHERnim	*Ethernet Network Integrity Monitor.* A Digital product for monitoring Ethernets.

Ethertype	Field in version 2.0 of Ethernet that indicates the type of user (DECnet, NetWare, or TCP/IP, for example).
EVD	*See Event dispatcher.*
event dispatcher	A module on a node responsible for accepting event reports from different modules and dispatching them across the network to different event sinks.
event log	A record of significant events kept in the director.
event sink	The destination in the network where significant events should be sent. Examples of a sink are a file, a program, and a terminal.
exclusive lock	A lock on data that prevents other users from accessing it. Used for write operations. In contrast to a shared (read) lock.
executable image	A program that is ready to run on an operating system. A program starts as source code and gets compiled to generate object code. The object code is then linked to form an executable image.
External Data Representation	Presentation layer protocol developed by Sun Microsystems as part of NFS.
external name	The external representation of a name (that seen by humans) in the DNA Naming Service.
F.69	CCITT standard for telex addresses.
F.110	CCITT standard for maritime mobile service.
F.160	CCITT standard for international public facsimile services.
F.200	CCITT standard for teletex services.
F.201	CCITT standard for internetwork teletex and telex services.
F.300	A set of CCITT recommendations for Videotex systems.
F.401	CCITT standard for the naming and addressing public message-handling services.
F.410	CCITT standard for the public message transfer service.

F.415	CCITT standard for intercommunication with public physical delivery services.
F.420	CCITT standard for the public interpersonal messaging service.
F.421	CCITT standard for communication between the X.400 interpersonal messaging service and the telex service.
F.422	CCITT standard for communication between the X.400 interpersonal messaging service and the telex service.
F.500	CCITT standard for international public directory services.
F.60	CCITT standard for telex services.
FADU	*File access data unit.* The unit of access in the OSI FTAM service.
FAL	*See File Access Listener.*
fault tolerance	An attribute of a computer system that reflects its degree of tolerance to hardware and software failures while continuing to run.
fax	*Facsimile.* A messaging service based on transmitting bit maps of 200 dots per inch across dial-up telephone lines.
FC	*Frame control.* Token ring field that indicates whether the packet is a MAC-layer management packet (i.e., a token, beacon, AMP, or SMP) or is carrying LLC data.
FCL	*Forms and Command Line module.* Presentation module in DECmcc.
FCPLT	*Faceplate.* Abbreviation used in DECconnect.
FCS	*Frame check sequence.* A mechanism like a CRC or checksum to guarantee the integrity of a packet of data.
FDDI	*See Fiber Distributed Data Interface.*
FFFF	*15 15 15 15.* A hexadecimal number. Hexadecimal is base 16 numbering in which the symbols A through F are used to represent the digits 10 through 15.

FFT

Final form text.   A version of IBM's Document Content Architecture (DCA).

Fiber Distributed
Data Interface

A 100-Mbps fiber optic local area network standard based on the token ring.

field

A term used in designing forms-based systems such as database applications. A field is a portion of the screen used for data input that is automatically mapped to a variable. The field may have attributes such as reverse video or default values.

FI.FMD

Function Interpreters for Function Management Data.   IBM's presentation layer protocol for SNA.

File Access Listener

A process invoked across the network by a user trying to access data on nonlocal systems using Digital's Data Access Protocol. A FAL is a remote DAP-speaking process invoked by the Record Management Services on the local node.

file cache

Keeping portions of files in main memory. When the computer requests data, if it is in the cache, it alleviates the need to refetch it from the much slower disk drive.

File Sharing
Services

Digital term for a distributed file service.

file system

The portion of an operating system that is responsible for storing and retrieving pages of data onto a disk.

FIMS

See Form Interface Management System.

finite state
machine

A way of describing a network module as a set of states that, based on inputs and conditions, perform transitions to other states and outputs.

FLASH/IMS
Programming
Interface

DECnet/SNA software product layered on top of the LU0 Application Programming Interface allows access to IBM IMS database systems.

floating point

A native data type on most operating systems. A floating point number is one that can have numbers after the decimal point, in contrast to an integer, which cannot.

flow control	A set of rules that allows a module to control the flow of data from another node. Flow control prevents limited buffer space from being filled, which means additional data received has no place to be stored.
FM	*See Function module.*
Form Interface Management System	Draft ISO standard for forms management.
fourth-generation language	A group of new languages often linked with database packages such as Ingres or Oracle. In contrast with FORTRAN and other third-generation languages.
FPI	*See FLASH/IMS Programming Interface.*
frame	A series of bytes of data encapsulated with a header. The data link layer sends frames of data back and forth. "Frame" is often used interchangeably with "packet," although technically a packet refers to data from the network layer of the protocol stack. A packet is thus usually contained inside of a frame.
front end	A program with which a user interacts. The front end sends off requests to the back end for data.
FS	*Frame status.* Token ring field that indicates whether the address on a packet has been recognized by a station and if the data have been copied.
FSZ	*Fixed Part Size* Abbreviation used in DAP to refer to the header portion of a variable record file.
FTAM	*File Transfer, Access and Management.* The OSI application layer service that provides access to virtual file stores on foreign systems. Similar to the DNA DAP protocols in purpose.
FTP	*File transfer protocol.* An upper-layer TCP/IP service for copying files across the network.
full-duplex	A data communications term that indicates both ends of a communications link can transmit simultaneously. Contrasted with half-duplex, where only one side can transmit at one time.
full name	A unique, unambiguous name in the namespace.

function	Takes a piece of data as input and returns a value. For example, the query language has functions that can accept a date and return the day of the week that the date falls on.
function module	A part of the EMA architecture. The function module is responsible for high-level management functions, such as configuration, security, or historical event reporting. *See also access module* and *presentation module.*
GAP	*Gateway Access Protocol.* A protocol used by applications software to access DECnet Gateways. The 3270 access routine, for example, would use GAP to access an SNA Gateway.
Gateway	There are two somewhat conflicting definitions of gateway, both used in networking. In the general sense, a gateway is a computer that connects two different networks together. Usually, this means two different kinds of networks such as SNA and DECnet. In TCP/IP terminology, a gateway connects two separately administered subnetworks, which may or may not be running the same networking protocols.
Gbyte	*Gigabyte.* One billion bytes of data.
GGP	*Gateway to Gateway Protocol.* An obsolete interior protocol in TCP/IP similar in functionality to RIP.
GID	*Group identification.*
gigabyte	One billion bytes of data.
GKS	*See Graphical Kernel System.*
GKS-3D	*Graphical Kernel System for Three Dimensions.* 3D extensions to the GKS standards.
global entity	The top level of the entity tree for management purposes. A node is an example of a global entity, with subentities including modules such as routing, MOP, and LAT.
GOSIP	*Government OSI Protocols.* Government-specified subset of the international OSI standards.

granularity	A term used in lock managers on an operating system. When the lock manager locks an entire file, this is locking with course granularity. When the lock manager locks a single record, this is fine granularity. Granularity is one of the factors that influences the performance of a particular application such as a DBMS.
Graphical Kernel System	ISO standard for the creation and manipulation of 2D objects.
H4000	Digital's baseband Ethernet transceiver.
H4000-BA	Ethernet transceiver for DELNI and DEMPR units.
half-duplex	*See full-duplex.*
handle	A number used to refer to a file or directory that is being remotely accessed on the network.
HASP	*Houston Automatic Spooling Program.* One of the original implementations of the remote job entry function on IBM equipment. Still used in conjunction with bisync as a lowest common denominator of interoperability.
HDLC	*High-level data link control.* ISO's data link protocol. Used in OSI and X.25 networks. Alternative protocols include SDLC in the IBM networks and DDCMP in the Digital networks.
HDR	*Historical Data Recorder.* Function module in DECmcc.
heap	A storage structure for data, where data are not placed in any particular order, requiring a scan of the entire table for every retrieval.
HEPnet	*High Energy Physics network.*
heterogeneous	Different.
heterogeneous network	A network consisting of different network protocols or kinds of computers. A network combining SNA and DNA protocols using an SNA gateway to connect the two is a heterogeneous network.

hierarchical database	A database that structures data as a hierarchy instead of in tables. Programmers then navigate the hierarchy to retrieve a particular row of data. IMS is an example of a hierarchical database system.
hierarchical routing	Routing based on domains. Interdomain routers are responsible for getting data to the right domain. There, an intradomain router takes responsibility for routing within the domain.
Hierarchical Storage Controller	Standalone disk and tape controller used in clusters using the CI bus. The HSC is actually a modified PDP computer that has been optimized as a mass storage controller.
HL	*High-Loss Transceiver Cable.* DECconnect abbreviation.
homogeneous	The same.
hooks	Programming technique. Allows a programmer to add new code to an existing program. The existing program has hooks that execute any additional code.
hop	A term used in DECnet routing calculations. A hop is one data link. A path to the final destination on a DECnet is a series of hops away from the origin. Each hop has a cost associated with it, allowing the calculation of the least cost path.
host	A computer that provides services directly to users (as opposed to a behind-the-scenes dedicated server).
HSC	*See Hierarchical Storage Controller.*
hub	A device connected to several other devices. In ARCNET, a hub is used to connect several computers together. In a message-handling service, a hub is used for the transfer of messages across the network.
I.120	CCITT description of ISDN.
I.230	Description of ISDN bearer services.
I.240	Description of ISDN teleservices.
I.250	Description of ISDN supplementary services.

I/O	*See Input/Output.*
IBM PC LAN	IBM PC network using broadband.
IBM Token-Ring	IBM token ring network.
IBM Token-Ring Adapter	Token ring controller card sold by IBM.
ICD	*See International Code Designator.*
ICMP	*Internet Control Message Protocol.* Protocol used by the IP layer of TCP/IP for exchanging routing control messages.
icon	A small pictorial object on a workstation used to represent a closed window. The user points to the icon, clicks the mouse button, and a window opens.
idempotent	A characteristic of an operation where it will yield the same result if it is executed more than once. Change X to 25 is idempotent. Add 25 to X is not.
IDI	*Initial domain identifier.* Part of an OSI address. Goes after the authority and format identifiers. For example, the IDI for a telephone address might be the country code.
IDL	*identifier list* Digital Naming Service attribute used for access control. A user's IDL is compared with the ACL of the object requested to determine if access is granted.
IDMS	Cullinet's database management system for IBM systems.
IDP	*See Internetwork Datagram Protocol* or *initial domain part.*
IEEE	*Institute of Electronic and Electrical Engineers.* A leading standard-making body in the United States responsible for the 802 standards for local area networks.
IEEE 488	IEEE standard for real-time data acquisition.
ILV	*indicator, length, value* Way of encoding parameters in DECmcc.
IMS	*Information Management System.* Database management software from IBM based on the hierarchical data management model.

index

A direct access method to data. An index has a key value and a pointer to the row of the table that contains data with the key value. An index can be a primary index, where it is part of the storage structure of the actual table, or a secondary index, which is a separate table in the database with pointers to the base table.

information manager

A module within the DECmcc software responsible for scheduling requests received from management modules.

Ingres

A popular relational database management system that runs on a variety of operating system platforms. A famous nineteenth-century French painter.

initial domain part

The first part of an ISO address. The IDP is made up of an Authority and Format Indicator and an Initial Domain Identifier. *See also domain specific part.*

initialization packet

A token ring packet used when a node joins the network.

input/output

Generic term for transfer of data from main memory to either a disk drive, terminal, printer, or other device.

Integrated Services Digital Network

An emerging international communications standard that allows the integration of voice and data on a common transport mechanism.

interactive terminal

A traditional terminal with a human being hitting keys. Contrast with application terminal. Used in LAT.

interchange key

A cryptographic key shared by two or more parties.

internal name

The internal representation of a name as stored by the DNA Naming Service.

International Code Designator

An ISO-administered four-digit unique ID based on organizations (as opposed to the Data Country Code which is based on geographic location).

International Organization for Standardization

International standards-making body responsible for the Open Systems Interconnection network architecture.

International Telegraph and Telephone Consultative Committee	English name for the CCITT.
Internet	A collection of networks that share the same namespace and use the TCP/IP protocols. The Internet consists of more than 5000 interconnected networks. The Internet should not be confused with internet (lowercase) which refers to any collection of networks with a path between them.
internetwork	A collection of data links and the network layer programs for routing among those data links.
internetwork address	An address consisting of a network number and a local address on that network. Used by the network layer for routing packets to their ultimate destination.
Internetwork Datagram Protocol	Network layer protocol in XNS.
Internetwork Protocol	Network layer protocol in TCP/IP.
interprocess communication	Communication between two processes by passing parameters and return values. Remote calls are a special case of an interprocess communication mechanism.
IOCTL	*I/O Control.* Unix function call used to control a device.
IOP	*Input/output processor.* Term used by Unix-based minicomputer manufacturers to refer to the I/O subsystems.
IP	*See Internetwork Protocol.*
IPC	*See Interprocess Communication.*
IPDS	*Intelligent Printer Data Stream.* A component of IBM's System Application Architecture (SAA).
IPMS	*Interpersonal messaging service* The part of the X.400 protocols that defines what the header of a message looks like. The message transfer service (MTS) then defines what the envelope the message goes in looks like.

IRDS

Information Resources Dictionary System. An ANSI and ISO standard for data dictionaries.

IS

Intermediate System OSI term for a router.

ISAM

Indexed sequential access method. A file structure that allows random access to data via an index then sequential access to data after that.

ISDN

See Integrated Services Digital Network.

ISH PDU

Intermediate System Hello PDU. From OSI Network Service Definition.

IS-IS

Intermediate System to Intermediate System An OSI protocol for routers to dynamically exchange topology information.

ISO

See International Organization for Standardization.

ISPF

Interactive System Productivity Facility. An IBM product that runs on the TSO and CMS user environments. ISPF provides a series of menus (dialogues) for use on a 3270 terminal that allow the user to bypass a command language interface to the operating system.

ISV

Independent Software Vendors. Third party software developers. Sometimes known as VARs, OEMs, or third party software developers.

ITT

Invitation to Transmit. ARCNET equivalent of a token.

ITU

International Telecommunications Union UN agency that administers the CCITT.

JCL

Job Control Language. Language used for batch processing on IBM mainframes.

JES

Job Entry Subsystem. Types of processes on IBM mainframes that accept JCL.

job queue

A method of letting multiple requests for a scarce resource queue up, as in the case of a print queue.

JTM

Job transfer and manipulation. An OSI layer 7 standard similar in function to a remote job entry (RJE) service.

kbps

Kilobits per second. Thousand bits per second.

kbytes

Kilobytes. Thousands of bytes of information.

KDC

See VAX Key Distribution Center.

keep alive message

A message sent over a network link during periods when there is no traffic between users. The message tells the remote node this computer is still in operation.

Kerberos

A component of MIT's Athena project. Kerberos is the security system, based on symetric key cryptography. Contrast with the RSA public key cryptography techniques.

Kermit

A popular file transfer protocol developed by Columbia University. Because Kermit runs in most operating environments, it provides an easy method of file transfer.

kernel

A term used in operating systems. The kernel shields the low-level functioning of the operating system from high-level interfaces such as user shells.

LA100

A Digital dot matrix printer commonly found in machine rooms as console printers.

LAD

Local Area Disk Driver. Protocol used for remote booting of PCs in DECnet/DOS.

LAN

Local area network. Usually refers to Ethernet or token ring networks.

LAP

Link access procedure. A protocol for accessing a data link. Examples are LAP B used in the X.25 environment and LAP D used in the ISDN environment.

LAPB

Link Access Procedure, Balanced. A subset of the HDLC data link standards.

LAPX

Link Access Procedure, Extended. Similar to LAPB but with extended sequence numbers.

LAST

Local Area System Transport. Protocol for remote booting in DECnet/DOS.

LAT

See Local Area Transport.

latency buffer

Token ring concept. The buffer is maintained by the active monitor and is used to compensate for variations in the speed of data on the network.

LAVC

Local Area VAX Cluster. An adaptation of the System Communication Architecture (SCA) to run over the Ethernet instead of a CI bus. Used to enable MicroVAXs to operate as diskless nodes.

LF

line feed

LI

Length Indicator. Used in the ES-IS protocols in the OSI network layer.

little endian

A multiple-octet piece of data where the lowest addressed octet is the least significant.

LL

Low-Loss Transceiver Cable. DECconnect abbreviation.

LLC

See Logical Link Control.

LN03

Digital's first eight ppm laser printer. LN03 is a proprietary language that has been superseded by the Scriptprinter, which uses the same engine and the Postscript page description language.

Local Area
Transport

Protocol developed by Digital for communication between terminal servers and hosts on an Ethernet.

LocalTalk

Data link developed for AppleTalk that uses ordinary twisted pair cabling.

locking

Preventing another user from accessing a piece of data.

lock manager

Part of the operating system that ensures multiple requests for the same data are not serviced in a way that will damage the integrity of the data.

logical

Without reference to physical details. Asking for data in a logical manner, for example, means not having to know where the data are located or how to get them.

Logical Link
Control

The upper portion of the data link layer defined in the IEEE 802.2 standard. The logical link control layer presents a uniform interface to the user of the data link service, usually a network layer. Underneath the LLC sublayer of the data link layer is a media access control sublayer. The MAC sublayer is responsible for taking a packet of data from the LLC and submitting it to the particular data link being used (such as Ethernet or token ring).

LAVC

Local Area VAX Cluster. An adaptation of the System Communication Architecture (SCA) to run over the Ethernet instead of a CI bus. Used to enable MicroVAXs to operate as diskless nodes.

LF

line feed

LI

Length Indicator. Used in the ES-IS protocols in the OSI network layer.

little endian

A multiple-octet piece of data where the lowest addressed octet is the least significant.

LL

Low-Loss Transceiver Cable. DECconnect abbreviation.

LLC

See Logical Link Control.

LN03

Digital's first eight ppm laser printer. LN03 is a proprietary language that has been superseded by the Scriptprinter, which uses the same engine and the Postscript page description language.

Local Area
Transport

Protocol developed by Digital for communication between terminal servers and hosts on an Ethernet.

LocalTalk

Data link developed for AppleTalk that uses ordinary twisted pair cabling.

locking

Preventing another user from accessing a piece of data.

lock manager

Part of the operating system that ensures multiple requests for the same data are not serviced in a way that will damage the integrity of the data.

logical

Without reference to physical details. Asking for data in a logical manner, for example, means not having to know where the data are located or how to get them.

Logical Link
Control

The upper portion of the data link layer defined in the IEEE 802.2 standard. The logical link control layer presents a uniform interface to the user of the data link service, usually a network layer. Underneath the LLC sublayer of the data link layer is a media access control sublayer. The MAC sublayer is responsible for taking a packet of data from the LLC and submitting it to the particular data link being used (such as Ethernet or token ring).

kbytes

Kilobytes. Thousands of bytes of information.

KDC

See VAX Key Distribution Center.

keep alive message

A message sent over a network link during periods when there is no traffic between users. The message tells the remote node this computer is still in operation.

Kerberos

A component of MIT's Athena project. Kerberos is the security system, based on symetric key cryptography. Contrast with the RSA public key cryptography techniques.

Kermit

A popular file transfer protocol developed by Columbia University. Because Kermit runs in most operating environments, it provides an easy method of file transfer.

kernel

A term used in operating systems. The kernel shields the low-level functioning of the operating system from high-level interfaces such as user shells.

LA100

A Digital dot matrix printer commonly found in machine rooms as console printers.

LAD

Local Area Disk Driver. Protocol used for remote booting of PCs in DECnet/DOS.

LAN

Local area network. Usually refers to Ethernet or token ring networks.

LAP

Link access procedure. A protocol for accessing a data link. Examples are LAP B used in the X.25 environment and LAP D used in the ISDN environment.

LAPB

Link Access Procedure, Balanced. A subset of the HDLC data link standards.

LAPX

Link Access Procedure, Extended. Similar to LAPB but with extended sequence numbers.

LAST

Local Area System Transport. Protocol for remote booting in DECnet/DOS.

LAT

See Local Area Transport.

latency buffer

Token ring concept. The buffer is maintained by the active monitor and is used to compensate for variations in the speed of data on the network.

Logical name	A Digital Command Language feature that allows the logical naming of devices, permitting a layer of separation between the physical configuration of a system and the logical view seen by the user process. Similar to the Unix concept of an environmental variable.
LSP	*Link state packet.* Routing control information message exchanged in a Phase V DECnet.
LTM	*LAN Traffic Monitor.* Digital software that uses a LAN Bridge 100 to monitor an Ethernet network.
LU	*Logical unit.* An IBM term in SNA which refers to a software or microcode program that uses the network. For example, a terminal connected to a 3274 cluster controller is represented by an LU2 on that cluster controller.
LU 6.2	*Logical Unit 6.2. See APPC.*
MAC	*See Medium Access Control.*
MAC-layer bridge	A device that connects two or more similar data links in a way that is transparent to the user of the data link service (the network layer).
mail-11	The original mail routing protocol used on VMS mail. Mailbus is a more modern message-handling architecture.
mailbox	A VMS concept used for interprocess communication. Processes leave messages for each other in a mailbox.
MAILbridge Server	A series of SoftSwitch products used for connecting different message handling environments.
MAILbus	A Digital architecture that provides a common message-handling system on a DECnet.
Maintenance Operation Protocol	Special-purpose DECnet protocol used for remote booting on the network and attaching a console onto a station remotely.
management description language	A formal language for describing the management. information and operations for an entity. *See also management specification.*

management information repository	A component of the DECmcc software. The MIR keeps information about entity classes, entity instances, entity attributes, and miscellaneous data.
management module	One of the plug-in modules in DECmcc. There are three types of management modules: function modules, access modules, and presentation modules.
management specification	A formal lananguage used in DECmcc to specify the structure, interfaces, and attributes for an entity class.
management specification language translator	A DECmcc program that loads a management specification into the DECmcc dictionary.
MAP/TOP	*Manufacturing Automation Protocols/Technical Office Protocols* Subsets of OSI promoted by General Motors and Boeing.
marshalling	Term used in RPC calls. Marshalling is taking a local procedure call and packaging it into a form for sending over the network.
master replica	The copy of a directory in the DNA Naming Service that can perform all actions, including child directory creations and deletions. *See also read-only replica and secondary replica.*
MAU	*See multistation access unit.*
MB	*Megabytes.* Million bytes of information.
Mbps	*Million bits per second.*
Mbytes	*Megabytes.* Million bytes of information.
MC	*Modem Control.* DECconnect abbreviation. DECserver with Modem Control
MCC	*Management Control Center. See DECmcc.*
MCI	Long distance telephone company.
MCI Mail	Commercial electronic messaging service.
MD	*See management description language.*
Media Interface Connector	The optical fiber connector that connects the fiber to the FDDI controller.

management information repository	A component of the DECmcc software. The MIR keeps information about entity classes, entity instances, entity attributes, and miscellaneous data.
management module	One of the plug-in modules in DECmcc. There are three types of management modules: function modules, access modules, and presentation modules.
management specification	A formal lanaguage used in DECmcc to specify the structure, interfaces, and attributes for an entity class.
management specification language translator	A DECmcc program that loads a management specification into the DECmcc dictionary.
MAP/TOP	*Manufacturing Automation Protocols/Technical Office Protocols* Subsets of OSI promoted by General Motors and Boeing.
marshalling	Term used in RPC calls. Marshalling is taking a local procedure call and packaging it into a form for sending over the network.
master replica	The copy of a directory in the DNA Naming Service that can perform all actions, including child directory creations and deletions. *See also read-only replica and secondary replica.*
MAU	*See multistation access unit.*
MB	*Megabytes.* Million bytes of information.
Mbps	*Million bits per second.*
Mbytes	*Megabytes.* Million bytes of information.
MC	*Modem Control.* DECconnect abbreviation. DECserver with Modem Control
MCC	*Management Control Center. See DECmcc.*
MCI	Long distance telephone company.
MCI Mail	Commercial electronic messaging service.
MD	*See management description language.*
Media Interface Connector	The optical fiber connector that connects the fiber to the FDDI controller.

Logical name	A Digital Command Language feature that allows the logical naming of devices, permitting a layer of separation between the physical configuration of a system and the logical view seen by the user process. Similar to the Unix concept of an environmental variable.
LSP	*Link state packet.* Routing control information message exchanged in a Phase V DECnet.
LTM	*LAN Traffic Monitor.* Digital software that uses a LAN Bridge 100 to monitor an Ethernet network.
LU	*Logical unit.* An IBM term in SNA which refers to a software or microcode program that uses the network. For example, a terminal connected to a 3274 cluster controller is represented by an LU2 on that cluster controller.
LU 6.2	*Logical Unit 6.2. See APPC.*
MAC	*See Medium Access Control.*
MAC-layer bridge	A device that connects two or more similar data links in a way that is transparent to the user of the data link service (the network layer).
mail-11	The original mail routing protocol used on VMS mail. Mailbus is a more modern message-handling architecture.
mailbox	A VMS concept used for interprocess communication. Processes leave messages for each other in a mailbox.
MAILbridge Server	A series of SoftSwitch products used for connecting different message handling environments.
MAILbus	A Digital architecture that provides a common message-handling system on a DECnet.
Maintenance Operation Protocol	Special-purpose DECnet protocol used for remote booting on the network and attaching a console onto a station remotely.
management description language	A formal language for describing the management. information and operations for an entity. *See also management specification.*

Medium Access Control	The bottom half of the ISO data link layer. *See also Logical Link Control.*
MEN	*Management event notification.* Part of DECnet Phase V network management. Used for sending information about events across the network. *See MICE.*
Message-Handling Service	Action Technologies' product for message handling, bundled into Novell networks as NetWare MHS. To be contrasted with the generic message handling service, which includes X.400 and other standards.
message-handling system	A system of protocols such as X.400 used to exchange messages such as electronic mail.
Message Router	Digital product that implements the MAILbus architecture. Message Router is analogous to the X.400 Message Transfer Agent.
Message Router Facsimile Gateway	Digital product that links the Message Router to Group III facsimile machines.
Message Router X.400 Gateway	Digital product that connects X.400 and Message Router.
message transfer agent	An X.400 term referring to the collections of network members responsible for transferring messages. The final MTA delivers the message to a user agent which is concerned with reading, editing, and other types of interaction with the end user.
MHS	*See Message-Handling Service or message-handling system.*
MIC	*See Media Interface Connector.*
MICE	*Management information, control, and exchange.* A DECnet Phase V network management protocol. *See also MEN.*
MicroVAX	A series of Digital processors usually used as workstations or small servers that compete in the marketplace with Sun and Hewlett-Packard/Apollo.
Minitel	A French terminal used for Videotex applications.
MIP	*Million instructions per second.* A measure of the speed of a CPU.

MIPS

Million instructions per second. A measure of CPU processing power. Different machine architectures use different instruction sets, so comparison of MIPS across architectures is highly misleading. MIPS also do not take into account the speed of other resources on a system such as bus speeds, I/O processor speed, disk drive throughput, or main memory access times.

MIR

See Management information repository.

mirrored

A disk drive is mirrored when two identical copies of the data are kept on two different disk drives. If one fails, the other can keep operating.

MIS

Management Information System. A database system used to provide information to managers in an organization. The term has come to refer to the department in an organization responsible for computing.

MLAL

Multiletter acronym listing.

MM

See management module.

MMJ

See modified modular jack.

MMS

Manufacturing messaging service. Part of the MAP protocols used for communicating with robots, programmable controllers, and other devices.

modem

Modulator/demodulator. A device that takes digital data from a computer and encodes it in analog form for transmission over a phone line. Modems are also used to connect computers to an analog broadband system.

modified modular jack

A DECconnect term for the connection on the faceplate used to connect a data cable.

MONITOR

A VMS tool used to examine the current status of a system.

monitor bit

Token ring concept. The monitor bit is flipped by the active monitor to prevent a frame of priority greater than 0 from circulating continuously.

MOP	*See Maintenance Operation Protocol.*
mount	Term used in the Network File System for making a remote file system appear as if it were a local disk drive. A Digital Distributed File Service Control Program (DFSCP) command to take a remote file system and make it appear to be locally attached.
mouse	A pointing device used on workstations.
MPR	*See multiport repeater.*
MPT	*See multiport transceiver.*
MR	*See Message Router.*
MR/FAX	*See Message Router Facsimile Gateway.*
MR/P	*Message Router PROFS Gateway.*
MRS	*Maximum Record Size* Abbreviation used in DAP.
MR/S	*Message Router SNADS Gateway.*
MR-TELEX	*Message Router TELEX Gateway.*
MRX	*See Message Router X.400 Gateway.*
MSCP	*Mass Storage Control Protocol.* The protocol used by HSC storage controllers to communicate with device drivers on the VAXs in a cluster.
MS-DOS	*Microsoft–Digital Operating System.* Microsoft's version of PC-DOS.
MS-NET	Microsoft network architecture that includes the NetBIOS and SMB protocols.
MSL	*See Management specification language translator.*
MTA	*See Message transfer agent.*
MTP	*Message Transfer Part. See Q.701.*
MTS	*Message transfer service.* The X.400 protocols that govern the exchange of envelopes of information. The IPMS defines the content of the envelope.

multicast

An address to which several nodes will respond. Contrast to broadcast, where all nodes on a network will respond.

multicasting

A term used in Ethernet addressing. A multicast address is a group address meant for a certain subset of users on the Ethernet. LAT nodes communicate their current status with each other using a multicast address. To be contrasted with a broadcast address that is received by all users on the Ethernet.

multilink end node

An end node that has more than one connection to the network. The end node may send and receive data over any of the links but will not route traffic for other nodes.

multipoint

A data link layer concept in which multiple nodes share a common physical medium. In a multipoint situation, a single node is the controller of the line and polls all tributaries periodically to see if they wish to send data. This is in contrast to multiaccess media like Ethernet where any node may send without permission.

multiport repeater

An Ethernet repeater, typically for thinwire networks, that connects several segments together into a multisegment Ethernet.

multiport transceiver

Several Ethernet transceivers built into one device. Can operate as a concentrator on a cable or as a stand-alone Ethernet (known as Ethernet in a can).

multisegment Ethernet

Several segments of Ethernet connected together with repeaters. All signals broadcast on a multisegment Ethernet are received by all other nodes. This is in contrast to the extended Ethernet, where the MAC-layer bridge forwards only those packets destined for the other Ethernet.

multistatement transaction

Several different interactions with the database that are grouped into a single transaction. If any one of the operations are not carried out because of a user abort or system crash, the entire transaction is rolled back. In a multistatement transaction all or none of the operations is carried out.

multistation access unit

Token ring device used to connect several stations to the ring. Similar to the multiport transceiver for the Ethernet.

multitasking	When an operating system (and microprocessor) maintains its position in several tasks simultaneously. The microprocessor alternates between the different tasks under control of the operating system scheduling process. Unix is an example.
multithreaded	An operating system feature that allows a process to maintain several threads of execution, each under the control of the parent process. OS/2 is an example.
MUXserver	A Digital product that combines a multiplexer and a terminal server in one device. Allows remote multiplexed traffic to access LAT-based services.
MVS/TSO	*Multiple virtual storage/time sharing option.* MVS is an IBM operating system. TSO is the interactive subsystem, as opposed to a system like JES used for batch processing.
NAK	*Negative acknowledgment.* Response to nonreceipt or receipt of a corrupt packet of information.
Named Pipes	A process-to-process protocol that allows a full-duplex communication path to be maintained. The pipe is the endpoint of the communication path through which a process gains entry to the function. Names are maintained and registered on the network, allowing a pipe to access services.
name server	A node containing one or more active clearinghouses and the DNS name server modules for accessing those clearinghouses.
namespace	A term used in Digital's DNS name server that refers to the collection of all names on the network. The namespace is distributed among multiple clearinghouses.
Namespace Creation Time Stamp	A unique ID for a namespace that distinguishes it from all other namespaces.
NAS	*See Network Application Support.*
National Bureau of Standards	*See National Institute for Standards and Technology.*
National Institute for Standards and Technology	United States government body that provides assistance for standards making. Formerly the National Bureau of Standards.

NAU	*Network addressable unit.* The boundary of an IBM SNA network. Logical and physical units are examples of NAUs.
NBS	*National Bureau of Standards. See National Institute for Standards and Technology.*
NBS-AS2	*National Bureau of Standards, Abstract Syntax 2.* An abstract syntax developed by the NBS (now NIST) to make a file directory an entry that appears like a file, allowing remote FTAM systems to request a directory of files.
NCL	*See Network control language.*
NCP	*See Network Control Program.*
NCS	*See Network Computing System.*
NET	*Network Entity Title or NetBIOS* Sniffer Analyzer abbreviation for NetBIOS packets or OSI network layer network entity title. The network entity title is one of several possible network addresses on a particular node. The NET is a permanent, unambiguous reference to the node, similar to the DECnet Node ID.
NETACP	*Network ancillary control process.* A type of VMS process that provides the link between the user of the network and the I/O drivers (NETDRIVER).
NetBIOS	Network Adapter Basic Input/Output System. A Network protocol that allows a client program to find a server process and communicate with it. Similar to Named Pipes.
NETDRIVER	A VMS process that provides read and write services over the network for DECnet applications. NETDRIVER would then communicate with a physical driver that used Ethernet, DDCMP, CI, or another supported data link protocol.
NetWare	The networking components sold by Novell. A collection of data link drivers, a transport protocol stack, workstation software, and the NetWare operating system.
NetWare for VMS	Program for Digital's VMS operating system that makes the VAX look like a NetWare server. Ancestor of Portable NetWare.

network address	The number of the network the user is on. Each network (data link) in an internetwork has a number assigned to it. The full address of a station is the network address plus the local address of the node on that network.
Network Application Support	Digital standards to allow everything to work with everything. Similar in scope to IBM's SAA.
Network Computing System	Apollo's computing architecture. The Digital RPC mechanism is derived from the NCS RPC architecture.
Network Control Language	Command line interface to DECmcc.
Network Control Program	A Digital user interface to the network management layer of the Digital Network Architecture.
Network File System	A distributed file system developed by Sun Microsystems and widely used on TCP/IP systems.
Network Information Services	*See Yellow Pages.*
Network Loadable Module	Program on NetWare 386 that when loaded becomes a part of the operating system.
network selector	The part of an address at layer N that selects a particular user at layer N; in other words, the address of the next layer.
Network Services Protocol	DECnet transport layer protocol.
NeWS	*Network Extensible Window System.* A windowing environment from Sun Microsystems based on the Postscript language and a proprietary window control protocol.
NFS	*See Network File System.*
NFT	*Network file transfer.* An interactive utility that gives access to remote data using the DAP protocols.
nibble	Half a byte.

NIC

Network Information Center. A facility located at the Stanford Research Institute that administers Internet addresses.

NICE

Network Information and Control Exchange. A DECnet protocol used for the exchange of network management information.

nickname

A way of referring to a DNA Naming Service namespace. The nickname is locally maintained on a node and translated into the NSCTS for interaction with name servers.

NIS

Network Information Services. See Yellow Pages.

NIST

See National Institute for Standards and Technology.

NLM

See Network Loadable Module.

NMCC/DECnet
Monitor

Network Management Control Center. A precursor to DECmcc for network management. Includes multiple open windows, historical data display, alarm definition, and other features.

NML

Network Management Listener. A VMS process that communicates with a Phase IV network management interface on another node to provide information about the local node.

node

An individual item in a set. An Ethernet node, for example, is a device attached to the cable with a transceiver, including a repeater, bridge, or computer. A file system node is a directory or individual file.

nonexclusive
(read) lock

A type of lock on a file that permits other users to read information but prevents any write operations.

nonpersistent
binding

A style of binding in remote procedure calls where the connection is set up and torn down every time the remote procedure is called.

nonrestricted token

FDDI token in asynchronous mode available to all users.

nonrouting node

See end node.

NPID

Network Layer Protocol Identifier. Used in the ES-IS protocols in the OSI network layer.

NPS

NMCC protocol server. A portion of the NMCC software that interfaces to the network.

NPSI

Network Packet Switching Interface. A type of IBM software that allows SNA data to be carried over an X.25 network to another SNA environment.

N(R)

Receive sequence number. LLC field that indicates the sequence number of the last packet received.

N(S)

Send sequence number. LLC field that indicates the sequence number of the packet being sent.

NSAP

Network Service Access Point The access point to the network.

NSCTS

See Namespace Creation Time Stamp.

NSDU

Network Service Data Unit. From OSI Network Service Definition.

NSEL

See network selector.

NSFnet

National Science Foundation network. A research network established by the NSF to give access to supercomputer and other computing facilities.

NSP

See Network Services Protocol.

NSUID

Namespace unique identifier. It is possible (though somewhat unusual) to have multiple DNS namespaces on a single network, hence the need for a unique identifier. Most operations use the default namespace.

object

An entry in the DNA Naming Service. The simple name of the object, together with the names of all parent directories, form a unique full name in the namespace.

OCC

See office communications cabinet.

office
communications
cabinet

A DECconnect cabinet that provides the hub for up to 128 offices (or faceplates).

OLTP

On-line Transaction Processing. A term muddied by marketing department. Basically means an application that executes lots of small transactions rapidly.

ONC	*See Open Network Computing.*
Open Network Computing	Sun marketing term for the family of protocols that includes the Network File System.
Open Software Foundation	Nonprofit organization founded by Digital, IBM, and four other vendors to develop specifications for an open software environment.
Open Systems Interconnection	The ISO's standards for a heterogeneous, open network architecture.
O/R Address	*Originator/recipient address.* A valid X.400 address.
OSAK	*OSI Applications Kernel.* A set of program libraries sold by Digital as the interface to layer 5 of the OSI model.
OSF	*See Open Software Foundation.*
OSI	*See Open Systems Interconnection.*
outgoing connection timer	Session control term. When the session layer issues a connect request to the transport layer, it starts this timer. If an accept or reject indication is not received before the timer expires, session control issues a disconnect and informs the end user.
P1	X.400 protocol used between MTAs.
P2	X.400 protocol used between user agents (IPMSs).
PAB	*See Personal Address Book.*
Pack	Term used in remote procedure calls for translating data from the machine-dependent format into a machine-independent format.
packet	A general term used in networking to refer to a message sent to a peer entity in the network.
Packet Assembler/Disassembler	Special-purpose computer on an X.25 network that allows asynchronous terminals to use the synchronous X.25 network by packaging asynchronous traffic into a packet.
Packet Exchange Protocol	An XNS transport protocol that requires each packet to be separately acknowledged.

packet switching | A network that has packaged data into packets. A computer can handle many more virtual connections with packets than it can with dedicated connections (known as circuit switching). Packet switching forms the basis for X.25, as well as most network-layer protocols.

PAD | *See Packet Assembler/Disassembler.*

Paging | A memory management technique in a virtual memory operating system. Only a few parts (pages) of a program are actually in memory. When a new part is needed, it is paged into memory.

PAM | *Protocol assist module.* A piece of hardware on a DECSA to provide higher performance for protocol processing.

PAR | *Positive acknowledgment retransmit.* A method of assuring reliable communications used by the DDCMP data link protocol.

path | As a file system concept, the path indicates what set of folders or subdirectories a file is stored in. In the networking sense, a path is the route a packet takes from the source to the destination. The path is a series of data links or hops.

PBX | *Private branch exchange.* A telephone switch installed at the customer premises. Allows the organization to take control of many of its telecommunications functions.

PC-DOS | *Personal Computer–Digital Operating System.* IBM's version of Microsoft's operating system.

PCSA | *See Personal Computing Systems Architecture.*

PDL | *Page description language.* Postscript is an example of a PDL.

PDP | *Programmable data processor.* A series of Q-bus-based 16-bit minicomputers manufactured by Digital.

PDS | *Premises Distribution System.* AT&T cabling system.

PDU	*See Protocol Data Unit.*
PEP	*See Packet Exchange Protocol.*
permanent virtual circuit	A circuit kept up permanently, as in the case of a dedicated leased line on the telephone network.
Personal Address Book	The local directory facility in ALL-IN-1. *See also Distributed Directory Service.*
Personal Computing Systems Architecture	Digital architecture for the integration of PCs into DECnet.
PEX	*See PHIGS Extension to X.*
P/FM	*PBX/Facilities Management.* Digital software for managing PBX traffic.
P-G	*Plenum-Grade.* DECconnect abbreviation. Type of cable coating suitable for installation in environmental airspaces such as heating ducts.
Phase IV	The current phase of DECnet.
PHIGS	*See Programmer's Hierarchical Interactive Graphics System.*
PHIGS Extension to X	Extension to the X Windows System to incorporate 3D graphics.
PHONE	A VMS program that allows interactive two-way conversations over a DECnet.
PID	*Process identification.* Used to identify each process running on an operating system. The VMS lexical function F$PID returns the value of PID.
PIN	*Personal Identification Number.* A number used on ATM and smart cards to verify the identity of the user.
piggybacked	Added on to. A term used in protocols that require the acknowledgment of prior packets. The acknowledgment can often be piggybacked into the same packet as data headed in that direction.

ping-pong	A type of transport protocol that requires each packet to be individually acknowledged. Before a node can send another packet, it must wait for an acknowledgment.
pipe	*See Named Pipes.*
PM	*See presentation module.*
portal	There may be several different users of the Ethernet service, each with a portal, or identification number. Incoming packets are then distributed to the appropriate portal.
POSIX	*Portable Operating System Interface for Computer Environments.* IEEE-developed standards to provide a common interface to the operating system, thus making applications more portable.
PostScript	A page description language used on printers such as the Apple LaserWriter and on computer displays used in workstations from companies such as NeXT and Sun Microsystems. Similar in function to Xerox's Interpress.
POTS	*Plain Old Telephone Service.* As opposed to ISDN, Call Waiting, or any other modern marvels.
ppm	*Pages per minute.* Rating measure for laser printers.
PRDMD	*Private Directory Management Domain.* An X.500 administrative entity that is not a public carrier. See ADDMD and Directory Management Domain.
PrE	*Printer emulation.* Digital SNA access routine that allows a VAX to emulate an IBM printer.
presentation module	The module in DECmcc responsible for the interface to the user device.
presentation syntax	A standard method of representing data in a heterogeneous environment. The Abstract Syntax Notation 1 (ASN.1) is an example of a presentation syntax.
primitive	ISO definition: an element of a service provided by one entity to another one.
print spooler	A software program that accepts several jobs at once for printing. The spooler controls access to the printer and queues incoming jobs for execution.

PRMD

Private management domain. An X.400 domain. *See ADMD.*

PROFS

Professional Office System. IBM office automation package for the VM/CMS operating system.

Programmer's Hierarchical Interactive Graphics System

Imaging system providing sophisticated capabilities such as hidden-surface removal, shading, and depth cueing.

propagation velocity

The rate at which a signal propagates on a wire. Signals travel over a wire much like ripples in a pond after a stone is thrown in.

propagated updates

One of two ways in the DNA Naming Service a replica can be updated. Propagated updates are immediately sent to other replicas. A skulk runs periodically and updates replicas.

protocol data unit

A layer communicates with its peer by sending packets. Each packet has a header that contains information with which the peer will work, such as addresses or acknowledgment requests. It also contains data, the protocol data unit, that is passed up to the client of the layer.

protocol sequence

DNA Session Control term to indicate the protocols to be used at each layer of the stack to make communication practical.

protocol stack

A set of functions, one at each layer of the protocol stack, that work together to form a set of network services. Each layer of the protocol stack uses the services of the module beneath it and builds on that service.

PSI

Packet-switch interface. Digital software to allow a VAX to participate in an X.25 network. Also the name of a company that provides commercial TCP/IP services.

PSN

Packet switched network. An X.25 network.

PSTN

Public Switched Telephone Network.

PTT

Poste Téléphone et Télégraphe. A government provider of communications functions in most European countries.

PU   *Physical unit.* An SNA term used to refer to different types of hardware in the network. A 3274 cluster controller is a PU type 2 (PU2).

public domain   Intellectual property available to people without paying a fee. Most computer software developed at universities is in the public domain.

PVC   *Polyvinyl Chloride* or *see permanent virtual circuit.* Polyvinyl chloride is a type of cable coating unsuitable for environmental airspaces, but often used in offices. *See P-G (Plenum-Grade).*

Q.700   Introduction to CCITT SS number 7.

Q.701   The Message Transfer Part of Signalling System number 7.

Q.711   Signalling connection control part of Signalling System number 7.

Q.721   Telephone User Part of Signalling System number 7.

Q.730   ISDN supplementary services definition for Signalling System number 7.

Q.761   The ISDN user part of Signalling System number 7.

Q.930   CCITT standard for the ISDN user-network interface at layer 3.

Q-bus   The peripheral bus used on MicroVAX and PDP computers.

QIO   *Queue input/output.* Method used for an application to call a device driver directly in the VMS operating system. *See RMS.*

QOS   *Quality of service.* A series of negotiable parameters in X.25 and OSI network implementations.

RAM   *Random access memory.* Dynamic memory, sometimes known as main or core memory.

RARP   *Reverse Address Resolution Protocol.* A TCP/IP protocol that provides the reverse function of ARP. Used by diskless nodes when they first initialize to find their Internet address.

rcp

Remote copy program. An upper-layer TCP/IP service found in the Berkeley Unix implementation for copying files. *See FTP for the Arpanet equivalent.*

RDA

Remote Data Access. An international standard for access to databases in a heterogeneous computing environment.

Rdb

Digital's relational database management system. Rdb/VMS is the primary software, although there is a version for the ELN real-time operating system.

RDN

Relative Distinguished Name A name in an X.500 directory. It is relative to some well-known root.

RD PDU

Redirect PDU. From OSI Network Service Definition. Used to inform a system to redirect future PDU to another intermediate system. A primitive form of routing control.

read-only replica

A DNA Naming Service directory. The read-only replica is a copy of the other replicas, but cannot be directly updated. *See also secondary replica and master replica.*

ReGis

Remote graphics instruction set. A set of Digital protocols used in the VT240 and 241 graphics terminals.

register

The DFSCP command that publicizes the availability of a file system for remote mounts. *See mount.*

Relative Record Number

Form of variable file access method in DAP.

REM

See Remote Electronic Mail.

Remote Electronic Mail

An MCI Mail account used by companies that have several users.

remote procedure call

A set of network protocols that allows a node to call procedures executing on a remote machine. The Netwise RPC Tool, HP/Apollo RPC, and Sun's NFS RPC are examples of such protocols.

Remote Wall Enclosure

DECconnect wiring concentrator. Used to distribute a multilead cable to individual offices or as a twisted pair concentrator for Ethernet.

REP

Reply to Message Number DDCMP message to force acknowledgment.

repeater	An Ethernet device used to connect two or more segments of cable together. The repeater retimes and reamplifies the signal received on one segment before resending it on all other segments.
replica	A copy of a DNA Naming Service directory. *See master, secondary, and read-only replicas.*
replica set	A list of all DNA Naming Service clearinghouses that store copies of a particular directory.
Request for Comment	A document issued in the TCP/IP Internet environment. Some RFCs become part of the TCP/IP standards.
reservation field	A field in token ring packets that allows a node to inform the active monitor it has data of a certain priority to send.
restricted token	A special mode of asynchronous access in FDDI where the bandwidth is dedicated to an extended dialogue between two users.
RFA	*record file address.* The unique address of a record within a file. Used in Digital's RMS file system.
RFC	*See Request for Comment.*
RFT	*Revisable form text.* A version of IBM's Document Content Architecture.
RG–62	Grade of coaxial cable.
RGB	*Red, green, blue.* A method of representing colors as a mix of red, green, and blue. Used on monitors.
ring purge	A token ring packet that clears the network of data, similar in function to the ARCNET reconfiguration burst.
RIP	*See Routing Information Protocol.*
RISC	*Reduced instruction set computer.* Generic name for CPUs that use a simpler instruction set than more traditional designs. Examples are the IBM PC/RT, Pyramid minicomputers, and the Sun SPARC workstations.
RJ	*Reject.* A protocol data unit type in the OSI transport service.

RJ11

Standard modular jack developed by AT&T. Used for telephones and data communications. Being replaced by the RJ45, which is the same size but has more wires.

RJE

Remote job entry. Facility for submitting a job to a computer for execution. Card readers were early RJE stations. Usually means software that emulates RJE stations.

rlogin

Remote login. Berkeley TCP/IP command to log onto a remote node.

RMS

Record management services. A common I/O interface for VMS used for access to local data via QIO calls and remote data via the DAP protocol.

RNR

Receive Not Ready. HDLC frame.

root

Unix superuser. The one account on a Unix system that has privileged access.

root directory

The top of the DNA Naming Service namespace.

ROSE

Remote Operations Service Element OSI protocol for remote procedure calls. Also the name of the developer of ISODE.

rotary

Multiple instances of a service all accessible using one address. The service provider intercepts all requests for that address and farms them out to a specific instance. A common example of a rotary is when several outgoing lines are available for a dial-out service. Rather than make the user ask for each line by name, a rotary service connects the user to the first available line.

router

Dedicated hardware used to route traffic on a network. The alternative is to use a portion of a general-purpose system such as a VAX.

router hello

DECnet packet used by routers to let other nodes on the network know they are operating.

routing directory

A database maintained by the network layer to determine which paths to use to get to particular networks.

Routing Information Protocol

Several different protocols used in Novell's NetWare, TCP/IP, and Xerox's XNS to inform computers on a network of any changes in the topology of the network.

Routing Table Maintenance Protocol	AppleTalk protocol for the maintenance of routing tables.
routing tables	A directory maintained by the network layer that contains the address of nodes on the internetwork and how to reach them.
RPC	*See remote procedure call.*
RPC specification	The information prepared by a programmer as input to the RPC Compiler. The specification informs the compiler which procedures will be distributed.
RPC Tool	The RPC mechanism sold by Netwise, including the RPC compiler.
RR	*Receive ready.* An LLC field indicating the sending node is ready to receive data. Sometimes also stands for request response protocol.
RRF	*Response Requested Flag* LAT flag set by the slave requesting another packet from the master.
RRN	*See Relative Record Number.*
RS-232-C	A physical interface standard used frequently for connecting asynchronous devices such as terminals. Developed by the Electronic Industries Association to define the electrical and mechanical link between a DTE and a DCE.
RSA	*Rivest, Shamir, and Adleman.* The developers of a public key authentication technology that forms the basis for the Digital security services.
RSADSI	*RSA Data Security, Inc.* The firm started by Rivest, Shamir, and Adleman to capitalize on their patents.
RSM	*Remote Systems Manager.* Digital software for managing remote MicroVAX computers.
RSTS	*Resource-sharing timesharing system.* PDP-based operating system.
RSX	Another PDP-based operating system. VMS systems running in compatibility mode are able to execute RSX-executable images.

RTL	*Run-Time Library.*
RTMP	*See Routing Table Maintenance Protocol.*
RT/PC	IBM 32-bit workstation based on an RISC architecture.
RU	*Request unit.* A part of IBM's SNA architecture. A series of request units are sent from one session participant to the other, then processed by upper layers of the protocol stack.
RWE	*See Remote Wall Enclosure.*
SA482	Digital disk cluster with 2.5 Gbyte of capacity.
SAA	*Systems Application Architecture.* IBM architecture to present common user, communications, and programming interfaces across multiple hardware platforms and operating systems.
SABME	*Set Asynchronous Balanced Mode Extended.* Type of frame used in the LLC operation.
SAF	*System Authorization Facility.* A family of IBM security products.
SAP	*Service Advertisement Protocol* or *See service access point.* The Service Advertisement Protocol is a NetWare protocol.
SAS	*See Single Attachment Station.*
SASE	*Specific application service element.* Application layer concept in the OSI network architecture. Refers to special-purpose services such as the job transfer and manipulation (JTM) facility.
Satellite Equipment Room	DECconnect wiring concentrator. The Satellite Equipment Room consists of patch panels for high- and low-speed data and voice communications as well as active devices such as terminal servers, repeaters, DELNIs, and DEMPRs.
SCA	*System Communication Architecture.* The Digital architecture for Clusters.
SCCP	*Signalling connection control part. See Q.711.*
SCP	*Server Control Procedure* or *Session Control Protocol.*

SCS	*System communication services.* Software services used in a VAX Cluster to provide internode communication. SCS is the lowest level of the System Communication Architecture.
SCSI	*Small computer standard interface.* Pronounced "scuzzy." A standard for connecting disk drives to disk controllers, used typically in small multiuser computers.
SDLC	*Synchronous data link control.* IBM's data link protocol used in SNA networks.
SDU	*See Service Data Unit.*
search path	A mechanism in DOS, Unix, and other operating systems that allows a user to specify a command without knowing which directory it is stored. The operating system will search each of the directories in the search path for the command until it finds the file.
secondary replica	A DNA Naming Service replica capable of updates and object or soft link creations but not child directory creation. *See also master replica* and *read-only replica.*
semaphore	A synchronization mechanism operating systems.
Sequenced Packet Protocol	XNS protocol for reliable transfer of data at the transport layer.
sequence number	A unique number for every packet on a particular connection maintained by a reliable transport layer service. The sequence number allows the transport layer to see if any packets were lost or delivered out of sequence by the underlying network and data layers.
SER	*See Satellite Equipment Room.*
server	A program on a computer that provides services to workstations. File, database, print, and communications are just a few kinds of servers.
server message block	Microsoft protocol for data access which sits on top of NetBIOS.
server stub	A piece of software generated by the RPC Tool. The server stub emulates the calling application program to the remote procedure on the server.

service access point	The address for the user of a service.
service class	A concept in the LAT architecture to allow extensions for specific groups of applications, such as interactive terminals or windowing workstations.
service data unit	The information a layer accepts from its client and sends over the network. Contrast with header or control information.
session	Networking term used to refer to the logical stream of data flowing between two programs communicating over a network. Note that there are usually many different sessions originating from one particular node of a network.
Session Control Protocol	DNA session layer module. Provides name-to-address translation, process addressing, and access control.
SGML	*See Standard Generalized Markup Language.*
shell	A term that usually refers to the user interface on an operating system. On Unix systems, the C shell or the Bourne shell are the primary user interfaces. Contrasts with the kernel, which interacts with the computer at low levels.
Single Attachment Station	FDDI term for a station attached to the ring via a concentrator.
SIXEL	A standard format used for bit-mapped images. Complements ReGIS, which is a Digital format for line-oriented images.
skulker	A term used in Digital's DNA Naming Service. A skulker is a background process that assures that all replicas of a portion of the namespace are consistent with the master portion.
slot	An entry in a fixed-size table. Also a sublayer in the Local Area Transport architecture that allows multiple users to share a single datagram packet, each occupying a separate slot.
SMB	*See Server message block.*
SMP	*See Standby Monitor Present* or *Symmetric multiprocessor.*

SMS   *Site Management Station.* A bundle of products for an early version of DECmcc, including the NMCC/VAX ETHERnim, LAN Traffic Monitor, Terminal Server Manager, and Remote Bridge Management Software.

SMT   *See Station Management.*

SMTP   *Simple Mail Transfer Protocol.* The TCP/IP protocol for a message-handling system.

SNA   *See System Network Architecture.*

SNADS   *SNA distribution services.* An architecture used for transferring messages in an SNA environment, similar to X.400.

snail mail   The traditional postal service.

SNAP SAP   *Subnetwork Access Service Access Point.* A special form of Service Access Point where the first 5 bytes of the information field in the Logical Link Control data serves as the protocol identifier.

Sniffer   A network analyzer made by Network General. The Sniffer was used to produce the screen dumps of network packets in this book.

Sniffer Network   Network General product used to monitor many different
Analyzer   upper- and lower-layer network protocols.

SNP   *Sequence Numbers Packet.* DECnet/OSI Phase V packet used to keep track of link state packets.

socket   An entry point to a program. User programs communicate with transport providers such as UDP or TCP by means of sockets. Each user typically has a separate socket.

soft link   An entry in the DNA Naming Service that points to another part of the namespace. The soft link is an alias for another name.

SOH   *Start of header.* The beginning of a DDCMP message.

SOM   *Start of message.*

source address   The origin of a data packet on a network.

SPARC	*Scalable Processor Architecture.* A reduced instruction set (RISC) processor developed by Sun and licensed by several vendors including AT&T and Texas Instruments. Used in the Sun Sparcstation family of workstations.
spool	A place for a fast device (such as a software program) to leave data for later processing on a slow device (such as a printer).
SPP	*See Sequenced Packet Protocol.*
SQL	*See Structured Query Language.*
SRC	*Source address.* Sniffer Analyzer abbreviation for the source data link address.
SS7	*Signalling System 7.* Protocol related to ISDN. Directs how the interior of an ISDN network is managed.
SSAP	*Source service access point.* Address of the user of a service. *See also DSAP.*
SSCP	*System services control point.* A network addressable unit in IBM's SNA architecture. Resides on a mainframe and is the central point for that domain of an SNA network.
standard	A convention that people know about. The nice thing about standards is there are so many to choose from.
Standard Generalized Markup Language	ISO standard for the representation of revisable form text.
standby monitor	Token ring term for a computer waiting for the active monitor to fail and ready to step in if that happens. Kind of like a vice president.
Standby Monitor Present	Packet sent out by a standby monitor every 7 seconds to advertise its presence.
star coupler	Device used to connect different nodes of a VAX Cluster that use the CI bus.
station management	Part of the FDDI ring. The service that monitor activity and exercise overall control.

STE
: *Signalling terminal exchange.* Equipment in an X.25 network that forms the boundary of a network. Communication between different X.25 management domains is between STEs using the X.75 protocols.

stored upstream address
: Token ring concept. Each node on the token ring stores the address of the neighbor from which it receives data.

stream
: An interface to the transport service that allows its client to send data in a continuous stream. The transport service will guarantee that all data will be delivered to the other end in the same order as sent and without duplicates.

STREAMS
: An AT&T mechanism developed for the Unix operating system. STREAMS is a way of connecting a series of software modules, letting them send messages to each other.

Structured Query Language
: International standard language for communicating with relational database systems.

stub
: A piece of code used in RPC mechanisms. The stub appears like the called or calling procedure thus masking the details of the RPC implementation from the calling or called procedures.

subnet
: A term used to denote any networking technology that makes all nodes connected to it appear to be one hop away. In other words, the user of the subnet can communicate directly to all other nodes on the subnet. A subnet could be X.25, Ethernet, a token ring, ISDN, or a point-to- point link. A collection of subnets, together with a routing or network layer, combines to form a network.

subvector
: Portion of a MAC frame. For example, the token ring command to request initialization on the ring contains subvectors with the adapter software level, upstream neighbor address, and several other fields.

Sun Microsystems
: Makers of workstations and the Network File System.

SunOS
: *Sun Operating System.* Sun's implementation of Unix, TCP/IP, and other utilities, libraries, and programs.

SVC
: *See switched virtual circuit.*

SVID
: *System V interface definition.* AT&T-sponsored definition used to determine the compatibility of different implementations of System V.

switched virtual circuit	A virtual circuit that is set up on demand, as in the case of a dial-up telephone line or an X.25 call. *See permanent virtual circuit.*
symbiont	Symbiosis is the bringing together of two different worlds. A symbiont is a VMS process that takes disk files and prepares them for a printer.
symbol	The smallest signalling element used at the MAC layer of the network. The symbol is sent down to the physical layer for transmission. In FDDI, a symbol is five code bits at the physical layer.
symmetric multiprocessor	Term used by Digital for true parallel processing in version V of VMS.
synchronization	Coordination of tasks among multiple users. Synchronization mechanisms include locking and semaphores.
synchronous	An FDDI service class where each requestor gets a preallocated maximum bandwidth and hence a guaranteed response time.
SYS$COMMAND	A VMS logical name that points to the device that will be used to input commands for the Digital Command Language. Points to a terminal device (i.e., tta0:) for an interactive session or a command file for a batch job.
SYS$ERROR	A VMS logical name that points to the device used to output error messages for the current user.
SYS$INPUT	A VMS logical name that points to the device used to input data (as opposed to commands) for the current user.
SYS$LOGIN	A VMS logical name that points to the default login directory for the current user.
SYS$OUTPUT	A VMS logical name that points to the device used to output results (as opposed to errors) for the current user.
SYS$PRINT	A VMS logical name that points to the default print queue for the current user.
SYS$SYSTEM	A VMS logical name that points to the location of system executable images.

SYSGEN A program in VMS used to alter system-wide parameters such as AWSTIME.

System Network Architecture IBM's networking architecture.

T1 Digital telephone line operating at 1.544 Mbps.

T.4 CCITT standard for group 3 facsimile transmission.

T.6 CCITT standard for group 4 facsimile transmission.

TC *See transport connection.*

TCC *Telephone Country Code.* Part of an X.121 address signifying the country being addressed.

TCP *See Transmission Control Protocol.*

TCP/IP *Transmission Control Protocol/Internet Protocol.* Nonproprietary network architecture used extensively in Unix and heterogeneous environments.

TDF *Time Differential Factor.* The difference between the local time zone and Coordinated Universal Time (UTC).

Teamdata Digital-developed user interface for DSRI compatible relational databases.

Telenet Packet-switched network service offered by GTE.

Telex Messaging mechanism that predates fax or electronic mail.

Telnet Upper-layer TCP/IP service for Arpanet implementations. Allows users to log onto remote nodes.

TERM *Terminal.* DECconnect abbreviation.

terminal emulator A program that allows a computer to emulate a terminal. The workstation thus appears as a terminal to the host.

terminator Device on each end of an Ethernet cable to prevent reflections.

terrabyte One trillion bytes (1,000,000,000,000).

ThickWire   Another name for the 10BASE5 standard for coaxial cables
                         and Ethernet.

ThinWire   Thinner and less expensive version of baseband coax cable
                         used for Ethernet networks. Also called CheaperNet.

THT   *Token holding timer.* Token ring and FDDI term for the
                         amount of time a node can transmit data before sending the
                         token back out the ring.

TK50   Digital tape cartridge that holds 95 Mbytes of information.

TLI   *See Transport Level Interface.*

token bus   An alternative to token ring and Ethernet local area net-
                         works. Used in the MAP protocols. The token bus uses a
                         multiple access protocol, but the device that "owns" the to-
                         ken is the only one that can send data.

token ring   A local area network protocol in which computers are con-
                         nected together in a ring. A node waits until a token is
                         passed around the ring, at which point it may send data.
                         When it has finished sending, it releases the token and
                         passes it to the next node. *See FDDI.*

topology   A network topology shows the computers and the links be-
                         tween them. A network layer must stay abreast of the cur-
                         rent network topology to be able to route packets to their
                         final destination.

tower   DNA Phase V term for the sequence of protocol identifiers
                         and associated address information through which a par-
                         ticular module can be accessed.

TP   *See Transport Protocol.* Sometimes means twisted pair (or
                         toilet paper).

TPDU   *Transport protocol data unit.* A packet of information ex-
                         changed between two transport layer entities in an OSI net-
                         work. *See PDU.*

TPE   *Unshielded Twisted Pair Ethernet Adapter.* DECconnect abbre-
                         viation.

transaction   A series of one or more operations that form a logical
                         whole. The entire transaction or none of it must take effect.

transaction agent	The DNA Naming Service module responsible for processing requests received from clerks.
transceiver	A term used in Ethernet networks. The transceiver is the hardware device that connects to the Ethernet media, often a piece of coax cable. The transceiver is then connected to an Ethernet controller on the host system.
transceiver cable	A cable of up to 50 meters between the transceiver and the Ethernet controller.
TransLAN	A wide-area extended Ethernet bridge manufactured by Vitalink.
Transmission Control Protocol	The transport protocol in TCP/IP used for the guaranteed delivery of data.
transport connection	Virtual channel of communication between two users provided by the transport layer module.
Transport Level Interface	AT&T-developed specification for the interface between the transport layer and upper-layer users.
Transport Protocol	The OSI transport service classes, numbered from 0 to 4. TP4 is a reliable transport protocol.
transport service access point	The entry point to the transport module for a particular end user.
trap	Programming concept for a block of code executed whenever a specific condition, usually an error, occurs.
TRT	*Token rotation timer.* Token ring and FDDI term for the amount of time the token should take to go around the ring.
trunk cable	Used to distinguish the coaxial Ethernet cable (the trunk) from the attachment to the individual node (the transceiver cable).

TSAP	*See Transport Service Access Point.*
TSR	*Terminate and stay resident.*
TTRT	*Target token rotation time.* A term used in FDDI to set performance parameters. The TTRT serves as a measure of expected delay and is used, among other things, to set time-out parameters.
TTY	*Teletype.* A line-oriented terminal.
TUP	*Telephone User Part. See Q.721.*
TW	*ThinWire.* DECconnect abbreviation.
twisted pair	A pair of wires (or several pairs of wires) such as those used to connect telephones to distribution panels. Twisted pair is also being used as a physical transmission medium for Ethernet, token ring, and other forms of data links.
Tymnet	Public packet-switched network based on X.25 owned by McDonnell-Douglas.
U	*Universal Modular Jack or Unnumbered Frame* DECconnect abbreviation.
UA	*Unnumbered acknowledgment or user agent.* An unnumbered acknowledgment is type of frame used in the LLC operation. A user agent is part of a message-handling system.
UAF	*User Authentication File.* VMS file that holds user information.
UDP	*See User Datagram Protocol.*
UI	*Unnumbered Information.* Type of frame used in the LLC operation.
UIC	*User identification code.* VMS code used to identify every user on the system uniquely.
UID	*See unique identifier or User Identification.*
UIL	*User interface language.* A DECwindows concept that allows the user interface to be modified for different countries without modifying the source code of the program.

Ultrix	Version of Unix sold by Digital for VAX computers.
Unibus	A peripheral bus used on 11/780 and 8600 VAX processors.
unique identifier	DNA Phase V service that provides a unique ID over time and space.
Unix	Operating system developed and trademarked by American Telephone and Telegraph. The word Unix is a pun on the Multics operating system.
unpack	Term used in remote procedure calls for translating data from the machine-independent form into the form used on a particular computer.
update listener	The DNA Naming Service module responsible for receiving propagated updates and processing them. *See also update sender* and *propagated updates.*
update sender	The DNA Naming Service module responsible for immediate propagation of updates to other clearinghouses. *See also propagated updates* and *skulker.*
update time stamp	An indication of when an entry was last updated.
Usenet	Network of Unix users. Informal network of loosely coupled nodes that agree to exchange information in the form of electronic mail and a bulletin board.
User Datagram Protocol	Part of the TCP/IP protocol suite. UDP operates at the transport layer and, in contrast to TCP, does not guarantee the delivery of data.
User Identification	VMS method of identifying users. Each user has a User ID (UID) and a Group ID (GID).
UTC	*Coordinated Universal Time.* Coordinated international standard for time. Local time is the UTC plus a time differential factor.
UTP	*unshielded twisted pair*
UTS	*See update time stamp.*
UUCP	*Unix-to-Unix copy program.* The standard Unix utility used to exchange information between any two Unix nodes. Used as the basis for Usenet.

UUID	*Universal Unique Identifier.* Part of the Hewlett-Packard/Apollo NCS remote procedure call definition. Similar to a DNA UID.
V.21	CCITT standard for 300-bps duplex modem over the general switched telephone network.
V.22	CCITT standard for 1200-bps duplex operation over the general switched telephone network.
V.22 bis	CCITT standard for 2400-bps duplex modems over the general switched telephone network.
V.23	CCITT standard for 600/1200-baud modems.
V.24	CCITT standard for the definition of circuits between a DTE and DCE.
V.27	4800-bps modem over leased circuits.
V.27 bis	CCITT standard for 4800/2400-bps modem over leased telephone-type circuits.
V.27 ter	CCITT standard for 4800/2400-bps modem over general switched telephone networks.
V.29	CCITT standard for 9600-bps modem over 4-wire leased telephone circuits.
V.32	CCITT standard for a family of 2-wire modems operating up to 9600 bps over general and leased telephone circuits.
V.33	CCITT standard for 14.4-kbps modems over leased circuits.
V.35	CCITT physical interface standard for high-speed data transmission.
value-added network	A network on top of a network.
value-added reseller	Company that embeds another company's products into a more sophisticated product.

VAN	*See Value-Added Network.*
VAR	*See Value-added reseller.*
VAS	*VTX applications service.* A library used to develop applications on Digital's VTX software.
VAX	*Virtual address extension.* Hardware series made by Digital.
VAX 11/780	A single Vax processing unit (VUP) processor. Somewhat equivalent to a one MIP computer.
VAX 6200	A series of VAX parallel processors with 1–6 CPUs using the XMI bus.
VAX 8600	A 4-VPU computer.
VAX 8700	A 6-VPU computer that forms the basis for the Bi-bus-based VAX computers.
VAX 8840	A parallel processor with four 8700 CPUs. Roughly 24 VPU of power.
VAX Cluster	High-speed Digital network used to supplement DECnet for highly integrated systems.
VAXeln	Digital real-time operating system.
VAX Key Distribution Center	Software on a VAX that works with the DESNC encrypting Ethernet controller.
VAXlink	A family of products that allows access from a DSRI-compatible user interface to a series of IBM-based data repositories.
VAXmate	Digital 80286-based PC/AT clone, with the addition of an Ethernet controller and a different keyboard.
VAXNotes	Digital conferencing software.
VAXPAC	*VAX Public Access Communications.* Software to allow VMS users to initiate outbound modem connections.
VAXstations	MicroVAX workstations with a 15-inch or 19-inch bit-mapped graphic screen and graphics coprocessor.

VBN

See Virtual Block Number.

V,E,A tuple

Verb, Entity, Attribute Tuple. A DECmcc concept used to identify a service. The DECmcc dispatch tables keep track of the <V,E,A> combinations and the associated procedures to call.

VIA

VAX Information Architecture. A related set of software systems sold by Digital for data management systems.

VID

Video. DECconnect abbreviation.

VIDA

VAX IBM Data Access. Digital DSRI product that allows access to Cullinet IDMS databases using any DSRI user interface.

view

A database construct that makes a collection of one or more tables appear as a single database table.

virtual block number

Form of variable file access method in DAP.

virtual circuit

A service usually offered at the transport layer. The user of a virtual circuit is able to send data to a remote user and not worry about putting data in packets, error recovery, missing data, or routing decisions.

virtual memory

An operating system concept that refers to the address space of a program. A paging system maps virtual memory to the limited physical memory pages as needed.

virtual terminal

A service that allows a user on one system to log onto another for an interactive session.

VISTA

VTX Infobase Structure Tool and Assister. Software package for maintaining VTX databases.

Vitalink

Makers of the TransLAN wide-area Ethernet bridge.

VM

Virtual machine or *see virtual memory.* Virtual machine is an IBM operating system that permits guest operating systems, such as MVS, to reside on top of it. Usually used in conjunction with the CMS user interface.

VMS

Virtual memory system. A Digital proprietary operating system for VAX computers.

VMSmail	Digital electronic mail utility on the VMS operating system.
VMS/SNA	Digital software that allows a VAX with the appropriate synchronous communications board to function as an SNA gateway.
VOSAK	*VAX OSI Applications Kernel.* Digital programming library for the OSI session layer.
VOTS	*VAX OSI Transport Services.* Digital OSI software that implements layer 4 of the ISO reference model.
VPU	*Vax processing unit.* A Digital measure of processing power. The 11/780 is equivalent to one VUP. A VUP is roughly analogous to an MIPS, although these numbers cannot be compared across product lines because each computer has different instruction sets.
VSAM	*Virtual sequential access method.* File organization method used in IBM environments for direct access files. Similar to ISAM (indexed sequential access method).
VT	*See Virtual terminal.*
VT100	A series of Digital terminals. The VT300 series is the current family of Digital terminals. VT100 and VT200 are a de facto industry standard, meaning that most software packages include terminal drivers for these types of terminals.
VT200	Type of terminal developed by Digital for use on VAX computers.
VTAM	*Virtual Telecommunications Access Method.* An IBM software system that provides the interface to an SNA network.
VTP	*Virtual Terminal Protocol.* ISO standard for virtual terminals. Similar in function to CTERM and Telnet.
VTX	*Videotex.* Digital's Videotex software package.
WAN	*Wide-area network.* Sometimes also used to mean work area network or a small subnetwork for a work group.
watchdog program	A program, not associated with a user, that watches for specific events. A typical watchdog program looks for idle terminals and logs the user off.

wide-area bridge	A MAC-layer bridge that works on wide-area communications links such as T1 and dial-up lines.
work group	Trendy term for people who work together. Several computers may be isolated on a small network, known as a work group network. Whether anything is accomplished is another matter.
WORM	*Write once/read many.* A type of optical disk that can be written locally, contrasted to CD-ROM disk.
write lock	Prevents others from reading or writing the locked data. Also known as an exclusive lock.
X.3	CCITT standard for a packet assembler/disassembler (PAD).
X.12	ANSI committee for Electronic Data Interchange
X.21	CCITT standard for circuit-switched networks.
X.21 bis	Use of the synchronous V-series modems over public data networks.
X.25	CCITT standard for the interface between a DTE and DCE for terminals operating in packet mode and connected to the public data network with a dedicated circuit.
X.28	CCITT protocols for an asynchronous terminal to communicate with an X.3 PAD.
X.29	CCITT protocols for a synchronous DTE (a host) to control and communicate with an X.3 PAD.
X.75	CCITT standard for interconnecting separate X.25 networks.
X.81	Internetworking between an ISDN circuit-switched and a circuit-switched public network.
X.110	CCITT standard for routing principles on public data networks.
X.121	CCITT numbering plan for public data networks.
X.200	CCITT version of the OSI reference model.
X.208	CCITT version of the OSI ASN.1.

X.209	CCITT version of the OSI ASN.1 Basic Encoding Rules (BER).
X.211	Physical service definition for OSI for CCITT applications.
X.212	Data link service definition for OSI for CCITT applications.
X.213	Network layer service definition for OSI for CCITT applications.
X.214	Transport service definition for OSI for CCITT applications.
X.215	Session service definition for OSI for CCITT applications.
X.216	Presentation service definition for OSI for CCITT applications.
X.217	ACSE definition for OSI for CCITT applications.
X.218	CCITT equivalent of ISO 9066-1: Text communication—reliable transfer.
X.219	CCITT equivalent of the ISO Remote Operations Service Element (ROSE).
X.220	CCITT specification of the use of X.200-series protocols in CCITT applications.
X.223	Use of X.25 to provide the OSI connection-mode network service.
X.400	CCITT standard for message-handling services.
X.402	CCITT Message-handling system: Overall architecture.
X.403	CCITT Message-handling system: Conformance testing.
X.407	CCITT Message-handling system: Abstract service definition conventions.
X.408	CCITT Message-handling system: Encoded information type conversion rules.
X.411	CCITT Message-handling system: Message transfer system: abstract service definition and procedures.
X.413	CCITT Message-handling system: Message store: Abstract service definition.

X.419	CCITT Message-handling system: Protocol specifications.
X.420	CCITT Message-handling system: Interpersonal messaging system.
X.500	CCITT standard for directory information.
X.501	CCITT Directory: Models.
X.509	CCITT Directory: Authentication framework.
X.511	CCITT Directory: Abstract Service Definition.
X.519	CCITT Directory: Protocol Specifications.
X.520	CCITT Directory: Selected Attribute Types.
X.521	CCITT Directory: Selected Object Classes.
XDR	*See External Data Representation.*
Xerox Network System	A set of upper-layer (layers 3 and 4) protocols, plus some applications, typically used in conjunction with Ethernet. An alternative to DECnet or TCP/IP. The layer 3 and 4 protocols form the basis for Novell's NetWare.
XI	IBM product for using X.25 in a heterogeneous environment, as opposed to NPSI that uses X.25 as a transport mechanism for SNA.
XID	*Exchange identification.* An HDLC frame used when a new node attaches to the physical medium. The XID frame contains information such as the node ID or a verification password for the connection.
XMI	A 100-Mbps bus used to connect CPUs, BI buses, and memory on the VAX 6200 series of parallel processors.
Xmodem	A set of protocols used for error-free file transfer over voice grade lines. Similar to Kermit, Xmodem is used to transfer binary and ASCII files from different hosts that are not running a common set of networking protocols.
XNS	*See Xerox Network System.*
XNS Mail Transport Protocol	Message-handling service in XNS.

XQP   *Extended QIO processor.* A VMS service that receives re-
                        quests for data then passes them down to the device driver.

Yellow Pages   A set of services in the Network File System that propagate
                        information from masters to recipients. Used for the main-
                        tenance of system files on complex networks. Yellow Pages
                        are also known as the Network Information Services.

Index